NOTTINGHAMSHIRE

SAPIENTER PROFICIENS

The King's England

A New Domesday Book of 10,000 Towns and Villages

Edited by Arthur Mee

in 41 Volumes

NOTHING like these books has ever been presented to the English people. Every place has been visited. The Compilers have travelled half-a-million miles and have prepared a unique picture of our countryside as it has come down through the ages, a census of all that is enduring and worthy of record.

THE VILLAGE CATHEDRAL—SOUTHWELL MINSTER

THE KING'S ENGLAND

NOTTINGHAMSHIRE

The Midland Stronghold

EDITED BY
ARTHUR MEE

With 219 Places
and 109 Pictures

THE KING'S ENGLAND PRESS
1989

First Published 1938 by
Hodder & Stoughton Ltd

This edition published 1989 by
The King's England Press
37 Crookes Lane, Carlton
Nr Barnsley, S. Yorks

© The Trustees of
The Late Arthur Mee

ISBN 1 872438 00 8

Printed and bound by
SMITH SETTLE
Ilkley Road, Otley, West Yorkshire LS21 3JP

The Editor is greatly indebted to
CLAUDE and LOIS SCANLON
for their valuable help with this book

For the pictures to
SIDNEY TRANTER, ART EDITOR

and to the following for photographs:

Messrs Edgar Bull, E. J. Burrow, Brian Clayton, Fred Crossley, J. Dixon-Scott, E. Elcombe, C. H. Henson, Higson & Company, Alfred Loughton, W. F. Taylor, Nevil Truman; and to the Society of the Sacred Mission for the pictures of the sculptures by Charles Jagger, the Curator of the Nottingham Museum, and the Rev. W. J. Conybeare, Provost of Southwell.

Erratum to first edition:-

In the set of pictures beginning opposite page 200 the water at the University is, of course, the lake and not the river.

PICTURES OF NOTTINGHAMSHIRE

*Where the pictures are not on or facing the page given
they are inside the set of pictures beginning on that page*

PICTURES OF NOTTINGHAMSHIRE

PICTURES OF NOTTINGHAMSHIRE

The Midland Stronghold

ITS capital is the Queen of the Midlands, and she sits enthroned in what is truly a midland county, an average piece of this green and pleasant land.

We do not come to it for something wonderful beyond compare as when we go to Cornwall, or for the thrill of an ancient countryside like prehistoric Wiltshire, or for the natural charm of Sussex or the historic wonder of Kent: Nottinghamshire is not like these, and all too little does it see the traveller in search of what it has.

Yet in its 826 square miles Nottinghamshire has some things that are matchless and many things that are noble, and for the rest it may be said that it is a fair county and fairly represents the great backbone of England, north of its neighbour Leicestershire (so much like it), with the vast space and the illimitable glory of Yorkshire north of it, on the east the Fens between it and the sea, and on the west the county unsurpassed for beauty of its kind, Derbyshire. The county of the Queen of the Midlands touches them all, and though she is not famous like Warwickshire a little way off, and has no definite character like Gloucestershire, and does not draw a ceaseless multitude like Devonshire, it is not to be denied that England would be infinitely poorer if all that Nottinghamshire is and has been were blotted out. We look in this book at more than 200 of its villages and all its towns, and those who think this county dull may be prepared for much surprise. Nature has endowed it richly. Man has given it splendour upon splendour. Its Sherwood Forest has given the world immortal chapters of romance. It has everlasting names wrought into its story, and it has seen dramatic days which live for ever in the history of the nation and the evolution of the world.

If we think of Cricket, no county has played it better. If we think of Work, how many counties have four pillars of the Industrial Age to compare with Arkwright, Strutt, Hargreaves, and Lee?—William Lee who invented a machine on which he made a pair of stockings for Queen Elizabeth, Hargreaves the poor weaver who came to Nottingham to set up a spinning mill, Richard Arkwright who followed him and set up a mill driven by horses, and in 20 years saw it driven by steam, and Jedediah Strutt, whose mechanical genius brought him fame as the improver of Lee's frame. If we ask for Romance, where is a more romantic story than Robin Hood? And if we are not sure that Robin Hood lived, where is a more romantic life than Byron's? If we think of the Church, it was from one village here that Archbishop Cranmer came, and from another Thomas Secker, the scholar who became Bishop of Oxford, Dean of St Paul's, and Archbishop of Canterbury. If we think of Science, the first immortal Darwin was born here, the wonderful Erasmus who prophesied that men would ride in cars and fly into the clouds. If we think of Literature, it is here that we find the tomb of Lord Chesterfield who wrote the famous Letters to his Son, here that the poet Kirke White was born, here that Byron lies, here that lived the brave colonel whose biography has long been a classic, Colonel Hutchinson, his stainless fame so nobly set in English literature by his devoted wife. If we think of History, it is a dramatic chapter that Nottinghamshire gives to it, for in the marvellous castle of Newark died the king who raged and set his teeth as he sealed Magna Carta. Here there set out the pathetic procession with the coffin of Queen Eleanor, its resting-place each night marked by an Eleanor Cross until at last the coffin reached Westminster Abbey to lie in a matchless tomb. Here lived that William Brewster who did so much to shape the destinies of the English-speaking race across the sea, for he negotiated for the land in Virginia to which the Pilgrims of the Mayflower sailed, Brewster leading them. Here was the home of Admiral Howe of the Glorious First of June; and in his village church is an altar

2

cloth from one of his captured ships. Here Charles Stuart set up his standard and challenged Parliament to war; in Nottingham he stood defiant on his last day of peace, and from one of these villages he rode away, when the war was over, on his last day of freedom. Here is the home of one of the men who brought him low, Cromwell's friend Ireton, and a dozen miles away was living the man who was to lead him to the scaffold, Colonel Hacker. There is no county in the land with more dramatic links with the Civil War. If we think of Politics, it was Nottinghamshire which introduced Mr Gladstone to Parliament as the rising hope of the stern unbending Tories. If we think of Great Houses, there is no county in England that in so small a space can match the Dukeries, with three stately homes set in delightful woodlands. This county with so much surprise for those who think it dull has one of the finest of all our cathedrals yet one of the least known, though John Ruskin thought there was nothing in all England to surpass some parts of it. As for Nottingham itself, its castle is set on a rock and it has one of the youngest and proudest of our universities; and at the heart of the city are two streets in which Barrie wrote his way into journalism, General Booth started the Salvation Army, and Jesse Boot founded the marvellous group of shops that have become in fifty years the biggest chemist's business in the world.

It is not without significance that the population of this county increased by a third in the first third of this century, and that in the third decade of the century the proportional increase of the population was greater than that of any other English county except those which border on London and take its overflow.

The half-million acres of this midland county, the home of three-quarters of a million people, are mainly divided by the River Trent, running across them from south-west to north-east, and it may be said roughly that the south and east are agricultural and the west industrial. The southern part of Notts continues the Leicestershire Wolds, country well known to the hunting world; on the south-west is the River Soar with its

3

fertile pastures, and on the south-east the Wolds fall away into the fine farming region of the Vale of Belvoir. Even in this hilly part of Notts there is farming as good as can be found in England, and the farm lands continue along the course of the Trent to Newark, which for ages has been a market town. Beyond Newark the land northwards sinks gradually into a dead flat, and the Trent becomes a Lincolnshire river running through the Fen country.

On the west side of the river the life of the county is determined by the coalfield. First the sluggish Erewash River divides Notts from Derbyshire, and the boundary then becomes high land, rising to over 600 feet. The coalfield runs through these hills nearly all the way between Nottingham and Worksop, being worked for 25 miles from south to north. It is in this coalfield that the steady increase of population has occurred. In the heart of it, the Mansfield neighbourhood, close upon 100,000 people live; in the neighbourhood round Nottingham there are 120,000 more; and the city itself is 280,000 strong.

It is interesting to note that at the census of 1931 all but two of Nottingham's 26 census areas had grown in population, from which we may assume a general prosperity in this immense area of England.

With so rich a coalfield the county has, of course, a wide variety of trades and industries. Though it was here that the resentment against machinery reached its worst frenzy, and the factory system, with its child labour, was here stained with its most atrocious cruelties, machinery has built up a group of flourishing trades in the city and the county. The county of the inventor of the stocking-frame has long been one of the chief centres of the stocking trade, which has grown into hosiery and general clothing, and, though Nottingham has largely lost its wonderful lace trade through the changes of fashion, it has established a great business in the making of lace machines, so providing the world with the means to compete with itself. It has leather and printing industries second to none. There is hardly a town in the world to which things do not go from

Nottingham. The wheels of its cycles run everywhere. Its cigarettes are in every smoker's pocket. Its drugs are known throughout the world.

It is the central position of Notts that has made it an average kind of country and given it its striking place in history. In Roman days it was well served by the Fosse Way running from Exeter to Lincoln. When the Vikings came, by way of the Humber, Nottingham could be reached by river, and its commanding site was seized upon as a national stronghold. It was one of the most formidable of the Northmen's citadels, and became the central point of the Danish defence against Saxon invaders from the south. All through our country's history this doorstep of the north has been a busy place; it was the same motive that led the Viking to set up his standard here and Charles Stuart to unfurl his flag here when inviting his Parliament to war.

In the days when man sought security in castles, two of the strongest were built here. There was a castle on the highest point of Nottingham for more than 1000 years, and at Newark the great castle was long regarded as the Key of the North. Even today it is a stirring experience to visit this castle where King John died, and a man shudders as he stands in its dungeon cell. The history of the castle on the rock at Nottingham is one of the most remarkable examples of the way in which the Civil War cut through the life of England like a knife. Here was a peaceful and prosperous countryside, most of it owned by families widely respected. Colonel Hutchinson defended the castle for Parliament, and it happened that his village of Owthorpe was the neighbouring village to Colston Bassett, where the Royalist Sir Francis Golding lived. Six miles away was Shelford manor house, the home of the famous Stanhope family. The Stanhopes fortified their manor house, and, when the war was lost at Naseby, replied to Colonel Hutchinson's offer of peace by threatening to lay Nottingham Castle as flat as a pancake, whereupon the colonel stormed Shelford and burnt it to the ground, and the sender of the boastful

message died of wounds. When the Stuarts came back, nine
years later, Sir Francis Golding started proceedings against the
colonel, who was flung into prison, where he perished from ill
treatment. Such things did war with otherwise friendly neighbours. Those were the days of castle strongholds.

The old castle at Nottingham is no more, but nothing can
remove the rock on which it stood. The stronghold was
centuries older than the Conqueror, whose men rebuilt it so that
it stood repeated sieges. It was the scene of the seizure of
Mortimer and Queen Isabella, mother of Edward the Third,
and after its long history it passed into the hands of the Duke
of Newcastle, who replaced it with a noble house, which was
burned down by the mob when the Reform Bill was defeated in
1831. It is now rebuilt, and used by Nottingham as its Art
Gallery and Museum, standing superbly on its wonderful rock.

It is more than the heart of Nottingham and the epitome of
its history, for it takes the mind back to the time when men lived
in dens and caves. The rock beneath the castle, like the sandstone ridge on which central Nottingham is built, is excavated
into caves. The dungeons of the castle were hollowed from the
rock, and today its sides have shelters in which people used to
live, its base has been penetrated for places of storage, and there
are labyrinths of tunnelling in which thousands of tons of
material might be stored away. Below the castle on its western
side was the ducal deer park, now a residential quarter of the
city. Looking across the castle from another height is St Mary's
Church, the oldest great structure in Nottingham, and midway
between the castle and the church is the fine open space in which
the Council House rises, the central building of this central city.

Of Nottingham itself it is enough to say that the city is worthy
of its name and fame as Queen of the Midlands. She has been
transforming herself since the war and has acquired possessions
of great splendour. Her University rises on a little green hill
with a tower like a beautiful white lady, chief of the city's great
group of architectural spectacles—the University itself, the
Council House in the heart of the city, the Peace Memorial on

the banks of the river, the Medieval Church on the hill, and the Castle over all.

The churches of the county are a wonderful group; we find Roman, Saxon, and Norman work in them. Quite a hundred of them have Saxon or Norman craftsmanship, and about 20 have both. Among those with Saxon masonry are Carlton-in-Lindrick, East Bridgford, Plumtree, and Sutton-on-Trent. Fine fragments of Saxon crosses or carved stones are at Costock, East Bridgford, Kneesall, Rolleston, Shelford, and Shelton. Rampton has a massive pillar and a crude piscina which may be Saxon, and Thoroton has a tiny Saxon window admitting the dawn. Southwell has a Saxon tympanum. A Saxon tomb-cover in Hickling church is one of the finest in the land, and Stapleford has in its churchyard one of the oldest crosses.

The grandest of the many churches we may visit for their Norman work are Blyth, the incomparable Southwell Minster, and Worksop which is a splendid witness to the later Norman days. Littleborough and Sookholme are tiny and modest examples. Halam has what is believed to be a Norman bell. Notable among forty Norman doorways are those at Balderton, Carlton-in-Lindrick, Cuckney, Finningley, Haughton Chapel, Laneham (framing a Norman door), South Leverton, Winkburn, and Woodborough. Fine tympana are at Carlton-in-Lindrick, Everton, Hawksworth, Hoveringham, and Kirklington. South Scarle has one of the best examples of enriched Norman arcading, and Halam and Harworth have fine Norman arches. Annesley, Bole, Markham Clinton, Screveton, and Woodborough have some of the best of about 30 Norman fonts, among which that of Lenton is supreme; it is one of the finest in the country.

Harworth, Hayton, and North Leverton have lovely doorways built when the Norman style was passing. Attenborough, Marnham, Misterton, Rolleston, and South Leverton have some of the beautiful 13th century work to be found at its best in Southwell choir and in Thurgarton's western doorway. Half a dozen churches have splendid chancels bearing witness to the 14th century masons whose work is outstanding in

Notts, their genius unsurpassed in the chapter house at South-well. Some of the striking monuments in stone and alabaster for which the county is famed are to be seen at Averham, Clifton, Holme Pierrepont, Hoveringham, Langar, Laxton, Ratcliffe-on-Soar, Sibthorpe, Strelley, Whatton-in-the-Vale, Willoughby-on-the-Wolds, and Wollaton. Wall monuments with the kneeling figures typical of Elizabethan and Stuart days are at Gotham, Laneham, Newark, and Normanton-on-Soar.

The traveller who would run through Notts for historic and picturesque places will have many calls to make. Apart from such famous sights as the Dukeries, with a beauty it would be difficult to surpass, and such prehistoric places as Creswell Crags (which it shares with Derbyshire), or Southwell with its wonderful surprise, there are scores of villages that must be seen by those who know how captivating the county can be.

Worksop, the northern gateway of the Dukeries, has a stately fragment of the early 12th century priory, a charming gate-house, and a glorious nave. Newark has one of the finest parish churches in the land and the impressive ruin of a castle on the waterside. The two Retfords have fine churches, one with a splendid array of carving outside and in, another noted for its lovely tower and spire. Hawton has in its chancel carving almost without compare in any parish church. Hucknall has the tomb of Lord Byron, Newstead has his home.

Littleborough has Roman tiles in its church walls and the memory of a dramatic peep of a young Roman lady who vanished from sight when her coffin was opened. Clifton is one of our most characteristic English villages, with a dovecot, the maypole on the green, the famous grove the poet Kirke White loved, and a church with a marvellous array of monuments in brass and stone. At Hickling we can open one of the loveliest 14th century doors in England, with its original ironwork. Thrumpton is an oldworld village with a striking peace memorial and Radcliffe has a lovely memorial garden high above the River Trent. Attenborough has, near its beautiful church, the home of General Ireton, which Charles Stuart may have

8

passed on his last ride as a free man, and East Bridgford has the home of the Hackers, one of whom led the king to the scaffold. Owthorpe is a modest village with the grave of Colonel Hutchinson. Perlethorpe has a lovely modern church in the loveliest of churchyards, a delightful setting by Thoresby Park. Clipstone has the ruins of King John's palace. Averham has a beautiful church in a delightful setting. Shelford is a typical and pleasant village in the landscape seen from Malkin Hills. Wysall has the oldest wooden pulpit in the county, Laxton the only wooden figure, and Kingston-on-Soar has a pillared canopy with sculptures of 200 babes in tuns. Gedling has a renowned spire and Gotham's spire is unique.

Laxton is famous for a unique survival of the old system of open-field cultivation in strips, quite general in England in medieval and Saxon days, but now seen nowhere else in these islands. In all our countryside there is no more interesting old custom still prevailing. Wollaton was the home of the Willoughbys for six centuries, and their wonderful house may be seen by all. In Wollaton church is what is thought to be the figure of Hugh Willoughby who was frozen to death in his ship, and at Willoughby-on-the-Wolds is the figure of Richard Willoughby, the judge who was captured by outlaws and held to ransom. At Oxton we may see in the church the first flag to enter Bagdad in 1917, and at East Stoke, the scene of the literal ending of the Wars of the Roses, is a flag which floated over our Embassy in Washington. At Widmerpool is some of the most charming scenery out of doors, and indoors a beautiful lady sleeping in white marble, exquisitely carved on a tomb. At Kelham is a new chapel like no other in the county and in it sculpture like no other—a marvellous green bronze Crucifixion scene by Charles Sargeant Jagger, whose masterpiece is at Hyde Park Corner, and whose death robbed English sculpture of one of its most brilliant figures. How few see the mark of his genius in this village: how many pass it in the midst of the busiest throng of traffic in the kingdom! At Shelford lies the Earl of Chesterfield who wrote the famous letters, and Eakring has the grave of one of the most pathetic heroes in the history of our country-side, William Mompesson. Scrooby, with its lovely tower, is the home of William Brewster and the cradle of the Pilgrim Fathers. Harby is the place where Queen Eleanor died. At Screveton was born Robert Thoroton, the historian of Notts.

Of Southwell, which still has the room from which Charles Stuart set out to deliver himself up to captivity and death, it is enough to say that it has perhaps as great a surprise as any village holds for an English traveller, for here is the least known of our cathedrals, the impressive Norman Minster, with a doorway that John Ruskin never forgot and a chapter house with carving that no one ever forgets.

Sherwood Forest, the most remarkable natural area of the county, is the most impressive remnant surviving of the vast forests which once clothed the low-lying parts of England. It is famous over the world, for it is the home of Robin Hood. It is said that in the old days it covered nearly a fifth of the county, a tract of dense forest, heath, and woodland, about 25 miles long and ten miles broad in parts, stretching from Nottingham to Worksop. Belonging originally to the Crown, the right of hunting in it was reserved for the king, and cruel were the Forest Laws guarding this right. Its great oaks were felled for the navy in the Commonwealth, and it is believed that some of the beams in St Paul's are made from them. So it was for centuries till the great landowners began to enclose their parks. In 1683 the Earl of Kingston formed Thoresby Park with 2000 acres of forest land; a little later Clumber took half as much again; and with the Enclosure Acts of the 18th century came the disappearance of much more. Now Old King Coal has marred the beauty of much of what is left.

The chief remnant of the old Forest is the area known as the Dukeries, comprising the three great estates of Welbeck, Clumber, and Thoresby, with their magnificent group of houses; but it is not only the ancient forest we see here, for thousands of trees have been planted since the estates were enclosed. Of the old forest there is nothing grander than the two magnificent stretches of Birklands and Bilhagh, side by side; of the later trees there is nothing finer than the famous Duke's Drive, an avenue of lime trees with a double row on each side, making a crescent three miles long on its way through Clumber Park.

Those who would see the forest at its best should do so from Edwinstowe and Ollerton, on the edge of the Dukeries; they should leave the roads and seek the paths. Some trees long renowned still stand. The Major Oak (one of the most famous trees still left in England) is in Birklands; so too is the old oak known as Robin Hood's Larder. By the road from Edwinstowe to Mansfield are fragments of the Parliament Oak which story associates with King John. The Greendale Oak still grows in Welbeck Park, with an archway cut through it by the first Duke of Portland. One of the giants now gone was the Duke's Walking Stick, over a hundred feet high.

Man or myth, Robin Hood is for ever linked with Sherwood Forest. Such a forest demanded a romantic outlaw chief, and traditions in fable, legend, ballad, and plays furnish ideal heroes in Robin Hood with his Little John, Will Scarlet, Friar Tuck, and the rest of the Merry Men of the Greenwood. We have a Robin Hood literature which makes him a veritable King Arthur of the woodland bandits, who was ever chivalrous to women, who did no wrong to field or fold, who opposed oppression and the terrible Forest Laws, and robbed the unworthy rich to give to the deserving poor.

In our own time James Prior Kirk wrote delightfully of the manners and customs of the old forest in his Forest Folk, and Washington Irving as he wandered through the forest lived again in the days of Robin and his merry band, writing of them:

> *He clothed himself in scarlet then,*
> *His men were all in green;*
> *A finer show in all the world*
> *In no place could be seen.*

> *Good Lord! it was a gallant sight,*
> *To see them in a row;*
> *With every man a good broadsword*
> *And eke a good yew bow.*

And whether or not we believe the story of Robin's death at Kirklees, through the treachery of the prioress of the nunnery there, we like to remember his last words to Little John:

Lay me a green sod under my head,
And another at my feet:
And lay my bent bow by my side,
Which was my music sweet;
And make my grave of gravel and green
Which is most right and meet.

Let me have length and breadth enough
With a green sod at my head,
That they may say when I am dead,
Here lies bold Robin Hood.

Historians are not agreed as to the origin of Robin. Some see in him a myth surviving on the shores of memory from the time of our pagan ancestors. Modern research would have it that Robin was some benevolent wood sprite, deriving his name from the hood such little people wore. It is known that his Maid Marian springs from French gallantry, for French literature has a Robin too. Another authority holds that there have been real Robin Hoods, whose actual achievements give a foundation of reality to many of the stories. That is to say, a Robin Hood has succeeded a Robin Hood, inheriting name and fame, traditions and domain, as oak succeeds oak for a thousand years. Blidworth claims many associations and Edwinstowe his marriage to Maid Marian.

The country abounds with suggestions of Robin Hood, far beyond the confines of Sherwood Forest; but the favourite story brings Robin into prominence in the reign of Richard Lion Heart, the period which Scott has turned to such magnificent purpose in Ivanhoe. In Scott Robin is a figure of dignity as well as of valour and well-doing, but Scott, alas, denies him his Maid Marian, and pays tribute to the Yorkshire ambition to have the hero as a native of Loxley.

Whatever the foundation for the story, Robin stood to England for centuries as the embodiment of the resentment of the poor against the Forest Laws, the breaking of which involved loss of eyes and limbs. In his pillaging Robin is vindicating democratic right against tyrannous Authority. Patriotism, too, this woodland hero typifies, his superb feats of archery reflecting the national pride in the English bowman who has conquered France and is the finest soldier in the world.

Late Plantagenet or early Tudor, he held the imagination of poet, playwright, and broadsheet-writer for century after century. Games and festivals were organised all over the country in his honour, and so prevalent and absorbing were these games that Hugh Latimer raged, in a sermon he preached to Edward the Sixth, over an experience he had had in a village to which he had sent notice overnight that he would preach there in the morning, the occasion being a holiday. The church stood in his way, he said, and he took his horse and went thither, but found the church door locked. At last the key was found, and one of the parish came to him and said, "Sir, this is a busy day with us; we cannot hear you. It is Robin Hood's day. The parish are gone to gather for Robin Hood; I pray you hinder them not."

Robin Hood and his Merry Men have peopled the woods and the pages of our literature for some 700 years, and as long as children love a greenwood tale they will not let him die. He is one with this famous county, woven into the spirit of the greenwood near the very heart of England.

Byron's First Love

ANNESLEY. There is old and new Annesley, but it is the old that has come into story, for here with the ruined church is Annesley Hall, home of Mary Chaworth. It stands in a park with a lake, and has been the home of the Chaworth-Musters family since Byron's first love brought together the two families by her marriage. The Chaworths have lived in Notts since the Conquest, their chief homes being at Wiverton and Annesley.

The beautiful Mary was the last of her house, and the romance of Byron's boyhood love for the "bright morning star of Annesley" must always cling to this place. In the park is Diadem Hill, 578 feet above the sea and seen for miles round. It was here that Byron and Mary often met, and here they parted, after which Annesley lost its enchantment for the poet:

> *Hills of Annesley, bleak and barren,*
> *Where my thoughtless childhood strayed,*
> *How the northern tempests, warring,*
> *Howl above thy tufted shade.*

> *Now no more, the hours beguiling,*
> *Former favourite haunts I see,*
> *Now no more my Mary smiling*
> *Makes ye seem a heaven to me.*

He was genuinely in love with her, but she did not return his love, and before he went to Cambridge she had married John Musters, the sporting squire of Colwick Hall. She died in 1832 as a result of exposure during an attack on the hall by Reform Bill rioters.

Mary was the heiress of William Chaworth who was killed in a duel with his cousin, the 5th Lord Byron, great-uncle of the poet. The duel arose from an after-dinner quarrel at an inn in Pall Mall, Chaworth and Byron settling the dispute by fighting in a room lit only by a candle and a dying fire. Lord Byron was tried by the peers and found guilty of manslaughter, but the verdict brought only nominal punishment. Chaworth lies in the ruined old church.

15

In the old churchyard, under a monument showing an anchor on a piled heap of stones, sleeps that George Chaworth-Musters who was traveller and explorer and almost a king. Born at Naples while his parents were travelling, he became himself a great traveller, and while he was only 21, being then in the navy, he and a midshipman climbed the famous Sugar Loaf Mountain and planted the British ensign on the top, where it remained for years before anyone climbed up to bring it down. Out in South America he settled down sheep farming, and later began exploring. He lived on terms of great friendliness with the natives of Patagonia, who treated him as a king. He travelled 1400 miles on a journey which added much to our knowledge of South America and its people, and was given the gold medal of the Royal Geographical Society. On returning to England after his sojourn in Patagonia he found it hard to fall into civilised ways and used to sleep in the garden wrapped in a blanket.

Though the old church is unsafe now even for visiting, there is enough of it left to tell of its beauty. The 14th century tower still has its belfry windows, and the south aisle has a lovely east window and fine sedilia. This aisle was added in the 14th century as a chantry, and was known as Felley Chapel after a small priory founded two miles away in the 12th century. Only a few fragments of the priory are left, and on its site is a charming brick house with many gables, in lovely gardens and in a delightful situation. James the First gave Felley to Anthony Millington in 1603, and Anthony's son Gilbert signed the death-warrant of Charles Stuart.

Two treasures from the old church are in the new one high on the hilltop, its tower and spire a landmark. Built in 1874, and made new this century after a fire, it is spacious and full of light, with nave arches on clustered pillars and four canopied angels marking the entrance to the chancel. The glass of the great east window, which pleases both by its colour and its delicate treatment, is in memory of a vicar whose portrait is in it; ten Bible scenes and a Crucifixion glow in red, blue, green, and gold, and there are small medallion heads of disciples. Three charming windows at the west end show Our Lord with a child on His knee, an angel holding lilies and a crown, and a winged knight with scales and a sword.

One of the old treasures is a splendid Norman font like a tub, carved with lattice pattern and a band of stars. Another is the alabaster figure of a man wearing a round embroidered cap with scalloped edge, a sheet draped over him. A striking and unusual 20th century font of white marble has an oblong bowl carved all over with birds and animals in foliage. Among a number of brass inscriptions to the Chaworth-Musters family is one with little colour engravings of the regimental badges of four who gave their lives in the war. Three were brothers who lived at Annesley Hall, and one a cousin, all very young, and at the foot of the brass are the words, "In the morning of their lives."

Nottingham's Busy Neighbour

ARNOLD. From the earliest days of the stocking frame, invented by William Lee of Calverton near by, this once pretty village of Sherwood Forest has grown into a workaday place. It was one of the places which suffered from the machine-smashing Luddites of last century.

Nottingham has stretched out an arm to part of it, but we have only to follow the line of hills that shelter it to be soon in the heart of the country, and to find at Dorket Head one of the finest viewpoints of this countryside. Not far away is Cockpit Hill, climbing higher still to 500 feet above the sea, with remains of a Roman encampment. In the bounds of Arnold, at Red Hill, is an old brick farmhouse by the side of the Old North Road where the Mansfield coaches stopped for a change of horses, and here in still earlier days travellers called for guides to take them through the forest. The old stables and their clock are still in the yard, and the lookout balcony is over the porch.

In a big three-storeyed house rising above its neighbours in a quiet street was born Richard Parkes Bonington, whose pictures are among the treasures of our land and won for him imperishable fame as a painter. There is a bronze plaque of him on the house, his statue is in Nottingham, and his pictures are in the Art Gallery at Nottingham Castle and in the Wallace Collection.

Although much restored, Arnold's fine church is a link with faraway days. Part of it was here when Ralph de Arnehall was knighted by Edward the First, and it is said to have been originally built late in the 12th century. The pinnacled tower is 15th century; from the 14th come the nave and the beautiful chancel with its double piscina, blocked sedilia, founder's recess, and battered Easter Sepulchre. Lofty arcades between the nave and aisles are adorned with patriarchical heads.

The graceful chancel screen, with a vaulted canopy and a lovely cornice, the stalls, the reredos, and the marble pavement of the chancel were the gifts of Frank Evelyn Seely who was lay rector here and died in 1928. The ancient chapel of St Catherine is restored in memory of 250 men who did not come home from the war. One of the men who did come home was William Johnson, who won the VC towards the end of the war, having shown wonderful courage in capturing two machine guns and, although badly wounded, continuing to lead his men forward.

The new porch was built by the widow of Sir John Robinson of Worksop Manor, of whom we read that "he was born beneath the shadow of this church, and throughout his boyhood and youth passed continually through these doors." He was a great public benefactor, building almshouses at Sherwood and Daybrook and endowing a church at Worksop.

An interesting list of Arnold's vicars from 1250 is filled out with history and notes of contemporary events.

The Young Englishman in France

RICHARD PARKES BONINGTON was one of the painters of genius whom the Midlands added to the great school of English watercolourists of the first part of the 19th century, though his own painting was in oil as much as in water-colour, and the greater part of it was done in France.

There chance directed him. Born in 1801, the son of an Arnold man who was in turn the unsuccessful governor of a gaol, a painter who exhibited at the Royal Academy, and a lace manufacturer, he moved with the family to Calais in connection with the lace business.

But young Bonington, who from his earliest boyhood had shown a talent for drawing and an incurable propensity to improve it on every possible occasion, would have nothing to do with the lace factory, and fortunately gained encouragement and instruction from Louis Francia the water-colourist, and afterwards from the great Delacroix.

Delacroix saw him copying the Flemish landscapes at the Louvre, and a friendship sprang up between the two. Soon young Richard's water-colours commanded a ready sale. He still kept to his own line, and though, when he was 21, he exhibited at the Salon and won a prize, he continued to paint in the open air and to disregard academic tradition. In the year when he received a medal for two of his French coast scenes a similar honour was conferred on two other Englishmen, Constable and Copley Fielding, and he stands with them as the founder of the illustrious modern school of French landscape painting which eventually produced Rousseau and Corot.

But if we may say that his influence was great his life was short, for he died only seven years after his first Salon picture. He came to England, once with Delacroix, and exhibited at the Royal Academy, but France saw and collected the greater number of his paintings, which are now much scattered, though there is a noble and representative group of them gathered in the Wallace Collection and others in the Art Gallery at Nottingham Castle.

A Crime of Long Ago

ASKHAM. Orchards abound in this quiet place, which has little to show except a church with grey walls, red roof, and Norman walling in the nave.

Its 15th century tower has battlements and eight pinnacles, and a modern porch leads inside, where the great charm lies in eight fine windows which have filled the nave with light as long as the tower has stood. The 13th century chancel has a 14th century east window with beautiful tracery. The old priest's doorway is blocked. The spiral altar rails are 17th century.

On one side of the churchyard are three small almshouses rebuilt last century from a foundation of 1658 by one of the Elwes family who lived here. One of them who went from the village to a place in history was Gervase Helwys, baptised here in 1561, and Lieutenant of the Tower in 1613. He is said to have had something to do with the murder of Sir Thomas Overbury, and though it is hard to say how far he was guilty he was hanged on Tower Hill. His uncle Thomas Helwys formed what is thought to have been the first Baptist church in England.

Cranmer's Village

ASLOCKTON. Though this quiet village has little for us to see, it will ever be remembered for having given England a famous man who died for his faith, Thomas Cranmer. Here he was born and lived for 14 years, having lessons from the parish clerk, and exercises in manly sports with his father, whose portrait is engraved on the floorstone of his grave in Whatton church.

The old manor house of the Cranmers has disappeared; it was probably in a field where the path called Cranmer's Walk sets off to Orston. Near this path, just beyond the modern church, is a moated mound which may be part of an ancient earthwork. It is known as Cranmer's Mound, for it is said that as a boy the archbishop loved to sit here and look round the countryside as he listened to the bells of Whatton church ringing across the River Smite. Some thick walls of an ancient chapel Cranmer would know, desecrated at the Reformation, still remain in the village; they are part of a mission room.

It was in 1489 that Thomas Cranmer, first Protestant Archbishop of Canterbury, was born here. Sent to Cambridge at 14, he enthusiastically applied himself to the new learning. It was Cranmer who suggested that Henry, when deeply engaged with his efforts to divorce Catherine, should ignore Rome and have the legality of his marriage decided by English divines from the Scriptures themselves. Henry was delighted, ordered him to write a book on his idea, appointed him one of his chaplains, and sent him to Rome and Germany to expound it. While in Germany Cranmer married a second time. Returning to England, he was consecrated Archbishop, and a few weeks later declared the king's marriage invalid.

His first great act as Primate was, within a week, to publicly marry Henry to Anne Boleyn, having already been present (it is believed) at their private bigamous marriage four months before. Three years later Cranmer declared this bigamous marriage null and void, and in 1540 he presided over the convocation which annulled Henry's marriage to Anne of Cleves.

The die having been cast, Cranmer strove his utmost for the Reformation; he placed an English Bible within all men's reach: he urged Henry to dissolve the monasteries, with a view to devoting their revenues to religion and learning; and he denounced the distribution of lands and abbeys among Henry's friends.

Thrust against his will into statecraft, Cranmer was at heart a scholar-recluse, and was happiest when engaged in literary pursuits.

His melodious English lives in the Prayer Book, of which the Litany, the Articles, and most of the Collects are probably his work.

The conspiracy which induced Edward the Sixth to change the order of the succession once more betrayed Cranmer into weakness, and at the same time doomed him, for at Mary's accession he was arrested, with Latimer and Ridley. Sentence was passed, and there followed the melancholy spectacle of Cranmer's six abject recantations; and then, at the last minute, his declaration that he had abjured only to save his life, and that he died a Protestant. As the fire blazed up at Oxford (in March 1556) the courage that had so often failed him reached a height sublime, and he thrust his right hand first into the flame, because it had most offended. It has been said that his death advanced the Reformation perhaps more than that of any other sufferer for his faith.

Famous Brothers

ATTENBOROUGH. Proud of its possessions as it lies between the busy road and the river, it leaves the stir of the world, with the closing of the railway crossing gates, for the seclusion of charming houses and gardens, leafy lanes, and broad Trent meadows.

In the shadow of the church tower, its garden adjoining the churchyard, is a farmhouse which has still traces of the old home of the Iretons, and here were born two famous brothers, John who became Lord Mayor of London, and Henry who married Cromwell's daughter Bridget. Henry's baptism in 1611 and John's in 1615 are both in the register.

Henry studied law, and at the outbreak of the Civil War, when he was living here, offered his services to Parliament. He fought at Edgehill and Marston Moor, and was one of Cromwell's right-hand men. He signed the death-warrant of the King, died of plague, and was buried in the Abbey; and at the Restoration was taken from his grave, dragged to Tyburn, and hanged from sunrise to sunset. His brother John was thrown into prison and transported to the Scilly Islands.

The church so well known to those two brothers, in the nave of which Cromwell stabled his horses, is beautiful without and within; and, though its atmosphere is eloquent with the story of the years, it has been so cared for that it might have been built yesterday. It is a charming blending of stone and woodwork old and new, with lovely medieval windows.

The 500-year-old tower has a lofty spire and traceried windows. The rebuilt porch shelters a 14th century doorway and three gravestones carved in the 12th, 13th, and 15th centuries. Its great treasure is the door itself, with three iron hinges of simple scrolls, which may have belonged to the doorway now blocked in the north wall. If so it must be one of the oldest doors in the land, for the doorway comes from the age when the Norman style was passing.

The lofty nave has a 15th century clerestory with a window over the chancel arch, and two 700-year-old arcades which each lost half an arch when the tower was built. The hoods of the pointed arches have bold carving ending in fine corbels of heads and a grotesque. The striking carving of the capitals crowning the round pillars is a feature of the church, those on the south side being a little later and more grotesque than the others. Twelve extraordinary figures on the three south capitals, one at every corner, are all grotesque except for a bishop's mitred head, most of them heads with wings or limbs and no bodies. In company with the bishop is a pig-faced grotesque, a hooded man, and a jester with a wide grin on his contorted face. Others are a pig with cloven feet and a creature with a tiny head, features of a bird, a round body with wings, and huge hands or claws.

The east window, which has at each side an old bracket carved with a winged figure, sheds a golden light with its picture of two angels and the three Marys looking up at Our Lord risen from the tomb. Lovely glass in the north aisle shows Joseph in red and gold with a lantern and staff, and Mary in red and blue with the Holy Child. The peace window has St Nicholas, St George, and an angel with a crown, and three small scenes from the front. There are fragments of old glass.

Beautiful oak lines the chancel walls, adorns the organ, and makes the pulpit lovely with panels of intricate tracery. Four Jacobean panels, set in the splendid modern choir stalls, are carved with a mermaid, a merman with his tail in the mouth of a sea monster, and a dragon which seems to be charmed by a small figure blowing a horn. The old chancel screen has gone, but two splendid 15th century stall-ends over six feet high are by the priest's doorway. The nave and chancel have fine flat roofs, that of the nave keeping some of its old moulded beams. The massive altar-table is Elizabethan, the font is 600 years old, and the rood stairs and doorway are in the south aisle which is strengthened by two flying buttresses inside the church.

Into this peaceful churchyard, which is like a shaded garden and has an ancient yew, strife has come, for a simple cross and rows of graves tell the story of a terrible day in the Great War when many lives were lost in a frightful explosion in the munition works at Chilwell. Here we get a fine view of the wooded hills of Clifton, Barton, and Gotham across the river, and of Brent's Hill, which the Ancient Britons knew.

Cromwell's Right-Hand Man

HENRY IRETON, at the outbreak of the Civil War, was living quietly here on his estate. He had taken his Art Degree at Oxford and had studied law at Middle Temple without having been called to the Bar. He was made captain of the Commonwealth troop of horse raised by Nottingham, and fought with it under Essex at Edgehill.

He commanded the same force at Gainsborough, and from that time forward was closely associated with Cromwell, under whom he quickly distinguished himself as one of the officers of the New Model. During the battle of Naseby Ireton's left wing was ridden through by the terrific charge of Prince Rupert, but with his broken forces he went valiantly to the succour of a disorganised body of Roundhead infantry, when he had his horse killed under him and was himself run through the thigh and taken prisoner.

When Cromwell's courage and generalship restored the fortunes of the day and converted the Cavalier success into a rout, Ireton was still a prisoner and helpless. He told his captor that if he would carry him back to the Roundhead lines he should have his freedom.

The invalid was soon restored, resumed fighting, and played a major part in the negotiations which led to the surrender of Oxford. It was while fighting and parleying were going on there that Ireton was vouchsafed a brief remission from his military duties to marry Cromwell's daughter Bridget.

A sincere affection linked Cromwell and his son-in-law. "I write not to thy husband," runs a letter from Oliver to Bridget; "partly to avoid trouble, for one line of mine begets many of his, which I doubt makes him sit up too late." The younger man played an important part in the years which followed. He would have saved Charles if the king could have been relied upon; it is plain that Ireton could and would have preserved the dynasty but for Charles's failure to respond to generous treatment.

But when all else failed Ireton became one of the most energetic members of the court which condemned the king. Afterwards he accompanied Cromwell to Ireland, and on the return of Oliver to England remained there as Lord Deputy. In this office, says Ludlow, who was his colleague, he conducted himself with great ability, and with unbounded devotion to the public service.

When Parliament voted him lands and a life pension of £2000 a year he firmly refused both. His patriotism was untinged by motives of personal gain. The nation, he said, had many just debts which it should pay rather than offer land and money to him who had desire for neither.

He worked himself almost to death, and plague did the rest. He died at Limerick in 1651. His body was brought to London, where it lay in state at Somerset House, and was afterwards interred in Henry Seventh's chapel with a magnificent monument, such as his friends believed Ireton would have utterly disapproved. Nine years later his remains were dragged from the tomb, drawn on a hurdle to Tyburn, hanged on a gibbet and afterwards buried at its foot, where the feet of those who pass the Marble Arch trample over his dust.

The Proud Suttons

AVERHAM. Its glory is the exquisite setting of its fine little church, which stands high on a bank of the Trent with a wealth of trees in the churchyard, and a magnificent cedar in the lovely garden of the rectory lifting its branches above the tower. With the fine sweep of the river, and the view across the meadows of Newark and its tapering spire, it is one of the fairest scenes in the valley of the Trent. In a wall of the rectory garden is a 15th century window from Southwell Minster.

Herringbone masonry in the walls of the church takes its story back to early Norman or even Saxon days, and the rest of it is mainly 14th and 15th century. The tower comes from both these times, the 15th century storey crowned with rich battlements and pinnacles and adorned with quaint gargoyles. The nave and the porch, with the initials of its builder (Sir Thomas Sutton), are also 15th century.

The 600-year-old chancel, which has no arch, has a splendid east window, a priest's doorway, some fine old glass pieced together from fragments found at Kelham Hall, and a plain oak screen mostly 500 years old. There is a Jacobean altar table. Fine oak panelling and seating of this century are in memory of Joseph Walker, who was rector here for 51 years, as Richard Sutton had been before him till 1785.

There are many memorials of the Suttons, and the village is proud of its connection with this old family which has now become Manners-Sutton. They lived here and at Kelham, but only a few mounds are left to mark the site of their Averham house, which Cromwell's soldiers destroyed. Robert de Sutton had the estate in the 13th century after the death of his uncle, Henry de Lexington, the last of three famous brothers of Laxton whose name gave the Suttons the title of their peerage in the 17th century. Charles Manners-Sutton followed Richard as rector in 1785, and became Archbishop of Canterbury; his son became Speaker of the House of Commons, and his brother Lord Chancellor of Ireland.

On the floor of the chancel lies a stone figure with sword and shield, perhaps a warrior of the time of King John, and in a recess lies a bearded civilian of the 14th century.

On a great tomb with painted decoration lies Sir William Sutton in armour, a courtier of the time of Elizabeth. He is with his lady, and part of the inscription runs,

> *Thrice nine years lived he with his lady faire,*
> *A lovely, noble, and like vertuous pair.*

On the opposite wall of the chancel is a memorial to their son Robert who was MP for Notts, served Charles Stuart in the garrison at Newark till its surrender, and was created Baron Lexington for his help in raising money. His son Robert, who was born at Averham in 1661 and became 2nd Lord Lexington, was a great diplomatist, and lost his only son at Madrid while he was Ambassador there. The body was sent home in a bale of cloth, and both parents and son sleep at Kelham, where a great tomb keeps their memory green.

A Pilgrim Father

BABWORTH. A singularly charming spot it is, among gently swelling hills and lovely trees, quiet and secluded, though the stir of Retford is only a mile away. Swans glide by the wayside on the lovely winding lake, from which fine parkland rolls up to the creepered hall and to the many-gabled and many-chimneyed rectory.

To the little church hiding among its yew hedges, encircled by mighty horse chestnuts, sycamores, yews, cedars, and beeches in the grounds of the hall, William Bradford used to come from his home at Austerfield ten miles away. He became one of the most remarkable of the Pilgrim Fathers who sailed in the Mayflower.

The old church is adorned with battlements and pinnacles, and has a low 15th century tower. The ancient porch has a stone roof with four ribs ending in tiny corbel heads worth finding, among them being a dainty human face and a grotesque animal. The nave and chancel are all in one, and an old arcade divides the nave from a wide aisle, one of its arches resting on a huge grotesque. The most pleasing glass makes a patch of blue, red, gold, and green in the west window of the tower, showing Noah's Ark and the dove with a spray of olive, John the Baptist, and Moses with the Ten Commandments.

Of the many memorials to the Simpsons who lived at the hall (a small part of which comes from about 1600), two are in great contrast. One is an ornate monument with a painting on glass of the Resurrection, set in a stone wreath of flowers; at each side is an ungainly cherub, who has put down his harp and his scroll of music in order to weep more copiously. The other memorial tells of a little midshipman who died when only 15, from a fever caught at the Cape Verde Islands.

Into Babworth's little gallery of heroes comes Arthur Hardolph Eyre, who was 23 when he was killed in 1874 during the last engagement of the Ashanti War. He fell while leading the advance on Coomassie, and his memorial window shows two small scenes of the war. He was the brave son of a brave father, General Sir William Eyre, who fought in the Crimea.

We read of Harry Doad that he was 24 when he died at Baden-Baden while trying to save the lives of others; and an inscription in a fine alabaster frame tells of 18 men who died for peace.

Beauty on the Byway

BALDERTON. A close neighbour of Newark, it has unsuspected joys for those who leave the busy highway for its pleasant road. Into a glance come a pretty angle of 19th century almshouses, a house built 400 years ago and set in a lovely garden which may often be shared by lovers of flowers, and a church showing its beautiful north porch to every passer-by. Beyond the church is the Old Hall by the roadside, with a glorious cedar on its lawn. Balderton Hall, built nearly a century ago, is away from the village, off the Newark road.

The church has fine work in wood and stone, one of its lovely things the 500-year-old spire crowning a 14th and 15th century tower. The oldest story is told by the Norman doorways in the 14th century south porch and the rebuilt north porch, whose handsome entrance arch is carved with zigzag and beak-heads. The lovely north door, adorned with tracery, is perhaps 600 years old.

Some of the capitals of the old nave arcades are enriched with foliage. There are many medieval windows, and in one of the lancets of the chancel is some old glass. There are two old piscinas, a priest's doorway, and a 14th century font with ballflowers. The panelled oak pulpit is old, and rare treasures of 15th century woodwork are the splendid chancel screen with the figure of a monk on one side and the Madonna on the other, and about 40 fine bench-ends with traceried panels, many of their poppyheads formed by pairs of rabbits.

By the Willows

BARNBY-IN-THE-WILLOWS. A bright little village on the Witham, it is tucked away in a tranquil countryside, with a tower or spire adding to the friendliness of the scene on almost every hand. It has a fine old round dovecot with a red roof, a house with a quaint porch fashioned from a yew tree, a big house in a park a mile away, and a charming medieval church to which we come between deep yew hedges. Over the willow-lined stream bounding the churchyard we step into Lincolnshire.

The two-storeyed tower is over 500 years old, the 14th century south porch is much restored, and the splendid 15th century north porch has a niche on each side of its wide entrance arch. A lovely 500-year-old door opens to the charming interior, which has many old benches with a few modern ones, looking like a garden of wooden flowers, their traceried ends crowned with poppyheads. Some of these are carved with faces and figures. One has a smiling face very like Mr Punch, the head of a grinning youth with his tongue out is between the heads of two women, an old man with staring eyes has a grotesque for a companion; one has two dogs and another two girls with curly locks.

The chancel of about 1300 is notable for the singular treatment of its window tracery. A stringcourse round the walls forms a transom across the side windows, and sometimes the tracery is below this as well as above. Between three lancets in the east wall are strange little openings. Both sides of the chancel are alike, and each has an unusual recessed window shaped like a diamond and filled with quatrefoil tracery.

The font and the nave arcades are 14th century, the altar table and the panelling in the sanctuary are 17th, and the parish chest is over 400 years old. An ancient coffin stone under the tower has a fine cross and the head and shoulders of someone now forgotten, the features worn away but the hands still at prayer.

The Doomed King Passes By

BARTON-IN-FABIS (or we may call it Barton in the Beans) nestles under hills by lovely Trent meadows, a quiet gathering of old houses, thatched cottages and farms, a fine old church surrounded by limes and chestnuts, and the old rectory close by.

More than once it has come into story. Brent's Hill was the site of extensive British and Roman fortifications. Many coins have been found there, and at Glebe Farm there could be seen until recent years the remains of a tessellated pavement of small coloured cubes which may have been part of a Roman villa. It was discovered last century, and after varying fortune came to the unseemly end of being a sackful of bits at the rectory.

For 200 years Barton was the home of the great Derbyshire family of Sacheverells. Their manor house is gone, but the wall that surrounded it and the old brick dovecot are still here, and their memorials are in the church. Henry of 1598 and Rafe of 1605 have inscriptions, and the name Sacheverell is on a marble tomb. William Sacheverell of 1616 and his wife lie side by side in alabaster, their hands and feet gone, both in ruffs, and Tabitha in a pretty headdress and a long gown with rucked sleeves.

Another William who knew the old house and died here sleeps in Morley church, Derbyshire. It was he, perhaps the greatest of the family, who resisted the attempt of James the Second to give Nottingham a new charter, and was fined heavily when Judge Jeffreys was sent to settle the trouble. He was an incorruptible politician, and is remembered as one of the first of our great orators.

Most of the church comes from the close of the 14th century, but the clerestory and the fine flat roof of the nave are of the time of Henry the Seventh. The tower has buttresses and a stair turret climbing to the top, and a fine spire with a tier of windows. Two of the bells are 1617, and four ring out in memory of the men who died for peace three centuries later.

Entered by a porch of 1693, the church is full of light, the stone walls attractive with the lines of their irregular coursing. The splendid nave arcade has four lofty bays; the chancel has three sedilia, a piscina niche with tiny recesses, a priest's doorway, and a canopied niche by the east window. The font is as old as the church. There is a Jacobean table, and the Jacobean pulpit has new panels. An old door in the nave has still its old bar fastening, and across the lofty narrow chancel arch is the fine old oak screen with gates.

It may not be idle fancy to think that this little place has had a share in one of the great dramas of English history; that in the early hours of a May morning, nearly 300 years ago, the people may have been roused by the hard galloping of a small company of horsemen on their way to the river, little dreaming that a king was passing by on a fateful journey, his last ride as a free man. In 1646, when Charles Stuart had resolved to give himself up to the Scots, he set out for Southwell, reaching Stamford on the 3rd of May. It is believed he crossed the Trent near Gotham in his anxiety to miss Nottingham, and if this were so nothing is more likely than that he would cross by Barton Ferry and ride on past the very door of Henry Ireton's old home at Attenborough.

Beautiful Vale

BEAUVALE PRIORY. In a most-happily named stretch of the busy Erewash valley, in the charming seclusion of green fields and forest-side, stands all that is left of a priory which came into history six centuries ago. It was founded in 1343 by Nicholas de Cantelupe, a great soldier and friend of Edward the Third, whose castle was at Greasley a mile away.

It was the last priory to be founded in this county, and the first to be touched with the tragedy of the scaffold in Henry the Eighth's war on the monasteries. For nearly 200 years it was the home of Carthusian monks, who lived in seclusion from the world and gave themselves to hard work and great privation. Life in the Beautiful Vale perhaps consoled them for the austerity of their daily routine, and these great gardeners, whose beds were of straw and their raiment of hair cloth, made this lovely place blossom as the rose.

Tragedy came upon it in 1535, when Prior Robert Laurence and Prior Houghton went with Prior Webster of Axholme to put forward petitions concerning the king's attitude to the monasteries. When questioned by Thomas Cromwell they acknowledged their loyalty to the king but refused to regard him as head of the church, and they were condemned and hanged at Tyburn. From his prison window Sir Thomas More, who was to follow them in a few weeks, saw them led out to execution, and said to his daughter, "Dost thou not see that these blessed fathers be now as cheerfully going to their death as bridegrooms to their marriage?"

Today a farmhouse stands where the priory stood, and among the ruins seen in the outbuildings is part of the prior's house. Part of the remains have been roofed to house the cattle which come and go by the old doorways, and close by are great ivied walls with traces of a fine window.

In the woods behind the priory is a charming spot known as Robin Hood's Well, where forget-me-nots are a delight to see.

The Drum-Major's Daughter

BECKINGHAM. A mile and a half from the Trent and Lincolnshire, it is big and pleasant with trees, treasuring a beautiful old church which comes chiefly from the three medieval centuries, but has a plain tub font taking its story back to Norman days.

The lower part of the lofty tower is 600 years old, but its buttresses and the top storey are a century younger. There are windows of both these times, and the clerestory is 15th century. The two fine nave arcades with nail-head on the capitals are 13th and 14th century, and between the chancel and its chapel are two 15th century bays. The chancel, though much rebuilt, keeps three 13th century seats for priests, with richly moulded arches and detached shafts with capitals of natural foliage. The piscina is 700 years old.

A lovely medieval relic is part of the oak chancel screen, now across the tower arch and much restored. There is an ancient image bracket in the south aisle, carved with the strange figure of a little man armed with a sword, his crowned head stuck on to his body at a right angle. Four curious gargoyle heads outside the north aisle have staring eyes and bulging cheeks.

On the wall near the tower is a brass plate engraved with a sinking ship and three or four boats taking women and children from the wreck. Lined up on deck are the heroes who wait for death rather than crowd the boats, and others are clinging to the rigging. It is in memory of Marion Parkinson, one of the survivors of the troopship Birkenhead which was wrecked off the Cape in 1852; she was the daughter of the drum major. One of about 190 who were saved, she saw 500 soldiers and sailors stand in line to go down with the sinking ship. She lies in the cemetery near the church.

A Citizen of the World

BEESTON. The world's biggest drug factories have come to Beeston, with a floor space of over a million and a quarter square feet and weighing nearly 300,000 tons. Into its making have gone 20 acres of bottle-green glass, 37,000 tons of cement in bags which, placed in a row, would reach 320 miles (about the distance from Beeston to Paris), and 8800 tons of steel bars which would make a line 1700 miles long, from Beeston to Constantinople.

Looking out from the lovely boulevard between Lenton and Beeston is the bronze bust of the man to whose business genius this great building of glass and steel and concrete is a monument. He was Jesse Boot, Lord Trent, citizen of Nottingham and of the world, of whom the inscription says:

Our great citizen, Jesse Boot, Lord Trent. Before him lies a monument to his industry: behind him an everlasting monument to his benevolence.

His bust is at the entrance gates of the splendid University College which (with the whole of the Highfields estate now turned into playing fields, lovely gardens, boating lake, open-air swimming pool, and boulevard) he gave to Nottingham, his birthplace, where the dramatic story of his firm began.

The busy little manufacturing town reaches out to the meadows and fine reaches of the Trent, where a weir adds beauty to the scene. On the other bank Clifton Hall stands high in a wealth of trees, and down the valley, beyond the towers and spires of Nottingham, Colwick Woods and the Shelford hills can be seen. It is a favourite haunt of river lovers, gay in summer with houseboats and pleasure craft.

In a beautiful churchyard in the heart of the town is the spacious church with a massive tower, a stair turret climbing well above the battlements. Sir Gilbert Scott's restoration of nearly a century ago made the church almost new, except for the chancel, which, though modernised, has its 14th century sedilia and piscina, and an old image niche by the east window. The font bowl is 13th century, a pillar almsbox is 1684, and the altar table in the north aisle is Elizabethan. One of two old Bibles in a case in the porch is a first edition of the Authorised Version. In early days the church was subject to Lenton Priory, and the priory arms of an angel holding a shield with a Calvary cross are on the eastern gable of the nave.

The hamlet of Chilwell, now linked up with Beeston, has lost its big house, and we found the estate in the hands of the builder. From 1620 it was the home of the Charltons, of whom John was MP for London in 1318, Sir Richard fell on Bosworth Field, and Sir Thomas was Speaker of the Commons in 1453. The old house was spared the fate of Nottingham Castle and Beeston Silk Mill during the Reform Bill riots only because the head of the family lay dead when the mob reached Chilwell.

BESTHORPE. Near the Lincolnshire border is this quiet little place which sees the spire of Carlton-on-Trent's church rising from a green and pleasant land. It is a delightful spot when the sun shines on the Fleet and the wind sings in the rushes, for here the little river, running in an old channel of the Trent, widens out to a great sheet of water like a lake. It was here that the devastating flood of 1875 reached its height.

SILVER BIRCH TREES IN SHERWOOD FOREST

Stapleford   **The Hemlock Stone**

Holme
Porch and Nan Scott's Chamber

Attenborough
Henry Ireton's Church

Love in the Civil War

BILBOROUGH. Though it belongs now to Nottingham, four miles away, it remains a peaceful village, hiding its old church in a bower of trees at the end of a lane. One of the trees is a gigantic sycamore which overhangs the gate between the churchyard and the rectory lawn.

The embattled tower of the tiny aisleless building comes from about 1450; half a century older are the square-headed windows, the porch with its canopied entrance, and a blocked doorway in the nave. The font and the east window are 15th century, and a table is 17th. In the chancel is a marble memorial to Sir Edmund Helwys, who lived at Broxtowe Hall a mile from the church in Queen Elizabeth's century. So too did Thomas Helwys, who is said to have been chiefly responsible for the formation of the first Baptist church in England. In the time of the Helwys Broxtowe Hall was the hospitable meeting-place of the Puritan clergy of the district, and before them it had been the home of the famous navigator Sir Hugh Willoughby, who perished in his attempt to find the North-East Passage through the Arctic seas.

After becoming more and more a shadow of its old self while new dwellings have crept closer and closer to it, the venerable house with its stone gateway has lately been pulled down; but its proud name, taking us back to Saxon days, will not be forgotten. Here the Hundred met, and the oath of allegiance was given as each man raised his weapon.

The echo of a 17th century love-story with a sad ending belongs to Broxtowe Hall, which was a stronghold of the Parliament during the Civil War, under the command of Captain Thornhaugh. At the same time Aspley Wood Hall was held for Charles Stuart by one of the Willoughbys. As Captain Thornhaugh was strolling along from the Hall one day he heard the cry of a lady in distress, and went to rescue her from the attack of three ruffians. She was Agnes Willoughby, returning from Bilborough to her home, and the staunch Roundhead and the beautiful daughter of a Cavalier fell deeply in love. Fate stepped in to settle the difficult situation, for orders came for the Captain to proceed to an attack on a Royalist fort at Shelford, where he was killed by a bullet.

A Man Who Taught John Milton

BILSTHORPE. It lies on the border of Sherwood Forest, and the new Bilsthorpe which has grown up round the colliery has left the old village in its seclusion, with the church set high on a little hill.

There are shapely old yews and two splendid beeches among the fine trees in the churchyard. Part of the old Hall survives in the farmhouse facing the church, and it still has a cupboard in which Charles Stuart is believed to have hid during the Civil War. Traces of the moat which once surrounded the church and the hall can still be seen.

The tower of the tiny church was refashioned in the 17th century. The nave is partly 14th century, and the chancel a little later. The Norman font is set on a low base which may be part of a Saxon cross. Covered with glass on a wall of the tower is a tapering stone, crudely carved with a cross, which may also be Saxon. A floorstone in the nave, with a Calvary of unusual design, is perhaps 600 years old. Three solid oak benches, perhaps older than the Reformation, were used as penance seats. The fine old pulpit has panels of linenfold.

The Saviles, who have held the manor from the 16th century, have a modern chapel with four wooden angels on the ends of its oak roof beams. A fine stone tomb, carved with arcading, has a brass inscription to Henry Savile of Rufford Abbey, who died in 1881. A marble memorial to Augustus Savile, surmounted by a little owl, has a wreath sent by Queen Victoria kept under glass; he was one of her Masters of Ceremonies.

A wall monument has a Latin inscription to William Chappell, who found peace here when there was none for him elsewhere. Born at Laxton, he became a tutor at Cambridge, where he was famous for his skill in debate. He is said to have won an argument with James the First, and among his pupils was Milton, who seems to have had a great admiration for him. In 1638 he was made Bishop of Cork, but the Irish rebellion sent him back to England, where he suffered much persecution for his faith, and was glad to find a refuge at the big old rectory by Bilsthorpe church, where his friend Gilbert Benet always had a bed for him. He died at Derby, but they brought him here to rest in the spot he had come to love more than any other. One of the altar steps is edged with alabaster from his vanished tomb.

The Old-Fashioned Town in the Vale

BINGHAM. Rich in its memories of famous folk, and treasuring an old church as full of beauty as of human story, the Bingham of today is a quiet, oldfashioned town in the lovely Vale of Belvoir. But its streets rang with the sound of horn and galloping hoofs in old coaching days, and though the marketplace is deserted now we are reminded of its busier times by the picturesque Butter Cross, erected last century to one of whom we read that "To be beloved is better than all bargains."

Two of Nottinghamshire's great soldiers sleep in the church, and one of them has a place for all time in Shakespeare. Three of its rectors became bishops; another is remembered as one of the originators of the Poor Law system of 1834, the Bingham workhouse serving as a model for the Poor Law reformers of the day. The rector sleeps at Oxton, where his son Henry inherited an estate and took the name of Sherbrooke. It was another son, Robert Lowe, born at Bingham rectory in 1811, who became a brilliant Chancellor in Mr Gladstone's ministry.

A lychgate leads us to a churchyard like a garden of lawn and flowers, where many yews make sheltered walks. It is a charming setting for the cross-shaped church, its beautiful 13th century west tower and short spire equalled by few in the county. The spire has three tiers of windows. Buttresses in the middle of three sides reach the belfry windows, and others at the corners climb to the top of the tower, where a bishop and a priest keep company with two pinnacles. One of the charming things inside the church is the sight of its west lancet, curiously set in a buttress, lighting up a deep splay of wall eight feet thick.

Among the interesting capitals of the 600-year-old arcades is one with curious masks said to represent the Deadly Sins, one having foliage realistically carved as if blown by the wind from the doorway, and another, a fine example of undercutting, showing small animal heads eating the leaves. The sedilia and piscina and many windows are as old as the arcades; the east window is 15th century.

A cross-legged knight of 600 years ago, with praying hands, a shield on his arm and a lion at his feet, may be Richard de Bingham, son of the Nottingham wool merchant Ralph Bugge, who founded the Willoughby family. The fragments of another figure are 15th century. A worn floorstone in the chancel has something left of the engraved portraits of one of Nottinghamshire's most famous warriors and his wife. He was Thomas de Rempstone, who helped to put Henry the Fourth on the throne and was one of the band who set out with Henry from Brittany and landed with him at Ravenspur. The story of this adventure lives in Shakespeare's Richard the Second, where Sir Thomas's name is altered to John, perhaps for the sake of metre.

For his services Sir Thomas was made Constable of the Tower, Admiral of the Fleet, and Knight of the Garter, and he was brought here for burial after being drowned in the Thames. His son Thomas, who fought with Henry the Fifth at Agincourt, was taken prisoner and ransomed for an enormous sum; like his father, he is buried in this church, but his memorial has disappeared.

Stories of our time cling to some of the beautiful modern work enriching the church. The children gave the fine oak cover, nearly six feet high, for the Norman font, which they set on a new base. In memory of men who died for peace the massive base of the 15th century oak chancel screen was given its fine top with tracery and a beautiful cornice. Lovely glass in memory of Canon Miles shows Jacob asleep with his head on a rock, seeing in his dream the angels ascending and descending; and the face of Jacob is the likeness of the canon as a young man.

Given by the parishioners to commemorate the 700th anniversary of the church, the great oak reredos, carved and gilded, is a study in beautiful craftsmanship, and its story symbolises the history and industry of Bingham, and the church's dedication to All Saints. We see Robert Bingham, who began building the church while he was rector. Christ as the Good Shepherd, St Wolstan with a sickle, a sheaf of corn, and a fowl, remind us that this is an agricultural district. St Barbara, patron saint of weavers, holding a model of this church tower, is symbolical of the days when frame-knitting came next to husbandry here. St Hugh of Lincoln, the Madonna as patron saint of Southwell, and St Wilfrid of York with a fine miniature of his Minster, are also here. There is a row of ten quaint little people of all sorts and conditions, suggesting that saints are found in all walks of life, the company including a king and a queen, a merchant with his papers and his wife with a golden box, a shepherd carrying a lamb and a labourer his bricks, a farmer with his sheaves, a priest, a beggar, and a woman at her wash-tub.

When the war broke out and the young men left the countryside, an old craftsman took the place of a young one and fashioned the lovely oak pulpit with its traceried panels and gilded medallions of rose, shamrock, thistle, and symbols of the Evangelists, working on its mass of exquisite carving during the last days of his life, for he died a fortnight after his masterpiece was brought here.

The stalls are notable, and every choirboy on each front row sits under a canopy.

Bingham's most charming story belongs to a little old lady carved in oak near the chancel. Eighteen inches high, in bonnet and shawl, she stands with a stick in one hand and a large fish basket in the other, as she used to go about the town collecting odds and ends. She was Ann Harrison, who came to this church throughout her long life of all but a century, for she was born in 1829 and lived till 1928, out of the reign of William the Fourth into the reign of George the Fifth. All the money this devout and generous woman made from going round with her bag was put into one of the church collections as soon as it amounted to two half-crowns. After her death (she would not hear of it in her lifetime) her photograph was put at the beginning of an illuminated Book of Honour to the Fallen, which was paid for with her contributions. It rests on the splendid lectern given as a thankoffering by the men who came back.

Ann's old armchair is now in the church near her attractive little figure in oak. This chair, too, has an interesting story, for it is said that it was once claimed for unpaid chimney tax, after which it passed into the hands of the Lowes at the rectory.

In our own day Bingham was for many years the home of James Prior Kirk, who wrote stories of Nottinghamshire life and won fame with his Forest Folk. He lies in the cemetery here.

The Nottingham Knight in Shakespeare

SIR THOMAS REMPSTONE is in gallant company in the pages of Shakespeare. The scene in which John of Gaunt delivers his magnificent oration *This royal throne of kings, this sceptred isle*, closes as with a herald's clarion call. Harry, old Gaunt's son, and his fifteen knightly lances,

With eight tall ships and three thousand men of war,
Are making hither with all due expedience,
And shortly mean to touch our northern shore,

and Sir Thomas Rempstone (Ramston as Shakespeare calls him) is of the immortal company.

It is with no connivance of this knight of Nottingham that this land of such dear souls, this dear, dear land, is now leased out . . . like to a tenement or pelting farm. He has broad possessions in the county of his birth, and, rather than condone the avarice and lawless extortion of Richard the Second, he crossed the sea to Bolingbroke and is now on his way with him to Ravenspur, to aid him to recover his estates and to transfer Richard's crown to his own brow.

Henry kept about him the men who had hazarded all in his behalf, and Rempstone's reward was the Constableship of the Tower and the custody of Richard. He was present at the abdication, and signed as a witness the deed of resignation by which the fallen king renounced his throne.

Thereafter we see him moving in a pageant of history of the times, quelling treasonable practices in London, created an admiral and steward of the king's household, taking his place in the Privy Council. As Admiral of the Fleet from the Thames westwards, he experienced a year of strange and fatal vicissitudes. At the beginning of 1406, while crossing the Thames from Queenborough to the Essex coast, he was captured by French pirates, but was released and returned to London, taking ship again in the same year, when he was drowned.

The Way Paulinus Came

BLEASBY. Quiet and charming is this small village, with its church, an inn with white walls and red roof, and a hall about 400 years old, its embattled turrets peeping out from the trees.

Clustered on the hillside is the hamlet of Goverton, and on the other side a narrow lane winds to where the ferry crosses the Trent (flowing here at its swiftest) to a fine stretch of wooded bank. Bleasby claims that Paulinus baptised his converts in the river here as he went through Notts in the 7th century.

As high as the sturdy embattled tower is a fine old cedar in the churchyard, which has a peace memorial at its gate. The church has lost most of its original work, and has nothing older than the 13th

century arcade, with round pillars and capitals. There is an Elizabethan chalice. Bright inside when the sun shines, and filled with
mellow light from tinted glass when the day is dull, it has lovely glass
in a south window glowing red and blue and purple, with a charming
group of the Madonna and Child and a minstrel angel at each side.
It is one of the fine windows from the workshops of Christopher
Whall whose glass we so often come upon with pleasure in our
churches.

The Remarkable Story of a Church Window

BLIDWORTH. In the heart of Sherwood Forest, sharing with it
the spirit of the gentlest robber that ever was, stands this home
of legend and romance, looking out from its hill to the distant land-
marks of Newark's spire, the towers of Lincoln, and the walls of
Belvoir Castle.

How old Blidworth is no one knows. Some great natural boulders
at the foot of the hill have been called Druid remains, and one (nearly
90 feet round and 15 feet high) has a passage through the middle.
The Romans may have had an encampment here. At Blidworth Dale
King John had a hunting seat, and not far away is the Queen's
Bower where Elizabeth is said to have camped during one of her
progresses. Rainworth Lodge, a mile and a half away, has some
remains of Tudor days.

The church crowns the hilltop. Except for its plain 15th century
tower, it is mainly in the classical style of the 18th and 19th centuries,
but the lofty south arcade of round arches and pillars is said to have
been the work of a pupil of Christopher Wren. The 15th century font
has a bowl on which is carved the head of a child, and its modern
oak cover was made by the village carpenter.

On the wall above the font hangs what is called the Register of
Rockings, a reminder of an old custom revived here in our time after
a lapse of a century. Once a year, on the first Sunday in February,
the last baby boy to have been baptised is dedicated at the altar and
rocked in a cradle in the sanctuary. In olden days the Rocking was
observed as a simple miracle play, representing the taking of Jesus
to the Temple.

Built up in the churchyard are fragments of the medieval church
which collapsed two centuries ago, including many old coffin stones,

a doorway, a window, and a piscina niche. In the outside wall of the church is a tiny tapering coffin stone, and a 15th century floorstone in the nave has a hammer and a carpenter's square.

The oak panelling in the chancel, with a few richly carved panels, came from Southwell Minster. So, too, did the unusual oak pulpit adorned with 18th century plasterwork showing 31 tiny heads and a panel of the Madonna and Child. One very odd possession the church has, for the spring which carries the pendulum of the clock in the tower is made from a sword carried at Waterloo.

A slate tablet on the wall has a rhyming epitaph telling how Thomas Leake fell in single combat near the end of the 16th century. He was a Ranger of the Forest, and carved in the alabaster frame of his memorial are hunting trophies of horns, knives, long-bows and cross bows, and hounds, one hound chasing a deer. The massive stone cross in the churchyard was brought here from the spot in the woods where he fell.

Among many memorials of the Needs, a soldier family who lived at Fountain Dale, is a window filled with Munich glass which is both pleasing and interesting, recalling an odd tale of war. It shows St Anne teaching Mary to read, the mother wearing a red mantle over her white robe and an amethyst wrap over her head, Mary kneeling on a rich blue cushion. The glass was ordered from a firm at Metz before the Franco-German war, and was fashioned by the French during the Siege of Metz. After the war enquiries were made about it, and in due course it arrived at Blidworth. A few months later a second window, identical with the first, was received, the explanation being that the Germans carried on the industry when in possession of Metz, and took the letter of enquiry to be another order. The second window was returned, and found a place in Cologne Cathedral.

The old men here will tell you that Robin Hood's Will Scarlet lies in the churchyard, and whether it is true or not we think he would have been glad to have this resting-place so near the scenes of his great adventures. One of that band of outlaws about whom so much has been imagined and so little is known, he was a merry spirit who knew every path through the forest. In the hill on which the village stands is a cave where the outlaws are said to have stored their food, and the records of Edwinstone church tell how Robin Hood took Maid Marian to be married there from her home at Blidworth.

Nowhere do their memories cling more surely than at Fountain Dale (a mile or so from the village), the source of the delightful little Rainworth Water, in a lovely setting by Harlow Wood. Here Friar Tuck is said to have lived, and it is supposed to be the scene of his fight with Robin Hood, which ended in a friendship broken only by death. Till half a century ago the Friar's cell could be seen. His well and the moat into which Robin was tumbled after the fight are still in the woods; and in the old house of Fountain Dale (modernised now) Scott often stayed while writing Ivanhoe, gleaning local colour for his jolly friar.

The story of Blidworth will live in spite of the fact that a colliery has come to mar the rural scene, and the old village will long be loved as the setting of Forest Folk, a tale of Nottinghamshire life written in our own time by a Nottingham man, James Prior Kirk.

Village Charming

BLYTH. It is old and lovely, one of the most gracious villages in Notts. It has a road where the Danes came over a thousand years ago, a noble church with rare Norman remains, and a school with a doorway over 700 years old.

On the old highway from London to York, it was of great import-ance in early days, when it had a market and fairs, and was close to one of only five tournament grounds in England licensed by Richard the First. Now the wide road through the heart of the village is lined with trim houses, some of them clothed with creeper, some red-walled, others painted white, cream, and gold, and all red-roofed. On the long green island down the middle of the road is an elm plantation and a building with a roof resting on ancient beams, with mullioned windows in stone walls, and a beautiful 700-year-old door-way through which the children of Blyth go in for lessons and come out to play on the green shaded by three fine beeches. The building is said to have belonged to a Hospital of St John, founded for lepers in the 12th century; a farmhouse stands on the site of the hospital at the southern end of the village, and not far away is a row of six almshouses reminding us of the old charity.

The little River Ryton flows on three sides of the village, passing under the road near an old dovecot. From the three-arched bridge spanning it on the road to Maltby we see a delightful picture of the church and the great house, charmingly grouped with the river and noble trees.

The church is all that is left of the priory founded here in 1088 by Roger de Busli, as a cell of the Abbey of St Catherine at Rouen, but the strength and grandeur of what remains is eloquent of its magnificence. At the Reformation all the monastic part of the church was destroyed, as were the domestic buildings on the site where the hall now stands. The preservation of what is left is due to the fact that the nave and aisles served as the parish church, and it is in these that we see what is said to be the oldest example of Norman architecture in England in its style, though perhaps not actually in date. It is thought either that the plans used in the building of the Abbey of Jumièges in Normandy were borrowed for Blyth Priory, or that builders came over here for its construction. The abbey was built about forty years before the priory.

The pure work of very early Norman days, severe but majestic in its simple strength, is seen in the nave (with a splendid 13th century vaulted roof), the two arcades, the clerestory, the triforium on the south side, and the north aisle with its original vaulted roof. When this roof was moved to a lower level, the triforium openings on the north side had to be filled up, and 15th century windows were inserted under the round arches.

The arcades are of five bays with round arches on lofty pillars, and a sixth bay projects into the hall grounds. Among the heads enriching the capitals are two close together, perhaps representing Roger de Busli and his wife Muriel, who may be buried under two recesses in the outside north wall. The south aisle was enlarged to its present size in 1290, whence come its five windows, and seven gargoyles of ugly winged animals and a bird. The fine porch is also of this time.

The beautiful west tower, 100 feet high and a landmark, comes from the close of the 14th century. Eight pinnacles crown its charming parapet of open arcading; it has buttresses of seven stages, a canopied doorway, a west window with a niche on each side and another above it, and a great arch reaching to the nave roof.

The 17th century font has a bowl with cherubs, a base which may be Norman, and a Jacobean cover. The round bowl of a Norman font lies on the floor. The oak pulpit and a table are 17th century, an old almsbox is heavily banded with iron, and two quaint collecting boxes of 1661 are still used. The oak panelling on a wall of the chancel is part of the 17th century box-pews, as are the backs and ends of some benches. On the east wall are faint traces of 15th century paintings of Time, Judgment, and Eternity.

The east end of the south aisle forms the chancel, and has a beautiful 15th century oak screen with tracery and a vaulted loft. Six of the old paintings on the base panels are still clear, showing Stephen with stones, a woman slain with a sword, St Edmund crowned, St Helena, St Barbara with a lamp and a palm leaf, and St Ursula with eleven maidens. With the old work still left in the screen across the nave are eleven paintings of saints.

Lovely modern glass has a share in the glory of Blyth. In the five windows on the south side of the church are about 150 figures in Bible scenes. We see Samuel being taken to Eli, Moses found in the bulrushes, Joseph cast into the well, Abraham with Isaac carrying wood to the altar, the anointing of David, and scenes telling the story of Jesus. The beautiful west window of this aisle frames ten splendid figures.

Three ancient floorstones are carved with crosses. The battered knight wearing armour with a great shield and an unusual square-topped helmet was perhaps a Fitzwilliam of the time of Richard the First. On the projecting tomb of a big monument with a long inscription reclines the short, stout, cross-legged figure of Edward Mellish, who has been sleeping here since 1703. After making money in business in Portugal, he rebuilt Blyth Hall, which was enlarged during the next century and was wanting a tenant when we called.

Hodsock Priory (which never was a priory) stands at the end of a beautiful shaded lane two miles from Blyth. It is a modern house in lovely gardens, on the site of the old home of the Cressys and the Cliftons, and was the home of the Mellish family when we called. Here is still the water moat, crossed by a small stone bridge in front of the lovely Tudor gateway, which has 15th century windows and an embattled turret on each side of the archway.

The Story on the Pulpit

BOLE. It lies at the end of the road, with the Trent a mile away dividing the county from Lincolnshire. It has little but a simple church, yet its snow-white walls shelter two treasures worth finding. The tower, crowned by eight pinnacles, is 14th and 15th century, and a few old windows remain.

At each side of a brass on a window-sill, with an inscription to John Danby who died in 1400, is a tiny brass engraved with an angel and a bull. On the front of a pew near the pulpit is an old oak panel carved with the letter B and a tun, the rebus of the Bartons, who lived at Holme in the 15th century.

The royal arms are a curious amalgamation of those of Queen Anne and George the First, the king's white horse painted over the middle to save expense. The rose and thistle badge of Queen Anne remains, though she was the last sovereign to have a personal badge, and it should have been painted out.

One of the treasures here is a massive Norman font with double arcading round the eight sides of its bowl; the other is the pulpit, with four 17th century Flemish panels. Elaborately carved in relief, with eight figures and eight cherubs in the ornamental arcading, they tell the story of Esther and Haman in scenes in which 19 vivid figures take part. We see King Ahasuerus sitting under the canopy of his tent, and a man behind him with a halberd. Esther, who kneels before him, is attended by two maidens, and has come to use her influence on behalf of the Jews. We see Haman summoned to advise the king how to deal with a man he wishes to honour, and Haman, thinking the honour is to fall on his own shoulders, suggesting that the royal crown and raiment be put on the man and that he should ride through the streets on the king's horse. The next scene shows Haman, with drooping countenance, leading the king's horse, on which rides his enemy Mordecai in the royal apparel. In the last picture the king and Esther are sitting at the banquet with Haman. Ahasuerus is handing a cup to Haman, who now looks mightily pleased at the honour shown him in being the only guest at the feast, little suspecting that soon he is to be hanged on the gallows he has prepared for Mordecai. The gallows is in the background, with Haman's tiny figure hanging from it.

The Saxon Track

BOTHAMSALL. It lies on the slope of a valley in which the Meden and the Maun flow side by side to become the River

Idle, and, coming to it by the lane from the lovely road between Ollerton and Bawtry, there are two things to see.

One is Conjure Alders, a charming spot where the two rivers run as one, shaded by ash and alder trees, and spanned by a wooden bridge. The grassy track bringing us to it from the lane is one of the oldest ways in the county, and was carried over the river here by an ancient ford known by the Saxon name of Coningswath.

The other is a fine green mound by the wayside, known as Castle Hill. A dry moat runs all round it, splendid sycamores, beeches, oaks, and elms grow all over it, and a grand old oak rises from its hollowed crown. The site of an ancient camp or a fortified place, it looks out on a great panorama of fields, patches of woodland, and stretches of forest; and sees, close by, the little rivers in the valley, and the tower of Bothamsall peeping from a mantle of trees.

It is a neat village. The 19th century church looks its best outside, with battlements and buttresses and a tower with a clock in memory of the men who did not come back. Among the few relics of the old church are two floorstones with crosses in the chancel, a fine 600-year-old font, and an old pewter flagon. In the vestry is the tomb of Henry Walters, who gave the church its silver paten of 1698. A floorstone marks the resting-place of Sir Charles Gregan-Craufurd who died in 1821 after a notable military career, and a brass plate with arms has an inscription to him and his wife.

The Solitary Tower

BRADMORE. A neat little village on the road from Nottingham to Loughborough, it has a surprise for us as we climb from Bunny to what seems to be a church beckoning from the hilltop.

Here indeed we find an ancient tower and spire, but they are without a church, standing like a monument to the fire which destroyed the rest of it, as well as most of the village, over 200 years ago. For many years the solitary tower and spire, with remains of 14th century tracery in a window, stood useless and forsaken till it found a link with the world again in 1880, when a small mission room was built on to it.

The Ancient Sentinel

BRAMCOTE. It has much charm for those who find it, and magnificent views from its hilltop of villages and towns and streams, great houses and castles, in the wide Trent valley. We look from here into five counties.

The delightful Elizabethan manor house with its red brick walls and gables has made itself a fairyland, its old buildings transformed into charming dwellings round a rock garden with pools and flowers. The road by the old church leads to the modern Hall among the bluebell fields: it is now a school. Bramcote Hills, a fine house nestling in the trees beyond the Nottingham Road, is famous for its rhododendrons. Not far away we see at night the glowing fires from Stanton furnaces.

A low 600-year-old tower in a closed churchyard is all that is left of the ancient church, though its 13th century font and some of its monuments are in the new church which took its place: it is 19th century, its pleasing spire a landmark. One memorial has a curious epitaph in which the first letters of the lines spell the name of Henry Hanley, who is said to have built the manor house about 1600. His memory is kept green by his almshouses in a street named after him in Nottingham.

To Bramcote belongs the famous Hemlock Stone, a natural phenomenon 30 feet high, rising from a green mound near Stapleford. It is a great mass of red sandstone rock which has resisted the action of rain and frost longer than man can tell, and its strange shape makes a curious feature of the landscape for miles round. For thousands of years nothing has disturbed this solitary sentinel, which is about 70 feet round and is said to weigh over 200 tons.

Links with Rome

BROUGH. Believed to have been the Roman station of Croco-lana, it is now a hamlet on the Fosse Way, two miles from the Collinghams. Here have been found many Roman coins (called Brough pennies here) and remains of Roman dwellings with stone foundations and timber walls.

It is the tiny church of St Stephen, standing with a cluster of houses and a school, that brings us here today. Built of brick half a century ago, it is neat and trim and surprisingly pleasing, just a chancel and nave divided by an ironwork screen, and lit by 42 candles in candelabra wrought with leaves and scrolls. Among the saints shining in most of the windows are Catherine with her wheel, Agnes with a lamb, Margaret on a dragon. Stephen and Alban and

Our Lord with a sphere are in the east window. It is curious to see in another General Gordon, wearing a red fez and holding his stick, standing astride a cannon. Very charming is the Christopher Whall glass in two lancets, showing the Madonna and Child in blue and white looking to St Hugh in mitre and rich green robes; a great swan at his side is trying to reach the golden chalice the saint holds. An angel at prayer crowns the cover of the font.

A bronze plaque by Sir George Frampton has figures of Fortitude in armour and Sympathy with a wreath, and an inscription to Thomas Smith Woolley telling us that he served this hamlet for 38 years and built the church and school.

High on the Wolds

BROUGHTON SULNEY. Also known as Upper Broughton, it is perched high on a steep slope of the border Wolds, a pretty village with a little amber-coloured church clinging to the hillside as it looks over a green valley into Leicestershire.

One of its memories is of its good fortune six centuries ago, for, standing on a grassy slope in the heart of the village, is the pillar of an old cross said to have been placed there as a thankoffering because the Black Death passed the people by. In front of a house near the cross is a fine relic of 1777 in a lead cistern ornamented with the Signs of the Zodiac. At this time Charles Wildbore, a clever mathematician, was serving his 35 years as curate here.

The porch by which we come to the church was made new in 1733 and given a classical entrance, but it keeps fragments of the old work, and has in its east wall crudely carved stonework which may have belonged to a tomb of 400 years ago. The low tower with quatrefoil moulding under its battlements is 13th and 14th century, and a medieval arcade leads to the north aisle, which, like the chancel, was made new last century. The oldest part of the church (now built into the south wall) is a fragment of an arcade set up when the Norman style was passing; it led to an aisle which was pulled down probably when the porch was made new. The traceried bowl of the font is from the end of the 14th century.

The Lovely Lake

BUDBY. Great stretches of forest and the parklands of ducal homes surround this beauty spot where the little River Meden runs by the road under a bank of trees, making a sharp bend at the old stone bridge under which it flows to Thoresby Park. A few hundred yards through the park it runs through the arch of another picturesque bridge to fill a lake a mile long and girt with trees, where countless swans gleam snow-white in the sun. We pass a grand old oak on the way to the lake, and catch a glimpse of Castle William on the hill, a grey house with battlements and turrets.

BULCOTE. Till the coming of the new road every traveller between Nottingham and Newark knew the sharp turn in this small place nestling under the hills. A stream wanders by the wayside facing the manor house and a row of ivied cottages, and the little church stands high on a wooded slope, catching lovely glimpses of the gleaming Trent. The church took the place of an ancient chapel.

Battles Long Ago

BUNNY. A lovely village near Fairham Brook, flowing through willows and rich meadows, half a mile from the famous hill which was the despair of the old coach and the early car, it has famous names among its landlords, the memory of Henry the Seventh's soldiers spending the night in Bunny Wood before the last battle of the Wars of the Roses, and the echo of Royalist and Cromwellian troops passing by in the Civil War.

Bunny owes much of its beauty and interest to the Parkyns, and we are glad to have known it before the builder disturbed its dress of mellowed brick, which was a testimony to one of the strangest of Nottinghamshire men, Thomas Parkyns, the Wrestling Baronet. It was a later member of the family, Lord Rancliffe, who made himself a lasting memorial by planting Rancliffe Wood and clothing Windmill Hill with trees.

Sir Thomas was the second baronet of a family honoured by Charles the Second for their service in the Civil War, especially that of Colonel Isham Parkyns, who was Governor of Ashby de la Zouche. After his father's death he began to improve the village and the lot of his tenants, and for the rest of his 78 years was a good friend to Bunny. He gave two bells to the church, restored the chancel, built a vicarage, rebuilt nearly all the farmhouses and dwellings, and made plantations. He lived at the hall, a strange mixture of brick and stone, and gave it the curious tower we see, with its elaborate

The Flag of St George on the 14th Century Tower

The Norman Nave   The Norman North Aisle

THE NOBLE CHURCH OF BLYTH

Ratcliffe-on-Soar   **Sacheverell Tomb**

Kingston-on-Soar Babington Tomb

Bunny Parkyns Monument

coat-of-arms and a fine oak staircase climbing to the top. He enclosed its lovely park with a wall three miles long which took three years to build, said to be the first wall in England to be built on a foundation of arched brickwork. The tops of some of the arches are plainly seen where the wall runs by the lane.

The gem of all his building is the charming block of four almshouses and a school at the church gate, with tiny leaded windows (round and square), and quaint dormers in the mottled roof. On the school, now used as a village room, is one of the Latin quotations of which he was fond, " Learning has no enemy except ignorance." He was a great student and compiled a Latin Grammar for the benefit of his grandson, but it was through his passion for wrestling that he won his reputation.

Lovely outside and in, the church is adorned with pinnacles, battlements, and bands of quatrefoils. The 14th century tower, with a graceful spire, has a lofty archway opening to the nave with 14th century arcades. One of its glories is the 15th century porch, of exceptional size and beauty, with a big window each side and a stone vaulted roof. The other is the great white-walled chancel, which was delayed in its building by the coming of the Black Death : it has lovely sedilia and a double piscina, and many windows filling it with light. The frame of the old chancel screen remains, with some original tracery and carved spandrels, but it has been given a poor modern cornice. There is an old chest, a new font, and a good old font.

In the chancel are many of the Parkyns memorials. Richard of 1603, Recorder of Notts and first of the family to live at Bunny, kneels facing his wife, the tiny figures of their eight children with them. A blue and white monument has a lovely draped figure bowed over the bier of the last Sir Thomas, who was so fond of hunting that in his old age he used to put on his scarlet coat and his cap to watch the hounds from his window. He died soon after Trafalgar.

Looking out from the wall as she kneels, with a wrap over her head, is Dame Anne Parkyns, the Lady Bountiful of Bunny. She was the mother of the Wrestling Baronet, and his helper in all his good works. She died in 1725, and we read that she came as a blessing into the family, and God drew out her precious life to 92 years. Her face is very beautiful.

But the monument that draws all eyes is that of her son, who

E   49

stands ready for a wrestling bout, a lifesize figure, while at the side we see his tiny figure stretched out on the floor, defeated at last by Time. Part of his epitaph runs:

That Time at length did throw him it is plain,
Who lived in hope that he should rise again.

It is said that Sir Thomas had the monument made before his death and set up in the chancel; now it is in the north aisle. He lies in the vault he built, in one of the stone coffins he used to collect.

The Wrestling Baronet

THOMAS PARKYNS, one of Nottinghamshire's oddities, was born in 1663, and educated at Westminster School and Trinity College, Cambridge. He studied law at Gray's Inn, was a lover of Latin, and had a knowledge of mechanics, mathematics, and architecture.

Whatever this man of vigorous mind and generous spirit did he did thoroughly. Interesting himself in education, he compiled a Latin Grammar which was one of the earliest books published in Nottingham. He was a keen magistrate, and a student of the economics of his day: and he learned something of the art of medicine so that he could prescribe for the poor. He bought many neighbouring manors, and used much of the fortune he inherited in good works. One of his eccentricities was his fondness for displaying Latin quotations about his estate; another was his habit of collecting stone coffins, which he gave to anyone who wanted one. A fine athlete, he never had a day's illness till he was 78, and even in middle life was a good runner and a tireless bellringer.

But his fame lay in his love of wrestling. He is remembered as the Wrestling Baronet; he called himself Sir Thomas Luctator. He established an annual wrestling match in the village for which the prize was a gold-laced hat, and the practice was kept up for nearly a hundred years after his death. He kept two wrestlers at Bunny to give him exercise and to train likely pupils, taking into his service those who could give him a fall. His own notions about the rules of the game he put in the curious book he wrote to make wrestling popular, calling it the Inn Play or Cornish-Hugg Wrestler.

One of the most remarkable squires of his day, he was like Sir Roger de Coverley, with many eccentricities but with a heart of gold.

The Vale of Trent

BURTON JOYCE. A new road has straightened its old winding way between a low ridge of hills and a bank of the Trent; and many new houses with trim gardens keep company with old cottages.

One of England's great cricketers knew the village as it used to be, for he was born here. He was Alfred Shaw, Emperor of Bowlers, who sleeps at Gedling.

In a churchyard where we look over the wide Trent vale to the Malkin Hills and the fine tower of Shelford is the much-restored old church, largely built during the 14th century. The low spire, with two tiers of windows, was struck by lightning half a century ago, and eight feet of the top was taken down and built into a pyramid near the porch.

As old as any part of the building is the beautiful east window of the north aisle, coming from the time of Edward the First. The bowl of the font and the middle pillar on which it rests are 13th century; so is a floorstone carved with a cross in the north aisle. Leaning against the wall of this aisle is the massive stone altar with two consecration crosses found when the church was restored. Here, too, is a great peephole like a window, and by it an old piscina.

The dim but pleasing little chancel has linenfold panelling on the walls, and surmounting the richly traceried panels of the reredos is a deep border like lace in the delicacy of carving. The east window has a lovely Crucifixion and figures of St Helena and Paulinus, who is said to have baptised his converts in the Trent hereabouts. Beautiful glass shows St Edith of Wilton and St Elizabeth of Hungary, and another window has Mary and Martha of Bethany. The pulpit and lectern were made from beams of the old roof.

On a stone tomb lies Robert de Jortz de Bertune, a 13th century knight of the powerful family who gave the village its name (Bertune Jortz). He wears plate armour, and his belt is of flowers. His head is remarkably small for his body.

The portrait of Sir Brian Stapleton, who died in 1550, is engraved on an alabaster stone, showing him in armour with dogs at his head and feet. His son Brian was one of the husbands of Alis Roos, whose figure has almost vanished from a very worn stone.

William Lee

CALVERTON. An old village straggling along at the foot of friendly hills (now being developed by a colliery and a housing estate), Calverton is remembered for its association with a man who died in poverty though he made many rich. He was William Lee, whose epoch-making stocking-frame brought him disappointment and a broken heart.

Though it is generally accepted that he was born here, some claim Woodborough as his birthplace. There is some uncertainty, too, as to whether it was of Calverton or Woodborough that he became curate after taking his degree as Master of Arts of Cambridge. And whether his invention was cradled in romance or in dire necessity depends on which of two stories we believe to be true—one telling how the constant knitting of a lady indifferent to his wooing drove him to the creation of a machine to take the place of her needles; the other how the poor curate found his inspiration in watching the nimble fingers of his wife whose knitting eked out his scanty income.

After working here with his wooden frame for about two years, using rough tools and wool spun from the backs of local sheep, Lee sought the patronage of Queen Elizabeth, who saw the frame at work but, disappointed that it did not make silk stockings, refused to grant a patent. Then the inventive parson made the frame produce silk stockings as easily as woollen, but the queen, fearing that it would throw the hand-knitters out of work, again refused a patent.

Through the mediation of the French Ambassador, Lee in his despair accepted the invitation of Henry the Fourth to France, and, with the help of his brother James and a few workmen, set up the frame at Rouen. There the help promised him did not materialise owing to the king's assassination, and Lee was left penniless in Paris, where he died about 1610 and was buried in an unknown grave. The frame was brought back to London, and eventually hosiery became a staple industry of Lee's own county.

His lasting memorial is in the great power machines which knit and make lace for the world today, for they had their beginning in his stocking-frame, one of the most astonishingly complete inventions ever devised at a single operation, and the first machine ever made to produce a looped or knitted fabric. Power machines are making hosiery in Calverton now, but we are back in the days of William Lee as we listen even yet to the rattle of the hand-frames in some of the cottages with wide windows, where globes of water are hung by the frames to catch the light and throw its beams on to the needles. His only actual memorial here is an addition made to the village school. In one of these cottages there died in 1938 an old man who kept in his home some of the original stocking-frames of William Lee, on one of which is the mark of a bomb thrown in the Luddite riots.

The church came into Domesday Book, but only a few things are left of ancient days. The church the Normans left was made new in the 14th century and again in the 18th. Fragments of Norman moulding are in the north wall: the sides of the chancel arch are Norman, and on one of the capitals is a tiny panel carved with two figures believed to be St Wilfrid and a convert.

Built into the belfry are seven stones carved by a Norman mason to illustrate the occupations of the months. January is represented by a man sitting at a table laden with food, while his hawk looks on; February is a man in a tunic, cloak, and heavy boots, warming himself at a fire under a tree; for March or April a man is pruning a tree with a big knife; another in June seems to be hoeing among growing crops; August is a man in a big hat, reaping corn with a sickle; and two panels represent September with two men threshing corn with flails. An eighth stone has a man on horseback with his hawk on his wrist, and a dog with tufted tail holding a hare or a rabbit.

Between the Parks

CARBURTON. Its old church is outlined on the rising slope, and it has a lovely view between the gracious parks of Welbeck and Clumber.

Side by side through the village run the road and the little River Poulter till they enter Clumber Park, where one goes to feed a great lake of nearly 90 acres, and the other to find the magnificent Duke's Drive, which stretches, with a double row of limes on each side, for three miles to Apleyhead. It is a splendid ride which all may take.

A busy little river is the Poulter, though placid enough as it flows through the village. It feeds the lake at Welbeck as well as that of Clumber, and the fine stretches known as Carburton Forge Dam and Carburton Dam remind us of the days when it worked an iron forge here, the iron being brought from Derbyshire and smelted by charcoal.

In a churchyard bounded by the Flood Dyke is the small chapel of Norman foundation, with nave and chancel under one roof, a square bell turret at one end, and a little porch: quaint in its simplicity, but, like the poet's old thatched cottage, wondrous neat and clean. A plain Norman doorway lets us in, and three tiny Norman windows are still here, a 13th century lancet between two of them in the east wall. The west window is 600 years old, and the tub font is Norman. There is a double sundial on a corner of the church, and just inside the door is part of an ancient gravestone.

The rare possession of the church is a register dating from 1528, said to be one of only three existing of this time. A second is at Perlethorpe three miles away, and the third is at Elsworth in Cambridgeshire. The date from which registers were kept by order of Thomas Cromwell was 1538, so that these three are ten years older than the oldest official record.

The Thorough Dr Thoroton

CAR COLSTON. Not far from the Roman Fosse Way is this pretty village of many interests, its seclusion guarded by gates at the ends of the lanes that lead us to it. Cottages and little inn, fine houses and the old stocks, make a picture of old-world charm as they gather round the biggest green in the county. There is a handsome modern hall in Elizabethan style, and at the Screveton end of the village is part of the 17th century home of Dr Brunsell, who is said to have been a kinsman of Christopher Wren.

Here for many years lived Dr Robert Thoroton, whose famous Antiquities of Notts was published the year before he died in the village. He was born at Screveton in 1623, and after studying medicine in London he returned to his native county to practise. But his love was for antiquities, old churches, and old families, and he decided to interest himself more in the dead than in the living. The Civil War interrupted his work for a time, but after years of patient and careful study, during which he paid many assistants to gather information, he produced a magnificent work which was the first history of its kind and was long the chief authority of the county.

It is thought that in the farmhouse just beyond the church may be remains of the old Moryn Hall where Thoroton lived, and there are several reminders of him in the church. Here is the massive stone coffin he had made six years before he died, so that his body might rest undisturbed. He was buried in the coffin in the churchyard near the priest's doorway of the chancel, but when the churchyard was being lowered last century the coffin was taken up and placed in the church. Cut in the floor of the coffin is the inscription expressing his desire to lie undisturbed, and on the coped lid are his arms, his name, and the date of his death. The stone which marked his grave was found to be part of the old altar with two consecration crosses, and this also is in the church, where the Thoroton Society have set up a tablet to his memory.

On a buttress outside is a stone Dr Thoroton set up to mark his family's resting-place, telling that his grandfather Robert Thoroton was a loyal servant of King and Church, and that his great-grandfather Robert died of plague and was buried here.

Round this fine little church runs an exceptional plinth moulding six feet high. The beautiful tower with slender belfry openings and a low pyramid roof belongs to the 13th and 15th centuries; other 13th century remains are the entrance to the south porch and the doorway within it which has an original door with later hinges. From the 14th century come the lofty nave arcades, the clerestory windows on the south, the north aisle windows, and its blocked doorway.

The glory of the church is its chancel, though its beauty is marred by the organ. Built in the 14th century, soon after the Black Death, it is typical of the fine work of this time in Notts, and has great gabled buttresses and lovely window tracery, the handsome sedilia and piscina being adorned with canopies, pinnacles, and finials. A grimacing man is peeping from one corner. The graceful altar rails are probably 17th century. There are a few old bench-ends, a poor-box 400 years old, parts of the old chancel screen in a dado, and carved Jacobean panels in the pulpit and a desk. The oldest relic is the round Norman font; one of our day is a wooden cross from a Flanders grave.

Ancient Treasure House

CARLTON-IN-LINDRICK. It is two villages with one church. South Carlton lies in winding lanes, a delightful picture (as we come from Worksop) of red roofs and grey church tower peeping from a great bank of trees. North Carlton is on the busy highway, and on a little green between the two is an elegant peace memorial cross.

The church looks across the stone-walled road to stately beeches in the grounds of the hall, a great house in the classic style looking down on a lake fed by a stream which works a mill near by. There are old yews among the glorious trees in the churchyard, and from a mighty beech at its eastern end we have the prettiest view of the all-embattled and pinnacled church, framed by magnificent cedars and backed by limes and beeches.

There is still much Saxon work in the lovely tower of this church, which came into Domesday Book. The masonry of one stage is almost all fine herringbone. Its handsome west doorway is Norman, with zigzag among the mouldings, and three detached shafts on each side with foliage capitals; it was once the south doorway of the church, sheltered by the porch. The early Normans built the tower arch with enriched capitals, and the top storey and the fine buttresses reaching to the battlements are 15th century.

As beautiful within as without, the church has a Norman arcade dividing the nave and north aisle. There is Norman work in the chancel arch, and on each side of a 13th century arch opening into the north chapel is a Norman light unglazed. One of the Norman treasures is the bowl of the font, with a band of scallop; another is a curious tympanum over the vestry doorway, carved with two medallions under an arch crowned by a tiny cross.

The north clerestory windows and three other windows are 15th century. A charming 13th century lancet in the chapel is filled with a medley of medieval glass in fragments of yellow and gold, with red and blue in the border, and three medallions. The east window, shining with modern glass, has Our Lord in robes of white and gold, and angels looking down on eleven men of Galilee who have watched Him taken up out of their sight.

Much 15th or early 16th century work remains in the fine roofs of the nave and north aisle, and in their splendid gallery of nearly 40 carved bosses are the arms of the Fitzhughs and of Lord Dacre, the bull and the greyhound (badges of the Nevilles), the Five Wounds, a rose, a thunderbolt, a lion with human face and tongue hanging out, flowers, and a face looking like Henry the Eighth's.

In a case hangs a small medieval sculpture of the Trinity, with figures of Mary and John and six angels, two catching the blood from the Wounds, two with the Holy Grail. An old altar stone with three crosses lies in a recess, a 15th century gravestone has remains of a fine cross, and there is an old chest with three locks. A charming little treasure is the cover of the Litany, the leather patterned with flowers and crowns and animals, the metal bosses engraved with roses; it is believed to come from the time of Henry the Seventh.

Gentlemen, As You Pass By

CARLTON-ON-TRENT. We found it all gabled and golden, shining among the trees, its church crowned by a prickly spire. A quiet oasis bypassed by the motor road, it has on one side the open Trent meadows where the ferryboat crosses the winding stream, and on the other it catches glimpses of the ceaseless traffic which now misses Carlton's stretch of the Great North Road, which enters the village as a lovely avenue of chestnuts.

The old inn, once astir with life, is now a golden farmhouse. The quaint wayside smithy is picturesque with a great brick horse-shoe round the entrance, painted black on golden walls and patterned to show the nails, its old rhyme beginning:

> Gentlemen, as you pass by,
> Upon this shoe pray cast an eye.

The stone church was built last century on the site of an old chapel of Norwell, of which the doorway is the only fragment left. It has a lofty tower and a graceful spire with two tiers of windows and a curious arrangement of rows of stone projecting like the spokes of a capstan. The altar table and two chests are 17th century, and a small old font, no longer used, looks like a huge egg cup with its bell-shaped bowl only 17 inches across. A window with a warrior at the foot of the Cross, and a brass engraved with arms, are in memory of George Brenton Laurie, who fought for his country in three wars and fell at last at Neuve Chapelle.

The Man Who Loved the Rose

CAUNTON. Here among the little hills, just off the lovely road from Newark to Ollerton, Caunton's red houses and small grey church are gathered pleasantly about the willow-bordered Beck. It is the village of the man Tennyson called the Rose King.

Hiding in splendid trees near the church is Caunton Manor, a pleasant old brick house with a stone portico, where the Holes have lived since the 15th century. Here Samuel Reynolds Hole lived for the greater part of his life (though born at Manchester), first as curate, then as vicar and squire, before serving as Dean of Rochester. Here he loved and studied roses, grew them, wrote of them, promoted societies for their cultivation and shows for their exhibition, and made himself the most famous of amateur rose-growers. We found roses blooming in his old garden when we called.

In a quiet corner of the grounds is a summerhouse where we found his portrait, an illuminated address congratulating him on becoming Dean of Rochester, a diploma awarded him in 1897, and, most interesting of all, an alphabetical list in his own handwriting of all the roses he was growing here in 1851, when he had 1027 trees and over 400 varieties. Since 1904 he has been sleeping in the churchyard, a granite cross marking his grave.

By the churchyard gate is a peace memorial of unusual interest, for the stones of its grey walling, fashioned like a monument, were once part of the 13th century church. On it we read:

> *These men of Caunton sought the glory of England.*
> *They found the glory of God.*

There is still much of 700 years ago in the little church, which is lighted by windows from the three medieval centuries and a 15th century clerestory. The chancel arch, the font, and the nave arcades are all 13th century, the south arcade a little older than the north. A fine elm grows near the 14th century porch which shelters an elaborate doorway of the same time. The tower and its arch are 15th century. There are three old piscinas, a founder's recess, an ancient bracket carved with a curly head, and quaint corbels on the hoods of the windows.

In memory of the Dean the chancel is neatly panelled in oak, and the beautiful glass in the west window shines red, blue, green, and gold, having portraits of Elizabeth of Hungary with roses and lilies, St Andrew with a book and a cross, St Dorothy with a spray of roses, and an angel with golden wings holding a scroll with the words, "The desert shall rejoice and blossom as the rose."

Dean Hole gave the poor glass of the east window and three

58

chancel lancets in memory of his parents, two sisters, and "a beloved friend John Leech," the famous Punch artist. The witty dean would help him with many of his drawings, and he enjoyed the strange distinction for a clergyman of being elected to Mr Punch's table.

There are many tablets and some attractive windows (one with St George), to the Bristowes who fought for Parliament in the Civil War, and have lived since the 16th century at Beesthorpe Hall a mile away. From the road to Maplebeck we see their big Elizabethan house, grey and gabled, in a wooded park laid out by Capability Brown. Another Elizabethan structure is embodied in a farmhouse known as Dean Hall, standing back from the Newark road.

Brave Parson Hodge

CLARBOROUGH. It has three things to see, a church and a yew and a glorious view of the countryside to Sherwood Forest.

Some say the yew is older than the church, and may have been growing a thousand years; it is still green and shapely, though its great days are gone and only half its hollow trunk is left. The much-restored church has a 15th century tower of two stages with a sundial on a buttress. From about 1400 come fine windows in the chancel and the very narrow aisles, the massive font with quatrefoils, and the south arcade. The 13th century north arcade is the oldest part. The only coloured glass glows richly in the east window, showing John the Baptist in raiment of camel hair, crying out as he sees Our Lord on the edge of a crowd.

A brass tells in quaint rhyme the virtues of George Mower, a boy of 14 who died in 1752; one of the Mowers gave the church an ancient silver chalice. A monument with a draped woman bowed over an urn has a long inscription to the Outybridge family.

Here there preached last century Parson Hodge, who proved himself a hero one terrible night. He was on board the Royal Charter when, after a voyage from Australia, she was wrecked off Anglesey in 1859. While a sailor tried to swim ashore with a rope, brave Parson Hodge calmed 500 terrified passengers by holding a prayer meeting. Before help reached them the ship was shattered on the rocks, and when morning broke only 39 people were left to tell the story of how Clarborough's parson spent his last moments.

Below the floor of a cottage on the lane to Welham is the once renowned well which gave that village its name. A flight of steps goes down to the water in a stone basin 12 feet square.

On a Roman Highway

CLAYWORTH. It lies along a stretch of the Roman road from Doncaster to Lincoln, and its old church is a charming wayside picture of neat grey walls and roofs, timber-fronted porch, and a fine line of windows six centuries old. Near it the Hall shines golden through the trees; and down a lane, where flowers bedeck the cottage walls, is red-roofed Royston Manor, with mullioned windows looking across a wide expanse of fields. Much of the old house has gone, but it still has something left of the Elizabethan home of the Otters, who have lived here nearly all the time since it was built in Queen Elizabeth's day.

The upper part of the tower, with eight fine pinnacles and eight quaint gargoyles, has been rebuilt, but in the base is some of the oldest work in the church, coming from early in the 12th century, or even from Saxon days. Part of the wall between the nave and chancel is of the same time, and has a little herringbone masonry near the arch. There are two Norman doorways, one with a later one built outside it, the other framing a fine old door with studded panels and restored tracery.

The 13th century nave arcades of wide and elegant bays have pillars on Norman bases, one pillar with five heads and three ornaments in place of a capital, another wreathed with foliage. A 13th century archway in the south wall of the chancel opens to a chapel shut off from the aisle by a simple stone screen which may have been set up about 1388, a rare possession for a village church. A 13th and a 15th century archway lead from the chancel to the north chapel, which has a 700-year-old arch between it and the aisle.

The clerestory is 15th century. The charm of many of the 14th century windows is enhanced by modern glass, saints and prophets and angels making a fine gallery, others showing Christ giving the keys to Peter, the Annunciation, and the Wise Men. The tower has a Jesse window, and in the 19th century east window are scenes of Our Lord washing the feet of the Disciples, Peter leaving the Judgment Hall, Gethsemane with the soldiers sleeping, and the Crucifixion. The upper half of the beautiful vaulted screen is new; the base, with its massive embattled rail enriched with floral medallions, is perhaps older than the Reformation. The new font has an old carved cover, and an old font has traces of painting.

The oldest memorial is a floorstone in the tower with a worn inscription to a rector of 1448. Under a great stone tomb carved with foliage and a shield of arms sleeps Humphrey Fitzwilliam, a Tudor judge, and on the tower wall is a memorial to William Sampson, a rector who founded a school and left behind 62 closely-written leaves of parchment giving a history of the parish from 1676 to1701. Among the memorials of the Hartshornes who lived at Hayton Castle (now a farmhouse between the village and North Wheatley), is a quaint brass with the tiny figure of Time lying on his back; he has his scythe, and the sands are run down in the hourglass at his feet. The rhyme on the brass tells us of the virtues of John Hartshorne of 1678.

There are memorials in the church of a Yorkshire family distinguished in the siege of Scarborough Castle during the Civil War, the Ackloms. They had the neighbouring Wiseton estate in the time of Charles the Second, and half a century ago built the handsome hall on the site of the older house in which they lived through the 18th century till the heiress married Lord Althorp, a well-known politician and an honest one. Lord Brougham was a frequent guest, and it has been said that perhaps the first Reform Bill was outlined under this roof. In the fine park is an old tulip tree and a magnificent fern-leaved beech.

Two brothers of the Otter family of Royston Manor are remembered in the church, and there is a wooden cross from the grave of one of them who fell in Flanders; the other was killed in an accident.

Proud Knights and Their Ladies

CLIFTON. Our countryside has few corners more beloved by those who know them, or more delightful for those who come upon them suddenly. Clifton, a mile or two from Nottingham, lives in poetry and in the hearts of all who come this way.

It is Nottingham's poet Henry Kirke White who has put it into literature in the dismal legend of the Fair Maid of Clifton, and in his finer poem on Clifton Grove, the far-famed view of oaks, elms, and beeches, planted two centuries ago and stretching for more than a mile along the top of a steep cliff overhanging the Trent, racing far below in one of its swiftest channels:

> Dear native grove, where'er my devious track
> To thee will memory lead the wanderer back.
> Still, still to thee where'er my footsteps roam,
> My heart shall point, and lead the wanderer home.

Other famous sights the village has. Who can forget the green on which every Mayday the children dance round the Maypole? Round it are gathered thatched cottages, gay gardens, the rectory, a pretty row of 18th century almshouses, and groups of stately trees; and on the green itself is a gabled dovecot lined with 2300 nests, a most remarkable number. It may be 18th century.

At the head of the famous Grove stands Clifton Hall, plain outside but packed with treasure. It has lovely gardens with flights of steps leading down from terraced lawns, and shaded by rows of yews. In the woods is a summerhouse two centuries old. But far older than the mellowed walls of the great house is the story of the Cliftons, who have known the village from medieval days and still live at the hall, though the last male of the line died in 1869. For centuries they have been figures at our courts and on our battlefields, and many of them have had their favourite name of Gervase. The first Sir Gervase was High Sheriff of Notts and Derbyshire. Queen Elizabeth called one of them Gervase the Gentle. Another Gervase, first baronet, born on the eve of the Armada and dying when London was burning, inherited the estates as a baby and grew up to marry seven wives. He offered a fortune to Charles Stuart when the king wrote for all the arms he could send, and was fined heavily at the end of the war for his loyalty; the king's letter is still kept at the hall. A portrait of this Sir Gervase hangs on the wall, and the story is told that he was much beloved for entertaining all who came his way, king or beggar.

In the hall is also a portrait of Sir Arthur Clifton, and near it is his uniform, with the banner of the regiment he commanded at Waterloo. He lived to be 99, and was uncle of the last baronet of the house, Sir Robert, who, having encumbered his estates in his youth by losses on the turf, opened the Clifton collieries in the hope of retrieving his fortunes. One of the greatest treasures here is Romney's painting of Frances Clifton, who in 1797 married Robert Markham,

Archdeacon of York. Their son became rector of Clifton, built the rectory, and laid out its grounds.

We meet some of the Cliftons in the church, where a wonderful array of monuments are links of brass and stone in their story. It is a beautiful building with a 14th and 15th century tower rising from the middle of a cross, and a lovely gable cross with a crucifix, over 400 years old, is on the west end of the nave. Like most of the church, the south arcade with finely carved capitals is 14th century, the clerestory coming from its close. The oldest part is the north arcade, with round pillars and pointed arches, built when the Norman style was passing.

Very charming is the effect of the lofty arches of the tower, framing a view of the much-restored 15th century chancel with its great windows and lovely roof. The roof was built in 1503 by a rector who signed it with his name and his quaint portrait. Under the brilliant east window is a splendid reredos of Derbyshire alabaster, coloured blue and gold. The stalls and screen are modern, and a fine chest is over 400 years old.

Most of the old monuments are in the north transept. The knight lying in an alabaster tomb with his head on a peacock, his feet on a weary lion, and the Clifton lion rampant on his surcoat, is either Sir Gervase, who died under Richard the Second, or Sir John, who fell at the Battle of Shrewsbury. The fine brass portrait of Sir Robert Clifton of 1478 shows him in armour with his head on a helmet and a greyhound at his feet; another brass is of his son Gervase, knighted at the coronation of Richard the Third. Very lovely is the smiling figure of his wife, Alice Nevill, who lies on an alabaster tomb, wearing a long-sleeved gown of smooth folds.

"Gervase the Gentle" lies magnificent with his two wives, all three in ruffs and wearing a remarkable number of rings, one wife having 11 and the other 8. On one side of the tomb are the five children of his first wife, and on the other is the second wife's son George, who was only 20 when he died a few months before his father, leaving the baby Gervase as the heir, who was to grow up to marry seven wives. We see George again in a brass portrait with the wife he married when he was only 14; he wears a short cloak and a big ruff, and she has a cap with her gown and embroidered petticoat. Close by is the floorstone of Dame Thorold, the grandmother who cared for the baby heir.

Grown-up, the much-married Sir Gervase set up an elaborate monument to his first three wives in 1631, showing their arms on a black sarcophagus with a medley of bones and skulls below; and built a vault in which he buried six wives, the seventh outliving him. At his own death in 1666 his bust and the arms of all the wives were placed over the chancel doorway to the vault. He is said to have left a thousand pounds for his funeral, which was attended with great pomp and ceremony.

There are many later memorials to the Cliftons, and one more relic of old days is a leaden case thought to contain a heart, perhaps of Sir William Clifton, a crusader. They had a negro servant in the 17th century, and it is said the initials J. P. on the entrance to the porch mark his height of 6 feet 4 inches. A floorstone in the south transept covers his grave, and tells us that Joseph, commonly known as the Black Prince, was converted to the Christian faith and died in the hope of a better life.

A charming memory of Clifton is the peep over the churchyard wall to the grounds of the hall, with a glimpse through the trees of the river shining below.

The Church Between the Villages

CLIFTON. It is Clifton North and South, a mile apart, each having a long shady lane between it and a fine stretch of the Trent, and both sharing a pleasing old church standing between them, near the river and the long line of arches on which the trains run.

A screen of fine elm, beech, and fir trees climbs as high as the eight tall pinnacles crowning the splendid tower, which is chiefly 15th century with some remains of the 13th; in its west doorway hangs a worn old door, and its fine arch to the nave is adorned with shields and embattled capitals. A porch made new and a 13th century doorway lead into the nave, where a beautiful arcade has 13th century arches resting on massive Norman pillars. The 500-year-old chancel arch has sides and carved capitals two centuries older. Worn heads adorn the hoods of the windows (many of which are 15th century), an old chest is like a trunk, and there are some old timbers in the aisle roof. Stone heads of kings and a queen support the modern roof of the chancel, which has a cornice of vine and grape.

The oak reredos, elaborate with paint and gilt, shows the Nativity.

The Dukeries
The Duke's Drive at Clumber

Retford
The Church of St Michael

Clifton   **The Famous Grove**

Gotham

Ancient Well and Sign of the Cuckoo Bush

Hawton
Figure on Tomb

Hawksworth
Norman Tympanum

Hawksworth
Gargoyle

Newark

White Hart Inn

Stapleford

Cross

Hickling

14th Century Doorway

The old piscina is like a tiny font, its round bowl on a tapering shaft and set in a rounded niche; and very quaint is an old image bracket in the aisle, carved with flowers and a cat-like face with its tongue out and its pointed ears upright; seeming to watch us come and go.

King's Palace and Parliament Oak

CLIPSTONE. Part of a storied countryside, it sees the glories of the Forest as it lies in the valley of the Maun. The fine meadows through which the river flows, at the foot of the village, are famous for having been reclaimed from swamp and heath and gorse by the irrigation canal built to distribute the waters of the stream. Known as the Flood Dyke, it stretches nearly from Mansfield to Ollerton, passing through Clipstone.

In a cornfield above the small iron church are the scant ruins of what was a great building long ago. Still dignified by the name of King John's Palace, the rough grey walling, with jagged openings once doorways and windows, is impressive in the suddenness with which it rises against the sky as we see it from a narrow lane. It is said that kings of Northumbria built it and lived here. It was built at any rate before the time of King John, who used it as a hunting lodge. Henry the Second improved it and gave it a park. An English and a Scottish lion met here when Richard Lionheart talked with William the Lion on his return from the Crusades in 1194. Edward the First held a Parliament at Clipstone in 1290. The building began to decay in the time of Henry the Fourth.

Two miles away, in a grassy bay of the road to Mansfield, are the remains of another vanished glory—the lifeless fragments of the gnarled and twisted trunk of an ancient oak, supported by props and fastened by chains to a younger oak. It is called the Parliament Oak, because Edward is thought by some to have held his parliament here and not at the palace. Another story is that by this tree King John (who was staying at his hunting lodge at the time) had a meeting with his nobles after hearing the news which led to the execution of 28 Welsh youths at Nottingham Castle.

Between Clipstone and Edwinstowe is a fine Gothic archway known as the Duke's Folly or the Duke's Archway, built by his Grace of Portland in 1842 after the style of the old Priory Gatehouse at Worksop. With buttressed walls, and rooms with traceried win-

F
65

dows on each side of the central arch, it breathes the spirit of the Forest in the splendid figures niched on its north and south sides, and the stone hares that sit above the projecting bays. Richard the First is here in chain armour, with unsheathed sword; Friar Tuck with folded arms looking quizzically down; Allen-a-Dale with his harp; charming Maid Marian; Robin Hood himself with a feather in his cap, and Little John, like Robin, with his bow and quiver of arrows.

The arch looks one way to Clipstone, the other along an undulating grassy stretch, lined with oaks, running straight as the crow flies to the Mansfield road. It is said that the duke meant this broad turf ride to be part of a direct drive from Welbeck to Nottingham, passing through his Archway.

Prince Rupert's Strategy

CODDINGTON. From miles around we see the windmill of this pleasant red-roofed village on a hill, part of which Walter de Maresco received in the time of Henry the Third for giving the king a pair of scarlet breeches every year. With Beacon Hill close by, it has seen stirring times in days gone by, and shared in one of the most brilliant exploits of the Civil War.

It was in 1644, when Newark was besieged by 8500 Roundheads and was almost on the point of surrender, that Prince Rupert was sent to its help by Charles Stuart. The prince drew up his men at Coddington, and, rushing down Beacon Hill, delivered a rapid attack which so surprised the enemy that the town was saved. Two years later, during the final siege of Newark, some of the Roundheads were quartered in the village.

Eight fine pinnacles crown the low church tower, which rises above the steep red roofs of nave and aisle, and is, like the rest of the building, much renewed. It is a wide and pleasant place, entered by the enriched 13th century doorway inside a modern porch. The nave arcades are 13th century, the north a little older than the south. There are stone seats round the pillars of both arcades. The font is 700 years old.

The modern chancel has a wagon roof painted in medieval colours with much gold. The traceried panelling of the sanctuary walls, and the reredos with roses among its carving, are adorned in similar style. Very beautiful are the oak sedilia with a coved canopy and a rich cornice. The lofty chancel screen, with gilded tracery and four figures of bishops, was one of the gifts of the Thorpes, who have been benefactors to church and village. One was John Somerled Thorpe who fought in the South African War and fell on the Somme in 1916, and attached to his memorial here are his three actual medals, including the MC. Among so much that is new in woodwork a little old is treasured in six traceried bench-ends.

With the farm buildings close to the churchyard is a gabled dove-cot, one of the oldest in the county, and used now as a little house.

She Walks in Beauty

COLSTON BASSETT. She walks in beauty; this charming patch of a secluded countryside has beauty at every step. In a lane like a grove of trees, where a stepped wall runs by the grounds of the hall in its park of 90 acres, a stone bridge spans the tiny River Smite. In a delightful setting where the ways meet is the charming old cross, rising with slender grace from a flight of steps. It is 15 feet high, and was rebuilt on the ancient base about a century ago. By another road embowered in trees (planted in 1710) is the stone church built in 1892 in memory of a beloved wife and her son, looking across the park to the fine old house where they lived.

Rich with elaborate battlements and pinnacles, the church has a central tower resting on lofty arches and crowned by a spire rising to 150 feet. The transomed east window glows richly with eight scenes from the life of Our Lord. The great attraction of the church is the fine carving in stone, especially notable in the undercutting of the capitals of the nave arcades and in the stone base of the oak pulpit, where the luxuriant foliage seems to be symbolical of the wealth of trees in the village. On the slender pillars supporting the roof are four angels, and the stone reredos has coloured panels of Our Lord and the Four Evangelists. The Hall pew has an elaborately carved oak canopy.

A lovely winged figure in the chapel, sculptured in marble, is to Alice Catherine Knowles; it was in memory of her and her son that her husband built the church. The son was drowned in Cumberland when 21, and there is an inscription to him and to a brother who fell in the Boer War.

We read on the wall of Joshua Brooke, who followed his father as vicar and served for 53 years before he died in 1888. It was another church he knew, and it is sad that the coming of this new church meant the loss of the old, which is falling in ruin. High up on the edge of the park, in a glorious situation, are the pitiful remains of the 13th and 14th century church of St Mary, which once had the shape of a cross and was one of the most beautiful in the county. The walls are overgrown with creeper, but we can see the embattled parapet and two pinnacles, remains of fine windows, and fragments of a still earlier church in the capitals of two Norman pillars. Of its famous peal of bells, five now make melody in the new church, and the old font has found a resting-place in the new churchyard, where there is a fine cross to 14 men who did not come back.

From the personal history of this place we gather that Francis Hacker, who led Charles Stuart to the scaffold, inherited land here from his father; and that in a skirmish here in 1643, when Francis and his brother were fighting on opposite sides, Thomas was killed. Here before the Hackers were the Bassetts, who gave the village part of its name. The founder of the house was Ralph, Chief Justice in the reign of Henry the First, remembered for the severity of his rule. He was responsible for carrying out the king's orders for the punishment of robbery, and we read in the Saxon Chronicle that "Ralph Bassett and the king's thanes held a Witenagemot in Leicestershire, and hanged four-and-forty men, and deprived six of their eyes and certain other members."

The Home of the Byrons

COLWICK. There is old and new Colwick. The old, with hall and church and park, has been drawn into Nottingham; the workaday part and the rambling old rectory by the Trent are left to the county. The herons still nest in Colwick Woods.

The hall and the church are close companions, with great beeches between them, but the great days of both are gone. One is a hotel, attached to the racecourse in Colwick Park, and the other we found in sorry plight, deserted for a mission church in the busy part of the village. Even before this book appears its monuments may be gone.

Built in 1776, and keeping still a splendid staircase and fine rooms with fireplaces in the style of the Adam brothers, the Hall is full of story, for the place where it stands is said to have been lived on since Saxon days. It was a home at the time of Domesday Book, when there was a mill by the Trent. Among the many owners who followed were the De Colwicks, who held it for a rent of 12 barbed arrows supplied to the king when he came to Nottingham Castle; then came the Byrons and the Musters, through whom it became the home of Mary Chaworth, the ill-fated heiress of Annesley immortalised in Byron's poems. She was his early love, but came here as the bride of the sporting squire, John Musters. She was here when the Reform Bill rioters looted and fired the hall, and the exposure she suffered then brought about her death a few months later at Wiverton Hall.

From the churchyard gate, a fine example of the ironwork for which Nottingham was then famous, we see the city's towers and spires, its castle high on a rock, the splendid dome of the new Council House, and the last of its old windmills at Sneinton. The church came into Domesday Book, but rebuilding by the Byrons in the 16th century and by the Musters in the 17th left it with little interest except for the monuments in a chancel almost too dark for them to be seen.

The Byrons were at Colwick for nearly 300 years, and there are monuments of three generations here. On an altar tomb are the elaborately engraved figures of Sir John Byron of 1576 and his two wives. Sir John, a knight in armour, was a favourite of Henry the Eighth, who granted him Newstead Priory in 1540. He was known as Little Sir John of the great beard, and, though he has no beard on the top of his tomb, he has one on the front, where we see him with his sons. With this group are three daughters and their mother, all in ruffs.

The fine alabaster figures of his son (Sir John of 1609) and his wife Alice Strelley lie under the pillared canopy of a great monument across the chancel. The knight is in armour, wearing ruffs and a triple chain, and has an extraordinary moustache and a very long beard. His lady has a ruff and a double chain round her neck. Their son, another Sir John, is kneeling with his wife on a wall monument, both having died on the same day in 1623, and below them kneel their son and a granddaughter.

Among the Musters memorials is a bust of Sir John de Monasteries of 1680, who repaired the church. An elaborate monument has the absurdly theatrical figures of his son and his wife in robes and sandals kneeling lifesize on a projecting tomb. At one side of the altar stands (or stood when we called) the draped figure of Mary Ann Chaworth-Musters, Byron's Mary of Annesley. At the other side sits Sophia Musters of 1819, with three children at the foot of the monument, one dancing, one with a harp, and one with a board and easel. This accomplished lady painted the unusual east window, glowing with golden light below grey clouds, showing a dove looking down on Unica with the lion, the Flight into Egypt, and figures representing Justice, Faith, Hope, and Charity. She took for her inspiration the window designed by Sir Joshua Reynolds in the Chapel of New College, Oxford.

An odd thing we found in the church was a thankoffering for the coming back of the Stuarts, a dado in the nave of 31 carved oak panels, and five larger panels in the chancel, brought from Colwick Hall in 1661 by Sir John Musters. Worn and shabby with time, they were destined to be removed to Annesley Hall. This sad church may perhaps be pulled down when a new one is built, and the Byron monuments are to find a home in the crypt at Newstead Abbey.

The Valour of John Shaw

COSSALL. They say the first coal in Notts was dug up in this border village seven centuries ago, and there are collieries still round about it, though the old village is in surprising seclusion on a green hilltop, looking to Ilkeston a mile away. It is a delightful picture as we come from Trowell, crowning a slope down which the canal winds like a serpent through the meadows.

Except for the 13th century tower and the low spire with dormer windows, the tiny church is not yet a centenarian, having been rebuilt in 1842. Under an arched recess in the sanctuary is a marble tomb of the Willoughbys, remembered for the fine almshouses near the church, founded by George Willoughby in 1685. In an aisle window is St Catherine in ancient glass. The bowl of the font is 15th century.

Cossall is proud of the great oak reredos, for its work was all done by village carvers. The cornice has roses, and among the fine bits of carving is a panel of passion flowers and leaves trailing over a cross, under a pinnacled canopy with a splendid finial.

It is strange to find in this little churchyard reminders of three wars. One is to 13 "lads of the village" who died for peace; another is to one who served all through the Crimean War; the third is a marble monument with helmet, cuirass, and crossed swords to three men who fought at Waterloo. Of these one lies buried here; the other two fell gloriously in the fight, and the daring deeds of valour of John Shaw the Lifeguardsman have given him a place among the brave for all time, and a lasting memory, in the words of Scott:

> Nor 'mongst her humbler sons shall Shaw e'er die,
> Immortal deeds defy mortality.

A giant of physical strength, it is said that he put out of action eight Frenchmen, refusing to retire from the field to have his wounds dressed, and only stopped fighting when he fell from sheer exhaustion. He was born in 1789 at a farmhouse.

A Saxon Fragment

COSTOCK. It is pleasant with cottages and farms, a little church in a narrow lane, and a charming Elizabethan manor house with a quaintly gabled roof, velvet lawns, a grand old chestnut tree, and a newel staircase made from a single oak. We were told that it was one of the first of its kind.

What is old in the church is mainly 14th century, including the bowl of the font, but a lancet window is 13th, and the aisle and the porch are 19th. In a richly canopied recess in an outside wall lies the battered figure of a priest in robes; it is said that his head was knocked off by soldiers in the Civil War. Built into the wall near this recess is a lovely fragment of a Saxon preaching cross.

The church has what we may call a garden of poppyhead benchends, six of them 15th century, and over 60 the work of a rector who died just before the war. He was Charles Sutton Millard, and very good his work is, the ends well carved, and no two of all the poppyheads alike. We may call them a garden because most of them are floral, but they have also quaint heads of animals, heads of men, and angels. One has trees of the forest and St Giles (the patron saint) with his hind.

The east window with the Crucifixion is in memory of the clever parson, and the east window of the aisle is in memory of nine men who did not come home again; in it are St George and St Michael, and Christ crowned.

King Charles's Rules

COTGRAVE. Reached by pleasant lanes in a countryside of fields and copse and cover, near the Fosse Way, it gathers trimly round its little square. Its prettiest corner is in a leafy lane where great limes and elms guard the church, and a lychgate leads to a burial-ground.

A gnarled old walnut tree stands near the tower, and an ancient yew shelters the chancel. Like most of the old work left in the church, both tower and spire come from the 14th century, the tower buttressed to the battlements and opening to the nave by a lofty arch. Of about the same time are the nave arcades with clustered pillars, and the chancel arch whose sides and capitals come from the close of Norman days.

An oak panel has the names of men who fell in the Great War, and of five women among those who served. We read in the tower that the bells were rung for an hour and 20 minutes, half muffled, in memory of Dorothy White, who died in 1918. Cotgrave has always been proud of its peal of bells, and she was one of the ringers. Another inscription tells that they were rung for over three hours in 1927 in memory of Pryce Taylor, one of the bell-founders of Loughborough, who died in Canada. Under the tower hang King Charles's Rules:

> *Profane no Divine Ordinance*
> *Touch no State matters*
> *Urge no Healths*
> *Pick no quarrels*
> *Maintain no ill opinions*
> *Encourage no vice*
> *Repeat no old grievances*
> *Reveal no secrets*
> *Make no comparisons*
> *Keep no bad company*
> *Make no long meals*
> *Lay no wagers*
> *Do nothing in anger*

Cotgrave finds its way into many parts of the country with marl for cricket pitches; it is found in a pit here.

For the White Rose

COTHAM. It overlooks the lovely vale of Belvoir from its place between the River Devon and the Lincolnshire border, and has a reminder of its story in a lonely church across a field.

The modest home of only a few folk, it has little claim to distinction now, but it was a proud village five centuries ago when it became the seat of the Markhams. William was Lord Treasurer of Edward the First, and in the church of East Markham, the village from which they sprang, lies the Judge Markham who drew up the document for deposing Richard the Second. Sir Robert, a supporter of the White Rose, was knighted after the battle of Towton Field, and his son John, set out from his home here to distinguish himself as a leader in the terrible battle when the White Rose met the Red for the last time at East Stoke, three miles away.

No trace of their splendid house is left, but in the ivied church near which it stood we see Anne Warburton kneeling with three sons and four daughters under the canopy of a wall monument; she was the wife of Robert Markham, whose unthriftiness brought to an end the glory of his house in the last years of Queen Elizabeth.

The church is only a shadow of its old self. Towards the end of the 18th century it lost two aisles as well as its tower, from which two gargoyles now guarding the churchyard gate are said to have looked down for over 500 years. Some of the old aisle windows are in the nave walls, and two 14th century relics are the massive font and the charming piscina. Two marble tombs, one of which has lost its brass portrait of a 14th century knight, may belong to the Leekes, who lived here before the Markhams came.

COTTAM. Its few houses line one side of the road and look over meadows stretching nearly a mile to the Trent, dividing Notts from Lincolnshire; and its tiny church, guarding a precious doorway of 800 years, hides from all who hurry by.

A lychgate at the end of a wayside path brings us to the simple building, with walls aslant, nave and chancel under one steep roof on four massive old beams, and a turret for one bell. A porch shelters the Norman doorway, which has crude chevron mouldings boldly carved, and pillars on each side with scalloped capitals. The bowl of the ancient font is outside the porch, set on a new base.

A Gem From Pin Hole Cave

CRESWELL CRAGS. They belong to Derbyshire as well as Notts, the boundary running through them on the verge of Welbeck Park. At their foot are the famous caves where remarkable treasures made by the earliest men in Britain have been found. These caves have names of their own, Robin Hood's Cave, Church Hole (named from its narrow tapering entrance), Mother Grundy's Parlour, and the Pin Hole.

Nearly 50 years ago Sir William Boyd Dawkins began to dig in these caves, and among many treasures he found the earliest example of pictorial art discovered in our land, a piece of smooth bone three inches long and an inch deep, on which had been scratched the head and shoulders of a horse. The mane of the horse is remarkable; the hair stands up straight.

Inch by inch the soil from the first three of these caves was removed and sifted, down to the white sand in which there were no remains. Above the white sand and red sand were bones, and one or two rude implements of quartzite which were also found in a layer of red clay above. The remarkable thing about these bones is that they belonged to the hippopotamus and the rhinoceros, animals which needed a far warmer climate than ours. Hyenas shared the cave with them, the marks of their teeth being on the larger bones. The hippopotamus is a survivor of the Pliocene into the early Pleistocene age, and the man who made these quartzite implements before the ice ages descended on the land must have had a hot meal from the flesh of these beasts, for signs of fire remain on the bones.

Above the clay we come to the mottled and light-coloured cave earth with implements in a higher stage of manufacture. The hare was the chief food of these men. On a higher layer still is a red cave-earth in which charcoal fragments and blocks of limestone occur with the bones, with implements made of flint brought from a distance. The men who made these were the artists, and used implements of bone as well as of flint. The top layer of all consisted of stalagmite material and other worked flints. Most of these objects are at the British Museum.

A few years ago Mr Leslie Armstrong decided to excavate Pin Hole Cave, which had been left as not worth troubling about. It has proved the richest of all, and from it we have evidence that at least two glacial periods have passed over Creswell Crags, driving men from it. Thousands of years separate the periods of its habitation.

The gem of Pin Hole was an engraving of a masked man or woman on the bone of a reindeer. The figure is standing erect, apparently engaged in ceremonial dancing of the kind Australian or African natives enjoy today. Other engravings worked on ivory, and the beautiful flint tools with which they worked and hunted and fished 20,000 years before the birth of Christ, were found in the upper layer of this cave, which has proved one of the most valuable records we have of the men of the Old Stone Age over a period of nearly a thousand centuries.

A Home of the Cromwells

CROMWELL. With the old brick dwellings making a red patch on the Great North Road is the grey stone church in a churchyard surrounded by fine elms, a splendid beech, and a chestnut. Its name is its distinction. In the old house by the churchyard, once the rectory, are foundations which are said to be part of the old home of the Cromwells, of whom the last and most famous was Ralph, Lord Cromwell. Treasurer to Henry the Sixth, Constable of Nottingham Castle and Keeper of Sherwood Forest, he was a man of wealth and a great builder. He built Tattershall Castle in Lincolnshire, and the greater part of Wingfield Manor in Derbyshire.

Here sleep three members of a family who left their mark on the village and were rectors from the eve of the French Revolution to the eve of the Great War. The first was Charles Fynes Clinton, whose son Henry, a famous classical scholar, spent some of his boyhood here. The second was another Charles Fynes Clinton remembered for a book of sermons, and for editing the book on Roman chronology which his brother had begun. Henry Fynes Clinton followed them till 1911; he lies in the churchyard, the others in the chancel.

A 15th century embattled tower crowns the pleasing little church, which was restored 60 years ago, when the 14th century arcade of two bays was opened out in the chancel, and the chapel built on old foundations. From the 13th century come the south doorway, the nave arcade, and some lancet windows. Among other medieval windows are two in the chancel with the graceful flowing tracery of the end of the 14th century, and in a tiny roundel of old glass is a rose. The low iron chancel screen with gates, wrought with delicate scrolls, was made in the village smithy in 1890.

We understand that all the men of Cromwell came home from the war, but that one died afterwards from wounds. It is one of the few villages without a memorial of the war.

The Carpenter's Whim

CROPWELL BISHOP. It belongs to the byways, and in the days gone by the bells of its interesting old church were rung for an hour every Saturday night to guide the villagers home from Nottingham market.

The fine tower rising above the trees and red roofs is 15th century, the chancel is 14th (and restored), and the nave arcades with round pillars are 13th. The font (with a 17th century cover) and two piscinas are 600 years old, and from the same 14th century come most of the windows, except for the 500-year-old clerestory. The only colour in the windows are a few fragments of old glass, and the peace memorial window of St Nicholas with a ship, St George in armour, a soldier helping a comrade on the battlefield, and an angel with the crown of life.

In the nave are ten gnarled oak benches of about 1400, their poppyheads carved with flowers, faces, eagles, and little men with their legs doubled up. The chancel screen, a patchwork of old and new, has fragments of medieval tracery, faces of two men, and symbols of the Last Days in Jerusalem. Eight fearful stone grotesques support the lovely Tudor roof of the nave with its richly moulded beams and leafy bosses. It is odd that on a later beam than the rest the carpenter carved the date backwards, as if not quite sure how it would read from below: it runs 4671 instead of 1764. The oldest woodwork here is about 12 feet of wallplate from the middle of the 13th century.

In the great mill by the Grantham Canal plaster is worked from gypsum found near by. Cropwell Butler, a pleasant residential village a mile away, takes its name from the old family of Botiller.

The Greendale Oak

CUCKNEY. Here many ways meet on the edge of the Dukeries, with lovely views of their woodlands. Skirted by the River

Poulter on its way to Welbeck and Clumber, it is pleasant with red-roofed houses in stone-walled gardens, set in haphazard array.

At a charming corner a shelving cedar stands facing an inn with cream walls and a swinging sign of the Greendale Oak. A mile and a half away, near Welbeck Abbey, is the famous tree to which the name belongs, so old that none can tell its age, its hollow trunk propped up but with life still flickering in it. It has a strange tale to tell. In 1724, as the result of a wager by the Duke of Portland that he could drive a coach and four through one of his trees, an archway ten feet high was cut in the massive trunk, which was then about 35 feet round above the opening. One of the treasures of Welbeck is the Greendale Cabinet made of timber from this tree, inlaid with panels showing it in its prime, with the duke driving a coach and horses through the archway.

Into Cuckney's old story comes a Saxon knight who was allowed to keep land here after the Conquest in return for shoeing the king's palfrey when he came to Mansfield, being given a horse if he did his work well but forfeiting one of his own if he did not please. In the 12th century Thomas de Cuckney, founder of Welbeck Abbey, was lord of the manor, and a moated mound in the churchyard is said to be the site of his castle. The church was made new in his day, and treasures fine Norman remains.

It is a rare thing to find Norman work in a porch, but, though this porch was made new 700 years ago, it keeps an original string of Norman ornament which makes a dainty trimming for the top of the side walls, and also round the gable. A lovely Norman doorway, with zigzag and cable mouldings and a hood ending in grotesques, lets us into the church, where the long nave is divided from its aisle by an arcade of six round arches on pillars of varying shapes. Except for one round pillar which is earlier Norman, this arcade was built when the Norman style was changing to English, and the priest's doorway is of the same time.

From the 15th century come the top of the sturdy tower (on a 13th century base) and many of the windows. One frames a lovely Annunciation, and another, glowing red, blue, green and gold in memory of the men who did not come back, shows St George and St Alban with Our Lord.

There is an unusual piscina with worn ornament about 700 years old, and the broken remains of a fine stoup or font have been brought to church after being dug up in a garden. Three coffin stones form window-sills in an aisle, and part of another is in the nave floor. There is some old tracery in the tower screen.

A stone with a story lies in the middle of the chancel floor, so worn that its inscription is gone. It marks the resting-place of Robert Pierrepont, who became Earl of Kingston-upon-Hull in 1628 and was killed in the Civil War. One of his sons was for Parliament and one for the King, but the Earl tried to remain neutral and is reputed to have said, "When I take up arms with Parliament against the King, or with the King against Parliament, let a cannon ball divide me between them." Strangely enough it came to pass. After having at length declared himself on the side of the King, he was taken prisoner at Gainsborough, put in a boat to be taken to Hull, and was literally cut in two by a shot fired at the pinnace by Royalists on the bank.

A Knight and His Lady

DARLTON. Midway between Lincoln and Worksop, quiet little Darlton has wide views of the countryside, a small ancient church made partly new, and a house with something left of the days when it knew King John. The house is now a farm (called King-shaugh), and part of its walls and some of the outbuildings are the ancient stone of King John's hunting lodge.

Two lofty limes are guarding a 19th century lychgate, which frames a small 700-year-old lancet in the tower as we draw near. The tower is old and unbuttressed, and wears a new pyramid cap of red tiles. The great possession of the church is the lovely south doorway letting us in, built at the close of Norman days, and having a hood of fine moulding over a round arch resting on detached shafts. A tiny medieval arcade divides the nave from the aisle, and a big window a hundred years older lights the east wall. The old aumbry has flowers in the spandrels. A cup and its cover are Elizabethan.

On the wall of the chancel are fine brass portraits of a knight and his lady, both with praying hands, and standing erect on grassy ground. The knight is in plate armour with a sword, his hair falling on to his shoulders; the lady has a long gown with an embroidered belt from which hangs a chain with an ornament, while from her pointed headdress two streamers fall to her elbows. They belong to about 1510, and are probably Sir William Mering and his wife.

The Three Stately Homes

DUKERIES. All travellers in Notts come to the Dukeries, one of the loveliest patches of our Motherland, and one of the richest in associations, for this remnant of old Sherwood Forest has become the glorious domain of the three stately houses of Welbeck, Clumber, and Thoresby. Their spacious deer parks, woodlands, gardens, and lakes cover the greater part of a rough seven-mile square, divided almost in two by the highway from Ollerton to Worksop, and threaded by other roads where we may ride, and paths where we may walk among the hoary oaks, the stately beeches, and the countless silver birches. None of the old trees make a braver array than those at Bilhagh and Birklands, which are on each side of the road as we go from Edwinstowe to seek the Major Oak.

The River Poulter fills a string of lakes as it flows through the parks of Welbeck and Clumber; the River Meden forms Thoresby's beautiful lake. Rufford Abbey at the south-east, and Worksop Manor at the north-west, are worthy neighbours of the three lordly homes of the Dukeries, owned by the Duke of Portland, the Duke of Newcastle, and Earl Manvers.

Welbeck Abbey is an imposing pile, reflecting the changing taste of its owners through three centuries, for there is little left of its earliest days, when it was actually an abbey. It was founded in the middle of the 12th century by Thomas de Cuckney, and was the head of the Order till the destruction of the monasteries by Henry the Eighth, when it was granted to Richard Whalley. He became involved in the troubles of his relative the Duke of Somerset, was imprisoned, and so heavily fined that he had to part with Welbeck. Bess of Hardwick bought the estate and left it to her son Sir Charles Cavendish, whose son Sir William was made Duke of Newcastle for his services to Charles Stuart. It was he who built the old riding-school at the abbey. His wife idolised him and wrote much in his praise, thus earning the contempt of Pepys; she also wrote poems and plays.

Welbeck passed into the hands of the Earl of Clare, and the Earl of Oxford whose wife was the "noble lovely little Peggy" of Matthew

Prior's poem. It was their daughter who brought Welbeck to the Bentincks by her marriage with the second Duke of Portland.

Though part of the great house was begun in 1604, most of it is later, with some remains of the original building in the walls inside, the refectory being now the servants' hall. It was partly rebuilt after a fire in 1900 which destroyed most of Lady Oxford's work.

The west front has embattled parapets and a great square tower from which the duke may display his banners. The east front, rising from a broad terrace over the lawns to the lake, has a gabled roof. The south front, with balustraded parapets, is in that Italian style which during the 18th century changed the appearance of so many English homes.

There is another aspect of it less visible and in some way more remarkable, the underground Welbeck. The ceremonial way to the abbey is through the iron gates of the Lady Bolsover Drive, but once it was through a tunnel under the lake, two miles long, lighted artificially and by skylights in the roof. It was wide enough for a horse and cart then, and is wide enough for a motor-car now. This is only one of the labyrinth of underground tunnels and rooms dug to the order of the fifth duke, who employed thousands of men and spent colossal sums of money on these undertakings. He was a recluse, and because of his unusual style of building was generally regarded as extremely eccentric.

The truth was otherwise. Great numbers of Nottinghamshire weavers, especially about Worksop, had lost their livelihood through the introduction of machinery. The duke sought to help these poor neighbours by giving them work to do, and he found it by employing them to dig the tunnels in many directions, and to excavate a vast underground chamber, 160 feet long and 63 wide, now used as a picture gallery and a ballroom. It is the biggest room in England without pillars, and one of the finest private apartments. The duke built the underground riding-school, 400 feet long and 106 wide, with a roof in three divisions supported on fifty pillars; the centre division, of iron and glass, is arched, and decorated with a frieze showing animals, birds, and foliage.

Of the portraits hung in the remarkable ballroom the earlier ones of the Bentincks are by Dutch artists. Later artists portrayed the members of families with whom the Bentincks claimed connection by

Dukeries   **Clumber Church**

Perlethorpe   **Modern Church**

The Stately Welbeck Abbey

Thoresby House

Rufford Abbey

Clumber House and its Lovely Lake

FOUR OF NOTTINGHAMSHIRE'S MAGNIFICENT HOMES

marriage: Cavendishes, Holles, Talbots, Harleys, Veres, and Villiers, so that the collection of portraits is like the pedigree of the Dukes of Portland.

A sumptuous room is the dining-room, where hang the Van Dyck of Prince Charles and the Kneller of the first Earl of Portland. The Gothic Hall is remarkable for the fan-vaulting of its ceiling, the drawing-rooms for their exquisite decoration and French furniture. The library and chapel were once the old riding-school and stables built by the first Duke of Newcastle before his fortune was sacrificed to the Stuarts. The beauties of panelling and painted roof are plain for all to see, but the things beyond price in the library are the collections of letters written to the Portlands through seven reigns. They begin with the letters of William the Third (in his own hand) to William Bentinck, the companion of his boyhood, the adviser of his manhood, and the faithful soul for whom he sent on his deathbed, and continue to the William Bentinck who governed in India in the 19th century.

These are some of the heirlooms of a family prominent in English affairs since the days of the Stuarts, but there are others of a different kind, including a collection of beautiful miniatures, the pearl earring worn by Charles Stuart on the scaffold, the chalice of his last Communion, a rosary of Henrietta Maria, the enamelled seal of Charles the Second, the ring Dutch William gave to his Queen Mary (which she always wore), and a dagger of the insatiable Henry the Eighth.

The gardens of Welbeck are most beautiful, massed with flowering borders, a triumph of modern gardening; there are vineries, conservatories, and orangeries. One of the famous oaks in the park is the Greendale Oak, past its old glory but still with the archway cut through its trunk in 1724 by the first Duke of Portland. One of the treasures of the furniture in the abbey is a cabinet made of oak from this tree, with many panels showing it as it stood in its greater days. Near the lakes, which wind for over four miles, is a bronze medallion in memory of Lord George Bentinck, son of the fourth Duke, who was famous at the time of the Corn Law agitation and died here suddenly when walking to Thoresby.

Clumber Park is eleven miles round, and through it runs the noble Duke's Drive, an avenue three miles long, with a double row of limes on each side. It was a barren waste and a rabbit warren till about

1770, when the Duke of Newcastle built Clumber House. It has four wings round a central block, and was designed by Stephen Wright, who was responsible for the Cambridge University Library. Fires last century and this have left old work only in the wings. The library, state drawing-room, and great hall have all had their glories, but a sad day has come for them, for the house is now a shell emptied of its rich store of treasure. Its charming church with a delicate spire, built half a century ago, is closed. But church and great house, and the beautiful Lincoln Terrace built of stone brought from Italy a century ago, are still a rare picture mirrored in a lake of nearly a hundred acres. Many of the rare collection of famous pictures have been lent for some years to Nottingham Castle.

Thoresby Park, formed in 1683 by the Duke of Kingston, is the most richly wooded of the ducal estates. Bounding it on the south is Bilhagh (entered by the quaint gates crowned by two stone deer), with its ancient oaks from medieval days, and the glorious Ollerton beeches, which form a forest cathedral unsurpassed. It may be doubted if there is in England a more impressive natural nave than this. On the west of Bilhagh are the Birklands, renowned for their slender silver birches.

The splendid house stands near the lake of about 65 acres, and a road running east through the park from Budby passes near by. It was built about 1870, near the site of a brick mansion which followed an older house burned down in 1745. It was in the older house that Lady Mary Montagu passed her girlhood years with her father.

The chief rooms of the house we see have decorated ceilings and floors and panelling of oak, walnut, or maple. There are fine carved mantelpieces in white marble, and the library chimneypiece shows a scene in Sherwood Forest. It is the home of Earl Manvers, whose family name is an honoured one in the county, for there have been Pierreponts in Notts from very early days.

A Fine Sweep of the Trent

DUNHAM. Its medieval tower calls us from afar and arrests us when we reach it. Keeping company with slender firs, it is a charming picture from the road beyond the gay flower garden of a cottage, or through the old stone archway opening to the churchyard, its great capitals carved with grotesque animals and foliage.

The tower is a noble tribute to the builders of the 15th century, and finds its glory in windows remarkable for their size and beauty. Four transomed windows light the upper storey, filling the walls to such an extent that from a distance the top of the tower seems almost detached from the rest. Another splendid window is over the west doorway, and between them is a small canopied niche. Its lofty archway, reaching to the roof of the nave, is as wide as the tower itself, and has foliage capitals. This ancient tower is all that is left of an old church twice rebuilt last century, and it was sad to find it calling for help with the pathetic appeal, "It is unsafe, so that we dare not ring the bells."

There is good carving of last century in the shallow sedilia, adorned with four-leaved flowers, and in the piscina with a band of ballflowers.

The village is neat and trim, delightfully set on the bank of the Trent. An ugly toll bridge which carries the road across to Lincolnshire has the saving grace of being a fine place from which to see a lovely panorama of our green and pleasant land, with the river sweeping grandly to flow in fine reaches to Laneham. We see Laneham church on one hand, and on the other Fledborough with its church and its countless string of arches over river and bank; across the river is North Clifton's church in Notts and that of Newton in Lincolnshire. The wooden stakes of the ferry can still be seen near the bridge. It was at this spot that a duke and his retinue met William of Orange to escort him to Welbeck.

The Village Afraid of a Hero

E AKRING. With red-roofed houses lining the road, and fine views of the Forest countryside, it is the resting-place of a hero whose story lives undying in the annals of human courage. Yet Eakring was afraid of him and kept him from them, like a leper in a hut.

At the foot of the village, by the rectory, stands the church, much restored and made new. The tower has a 15th century top storey on a 13th century base which has a carved stone over its doorway showing traces of a figure. The sides of the tower arch are perhaps Norman, and there are three 13th century lancets in the chancel. There is a fine little Jacobean pulpit with a canopy, a poor-box of 1718, a small old chest, and a 17th century font like a pillar. The arms of Charles the Second are in the church, and in the porch are those of Elizabeth, brought from a house in the village which was once an inn where the queen is said to have stayed. Two stone corbels on an outside wall show a woman's worn face and a demon with bared teeth.

A brass plate tells us of George Lawson who gave the church a silver chalice; he was rector here before the coming of a new rector who was told that he must not enter the village. He was William Mompesson, who from September of 1665 to October 1666 had laboured in plague-stricken Eyam, ministering to his pitiful flock as they awaited their dread fate and perished one by one, till less than 40 of Eyam's 350 folk were left alive.

Three years had passed since the plague when he came to Eakring, but the people were afraid of infection, and Mompesson had to live for a time in a hut in Rufford Park. It is one of the saddest examples we have come upon of the superstition of country folk. He remained at Eakring for 38 years and died in 1708. On the chancel wall is the brass plate which used to be in the floor over his grave, and a modern inscription tells of his ministry at Eyam. The poor glass in three lancets is his memorial.

The scenes through which this devoted man and his wife chose to live were almost too appalling for description. It was difficult to bury the victims, for no one dared to touch them and there was no possibility of making coffins for them all. One wife and mother buried her husband and six children in eight days.

Perhaps the story of this brave rector comes nearest our hearts as we stand in the fields with only the sky above us, where a simple rustic stone cross marks the spot at which he used to preach during his pathetic exile from the village. Near the cross is a young ash tree which has replaced the old one under which he used to stand. It was known as Pulpit Ash, and was destroyed by lightning some time ago.

From this rough cross, which stands at the head of a field at the top of the village, we have a pretty view of Eakring among the trees, and a fine one of the countryside.

He Led the King to the Scaffold

E AST BRIDGFORD. This charming old village, full of story, stands high on a wooded cliff overhanging fine reaches of the

Trent. The main road has passed it by since the coming of the new bridge at Gunthorpe, but its delightful green lane still drops sharply down to where the old toll bridge spanned the river. In a field by the church is a windmill without sails; at Newton near by is another with no sails, a fine old giant and a landmark for many miles. It is said to have been one of the string of windmills which stood on the ridge overlooking the Forest at Nottingham.

The oldest story of the village is being revealed in our own time by the excavation of Margidunum between the village and Bingham— one of the line of Roman forts built along the Fosse Way, Britain's straightest road. Over twenty years of patient digging and research by Dr Felix Oswald have brought to light many relics now housed at Nottingham's University College, indicating the importance of the site in the Stone and Bronze Ages.

The next step in the story is the church, which is old enough to have been burned by the Danes. The Civil War touched the village very closely; in a skirmish here Colonel Ferninando (son of the Earl of Chesterfield) was killed, a year before his gallant brother fell in the storming of Shelford House near by; and it still has a house where lived a man who listened to some of Charles Stuart's last words.

For the Old Hall of mellowed brick, at the end of a rose-bordered drive not far from the church, was the home of the Hackers, and is little altered (except for additions) since their day. Here about 1590 came to live John Hacker, a rich man and the head of a family who were all Royalists but one. The Roundhead member of the family was Francis Hacker, who married Isabella Brunts of East Bridgford; there is in this church a memorial to her father Gabriel Brunts. Hacker was a firm supporter of the Parliament. A fine soldier, he is reported to have given all the prizes he took to the State and to his men, and the king is said to have offered him the command of a choice regiment of horse if he would serve him. He remained faithful to his cause, however, and at the trial was one of the officers charged with the custody of the king, escorting him daily to and from Westminster Hall. The king's death-warrant was addressed to him and two others.

Thomas Herbert, the faithful servant of the king, who lay at his bedside on his last night, tells us that Colonel Hacker wished to place two musketeers in the king's bedchamber, at the thought of which the king gave a sigh, but the bishop and Mr Herbert, resenting the barbarousness of such an act, never left the colonel till he withdrew these men. The next morning, Thomas Herbert tells us, Colonel Hacker knocked at the chamber door, and Mr Herbert would not stir to ask who it was, but at a second knocking the king bade him go to the door, and the colonel said he would speak with the king. The king said, Let him come in. The colonel in trembling manner came near and told his Majesty it was time to go to Whitehall. The king bade him go forth: he would go presently. They walked through the park and the king arrived and went to his bedchamber, where after some time Colonel Hacker attended at the chamber door, and the king took notice of it saying, Open the door, and bade Hacker go and he would follow:

A guard was made all along the galleries and the banqueting hall, but behind the soldiers abundance of men and women crowded in to behold the saddest sight England ever saw, and as his Majesty passed by with a cheerful look he heard them pray for him, the soldiers not rebuking any of them.

It was this East Bridgford boy who led this sad procession to the scaffold, and who later was to be led to the scaffold himself, for after the Restoration his name was on the list of those who were to die for having encompassed the death of the king. It transpired that the death-warrant of the king was in Hacker's house, and his wife was sent to fetch it. She delivered it in the hope that it would save him, as proving that he acted only as a soldier under orders; but nothing could save him, and he was hanged on October 19, 1660, his body being given to his friends for burial, and laid in the church of St Nicholas Cole Abbey, London.

Although a number of the Hackers lie in East Bridgford church, their only monument is to John, the first to live here. He kneels with his wife at a desk, with four sons and two daughters below them. He died in 1616, the date of the monument being wrong. The eldest of the sons was father of Francis; he died in 1646 and sleeps here with his wife. Two brothers of Francis who sleep here are Thomas (killed in a skirmish at Colston Bassett when Francis was fighting on the other side) and Rowland, who lost his right arm defending Newark and lived till 1674. After Francis Hacker's death, Rowland was allowed to buy back most of the family estates.

The battered stone figure of a cross-legged knight, wearing chain-mail with surcoat and shield, was found in the garden of East Bridgford Hall; he may be Sir John Caltoft, a medieval lord of part of the manor. On the wall above the recess in which the figure lies are the arms of John Babington of 1409, owner of a small estate here. His son William was Chief Justice and Baron of the Exchequer.

In the wise restoration of the church early this century 12 feet of Saxon walling 34 inches thick was found below the chancel floor, with other stonework which showed that the chancel of the church that came into Domesday Book was only eight feet wide. Traces of fire here led to the belief that the ancient building had been burned by the Danes. Two fragments of a Saxon cross, and a 13th century headstone (buried in an upright position in the churchyard) were found at the same time, and are in the church for us to see.

The chancel was rebuilt on a bigger scale about 1200, and was given its charming priest's doorway later in the 13th century. The middle portion of its 14th century arch is nearly a thousand years old; the 14th century sedilia and piscina were restored after being found in the rector's garden. A fine roof with angels at the ends of the beams looks down on the nave with 14th century arcades and a clerestory of the 15th. The porch with gargoyles and a niche with a modern figure, and some tiles with many patterns, are also 14th century. The tower was rebuilt in 1778.

Here Were the Romans

EXCAVATIONS at East Bridgford have brought to light the Roman Posting Station Margidunum established beside the Fosse Way, the great road constructed by the conquerors of Britain from Exeter to Lincoln, the straightest road in our country.

But before this place became a posting station it was a Roman Camp, perhaps one of the forts referred to by Tacitus as erected on this side of the Severn and the Trent for keeping the enemy in check. Margidunum appears to have been established about the middle of the first century, during the invasion by the legions of the Emperor Claudius, and the excavations by Dr Felix Oswald have confirmed this view.

Arrowheads of the Bronze Age have proved that the site is an ancient one, obviously chosen for its easy defence, having marshes on two sides and good drinking water twelve feet down. The Roman legionaries at once sank wells, and one of the most remarkable discoveries made by Dr Oswald is the oldest of all on the site, a well lined with a square casing of oak planks. It is clear that when this lining of oak had been placed in position clay was rammed round it, and the oak has been wonderfully preserved; we may see it with the other relics of the station at University College, Nottingham. After about 19 centuries they still show marks of the workman's tools.

The age of the pottery found in the well indicated that it had been filled in about the time of Boadicea's rebellion, when Margidunum was abandoned and burnt by the British.

The Romans returned to the camp and lived in it for another fifty years, when, not requiring it for military purposes, they appear to have razed it to the ground. The foundations of the walls they built, of stone-lined wells and cellars, and a great number of pots of various shapes and sizes, have been dug up. Many potter's marks have been deciphered by Dr Oswald, who is famous for having printed with his own hands, page by page, an authoritative book on this subject. The task he set himself was nothing less than the collecting of about 20,000 stamps of Roman potters, arranging them alphabetically, and recording the shapes of some of the vessels on which they occur; and when this vast index was ready, and was found too great an undertaking for a publisher, Dr Oswald set it up in type himself.

When Margidunum became a posting station the Fosse Way was reconstructed straight through the old camp, and by the time of the Emperor Constantine it had become a flourishing little place, judging from the things discovered there—urns with moulded human faces, the Samian bowls, and other pottery of the period found here. In the year 367 the Picts and Scots swept through Britain, and the concrete foundation and part of the stone rampart built at this time to defend Margidunum has been revealed. Close up to this wall (which was probably 18 feet high) the remains of a building set up on the site of a former bath-house have been found, the floors composed of pink concrete on which lay fragments of wall plaster decorated with bands of red, orange, and green. There were thick roofing slates, which are known from the positions of the nail-holes to have been arranged in diamond pattern, and on the floor of one room was a newly-minted coin of the Emperor Valens.

Among other objects found by Dr Oswald on this interesting site were bronze ornaments, an iron sword, a gridiron, a bucket handle, a spring lock, some keys, a bronze pin with a head like an outstretched hand, and an enamelled seal-box of native British workmanship. Altogether Margidunum, though covering about seven acres, has revealed much of the life and history of this county during the Roman occupation of Britain.

E AST DRAYTON. Gathered pleasantly about its quiet cross roads, it is proud of its wayside church, a fine all-embattled pile of grey stone inside and out, filled with light from windows which all have clear glass and come from the end of the 15th century.

The tower is 14th and 15th century. The handsome porch of the 15th has elaborate buttresses and pinnacles, and a stone roof with ribs ending in tiny corbel heads showing grotesque and human faces. Other faces peep out from foliage in bosses of the nave and chancel roofs, where beams painted with scrolls and flowers are in rich contrast with grey walls.

The north arcade of the nave is six centuries old, and the south is five. There is a plain old font, and at the foot of the belfry stair is a small old door. Much of the lofty chancel screen is about 1500, and part of the old altar rails are in the south aisle.

The Vamping Horn

E AST LEAKE. Busy making baskets and hosiery, it lies in a dip of the Wolds nine miles from Nottingham. Its old manor house and huge barns in the middle of the village are now part of a farm. A fine cross and a charming wayside garden, with the Sheepwash Brook from Rempstone Hill running by its rockeries and pools, are in memory of the men who gave themselves for peace. On the opposite side of the road, in company with two towering sycamores, is the church, full of years and interest.

Its oldest story is told by two fine patches of herringbone masonry in the north wall of the nave, which come from early Norman or even Saxon days, and by two windows of the same time which frame modern pictures of Mary and John. The 13th century tower has a 15th century spire, and the nave arcade comes between the two. The clerestory is 15th century. The chancel, mostly made new last century, has a splendid 600-year-old east window and some 13th century lancets, one looking like a coloured pencil with its shining glass in memory of John Bley, who endowed a school in the village 200 years ago. The beautiful 14th century east window of the aisle glows with warm colour in memory of John Bateman, a rector for 46 years of last century.

The great font is over 700 years old; some of the poppyhead bench-ends and the splendid pelican on the pulpit are 500. The pulpit and the lectern are made of oak from the old belfry, and some open seats have been here since 1612. Part of a rare book called The Dippers Dipt, of 1645, is in the vestry; it was once chained.

East Leake's rarest treasure, in the church for all to see, is a long tin trumpet which is one of six left in English churches. Measuring nearly ten feet when extended, and twice as far across the mouth, it was used till 1855 for the principal singers to vamp through, making what the Psalmist would have called a joyful noise unto the Lord. The other five are at Bradbrook and Harrington, Northants; at Charing in Kent; at Ashurst in Sussex; and at Willoughton, Lincs.

The Fall of a King

EAST MARKHAM. Its orchards make it pleasant, it has two old windmills hard by, and memories of famous folk cling to two of its houses and its noble church.

One was a gracious lady who wrote books for children, and a history book without stories of cruel things, showing her love for the village by using Mrs Markham as her pen-name. She was Elizabeth Cartwright, whose father invented the power loom, and she spent much of her early life with her aunts at the big red house known as East Markham Hall. She has been sleeping in Lincoln Cathedral since 1837, but is remembered here by a window in the church.

In the stone foundations of the manor house close to the church are remains of the old home of two famous judges of the Markham family, father and son. The father was Sir John, who helped to change the line of kings by drawing up the document for deposing Richard the Second. The thought that he lies here carries the mind back to one of the most dramatic scenes in history and one of the most moving scenes in Shakespeare:

> *What must the king do now?   Must he submit?*
> *The king shall do it.   Must he be deposed?*

NOTTINGHAMSHIRE

The king shall be contented. Must he lose
The name of king? O' God's name, let it go:
I'll give my jewels for a set of beads,
My gorgeous palace for a hermitage,
My gay apparel for an almsman's gown,
My figured goblets for a dish of wood,
My sceptre for a palmer's walking-staff,
My subjects for a pair of carvèd saints,
And my large kingdom for a little grave,
A little, little grave. . . .

It was Judge Markham who gave the deposition of King Richard its legal basis by drawing up the document, and here they laid him when his exciting days were over; he lies in the chancel under an alabaster tomb with an inscription and plain shields. His son John, known as the Upright Judge, is said to have lost office through carrying out his maxim that no subject can be arrested by the king for treason. He sleeps in Lincolnshire.

Set in a floorstone in the south aisle is a beautiful brass portrait of the first Sir John's widow, who after his death married William Mering. The brass shows her in a high-waisted gown with hanging sleeves and a wide collar reaching to her shoulders. Her embroidered headdress is wired so that it looks rather like a canopy, and her hands are at prayer. The little dog at her feet, with bells on its collar, is charming.

In memory of the two Markham judges the east window of this aisle was renewed and filled with stained glass by their descendants last century. It has shields of arms and medallions of foliage; three of the shields are of old glass, and among old fragments in the tracery is St Scyth crowned. Of two other windows here (filled at the same time with similar glass), one is in memory of Elizabeth Cartwright and has old fragments in the tracery; the other is to John Kirke, a soldier of Trafalgar days, and his three sons, who died serving their country.

The chancel is beautiful with its modern glass. The east window, shining silver and gold, blue and green, has Mary and Jesus, St Hugh and his goose, John the Baptist, and St Cuthbert. Splendid figures of St Alban, St George, and St Martin, with small scenes from their lives, look out from a window in memory of Kenneth Markham Rose, who fell in action in West Africa in 1915. He was the only son at the manor house.

A great delight inside and out is the clerestory of 16 triple windows, a glorious traceried lantern which helps to fill this spacious place with a blaze of light. It is a worthy part of a 15th century embattled pile which is one of the finest churches of this countryside.

Eight pinnacles and gargoyles like winged demons adorn the massive tower, which has transomed windows, a recessed doorway, an archway of great height opening to the nave, and a small figure in a canopied niche. Projecting far from the chancel buttresses are four extraordinary gargoyles—a winged animal, a grotesque with a rope round its shoulder, a creature in armour with a battle-axe, and another with staring eyes and one hand in its wide-open mouth. In the gallery of heads at the windows are a king and a queen, a bishop, a lady in a frilled headdress and a crusader. On a battlement is an old sundial.

Great heads look out from the nave arcades with channelled pillars. Much of the old work is left in the oak screen of the south aisle, the old pulpit has carved borders, an old pillar almsbox has iron bands, and worked up into the Litany desk is part of an old bench-end carved with the head of a bishop, vines coming from his mouth. He is hidden from the casual eye. The modern roofs have rich bosses and carved borders, and on the ends of the nave beams are angels and heads of human folk, one a man with his tongue out.

Very striking is the massive and unusual font, looking like a giant spider, with a bowl of 1686 and a 14th century base which has a central pillar and eight legs bent outward, their feet resting on a stone carved with four-leaved flowers. It is crowned by an elaborate pyramid cover.

Set up in the north aisle is the ancient altar stone. We read in the church that its presence near the chancel arch was revealed to a vicar in a dream the year before it came to light in 1897.

Red Gutter and Deadman's Field

EAST STOKE. Its red-roofed houses gather pleasantly round the cross-roads on the Fosse Way, and its meadows are by pretty reaches of the Trent. Only a name or two remind us of a black page of history written here four and a half centuries ago, when six or seven thousand men were slain.

In 1486 Henry the Seventh had made his throne more secure by marrying Elizabeth of York, so ending the long struggle of the Yorkists and Lancastrians; but there was still unrest among the White Rose supporters, and a priest named Richard Simon planned to set up Lambert Simnel, son of an Oxford joiner, as the young Earl of Warwick, who, like the Earl of Lincoln, was a claimant to the throne. Simon hoped that if the plan succeeded he might become Archbishop of Canterbury.

Simnel was crowned king in Dublin, and an army of Irishmen with 1500 Germans invaded England and went to York. Led by the Earl of Lincoln and Viscount Lovell, they marched south and forded the Trent at Fiskerton to East Stoke, on their way to take Newark. But at East Stoke they were met by the king's army marching out from Nottingham, and for three hours there was stubbornly fought here one of the most terrible conflicts known till then, ending in the complete rout of the Yorkists and the shattering of their hopes for ever.

The fight probably took place about the cross-roads, and the rebels were driven to the steep track running down to the river meadows, still called the Red Gutter. Near the Fosse Way is Deadman's Field, where many of the bodies were buried.

Stoke Hall stands back from the river, in a thickly wooded park with lofty beech, elm, and chestnut trees, and the biggest heronry in the county. A magnificent cedar on the lawn is seen from the churchyard wall. The house was bought in the middle of the 18th century by Abel Smith the banker, and until recently was a home of his descendants, the Bromleys and the Pauncefotes whom we meet in the church.

Restoration and rebuilding have spared a little old work in the church, which stands by the lovely lane going to Fiskerton Ferry, passing on its way a grassy track to the meadows where the Red Gutter comes down. Great trees in the churchyard tower above the marshland, and all there is here to remind us of the old struggle are the stones in the porch which are said to have been hollowed out by soldiers sharpening their swords on them. From the close of the 14th century come the west window of the low tower and its arch on 13th century shafts, and the east window. There are fragments of old glass, a medieval piscina, and a chest 500 years old.

We found a framed copy of some extracts from Captain Scott's last message to the nation hanging here, and learned that Scott's friend Admiral Bromley gave it to the church when he left the Hall.

A story belongs to a great Union Jack hanging near the tower. It once floated over our Embassy in Washington, and when Lord Pauncefote, the first British Ambassador to the United States, died there in 1902 the flag covered the coffin in which he was brought home to sleep in this quiet churchyard. The flag is treasured in the church, and a beautiful bronze angel keeps watch over the Ambassador's grave.

The First British Ambassador to America

LORD PAUNCEFOTE was one of the illustrious peacemakers of last century, and he will go down in the annals of the English-speaking peoples as a statesman who brought together in friendship two peoples who were drifting into enmity. He will live also as a pioneer of world peace, for he represented his country at the first Hague Conference, where his wise counsel did much to establish the Permanent Court of Arbitration.

Born at Munich in 1828, he became a lawyer. Having proved his ability as Attorney-General at Hong Kong and as Chief Justice of the Leeward Islands, he was given posts in the Government at home until 1889, when a serious crisis arose with America, our minister there having been dismissed for interfering in a Presidential election. Pauncefote took his place, won back all the confidence that had been lost, and was raised to the rank of ambassador. It is difficult to realise now that at the time he was appointed there were no foreign representatives of Ambassador rank in the United States.

Two serious disputes between the two countries occurred while he was at Washington, but both were referred to tribunals of arbitration, and both parties accepted the awards. The first dispute concerned an American claim to prevent Canadian vessels fishing in the Behring Sea, and the second concerned the boundary between Venezuela and British Guiana. The boundary question needed very tactful handling, for President Cleveland had intervened in a challenging message to Congress which tactlessly invoked the Monroe Doctrine against the very country which had suggested it for the safeguarding of American security. Intense feeling was aroused on both sides of the Atlantic, and for a short time there were shadows of war, but wisdom prevailed and the British claim was upheld.

When Lord Pauncefote died his body was sent home in an American

94

warship, for he had then become widely popular. He had achieved three distinctions of which any man might be proud. He had been the first British Ambassador to America. He had steered us safely through the most war-menacing crisis between the two countries for a generation and more. He had brought the two countries together in the greatest arbitration treaty ever agreed upon, pledging them never to fight one another again.

The Battle of Nobles and Noodles

IN all our annals there is nothing stranger than the story which reached its fantastic conclusion here, the aftermath of the Wars of the Roses. Seldom has there been a more stubborn battle on English soil, never a stranger cause, never a more enigmatic squire than the leader of the defeated army, John de la Pole, Earl of Lincoln.

Head of a great house which in a century had risen from a family of Hull merchants to alliance with royalty, John de la Pole was the grandson of Alice Chaucer, Duchess of Suffolk, and Alice was the granddaughter of Geoffrey Chaucer. Her son married the Princess Elizabeth, a sister of Edward the Fourth. Their son, created Earl of Lincoln by his uncle, King Edward, was adopted by his other uncle, Richard the Third, as heir to the throne of England. He is the towering figure on this battlefield of Stoke.

It was as Heir Apparent, and one of the greatest forces in the realm, that Lincoln entered Bosworth Field, to see Richard slain, and himself dispossessed of all his hopes by the birth at Bosworth of the Tudor dynasty; he left that field dependent for his life on the clemency of the new King, Henry the Seventh. Lincoln took the oath of fealty to Henry and was spared; but, ambition smouldering, he struck, two years later, here at little Stoke, for a kingdom, under the most fantastic banner that ever led nobles and noodles to death. Aiming at the throne, Lincoln used the son of a joiner as a stalking horse. Lambert Simnel was made to personate, first the murdered little Duke of York, and then the Earl of Warwick whom he resembled. Visiting Brabant, Lincoln raised a force of 1500 mercenaries and took them to Ireland. There he arranged for Simnel to be crowned King of England, and with an army reinforced by some 5000 Irish he crossed to the Lancashire coast, landed at Furness, passed through Yorkshire into Nottinghamshire, and here at East Stoke on a blazing summer afternoon encountered the army of Henry.

During the ferocious fighting the aristocratic fellow-conspirators were cut to pieces, save perhaps Viscount Lovell whose fate has never been known for certain. Some say he was drowned in the Trent; others that he escaped to his home at Minster Lovell in Oxfordshire and died there in a vault where he hid. The priest was flung into a dungeon and never heard of again, and Simnel was derisively exhibited as a scullion in the king's kitchen. Lincoln, the proudest noble in England, was left to moulder into the soil of East Stoke, dead ignobly, fighting under the flag of a tutored Jackanapes whom he had intended to supplant as king.

The Battle of the Idle

EATON. It lies two miles from Retford, a tiny village of a few red houses, a great house with lovely gardens and walls glowing with gold as we see it through the trees from the Great North Road, and a small greystone church which has followed one of Norman days.

The church stands high in a churchyard where fine sycamores and a great horse-chestnut grow, looking down on the River Idle. A peaceful scene it was for us, with a flotilla of 30 geese on the stream flowing through the three-arched bridge, an ivied farmhouse on the other side, and woods and green meadows everywhere.

Yet this is the spot, it is believed, where more than 1300 years ago king met king in battle, one of them and the son of the other being slain. It was in 617 that the Battle of the Idle was fought in which Redwald of East Anglia slew Ethelfrith, the usurping king of Northumbria, but lost his own son Regnhere. Redwald had been sheltering Edwin, the true Northumbrian king, and as a result of the victory Edwin was restored to the throne. He married the beautiful Ethelburga, daughter of the Christian King of Kent, and was himself baptised by Paulinus.

The Great Sycamore Tree

EDINGLEY. Abounding in orchards, this trim little place between Southwell and Mansfield has a plain church which has something it has kept 800 years in spite of much change. It has lost a south aisle, but two wide arches and other fragments of its 14th century arcade are still seen in the wall; and though the chancel was

Thurgarton   **The Priory Church**

Cotgrave   **The Village from the Fields**

Trowell   **Church and Colliery Chimneys**

Edwinstowe   The Major Oak

Edwinstowe   Sunshine and Shadow

IN SHERWOOD FOREST

made new last century it has its old piscina and the priest's doorway, which is now blocked. There is a Norman west doorway with chevron and cable mouldings, and a small Norman window deeply splayed in the north and south walls of the nave.

A stream runs by the churchyard gate, and just within is a tremendous sycamore overhanging the road and dwarfing a shapely little yew; the big tree shelters a patch of ground 76 yards round.

Tiny Church With Walls Aslant

EDWALTON. Charming new houses and gardens line the busy highway, but the heart of the old village lies at the end of a leafy lane, three miles from Nottingham. Just beyond two delightful little homes in a garden (a memorial to the first Clerk of the County, Jesse Hind) is the old church enshrined in trees. Some of them make an evergreen avenue from a beautiful oak lychgate with a shingled roof.

Its story and its name are thought to go back to a Saxon settler named Eadweald, who reclaimed the land from a boggy marsh. With walls aslant and some of its windows askew, the tiny church is much changed since it was built about 800 years ago. The chancel collapsed in the 17th century, and the new one is of brick. The small red brick tower, diapered with black, is believed to be one of the rare examples of church building in the time of the terrible Mary Tudor.

A buttress of the aisle is 13th century. The bowl of the font, curiously shaped like a trough, may be as old, but its base is modern and its cover is Jacobean. An old hooded doorway lets us in, and between the nave and the very narrow aisle is a 14th century arcade. The brass lectern is the peace memorial, and rich glass of our day, showing one knight sheathing his sword and another kneeling at the Cross, is in memory of Colonel Arthur Brewill, DSO.

Rebecca Freeland, who lived through all but a century of history from the outbreak of the Civil War, has a slate in the churchyard with a curious epitaph.

The Biggest Oak

EDWINSTOWE. Pleasantly set on the River Maun, it is a gateway to some of the loveliest haunts of old Sherwood Forest.

Above the church and the charming hall the village opens out to a spacious common on the doorstep of Birklands and Bilhagh, two parts of a wonderful stretch of forest with a driving road between, and many a path which we may tread in the wake of Robin Hood and his Merry Men. Birklands has ancient glades and a wealth of oaks, beeches, and the graceful silver birches which give it its name; Bilhagh has the grandest remnants of the old Forest, with magnificent oaks which have seen medieval and probably even Norman days, splendid still whether in life or in decay. It is on record that in 1609 there were 21,000 oaks in Birklands and 28,900 in Bilhagh, as well as thousands of other trees.

Within a mile of the church is the Queen or Major Oak, an ancient tree of great renown; it is the glory of Birklands and perhaps the biggest oak in the land. No one knows how many years it has weathered, but it is hale and green and shapely yet in spite of having lost its top in a storm last century. Standing in a little clearing, with oaks and silver birches paying it homage at respectful distance, this Monarch of the Forest has a hollow trunk 30 feet round, strong enough to support unaided the mighty limbs which make a ring of about 260 feet. The branches are held together by a ton of iron bands, and are protected from the weather by 15 cwts. of lead.

A mile and a half west of the Major Oak is Robin Hood's Larder, the remnant of another great oak in which Robin is said to have hung his game. The shell of three-quarters of its hollow trunk is left, 24 feet round, still giving life to the green above. Near this tree, where the ways through the Forest divide, is a charming one-storeyed Russian cottage in a delightful setting of lawn and flowers and rambler roses, backed by beech, birch, and chestnut trees. It is built of dove-tailed logs, adorned with splendid carving. The shutters are panelled and carved; the ridge of the steep tiled roof, the barge-boards and the decorative medallions are all like open embroidery. Made in Russia, and shown at a great Exhibition in England last century, it stands by the road for all to see, a gem worth finding.

On the edge of Birklands, set back from the Ollerton-to-Mansfield road, a tall iron cross painted white marks the site of a royal chapel, chantry, and hermitage dedicated to Edwin, King of Northumbria. A heap of old stones piled round the base of the cross is all that is left of the chapel where King John paid the hermit to pray for his soul.

Story says that the village itself owes its name to the Christian King Edwin, whose body perhaps had temporary burial here after he was slain in battle by Penda thirteen centuries ago. It was afterwards carried to Whitby for burial in the abbey between the moors and the sea.

The tradition of the Forest clings to the church, for here Robin Hood is said to have made Maid Marian his bride. Beautiful inside and out, looking younger than its years with restoration, its stone walls are of rosy hue with many delicate tints here and there. It came into Domesday Book, but has nothing older than the plain Norman priest's doorway in the chancel.

The lovely tower, over 700 years old, is a landmark with its stout broach spire adorned with fine pinnacles and windows between them. The spire was much rebuilt about 1680 after a storm, and at the same time the people petitioned the king for leave to cut enough of the forest oaks to pay for repair to the rest of the church. Two extraordinary heads, one with great staring eyes and the other with open mouth, are on the tower arch. Among the heads on the 13th century north arcade and the 14th century south arcade are mitred bishops, a pouting face, some with curly hair, and one with smartly trimmed beard.

Most of the windows are medieval, one having a little old glass, and the clerestory is 500 years old. A window with Gabriel, Michael, and Raphael is in memory of somebody from Kent who died on a New Year's Eve. The fine font with quatrefoils is 14th century. A piscina in the south aisle is of this time, and two aumbries here have floors formed by the two halves of a 700-year-old coffin lid engraved with shears by the stem of a cross. The medieval stone altar, with two crosses, has been set up after being found on the floor of the belfry. Fragments of the old chancel screen are in the organ case and over the altar. The altar table is Jacobean, and under glass on a pillar is a Cavalier's spur found in or near the church. A dwarf pillar piscina, only 16 inches high, has a four-clustered pillar between its head and base; it is 13th century.

An unusual relic is a stone, about 14 inches long, projecting from the north aisle wall, carved along the middle with a kind of milling pattern. It is possible it may have been used for measuring land, and to have been originally 18 inches long, which was the length of a forest foot.

A stone marks the grave in the churchyard of Dr Cobham Brewer, who, while living with his daughter, died at the vicarage here in

1897. A great scholar, he is remembered for his Dictionary of Phrase and Fable and his Reader's Handbook to Literature, two volumes still used by working journalists. A stone telling us that a native of Scotland lies here has a touch of the Scotsman's love of the land from which he comes away.

The Screen of Many Colours

EGMANTON. It lies in a hollow with orchards and trees, the pretty gardens of some of its houses reached by tiny bridges spanning a wayside stream. It has a fine little church with something of Norman days, and memories of a castle built soon after the Conquest. It stood on the green mound near the church, encircled by a dry moat and known as Gaddick Hill.

The church is by the great chestnuts overhanging the road in company with shapely old yews. The arresting thing about the interior is its medieval air, which comes chiefly from the red, white, blue, green, and gold of the modern oak screen, the organ case over the doorway, and the open pulpit—a most unusual blaze of colour for a church in this countryside. The handsome screen with entrance gates has beautiful craftsmanship in its tracery and fan-vaulting, and has a star-spangled canopy curving above a Crucifixion group on the roodloft.

We come into the nave by a Norman doorway on which are small crosses which may have been made by pilgrims. The panelled door is old. The nave arcade has the English pointed arches on the round Norman pillars, and the chancel arch, with a face at each side, comes from the same builders, the men who saw the Norman style changing into English. Most of the windows are medieval, old glass showing roundels with wreaths and part of a bird, a glowing little figure of St George, and perhaps St Michael. The massive Norman font has a beautiful modern cover carved with symbols, the rebuilt chancel has a 13th century piscina with two arches, and the 13th century Savile chapel has a charming trefoiled piscina and an aumbry. The old almsbox was made from a solid block of wood, the nave roof has old beams, and there is a Jacobean table.

A stone in the sanctuary floor has on it worn portraits of Nicholas Powtrell and two wives who lived at Egmanton Hall in the time of Queen Elizabeth; nothing is left of it now. Gargoyles of quaint heads, a muzzled bear, and a grotesque with its hands in its mouth look down from the tower.

The Three Bells

ELKESLEY. There is money in Elkesley belfry where three old friends keep company, and beauty all round this village of the old Sherwood Forest, lying between the lovely park of Clumber and the open country stretching to the Trent.

Its own beauty spot is by Twyford Bridge, where rivers meet and four roads converge. Here the little River Poulter comes its lovely way from Clumber, flowing under the road to find the waters of the Meden and the Maun and going on as the Idle. Here a charming road, like a grass-bordered avenue of sturdy limes, sets off to Ollerton.

The lofty 14th century tower serves as a porch with two doorways. One is 15th century, and in it hangs a fine panelled door of 1612. We come to its north doorway under an arch which is part of the 15th century nave arcade, left outside when the aisle was shortened. It is remarkable to discover that three of the bells have been ringing in this tower for 500 years, two of them inscribed, "I have the name of Gabriel who was sent from Heaven," and " This bell sounds for the praise of Holy Mary," and between the words are coins of their day.

The church was partly rebuilt last century, but it has some 15th century windows (including the clerestory) and a 14th century east window. The old nave roof has two bosses, and between the nave and chancel is an embattled beam. The chancel has no arch; near its entrance is an old niche, and above this is another niche which is the old rood-stair doorway with a new top. There is a Jacobean table, and a massive old oak bench like a glorified settle is crowded with carving. The small bowl of the old font has been set on a queer modern pedestal, after being used as a pump trough. The comical face of a man looks out from the nave arcade, and the quaint face of another smiles between two windows outside.

Darwin the First

ELSTON. Hidden from the Fosse Way by a great belt of trees is this charming village, where a windmill like a black giant still grinds the corn. Near a meeting of the ways where fine trees make vaulted arches in three directions stands the long grey hall, famous as the birthplace of great men; its lawns come to the edge of a low wall crowned by vases of flowers, and a splendid cedar, seen from the gate, stretches out its arms like a huge candelabra.

The house has grown up and been modernised while it has been the home of the Darwins from the 17th century. Here came William Darwin from Lincolnshire when he married the heiress of the Warings; and here to his son Robert (in whom began to develop the love of science which was to make the name a household word) were born two sons, Robert (who wrote the Principia Botanica), and Erasmus the physician, poet, inventor, and scientist.

Born in 1731, Erasmus had a successful career as a doctor in Lichfield. He won a reputation as a poet, and showed his love of living creatures in his Loves of the Plants (one of two parts of his Botanic Garden) in which he foretold steam locomotion and even the flying machine in these remarkable words:

> *Soon shall thy arm, Unconquered Steam, afar*
> *Drag the slow barge or drive the rapid car;*
> *Or on wide-waving wings expanded bear*
> *The flying chariot through the fields of air.*

He had wonderful powers of observation, and his mind teemed with far-reaching and potential ideas. He invented and suggested many domestic and industrial machines, and was a pioneer in sanitary reform as well as a great advocate of temperance in drinking. We remember him best for his anticipation of the theory of evolution, and for being, through his two marriages, the grandfather of the famous Charles Darwin and of Francis Galton. He spent his last years at Breadsall Priory in Derbyshire, and has been sleeping in Breadsall church since 1802.

The almshouses founded by Ann Darwin nearly two centuries ago are facing the church, which has four tiers of battlements and a slender tower with elaborate pinnacles. Beyond a row of yews is the grey stone rectory, gabled and stately, with flowers in fine array, and a splendid cedar on its lawn.

Though the church is much restored, the two lower stages of the tower are 13th century, the time of three lovely windows in the chancel which have foliage capitals crowning their shafts. The tiny font may be 600 years old. Among the Darwin memorials is one to the father of Erasmus.

In the lower part of the village is an ancient chapel standing in a field beyond a cluster of farms and cottages. Unused but cared-for, it has a lovely Norman doorway adorned with zigzag, two great 13th century buttresses, two 14th century windows, part of a coffin stone in a wall, and a pulpit with Jacobean carved panels.

In Belvoir Vale

ELTON. It is part of the lovely Vale of Belvoir, and peeps into the top corner of Leicestershire. All it has to show comes into a glance, its charming stretch of road between Bingham and Grantham, the inn, a row of white-walled dwellings, and a tiny church in a churchyard with a yew hedge trimmed like a battlement. Its old companion, the big house built by the famous Adam brothers, has been pulled down.

The church is only 15 feet wide, and has little claim to beauty. Three round arches built up in a wall, coming perhaps from the close of Norman days, tell of a vanished aisle, and in the modern porch is a 14th century doorway which was set back when the aisle was destroyed. The plain font may be 700 years old.

The heavy altar rails are Jacobean, and worked up into the high pews are parts of the medieval chancel screen. Two modern oak choir seats are interesting for their carvings of four heads above the names of Knox, Latimer, Cranmer, and Edward the Sixth, who is shown as a young king in cap and ruff. The oak pulpit is ornate with scroll-work panels, and the east window has Paul preaching on Mars Hill.

Jeremiah Carfinter's Half-Century

EPPERSTONE. A rare natural charm has this small village enshrined in trees, with old houses, an ancient dovecot, and the Dover Beck meandering through the willows. Opposite the church the manor house comes to the road, and through its beautiful gateway we see a fine drive of trimmed trees. From the path crossing the park to Woodborough we see the front of the house and its charming garden.

The church stands high above the road, a flight of steps climbing to the churchyard, where one of the fine trees is a magnificent cedar with propped-up branches sheltering a patch of ground about 90 yards round. Here, too, a shaded walk leads to the cottages beyond, and gives us a peep of the Old Manor below. There is a stone in the churchyard to Jeremiah Carfinter, who was over half a century at the rectory and died in 1840.

Among many corbel heads outside is a woman in a wimple, a head which has lost its features but has kept a crown, and a little fellow who has been looking across the churchyard for centuries. Crude gargoyles look down from the handsome 15th century tower whose spire has a 19th century top, and a king and a queen greet us as we reach the modern porch. A door with beautiful old timber inside opens to the dim interior, where the two finest things are the splendid tower arch, reaching to the roof, and the graceful 13th century nave arcade, with clustered pillars and unusual capitals. In the foliage of one capital is a fine head.

All that remains of the 14th century chancel is the east window. The font has a massive Norman bowl, and there may be some Norman masonry in the north wall. One of several coffin stones is a fine specimen carved 700 years ago. Two oak angels with wings look down from the chancel, and the oak pulpit has old panels with quaint figures said to have been carved by a sexton.

An inscription tells of John Odingsells who was member for Nottingham in the Barebones Parliament. The stone figure of a man with praying hands, wearing a long gown, may be one of this family, who knew the village for many generations.

The Two Dragons

EVERTON. Pleasant with its red roofs and winding ways, it lies in the valley of the River Idle, and looks across miles of re-claimed fenland which stretch as far as Yorkshire. It has an old windmill which has lost its sails, a wayside cross to men who died for peace, and a small church of which it can well be proud, for it has Norman remains and one treasure older still—an ancient tympanum belonging perhaps to Saxon days, crudely engraved with the heads of two dragons facing each other with tongues out-stretched. It is over the doorway through which we enter.

The lovely chancel arch and the fine little horseshoe arch to the tower are Norman. Both are adorned with zigzag and thrown into relief by the dim backgrounds of a 19th century apse and the old tower. Except for its arch and a Norman window, the tower is chiefly 15th century. The Norman arch frames a splendid tub font carved with arcading and bands of zigzag and cable. It is a 19th century copy of the original Norman font, of which a battered part is now in the church after a sojourn in the vicarage garden. A fine little arcade of about 1190 divides the nave and aisle, and a capital carved with foliage crowns the pillar between the two bays. From the 15th century come the clerestory and the windows of the nave and aisle.

There are four old armchairs, and a huge and rather battered stone has the worn portraits of a 13th century knight and his lady.

FARNDON. It lies between the old Fosse Way and an elbow of the Trent where the ferry crosses to Rolleston. In the middle of the village, at the end of a quaint avenue of lopped limes by high ivied walls, is the church, with fragments perhaps from Saxon days.

The tower is mainly 14th century, with later windows. A beautiful 13th century arcade with pillars of grouped shafts divides the nave from the south aisle. The other arcade and its aisle have been rebuilt, but it is in the north wall that we find the oldest work, in crude herringbone masonry, seen outside, and a simple round-headed doorway. They are part of the first church on this site and are early Norman or Saxon. There is a broken stone coffin in the church.

The clerestory and a few windows are 14th century. The font is as old, but its richly pinnacled cover, like the oak screen, is modern. The simple oak roof of the nave has richly moulded 17th century beams, and the chancel has its old piscina.

Exploring a Continent

FARNSFIELD. This fine red patch in a green countryside gave Australia a famous explorer and has traces of ancient camps round about.

One of the camps was where Combs Farm is perched on a hill, and is reached by a winding lane. Looking out on climbing woods carpeted with bluebells, it was one of two promontory fortresses in the county, used by the Romans but of earlier origin. On the other side of the village is Camp Hill, an ancient earthwork near the finely wooded Hexgrave Park where a bridle road winds through beautiful avenues of limes.

Attractive outside with red stone walls, gabled clerestory windows, and a spire, the church stands near the small three-cornered green in a churchyard with an ancient stone pillar and a slender peace memorial cross. The lower part of the tower comes from about 1400, and is all that is left of the original structure, the rest being rebuilt last century. A curious feature of the tower is that its north wall, with an outside buttress, is enclosed inside the new building. The font is the only old relic.

Here was born Augustus Charles Gregory, and here he spent his early days before going out to Australia with his father. A brave explorer and scientist, his long life of public service was a great asset to the new land. His father was head of an old Notts family, Lieutenant Gregory, who, wounded in Egypt, received in compensation a grant of land on the Swan River in Western Australia, sailed with Augustus and two other sons, and settled down to colonise in 1829, Augustus then ten years old. Their education completed, the three brothers entered the survey department, and from that time forth their names occupied a foremost place on the roll of men who, little by little, penetrated and revealed the mysteries, wonders, and grim terrors of the island continent. Augustus was the leading spirit; by instinct and training he seemed predestined for his formidable task.

His active work embraced twenty years of skilled and daring effort, and in that time he penetrated east, west, north, south. His first journey, beginning at Bolgart Spring, gave him his first shock, for his progress to the east was soon barred by an immense salt lake. North-west, however, they made the first discovery on the continent of rich seams of coal. In 47 days Gregory covered 1000 miles. More fruitful still was his expedition to explore the Gascoyne River. It was in 1848, when thrones were toppling in Europe, that Gregory saw what seemed a Promised Land inviting all who would to settle, the Murchison and Champion Bay areas with all their prospect of pastoral wealth. His fame had by this time reached home, and the Royal Geographical Society sent him forth in 1855 to explore the interior. Five thousand miles of territory were added to the map by this work, which brought its leader the founder's medal of the society.

This was Gregory's last addition to our knowledge of the unknown wastes, but he did valuable work as surveyor-general for Australia, as geological surveyor, as member of the legislature, as a protector of the aborigines, and as unwearying promoter of the scientific advancement of his adopted country. He died in 1905.

Martin Frobisher's Manor

FINNINGLEY. Three open greens adorn its winding ways, one shaded by a great oak, one where we turn by the school to find the church, and the biggest with its lofty elm in the middle of the village. Cottages, farms, and smithy are gathered about this spacious green, with a duck pond close by, and on one side the manor farm in company with four grand elms; it comes from a rebuilding of the old manor house half a century ago.

The manor was Swayne's before the Conquest, and its most famous owner since was Martin Frobisher, the intrepid seaman of Elizabethan days. It was held by his family till the end of the 17th century, when Cornelius Vermuyden, the great Dutch engineer, acquired land here in connection with the attempt then being made to drain the fenland east of the village.

Nottinghamshire's most northerly village, Finningley is part of a curiously projecting bit of the county which makes a right angle between Yorkshire and Lincolnshire. To reach it from the south we come through some miles of Yorkshire, and its station and one of its inns are actually over the border. The inn is called the Horse and Stag, and its metal sign, showing a horse holding down a stag with its foot, illustrates a story in the parish register of a horse coming to its master's aid when he was attacked by a stag in 1707.

Before the little school and its schoolhouse were built the school was in the churchyard, which served as a playground. We may be sure John Bigland would know the old school, for he was master here some years. He wrote a host of educational books, and is remembered as one of our forerunners, for he wrote a fine survey of Yorkshire in a wonderful series of books known as the Beauties of England a century and more ago.

Now all is peace in the churchyard, at the end of a little road overhung by the fine trees in the rectory garden. It is a fitting setting for the ancient church, which is of much more interest than its modest appearance suggests. Except for the embattled parapet, the Normans built the low tower with two tiny splayed windows in its west wall, belfry windows with central shafts, and a fine archway to the nave.

They built the beautiful doorway letting us in, with simple mouldings and capitals with worn carving. The plain font and some masonry in the south wall are also of their day.

The porch with a stone roof was made new last century, and has a timbered and gabled front. Built into its walls are four coffin stones and fragments of others engraved with crosses, one with a pair of shears by the stem.

The nave arcade comes from about 1280, as does the fine arch on clustered pillars opening to the 14th century chancel, which has three sedilia and a piscina with two drains. The only coloured glass fills the east window with realistic scenes of the battlefield, stark tree trunks and shattered buildings, and angels with trumpets above a figure of Our Lord whose hand is on the shoulder of a soldier. It is a tribute to those who served in the war, and to 22 who did not return. The oak pulpit was made in the year after Queen Elizabeth died, and from the close of that century comes a wooden memorial with a canopied frame.

Perhaps the chief charm of this bright place lies in the open timber roofs, with much fine decoration. Six kingposts in the nave have curved and carved braces, and on the tie-beams are medallions of flowers and floral bosses, one showing foliage coming from a quaint head. With the 17 floral bosses in the chancel is a crowned king with his sword and sceptre, and another has a bishop with staff and cross.

End of a War

FISKERTON. With its leafy road running along a bank of the Trent, its quay-like promenade above the river, and its pleasant houses with look-outs, it is a delightful little village, and fishermen love it well. The people go to the 18th century church at Morton.

It is all very peaceful now, but it looked out on a blood-stained land over four centuries ago, and saw many men drowned in the river where the ferryman crosses. At East Stoke across the river was fought in 1487 the terrible battle which finally brought to an end the Wars of the Roses, when the army of Henry the Seventh routed the Yorkists with the pretender Lambert Simnel. The rebels were driven from the old Fosse Way towards the river meadows, down a steep track which has since been known as the Red Gutter because of the ghastly slaughter there.   Looking on safely across the river, Fiskerton shared in the horror of the scene.

The Old Folk at Rest

FLAWBOROUGH. One of the smallest of Notts villages is this, where we see lovely views and hear that people never die. Into its panorama come Elston and Cotham, Shelton enshrined in trees, Sibthorpe and its fine dovecot, Thoroton's lovely tower, Belvoir Castle, and Bottesford's spire.

We can well believe the village is a good place for length of days, for, counting the ages on seven gravestones, we found the average to be 84. But someone found an answer as to why life even here must end, for another stone has the words:

> *It is no wonder we turn to clay*
> *When rocks and stones and monuments decay.*

The small church was made new a century ago, but a fine Norman doorway with zigzag in its arch lets us into the modern tower. The bowl of the font, enriched with interlaced arcading, is also Norman, and has a cover of about 1660. A plain chest is over 400 years old. The chancel has its old piscina and medieval tracery.

The Unknown Lady

FLEDBOROUGH. This home of a hundred folk who live in scattered dwellings has precious things to show to all who seek its lonely haunts.

At the end of a quiet lane leading to spacious Trent meadows we come suddenly upon a fine church full of interest, with a splendid chestnut and a lofty yew among the trees. By it is a deserted rectory with a score of chimney-pots, and near by is a pleasant manor farm. Clifton is over the river, spanned here by a railway bridge of about sixty arches.

So remote does it seem that we are not surprised to hear that it was a sort of Gretna Green in the 18th century, when a rector with the pleasant name of Sweetapple was willing to grant marriage licences to anyone. In the 19th century famous folk found their way here; Dr Arnold, the famous headmaster of Rugby, came to marry the rector's daughter in 1820, and nine years later came John Keble to bury the rector.

The church came into Domesday Book, but has nothing older than the low sturdy tower of about 1200. Except for the chancel and the 15th century porch, which are rebuilt, the rest of the church is 14th century. In the wall of the porch is an old sundial in pieces.

As the old panelled door opens, the light from beautiful windows shows up the lovely stone of walls and pillars, tinted with buff and green and rose. The arcades of the clerestoried nave have clustered pillars. There is an old stoup by the door, the font with a fine big bowl is 600 years old, the drain of a piscina, carved like a six-petalled flower, lies by the tower, and a pillar almsbox of 1684 says Remember the Poore.

Built into the chancel wall are fragments of a 14th century Easter Sepulchre, their delicate carving showing three sleeping soldiers under canopies, and angels carrying Christ away. The biggest fragment has been a doorstep at the rectory.

A great possession of the church is the beautiful 14th century glass in some of the north aisle windows, with canopy tops and heraldic shields. (A few of the shields are new.) Its east window, which has a canopied niche in place of a middle light, is a charming frame for glass in delicate colours of pale gold and silver-green, showing St John, St Andrew, the Madonna, and a knight in armour; it is both old and new, the old setting the pattern for the new, and making together a window typical of those which once filled the church. Two fine panels of similar glass in another window have the Madonna and Child, and the figure of a woman with a book.

In the old lancet in the tower modern glass with St Gregory glows red, blue, green, and gold in the setting sun; and there is many-coloured glass in formal design in an aisle window given by the villagers as a thankoffering for their escape from cholera in 1849.

A very lovely thing is a 700-year-old coffin stone under the tower, carved with a cross which has a stem branching into a luxuriance of flowers, and a head adorned with bunches of leaves. Here lies the battered figure of a knight, his hands broken but still at prayer, his legs gone. He may be one of the Bassets, who were lords of the manor for 300 years, their property being confiscated by Parliament.

There are medieval gravestones to a rector, Hugh de Normanton, and to Dame de Lyseus, and in an outside recess stands the fine figure of a 14th century lady carved in stone. She is quite six feet and has a natural and charming expression. She wears a wimple, a long gown, and a mantle with graceful drapery caught up under her arms. She holds a heart in her hands, and from the cushions under her head, held by small angels, we know that she was originally lying down. She is the Unknown Lady of Fledborough, and has been here while 20 generations have come and gone. Near her is a 12th century stone coffin.

The Battered Knight

FLINTHAM. It lies by a fine belt of woodland stretching to the Trent a mile away. From the Fosse Way we have a glimpse of the hall in its splendid background of trees; it was built last century on the site of the old home of the Hose family, who were its lords from the time of Henry the Third to Elizabeth's day. From the road below the village we have a lovely view of the park.

The church outside has little claim to beauty. The 13th century tower, with a pyramid roof, stands between the nave and the chancel, telling of the time when the building had the shape of a cross. The transepts were lost and the arches leading to them were blocked when the nave was made new over a century ago, but the two fine tower arches still left frame an effective picture of the chancel, with steps up to the sanctuary, some beautiful old lancets deeply splayed, and the old piscina. The reredos has old carving in the panels, the altar rails may be Elizabethan, a chest and the font cover are Jacobean, and the font itself is 14th century.

On a low tomb lies a battered stone knight in chain mail, his legs crossed. He belonged to the Hose family, and is precious to the village because he may have founded the 13th century church. A tablet tells us of Richard Hacker, who owned land here and was High Sheriff of Notts three years before his nephew led the king to the scaffold.

The Marvellous Scholar

GAMSTON. Trim and pleasant with many trees, it lies between the Great North Road and the quiet River Idle, on the border of the old Sherwood Forest.

As we come from Elkesley, the all-embattled church with its fine clerestory is a charming picture set in fields and woods, crowning a ridge which rises gently from the river. A round turret climbs at a corner of the nave. The massive tower, one of the finest in this countryside, has eight pinnacles 120 feet from the ground, and is a grand tribute to its early 15th century builder, who was perhaps Sir Nicholas Monboucher of 1385, owner of vast estates. The battered stone figure of a cross-legged knight lying in the aisle may be his.

Though much of the church is 15th century, the nave arcade, some walling in the aisle, and the chancel arch (one of its corbels having a face with bared teeth) come from the end of the 13th century. In the chancel lies a priest in robes, his tonsured head resting on a cushion held by two angels; and built into the chancel wall is a coffin stone showing the head and shoulders of a priest recessed in a quatrefoil. A later rector was Charles Fynes Clinton, whose famous son, Henry Fynes Clinton, the classical scholar, was born here in 1781.

His scholarly passion was for Greek, and it is recorded that while at Oxford he went through 5223 pages of Greek literature. In later years he drew up a list of Greek and Latin authors and took great pains to obtain the quantity of their writings that have survived. He set himself the curious task of reducing their folio pages to a standard page of 1002 letters, and in eight years he read Greek literature filling over 33,000 of these standard pages.

He kept a literary journal in Latin or Greek until the day before he died. He considered that a scholar in Greek or Latin could be completely equipped for every purpose with a library of six or seven hundred volumes. Few men have ever had a more complete knowledge of Greek poets and prose writers. He himself declared that at Oxford in seven years and eight months he read through 69,322 verses of the Greek poets. He lived out the Psalmist's span of life and gave nearly every day of it to scholarship.

A Cricket Pitch Between Them

GEDLING. The fine view of the Trent Valley as we drop down the hill from Mapperley Plains is not to be forgotten, nor the charming picture of Gedling nestling below, with its church spire soaring above the trees.

The tower and its lofty spire is part of a beautiful old church built of stone from a local quarry, now a green hollow a mile away. It is one of the earliest examples of a tower and a spire of the same time, for both are about six centuries old. The spire is renowned for

Hucknall   **Where Byron Lies**

Strelley   **The Way to Church**

Hawton   **The Famous Easter Sepulchre**

the pronounced bulging of its eight sides between its tiers of windows; in one of its image niches is a mailed knight, and below the battlements of the tower are 24 quaint heads. In a niche by the west window of the south aisle is a saint.

Though most of the church comes from between 1250 and 1340, there are traces of an earlier one in the lower walling of the chancel, and in a small window high up near the tower arch. A splendid stone-roofed porch leads us inside, where stately nave arcades of about 1300, below a 15th century clerestory, divide the nave and and aisles. The chancel, 50 feet long and half as wide, has beautiful lancets among its medieval windows, the east framing figures of Raphael and Michael as red-winged saints, and Mary and John by the Cross: it is the peace memorial. The sedilia and piscina, richly moulded, are 600 years old, as is the font. A coffin stone by the altar shows a deacon, perhaps of the 12th century, and another near the tower arch has the head and feet of a medieval priest. The fine pulpit was made from old carved bench-ends, and there is lovely modern craftsmanship in the chancel screen, the stalls, and the organ case with a figure of St Cecilia. The reredos and a silver hanging lamp are in memory of a rector's son who fell at Ypres.

On the hill from the Plains, not far from the church, is the delightful crescent of 12 Mary Elizabeth Almshouses with a steep roof and a Dutch gable at each end. There are lacy iron gates in the archways, and leaden window boxes embossed with vines; a rose garden is on the front terrace, and below is a sunken lawn. The charity was founded by the will of Mary Elizabeth Hardstaff, and the crescent has won for its architect, Mr T. C. Howitt (architect of the Nottingham Council House), the Architect's Bronze Medal.

In Gedling churchyard, which is like a rose-strewn garden, lie two great cricketers, their graves separated by about the length of a cricket pitch. They were Arthur Shrewsbury, whom Dr W. G. Grace described as the greatest batsman of his age, and his friend Alfred Shaw, who was known as Emperor of Bowlers.

Their friendship began in 1880, when they opened an athletic outfitter's shop in Nottingham. They went to Australia together four times, the great bowler and the great batsman sharing success and defeat. Shrewsbury's most brilliant year was 1887, when he scored 1653 runs, and before his last game in 1902 he had scored 60 centuries. A wonderful thing it was to see Shrewsbury, always cautious and patient, running up the scores, and Shaw knocking down the wickets with his untiring bowling.

The Tragic Story of the Mills

GONALSTON. It is on the road between Nottingham and Southwell, sheltered by low hills in pleasant countryside where the Dover Beck flows to the Trent.

Opposite its big house a flower-bordered walk leads down to the churchyard, which has a fine avenue of trimmed yew arches and a trickling stream. A tower and spire crown the little church, which was almost all rebuilt last century, and is surprisingly pleasing. Looking out from the hoods of the windows is a gallery of heads; a bearded man and a woman in a wimple greet us at the porch, and a laughing boy with his tongue out is not far away.

Most of the fine grey-walled chancel (built about 1300) still remains, now three steps lower than the rest of the building, and having in its north wall a blocked arch which led to a vanished chapel. The battered Norman font is kept but not used. There is an old pillar stoup, an old oak chest has an iron one for company, and an ancient altar stone belonged to a vanished hospital which stood between the village and Thurgarton. It was founded by William de Heriz, one of a family represented by three figures which were rescued last century from under the nave.

The finest of the three is of a beautiful woman wearing a draped mantle and a square headdress which shows her lovely hair and falls in rich folds to her shoulders; a dog is at her feet, and over her head is a splendid canopy. She was Matilda de Heriz, heiress of the last of the family, who died about six centuries ago. Near her lies a worn knight in chain mail, with a close-fitting helmet, a sword, and a broken shield; his legs are crossed, and his feet are on a lion. He may be John de Heriz of 1229, and the other knight in chain mail, also with a lion at his feet, is perhaps John de Heriz, who died a hundred years later.

Between the village and Lowdham, where the road is a tunnel of living green, is a gaunt old mill by the Dover Beck, bringing to mind a tragic tale. The mill is one of many turned by this stream in days gone by, and in the bad old days of child slavery waifs were sent to them from London. From St Pancras workhouse in 1799 about 80 wretched little ones came down to one of the mills here, and the experience of one of them who survived, though crippled and deformed by the life, is on record in a pamphlet called the Memoir of Robert Blincoe.

Robert was seven when he left the workhouse with the rest of the children, eager for the happy change of life that was promised them, but finding only too soon that roast beef, plum puddings, and rides on the master's horse became in actual experience daily toil of 14 or 16 hours at the machines, with thrashings for being too small to reach the work, and always insufficient food.

The children were apprenticed to the millowner till they were 21, but many died long before their time was up. Often their fingers were bruised and maimed by being caught in the mill, and when Blincoe lost the forefinger of one hand a surgeon put the joints together and sent him back to work. Once he tried to escape, but was found, brought back, and beaten, while the finder went off with five shillings reward—*singing hymns*.

But all this was gentle treatment compared with the treatment at Litton Mill, near Tideswell in Derbyshire, where they were sent to finish their time after the Lowdham mill closed down. At Litton Mill, which belonged to a magistrate, the day began at five o'clock with a horse-whip in the sleeping quarters, and continued under conditions of unthinkable horror. Slow starvation, filth, and brutality led to broken spirits, fevers, and death, until the millowner thought it wise to bury the dead in different churchyards to hide their ever-growing numbers.

So this old mill in this country lane brings to mind the thought of the slavery endured by our little ones at home even while our poet Cowper was writing "Slaves cannot breathe in England" and our statesmen were setting free the slaves abroad.

Merrie Tales of Gotham

GOTHAM. A commonplace village with its mining and plaster works, it has beauty on the hilltops, where the woods are richly carpeted with bluebells, and there are charming views towards Belvoir. It has an ancient church, an old well and a name which has been for centuries a household word to all who love a merry tale.

For Gotham was the home of the folk who did the simple silly things which brought much laughter into the world when the Merrie Tales of the Mad Men of Gotham were printed in the 16th century. Who has not heard of the Wise Men who tried to drown an eel in a pond, who burned down a forge to get rid of a wasp's nest, built a hedge round a cuckoo, and sent cheeses rolling downhill to go their own way to Nottingham?

There is no pool now to lend colour to the stories, and the old forge is gone; but Cuckoo Bush Hill and the Cuckoo Bush Inn are here still, and the Cuckoo Bush Mound, with tall trees rising from an ivy carpet, is set in a dense wood where the Wise Men might almost be forgiven for thinking they could keep the cuckoo captive. Not far from Cuckoo Bush Wood is Crow Wood Mot which takes us back a thousand years and more to the time when Saxon chieftains sat in judgment at the gatherings of the Hundred of Rushcliffe.

For five centuries Gotham has had a place in literature as the home of the men supposed to be capable of the maddest follies. As early as the 15th century the village was enshrined in the famous Townley mystery plays, where we see the village sages planting a hedge round the cuckoo so that it may sing for them all the year, and the village genius riding to market with two bushels of wheat, carrying the burden round his own neck so that his horse shall not have to bear the load. But it is believed that the Tales of Gotham are much older than the 15th century, for one explanation of them is that the Men of Gotham were not so mad as some of us imagine, but that they pretended to be a collection of fools in order to keep King John away, either because he was contemplating building a hunting lodge among them or because of the superstition that the ground which a king passed over must ever after be a public road. It was felt that if the king's messengers found nothing but fools in Gotham the king would not choose to live among them and all would be well.

The old village church had been restored when we came, and the stone of the inside walls shines with the fresh bloom of youth. It is chiefly 13th and 14th century, and has an unbuttressed tower and a sturdy broached spire of peculiar interest. They are believed to have been built from base to summit at one time, in the 13th century, the spire being one of the earliest stone spires in the country, and the only one in Notts to follow the design of the ancient wooden ones. It has two tiers of lights, and springs from a corbel table, its upper part having been made new. A 15th century clerestory crowns the nave with its arcades of the 13th and 14th centuries. One of the older capitals is entwined with foliage springing from four heads.

Of two monuments to the St Andrew family, who knew the village from the 13th to the 17th century, one has kneeling figures of William, his two wives, and their four children; the other shows John St Andrew of 1625, the last male of his line, kneeling with his wife under a canopy. With them are three daughters and a pretty babe in a cradle, the only son, who died 14 days old.

The chancel is striking with colour—a red and white panelled roof crowning grey walls and blue furnishings. The new east window frames an Easter morning scene in rich colours, with the three Marys and the angel at the tomb.

The Merman and the Mermaid

G RANBY. A village of narrow winding ways near the Leicestershire border, it is the home of a merman and a mermaid who have never seen the sea.

They are sheltered in the church, which is more pleasing inside than out, and has a shapely old yew for company in the churchyard. The lower part of the massive tower, with its wide arch to the nave, is 13th century; the rest of it is 500 years old, with battlements and pinnacles above a fine band of quatrefoils.

A blocked doorway and the wide chancel arch are 13th century, and a blocked archway in the chancel, which led to a vanished chapel, is 14th century. The north doorway may be 600 years old, and has its original door on two splendid hinges. Projecting from the north wall is a built-up arcade which divided the nave from a lost aisle, and four heads with human faces are still here. The bowl of the 14th century font has been turned upside down to make a base for a new bowl, the panelled pulpit comes from 1629, and the altar rails may be about 1700. A tall lancet is one of several medieval windows, but the east window is modern. A floorstone of 1749 is to Abigail Anna Frost, sister of Archbishop Secker.

Granby treasures 14 old benches with quaintly carved poppy-heads, showing heads of women in horned headdress, animals and reptiles, grotesque heads with protruding tongues, and others with foliage coming from their grinning mouths. Most interesting of them all is one with a merman and a mermaid, she with her comb and mirror as she has been pictured since men have gone to sea.

The Proud De Cantelupes

GREASLEY. From this hilltop, and from those of the neighbouring hamlets, are fine views of the hills and dales of the Erewash Valley. From the side of the great lake at Moorgreen close by are seen two charming houses on opposite slopes, Beauvale House delightfully set in High Park Woods, and Lamb Close House which has grown from a farmhouse and a shooting box.

Greasley's great days are gone, but reminders of them are still to be seen. Here in the 13th century came the Cantelupes, the powerful Norman family who rose to high place in Church and State. One was King John's steward and counsellor, another was Bishop of Worcester, another became Lord Chancellor, but most distinguished of them all was Nicholas, a man of great wealth, a stalwart warrior who fought for Edward the Third, to whom he was a confidential servant. He was summoned to Parliament between 1337 and 1354. During these years he made Greasley his home, and in 1340 had leave from the king to fortify his manor house, from that time known as Greasley Castle. Today a farmhouse stands on the site, but in the outbuildings are remains of the old walling of tremendous thickness and strength; and earthworks, fishponds, and part of the moat tell of its importance five or six centuries ago. It was this Nicholas who founded Beauvale Priory in his park, some remains of it still standing.

Four great beeches overhang the gate at which a pergola of roses leads to the church, which was much restored last century. Part of the chancel is old, and the fine tower, with a crown of eight pinnacles, is 15th century. The font, like a chalice, is perhaps as old as the tower. Among the memorials of the Rollestons of Watnall Hall is a bust of Lancelot of 1685, a high sheriff beloved by all who knew him. We read of John Hides who was vicar for 51 years of last century; and we remember that William Warburton, a Bishop of Gloucester famous for his books, was vicar here for a short time, and that a pastor of the Pilgrim Fathers, John Robinson, was married in this church, his bride coming from Beauvale Priory Farm.

There is history in the churchyard, for here lies Benjamin Draw-water, who died in Waterloo year, proud all his life that he had sailed with Captain Cook on his famous voyage to the Antarctic in 1772, when he saw icebergs over fifty feet high in a sea so rough that they were often hidden by the waves.

The Wonderful Panorama

G RINGLEY-ON-THE-HILL. Halfway between Bawtry and Gainsborough is this airy village of lovely views and steep and dangerous ways. It climbs the hillside and spreads along a ridge at the end of a long range of low hills which stretch from Nottingham; and in Beacon Hill, a green mound at the very end of the ridge, Gringley finds its glory.

From this site of an ancient encampment, where Prince Rupert is said to have camped before riding to the relief of Newark, is a matchless panorama reaching for 20 or 30 miles whichever way we turn. We see the gleaming towers of Lincoln, the Great North Road riding straight through the land beyond the valley of the River Idle, and the Cars which carry the eye to Yorkshire, a flat area like a great sea of reclaimed fenland, but a beautiful sight from Beacon Hill when the sun lights up the golden corn and shadows make waves on the fields.

Strikingly set where the road divides to make a dangerous bend and a steep drop, is the fine old village cross, and near it, standing well above the road, is the church, which has been restored this century from a pitiable plight to be a bright place not ashamed of its years. The tower, with battlements and pinnacles which were all in a heap inside it till the restoration, is mainly 15th century, though a built-up arch in the outside north wall may be Norman. Against this wall is an ancient stone coffin. From the 13th century comes an arch to the chancel chapel and the north arcade of the nave, its leaning pillars on massive bases. Among many medieval windows are those of the 15th century clerestory, and the east window of the new south aisle, with glass in memory of men who died or served for peace; it shows St George with the dragon, St Michael with scales and flaming sword, and Christ crowned.

A treasure of the church is a beautiful shaft piscina 600 years old, with natural foliage encircling the top of a round column. Some old timbers remain in the roofs of the nave and the north aisle, and of four old bosses in the nave one shows the grotesque head of an animal with its tongue out, and another a man's face with a great moustache and a small beard. A quaint face with pursed lips and goggle eyes looks tirelessly out from the wall over the small doorway in the tower. The modern screens are neat and good, and a charming little angel crowns the modern cover of the font.

The Tapestry Map

GROVE. Right well is it named, for this secluded hillside village is truly mantled in trees.

Above a delightful gathering of red cottages, white-walled farm, rectory, and church, where the road becomes a deep cutting at the top of the village, two flights of rough-hewn steps climb to a tall grey cross with a fine view of the countryside and a sight of Lincoln Cathedral when the day is clear. The cross is a tribute to men who went to the war, and a memorial to one who did not return.

A lychgate with stout oak timbers opens to the pretty churchyard, where the small aisleless church was built in 1882 in the style of 600 years ago. Its fine tower has a spire with two tiers of tiny dormers, and is very neat inside with its vaulted stone roof and a charming arch to the nave. There is rich carving in the font, and also on a niche on the porch, sheltering a crowned figure of St Helena.

The only relics of the old church, which stood close by, are two floorstones in the tower, one showing a chalice by the stem of a cross, the other with splendid portraits of Hugh Hercy of 1455 and his wife Elizabeth, restored by a descendant. Hugh is a knight in armour with sword and dagger, with a tam o' shanter kind of hat on his head, and his feet on a dog. His lady has a long pleated gown and a head-dress at a rakish angle.

The Hercys built the hall in the 16th century, but it is much changed since their day. It stands west of the church, hidden from the road in a park of rolling turf and fine old trees, and looking out to the dark woods of Sherwood Forest and the hills of Derbyshire. It still has some remains of the time of Henry the Eighth, and with the fine pictures and rare books treasured by the Harcourt Vernons, who live here now, are two unique tapestries worked by their kins-woman Mary Eyre 300 years ago. They make a complete map of Notts, with every place named.

North of the village, on Castle Hill, are traces of earthworks of Roman or perhaps earlier times, and a moat on the edge of the woods.

The Tribute of a Refugee

G UNTHORPE. Once owned by Simon de Montfort, it finds its beauty by a wide peaceful reach of the Trent where the river sweeps on its way to Hoveringham. Opposite Gunthorpe's quiet meadows are woods and cliffs crowned by the pretty village of East Bridgford.

Once there was but a ferry boat bringing the two villages together, but in 1875 Gunthorpe found a new importance, for with the building of an iron toll bridge (the first and only road bridge between Nottingham and Newark) all kinds of traffic began to pass along the river bank and down the village street. Half a century later came another change, and quieter days again for the heart of the village, and today the old toll house, bereft of its bridge, looks upstream to where growing traffic between north and south runs over the three wide spans of a fine new bridge.

In the little stone chapel of 1849, with just a nave and chancel and a bell in a gable, is Gunthorpe's roll of honour, the names of 58 men of whom 12 did not come back. They are set in a frame showing the arms of the Allies, the fine handiwork and gift of a Belgian refugee who lived here for a while, an architect of Ghent.

The Bell of a Thousand Years

H ALAM. Pleasant with its orchards and a stream flowing to the River Greet, sheltered by the low hills between it and Southwell, it is rung to church every Sunday by a bell known in the countryside as the bell of a thousand years. It hangs in a sturdy 13th century tower with pinnacles and a squat pyramid roof, a muzzled bear and a dragon among its gargoyles, and an arch all askew opening to the nave. The bell is said to be Norman and is still sound, though its 18th century companion is cracked and never struck.

The fine Norman chancel arch has scalloped capitals enriched with vandyke and diamond pattern. The font comes from the close of the 12th century; the beautiful little nave arcade from the end of the 13th was opened out when the aisle was made new half a century ago. A projecting piscina rests on a carved head, and there is a handsomely carved Elizabethan altar table. The oak lectern of our century has a splendid St Michael in a niche.

We see the patron saint again in a 13th century lancet. Four lovely panels in other windows, by William Morris and Burne-Jones, show Gabriel bringing the good news, the meeting of Elizabeth and Mary, the Transfiguration, and the Ascension. A window rather like a page in a child's picture book has the Nativity with a choir of angels, roses and passion flowers climbing round the stable at Bethlehem with the oxen, an ass, and a lamb standing by, a dove-cot and the doves, shepherds with an English sheep dog, and a shepherd with his crook. Four charming 15th century panels shining in a chancel window have Eve spinning, Adam digging, St Christopher carrying the Child, and St Anthony with his staff; birds are in the borders. On this window outside are two laughing faces, and on the north wall is a whistling boy.

A Poet's Thought of Earthly Things

HALLOUGHTON. Just off the highway to Southwell, its few farms and dwellings straggle along a winding lane, all up and down and buried in orchards, going to the pretty Halloughton Dumble.

The neat wayside church stands in a glorious company of elms and limes, silver birch and copper beech, an old yew, and a wide-spreading sycamore. It is said that Henry Kirke White loved to sit and dream in this charming seclusion. Here he may have sat and thought, as once he sat and wrote, that

Earthly things
Are but the transient pageants of an hour
And earthly pride is like the passing flower.

Though it was made new last century, the church keeps its original east end with two lancet windows. Its chief possession is the low 15th century screen, carved with tracery.

At one end of a farmhouse opposite the church is all that remains of a 14th century house associated with Southwell Minster, the home of a canon. Its stone walls are very thick, and some tracery is still left in one of its windows.

A Queen's Last Journey

HARBY. The memory of a queen clings to this small border village, for it was here that the gentle Eleanor of Castile died.

Here she came riding with Edward the First in September 1290 being detained by illness at the manor house of Richard de Weston while the king paid a round of visits. Here she died on the 27th of November with the king at her bedside, leaving him full of sorrow. "I loved her tenderly in her lifetime, and I do not cease to love her now she is dead," he wrote. From here they took her to Lincoln to be embalmed, and then by slow marches to Westminster Abbey, where she sleeps under a lovely tomb near the Coronation chair. The resting-places on the solemn journey were marked by what have come to be known as Eleanor crosses, the last of which gave its name to Charing Cross, where a copy of this last one stands.

In the field next to the churchyard is part of the moat which protected the manor house where she spent her last days, but nothing of the house is left. The old chapel in which the king founded a chantry to her memory has gone, save for two relics in the new stone church built near the old site. One is the plain Norman doorway opening to the vestry from outside; the other is the 14th century font. Here, too, are the only memorials Harby has to keep the queen's memory green, a small brass plate on the altar step telling us that she died here, and her little crowned figure in a niche above the tower doorway, with shields on each side of Castile and Leon, England and Ponthieu, as on her tomb at Westminster. Four tiles in the pavement near the brass inscription have similar shields.

The aisleless church is made into a cross by the vestry on one side, and the tower (crowned by a shingled spire rising 120 feet) on the other. A tiny old chest has a mass of carving on the front; the reredos of mosaic, set in the base of the east window, shows Matthew, Mark, Luke, and John and four angels; and the west window has figures of Hugh of Lincoln, Paulinus, and Augustine, and mothers bringing their children to Jesus.

Noble Trees and Old Masters

HARWORTH. Its collieries are forgotten when we climb from the pleasant village to the church among trees and green fields, set on a little hill where the Roundheads are said to have mounted their guns to attack Tickhill Castle.

It came into Domesday Book, but, though fragments of Norman work remain, most of it was made new last century, when the

Norman nave was pulled down, and transepts were added to give it the shape of a cross. The chancel was rebuilt in Norman fashion, but has still its lovely original arch, with unusual ornament and detached pillars, a very rare survival in two Norman sedilia, and the base of a Norman piscina given a new head. The fine south doorway, with its consecration cross, was built when the Norman style was passing into English.

All the walls are embattled, and eight pinnacles crown the tower, which has a modern west window in its 14th century base. Built into an outside wall is an ancient stone carved with a cross, and in a recess of another is a stone coffin.

We have from the road by Serlby Park a splendid view of the red brick hall at the head of terraced lawns, its gaunt lines softened by a frame of dense woods. The road becomes here and there a glorious aisle of beeches, then runs with the sparkling River Ryton to a stone bridge, where the river flows on to the Idle and our way goes to the Great North Road.

Oaks and beeches are grouped about the park in stately grandeur, and beech avenues come close to the house and thread the lovely woods. An old heronry in the park has many nests. The hall has been the home of the Galways since the 18th century, and was built on the site of the older house about 1770. Among the pictures here are a portrait of Henry the Eighth by Holbein and another of Charles Stuart by Van Dyck. Covering the end of one room is a great painting by Daniel Mytens, showing Charles Stuart and Henrietta Maria with two horses and dogs, and the famous dwarf Jeffrey Hudson (who hopped out of a pie), trying to keep the dogs quiet. Attached to the hall is a chapel panelled in old oak, and in the gardens is a mound on which stood the church of a lost village.

Great Days Gone

HAUGHTON. So secluded is this place that it is hard to imagine the great days when the Longvilliers, the Manlovels, and the Stanhopes were its lords; or the 16th century days of pomp and splendour when it came into the family of Holles, who had found wealth in London bakehouses and honour at the Mansion House, for one was Lord Mayor.

They rebuilt the old homestead of the Stanhopes in splendid style, and made it one of the most famous houses of the county, known far and wide for its hospitality. They even kept a company of players. Denzil Holles, most famous son of his family, the statesman who held down the Speaker in the Chair while the Commons passed the Resolutions against the Crown, was born here in 1599. He was one of the Five Members Charles tried to arrest. His grand home fell into decay when the family, then Earls of Clare, made Welbeck their home; its only remains are in the moat and the stone foundations of the buildings of a farmhouse on its site.

A walk across the fields, in company with the little tree-shaded River Maun, brings us to the farm; and just beyond it, on the brink of the river, is the roofless ruin of a Norman chapel, with mighty trees in its mantle of beech and yew, chestnut and sycamore. It saw Haughton's great days come and go.

Open to wind and sun and rain, and overgrown with weeds, it has still the old bellcot, herringbone masonry in the walls, a Norman doorway adorned all round with zigzag and cable, and the battered bowl of a Norman font. The traceried medieval windows are for the most part blocked, and in the nave wall are the short pillars and great capitals of an arcade which led to a vanished aisle. A fine pointed arch leads to the chancel, which has a tiny piscina and an image bracket. From the close of the 12th century comes an arch to the small north chapel, which has lost its east wall. A broken floorstone carved with a cross lies in the nave. One of three memorials to the Stanhopes is the broken figure of a woman in a long gown, her features worn, and her hands still at prayer; the others are gravestones, each showing the upper part of a figure recessed in a quatrefoil.

It is said that Sir William Holles, who died in 1590, was buried here. He was known as the Good Lord of Haughton for his display of hospitality; no one was ever turned from his door.

From Norman England

HAWKSWORTH. Two treasures in the little church bring us to this out-of-the-way village in the Vale of Belvoir. In a pretty setting is the low creepered manor house, shaded by giant chestnut trees, its orchard a riot of daffodils in spring. The house in a beautiful garden by the church was once the rectory.

The church has an older story than its brick tower and its chancel made new would lead us to think, for built into an outside wall of the tower is a splendid Norman tympanum. Round it are roses and stars, in the middle is a cross, and beneath its arms are smaller crosses and figures of the two thieves. In tiny medallions over the arms of the big cross is a holy lamb and an archangel, and on one side is a Latin inscription saying that the church was built by Walter and Cecilina his wife, who lived eight centuries ago.

The other treasure is under the tower, of which the basement forms the porch. It is a fine stone nearly six feet high, richly carved with plaitwork and knotwork, and a cross with a head at each end. It has served as the lintel for a Norman doorway to which the tympanum once belonged. Looking out from the south wall of the nave are three old gargoyles of huge grotesque animals.

The Sanctuary in Its Splendour

HAWTON. Well off the beaten track, where the River Devon flows two miles from Newark, lies this simple setting for rare gems in England's treasure-house. It has little but its church, but that is a shrine for some of the most exquisite 14th century stonework in the land. The house of the Compton and Molineux families has gone, but there is more than memory of them here, for a Compton gave the church a chancel of which a cathedral city might be proud, and a Molineux built a tower which is a landmark of compelling beauty.

Sir Robert de Compton's noble chancel was completed about 1325. A fine stringcourse runs under the windows and round the buttresses, in one of which is an image niche. The great east window of seven lights, with lovely tracery and shafts, is said to be one of the best of its time in England. It is difficult to do justice to the delicacy and richness of the sculpture in the chancel, thought to have been the work of that marvellous band of craftsmen who gave us the Chapter House of Southwell.

On the north side, under a carved cornice and all within a space 17 feet wide and 12 feet high, is Hawton's famous Easter Sepulchre, with a lovely founder's tomb recess and a most charming doorway, both with feathered arches. The doorway once opened to a now vanished chapel, and in the wall of the recess is the tiniest of peepholes, which gave the chapel a view of the altar. In the arch of the recess a man's face is peeping from the leaves, and two little women in wimples are reading books. On the finial stands a bishop, and within it lies the battered figure of Sir Robert de Compton in chain mail, his knees crossed. He died in 1330, and this glorious chancel is his lasting monument.

The Easter Sepulchre tells its story in three sections. At the foot four soldiers are crouching in sleep, each in a niche, and all wearing chain mail with helmets, swords, and shields carved with heads and dragons. In a canopied niche above them is Our Lord (now headless) rising from the tomb with one foot in the grave. At one side of Him are the three Marys, on the other side is an exquisite little niche where the Sacrament was kept from Good Friday till Easter Sunday. In the top compartment a fine scene of the Ascension shows the Disciples gazing up to catch the last glimpse of the Saviour's feet as they disappear into a cloud; an angel is at each side, and on the finial of the canopy below are His footprints.

In the opposite wall are the magnificent sedilia and double piscina, a gem of medieval art in perfect preservation. The three niches of the sedilia, with vaulted canopies and delicate leaf ornament in the hollow of the mouldings, are divided by shafted buttresses crowned by lofty pinnacles. Among their luxuriance of carving are two bishops and a king, two men on all fours among the foliage, two men gathering grapes (one cutting a bunch with his knife), and a fine pelican in her nest on the tree-top. Six saints, standing on little men and crouching animals, are being crowned by angels carved in the cornice above it all. A winged lizard and another winged animal are in the delicate capitals of the piscina, which has a quaint fiddler on one side and a harpist on the other.

The stately 15th century tower, wearing a crown of eight pinnacles and battlements above quatrefoil moulding and hooded belfry windows, was built by Sir Thomas Molineux. Descended from a warrior who came with the Conquerer, he was father of a famous judge, and ancestor of the Earls of Sefton. The original oak door, adorned with tracery and remains of a prayer, still hangs in the west doorway, which has Sir Thomas's arms and those of his second wife carved in the spandrels. In our own time bullets were found embedded in the old door, perhaps a relic of the Civil War, for only a mile and a half away is the Queen's Sconce, a famous fortification of the royal garrison.

The massive oak benches are as old as the tower, and so are the beautiful oak chancel screen (almost unrestored), a fine bracket and canopy over a lifesize figure in the south aisle, the clerestory, and most of the windows in the aisles. The east windows and a piscina in each aisle are 14th century, as is the font. From the close of the 13th century come the north arcade and the north doorway; the south arcade is a little later. The only colour in the windows is in a few old fragments of glass showing oak leaves in black and gold.

The Pinnacled Porch

HAYTON. It is three miles from Retford and one from the River Idle, a straggling village with surprisingly fine remains in its small church. In the churchyard lie three medieval stones with moss-grown figures carved in relief.

There is Norman masonry in the nave, and the lovely doorway through which we enter comes from the end of the 12th century, when the Norman style was passing. The splendid porch which shelters it is a rare posession for a village church; built about 1400, it has a stone-ribbed roof, and is enriched with pinnacles which are a study in themselves, for the crockets at the foot of every pinnacle are tiny sculptured heads of human folk and animals.

The beautiful nave arcade, 700 years old, has round arches and pillars, and one capital carved with foliage. The tower was built while Richard the Second was king. The fine font (about 1400) has a bowl carved with foliage and set on an arcaded stem. There are two old piscinas, a 13th century bracket carved with foliage, a Jacobean altar table, and a 500-year-old chest with a slot for Peter's Pence.

On a modern brass are two angels in memory of Percy Harts-horne Cooper, a High Sheriff of last century. The old moated home of the Hartshornes (Hayton Castle) has gone, but the name survives in a farmhouse. Another brass tells of William Chapman Mee, who was vicar here for 53 years of last century.

The Crown of Thorns

HEADON. It has a fine view-point at its little church, where for 600 years two stone faces have been looking out from the tower on a patchwork of fields and woodland.

An unusually spacious tower, it looks almost as wide as it is high;

it is thought that its builders meant it to be higher and perhaps to have a spire, and that the Black Death stopped the work, except for the addition of the embattled parapet. It has tiny lancets and a 14th century west window, and inside, with 17th century altar rails across its arch, it is a charming setting for the modern font mounted high on three steps, its bowl resting on a wreath of water lilies. From the 15th century come most of the windows and the arcades, their end arches on old and new brackets and fine heads of women and bearded men. The lovely Jacobean pulpit, with two grotesque figures supporting a canopy, is daintily carved with arcading. An old chest has six carved bosses which seem to be from the old roof, and there is a splendid dug-out chest shaped from the trunk of a giant oak, its wood seven inches thick in parts, the old hinges and hasps fixed on to a new lid.

At the foot of an oak crucifix hangs a small crown of thorns which were gathered near the spot where the Judgment Hall stood in Jerusalem when Christ was tried before Pilate. This crown must be very like the one He wore.

Sir Hardolph Wasteneys, the last male of his line, died in 1742 and has an inscription here. Headon had belonged to them from the 14th century, and Sir Hardolph rebuilt the old home, little dreaming that it would be pulled down before his century was done. Some of their trees live on, and one of seven fine avenues which used to radiate toward the hall is still here, over a mile from the village, where the road to Grove cuts through its splendid limes and chestnuts.

From a Saxon Tomb

HICKLING. On the edge of the Vale of Belvoir, sheltered by the Wolds, lies this border village where the basin of the canal, much beloved of fishermen, comes to the road. There are magnificent views of the wide green vale from the top of the rough road going south, and from the massive tower of the church standing in a square of fine trees. It has rare things in its keeping.

The tower has been rebuilt from its 14th century material, and a newel stair climbs from a small medieval doorway to the parapet, passing the works of the clock in a glass case. The chancel has been made new, but its arch, like most of the old work in the church, is 600 years old. The clerestory is 15th century.

The walls and arcades are leaning, and the tinted stone is charming against the plaster indoors. There is old timber in the roofs of the nave and aisles, and fragments of old glass are in a medley of new in the east window. A pillar almsbox is 1685, the font with angels under its bowl is about 1400, and three bench-ends of the same time have quaint heads on the arms and in the poppyheads.

One of the fine possessions here is the 14th century oak door letting us in, patterned all over with the delicate scrolls and leaves of the original iron hinges which have a charming lace-like effect. On the floor of the chancel is the brass portrait of a priest holding a chalice, one of only two priest brasses in the county. An inscription which seems to be upside down (for the head of the brass is toward the east instead of the west) asks us to pray for the soul of Master Ralph Babington of 1521, a rector here whose small figure we remember on his father's tomb in Ashover church, Derbyshire.

The oldest treasure, and one of the finest things of its kind in the land, is a relic of a thousand-year-old tomb, the coped cover of a Saxon coffin. It is 5 feet 6 inches long, showing in its mass of carving a fine cross, and animals enmeshed in interlacing knotwork. An animal at one end is biting its own tail. Very beautiful is a 600-year-old gravestone built into an outside wall, carved in relief with graceful branches of leaves growing from the stem and head of a cross. Some of the 18th century slate stones in the churchyard are remarkable for the fine lettering of their inscriptions.

HOCKERTON. This plain little village, with Southwell for a neighbour, has two things left of Norman days, both in the church which stands by two old yews. One is the chancel arch, the other a small window in the nave, its deep splay making a fine frame for a bright modern St George. There is a 13th century lancet in the same wall, and most of the other windows are 14th century.

The low embattled tower is 500 years old. The unusual font, with eight sides and a round rim, may be 700 years old. The old stoup is in the porch, a tiny old almsbox is set on a new pillar, and one of the bench-ends has been here since 1599. Pleasing for its glass and for its story is a window showing St Nicholas, the Madonna and Child, and St Cecilia with her organ. The face of Nicholas is that of a gracious old man, James Fuller Humfrys Mills, a much-loved rector who ministered here for 56 years. He came just before the Crimean War and died two years before the Great War.

A Story of the Plague

HOLME. Strange things have happened in this pleasant village of orchards and farms, which found itself at the end of the 16th century on the east bank of the Trent instead of the west, owing to the river having changed its course in a great flood. The plague came this way in 1666 and frightened an old woman into a queer hiding-place; and there is a tradition that Dick Turpin used to visit a cottage here, stopping to give Black Bess a drink on his famous ride to York.

Between the road and the river is Holme Old Hall, a creepered farmhouse with mullioned windows which has grown from the house where centuries ago the Bartons lived. With part of the fortune he made out of wool in the Calais trade John Barton rebuilt most of the church where he has been sleeping since 1491, and it is said that he put in a window of his house the words:

> *I thanke God, and ever shall,*
> *It is the shepe hath payed for all.*

One of his descendants married the Royalist brother of Lord Bellasis (who was Governor of Newark at the time of its surrender), and their son married Cromwell's daughter Mary. Lord Bellasis lived either at the Old Hall or in a house which stood where the red brick Holme Hall stands now.

After years of neglect, the wise restoration begun in 1932 by Mr Nevil Truman is bringing back the charm of the church John Barton left. It is one of the few complete Tudor church interiors, with all the fittings put here in 1485. With walls aslant, gabled red roofs, and big tilting 15th century windows letting in a blaze of light, it has something to show of all the building centuries from the 12th to the 15th. Below the east window inside are two fragments of Norman stringcourse. There is much 13th century masonry in the north wall and at the east end, and in the north doorway hangs the ancient door with its old bar fastening. The tower with its short sturdy spire and grinning gargoyles is 14th century, with buttresses and a west window a century younger. In the little gallery of sculpture on the hoods of the windows are quaint heads, angels with shields, and the laughing face of a man in a postman's hat. Over a window is a charming spray of a rose and leaves, and on a parapet is a grotesque with a human head and an animal's body.

The handsome two-storeyed porch is part of John Barton's rebuilding, which included the addition of the south aisle and the chantry chapel. Over the entrance is a fine band of seven shields, carved with heraldry, the initials of the Bartons and their badge of bears and tuns, the merchant's mark, with bales of wool, and the Staple of Calais with sheep below. Two gargoyles show a man with a book and a staff, and a grotesque struggling with a dragon.

The tragedy of a poor old woman clings to the upper room of the porch, known as Nanny Scott's Chamber, for it was here she fled (with food enough to last some weeks) when the plague was in the neighbourhood. From the window she would see a lovely view of the river close by, and the green fields and trees towards Newark, but the sight that arrested her old eyes was of her friends being carried, one by one, to their last rest. When hunger forced her to leave her refuge she found only one other left alive in the village, and, horror-stricken, she returned to this room and never left it till she died.

The nave arcade and the two bays between the chancel and the Barton chapel divide the interior of the church. The great east window of the chancel glows red, gold, blue, and brown with a fine medley of old glass. John Barton's memorial glass in the three middle lights shows initials, heraldry, bears and tuns, parts of big figures of saints, and small groups of women; the glass in the two outer lights belonged to Annesley's old church, now in ruins; it includes the Coronation of Our Lady (1363) and shields of arms.

The chapel has a handsome canopied niche on each side of the east window, and a lovely piscina niche with the drain cut in the middle of a flower. The massive benches and stalls are original, though very worn, with poppyheads of angels, birds, dogs, lions, and grotesques. Enclosing the chapel from the aisle and from part of the chancel is 15th century screenwork, and more of it divides the chancel from the nave, there being no chancel arch. Holding up the arch between the chapel and the aisle are two stone heads, one with bared teeth, one scowling; and a dragon and an angel support old brackets. The medieval stone altar has been set up for use in the chapel.

The benches are for the most part as in John Barton's day. The alter rails are 17th century. There is a battered old chest, and the tower screen has been made up of old panelling from another church. A pair of plain iron standard candlesticks is from the 15th century. There is a Queen Anne chandelier. A plain cross in the church was made from the lead which secured the shaft to the base of the old village cross, a fragment of which still stands by the wayside, where a grassy lane goes down to the ferry. The shaft and base were parted early this century in a vain search for a record of the age of the cross.

On a great stone tomb between the chancel and the chapel lies the church's benefactor, John Barton, with his wife; his feet are on a tun with a bar across the top, and hers are on a dog with a collar. John wears a long belted gown, Isabella a long-sleeved gown with cuffs and an ornamented waist-belt, her banded headdress falling in folds behind. Below the table of the tomb lies a shrivelled corpse on a sheet, a grim spectacle. In his will (the original of which is at Nottingham Castle) John Barton directed that his body should be buried " in my new tomb in the chapel newly constructed by me."

There is no memorial to Charles Stuart's General, Lord Bellasis, but a floorstone is quaintly inscribed:

> *Here lies interred the Bodys of John Belasys of Holme*
> *in the County of Nottingham Esq: and of Cathrine*
> *his wife. Catherine Dyed in 1716 and Mr Belasye 1717.*

King, Knight, and Poet

HOLME PIERREPONT. If the story is true which is here believed, a famous memory is enshrined in this village, delightful with quiet lanes, holly hedges, and great trees. Long the home of the Pierreponts, who became the Earls of Kingston, we found the great house silent, its ivied and embattled walls still charmingly grouped with the church.

The famous memory is of the founder of our Tudor dynasty, who is believed to have lodged here before the Battle of East Stoke which ended the pretensions of Lambert Simnel after the Wars of the Roses; Henry is said to have attended service in this church. He would see something that we see, though much is changed through rebuilding in the 17th century and restoration in the 19th. The massive tower and spire, the nave arcade with clustered pillars, and the great font are all 14th century, but the importance of the church is in its monuments, a fine group.

The oldest of all is a stone figure of an unknown civilian on the floor of the aisle. A battered alabaster knight is 14th century. The Sir Henry Pierrepont who fought against the Lancastrians in the Wars of the Roses and died in 1499 lies on a fine tomb, a knightly figure with long hair and a lovely collar of roses, his head on a helmet and his feet on a lion.

Sir Henry of 1615 lies on the projecting tomb of his splendid alabaster monument, wearing armour and a ruff. Above him is a great display of heraldry with an epitaph telling us that his wife was a daughter of Bess of Hardwick. On the front of the tomb are seven small figures, an infant, five daughters, and a son who became the first Earl of Kingston. The story is told that the son, trying to remain neutral in the Civil War, prayed that if ever he took up arms for either side a cannon ball should divide him between the parties. It came to pass that he joined the King's side, was captured, and was cut in two by a chance shot from his own side as he was being taken by boat to Hull. He lies in Cuckney church.

There is a massive monument to a 17th century Countess of Kingston, describing her as "the illustrious Princess Gertrude." A plaque with a weeping woman by a draped urn is in memory of the second and last Duke of Kingston, Sir Evelyn Pierrepont who fought at Culloden and was one of the husbands of the notorious Elizabeth Chudleigh.

A sculpture by Flaxman of a woman reading a book is in memory of William Saltren, who was drowned while skating on Thoresby Lake, and a tablet on a pillar pays tribute to poor John Oldham, the young poet befriended by the Earl of Kingston. He lived through 30 exciting years of the 17th century, from 1653 to 1683, but he is not among the brilliant poets and his life can hardly be called a success. He was a Gloucestershire Nonconformist minister's son, a Tetbury grammar school boy, and spent some miserable years as an usher at Archbishop Whitgift's school at Croydon. He mixed too much with the unpleasant wits of his time and made a reputation by his satires (one of them against Virtue), and he was, as Pope called him, a very indelicate writer. He died here of smallpox, and he is chiefly remembered now because Dryden wrote a beautiful farewell to his memory beginning:

> *Farewell, too little, and too lately known,*
> *Whom I began to think and call my own,*

and ending by calling him the Marcellus of our tongue:

> *Thy brows with ivy and with laurels bound,*
> *But fate and gloomy night encompass thee around.*

The lychgate opening to the peaceful churchyard is a memorial of the Great War, and another echo of strife comes with the massive tomb of a Frenchman who fled from his country during the Revolution and lived many years in England.

Elizabeth and Her Husbands

HOVERINGHAM. It lies in the rich meadows by a fine reach of the Trent, where the ferryboat crosses to a thickly-wooded cliff crowned by Kneeton's church, set like a sentinel.

The small brick church has none of the beauty of the old one it replaced last century, but it has a few treasures. Built into the outside wall over the north doorway is a fine Norman tympanum showing St Michael flourishing his sword as he attacks two winged dragons with curling tails. He is defending the church (represented by a holy lamb) from its enemies; over his head is the Hand of God, and at the sides are Peter with a key and a bishop with his hand in blessing.

The font belongs to Norman and 13th century days, and was brought back to the church from the Ferry Inn last century. Set in a wall is part of an ancient coffin stone with the fine head of a cross carved in relief.

On an alabaster tomb lie the battered but still fine figures of Sir Robert Goushill and his wife Elizabeth, the widowed Duchess of Norfolk. The knight, with a chest like a balloon, has plate armour, a pointed helmet, and an ornate belt with a flower on the buckle. His head is on his crest and his feet rest on an alert-looking dog with bells round its collar: he is wearing one of his gloves and holding the other. Elizabeth is a dainty lady in a mantle held by a cord and fine clasps, and covering a graceful gown. Her coronet is broken, her right arm is gone, and in the other hand she holds a tasselled cord; her pretty necklet, like a feathered chain, has a pendant. Her third husband was murdered after the Battle of Shrewsbury, and she married a fourth. Her father was the Earl of Arundel who was beheaded for treason in 1397; her second husband, the first Duke of Norfolk, who had been one of his accusers, was himself banished for treason.

Here Byron Lies

HUCKNALL. Its church has made this mining town a place of pilgrimage for over a hundred years, for here lies Byron, in a darkness made by stained glass windows. He lies with his mother and his only child under the chancel where some of his ancestors are buried, one of them the fifth Lord Byron (the Wicked Lord) who killed William Chaworth in a duel. The poet's bust is on the chancel wall, there are tributes to him from many famous men, a lovely lamp of beaten brass is for ever burning in his name, and in the chancel floor a wreath of leaves of brass is let into a stone sent by the King of Greece. The stone is part of the great block sent from Greece for the poet's statue in Hyde Park.

On this stone a little while before we called the Greek Prime Minister, Venezilos, had laid a wreath of laurel leaves that he himself had gathered on the banks of the river Ilissus, the inscription paying a tribute of homage "to the immortal champion of Greece, on behalf of the Hellenic nation."

At Newstead, his ancestral home, are such relics of Byron as Nottingham has. There he lived at times in his schooldays, and became attached to the beautiful Mary Chaworth from whom he parted in the year before Trafalgar on Annesley Hill, the hill "crowned with a diadem of trees," of which he wrote,

> *Now no more, the hours beguiling,*
> *Former favourite haunts I see,*
> *Now no more my Mary smiling*
> *Makes ye seem a heaven to me.*

This church which hides itself in darkness (but happily redeems itself by enabling us to flood it with electric light) has 25 painted windows by Kempe, with 350 figures in them. It is good to see their shining jewels giving a touch of brightness in the twilight gloom. In the north transept is one window with four lights filled with scenes of the Nativity and the childhood of Jesus, rich with shepherds and kings, chalices and caskets, lanterns and trumpets. In the great east window is a scene in which Christ appears to the disciples on the road to Emmaus, and the face of one of the disciples suggests Lord Byron!

Two corners of the church have a bright light—the lady chapel 600 years old, which has been restored as a peace memorial to Hucknall's 260 heroes, and the baptistry with its 600-year-old font. It is said that one of the three bells in the tower was ringing when the font was new. The tower itself was raised to its present height in 1320, its lower part (with a beautiful wide arch, only slightly pointed) being all that is left of the simple church built at the close of Norman days. The nave and north aisle are 14th century, the aisle windows and the clerestory are 15th. The south aisle and the transepts are additions of last century. The splendid timber-fronted porch has been here 600 years, and the stout oak door which was opened for Byron has been swinging on its hinges all the time. There are three stone coffin lids older still.

Two things Hucknall has from 16th and 17th century England, a sturdy chest with iron bands which has been recovered from a cowshed, and the lovely silver chalice given by Elizabeth Byron in 1664. One small possession it has from Jerusalem—a tiny cross made of glass mosaics, given by a Rabbi who received many kindnesses from the church, and said to have been in the floor of the Temple in the days of Our Lord. It is a thrilling fancy that if this is true Jesus may possibly have walked over them. There is some fine modern carving in wood and stone—stone corbels in the transepts, and on the chancel arch; wood panelling and screen work, carved figures on the pulpit, and an oak casket for holding the beautiful chalice. The reredos is a handsome gilded triptych.

A painting of Christ and Mary Magdalene by Daniel Maclise, RA, hangs in the nave, which has other Bible scenes in mosaic. On the tower wall in the vestry is a brass tablet to Elijah West, who rang the bells and sang in the choir for 50 years; and in the churchyard are the graves of three men whose names are familiar to Hucknall folk. One is Canon Godber, who gave the mosaics and the 25 Kempe windows. Another is Zachariah Green, the old stocking-maker who lies in the shadow of a Japanese cherrytree which was enchanting with blossom when we called. He has also a granite fountain with his portrait in Titchfield Park, the inscription saying that "he was gifted with the art of healing and spent his life in alleviating the suffering of his fellow-men." The third grave is that of Ben Caunt, a boxer who met the famous Bendigo of Nottingham three times in combat, and was boxing champion of England in 1840.

By the aerodrome on the edge of the town is what is left of Bulwell Old Hall, once a home of the Byrons, who built it as a Dower House. For years it has been growing sad and forlorn, and a recent fire has left it a roofless shell. Most of its old woodwork is gone, but its famous spiral stairway is still here, each wide tread a solid piece of oak resting on the one beneath, all climbing round a central pillar.

Lord Byron's Last Journey

BYRON threw himself wholeheartedly into the Greek War of Independence, but the fever-ridden swamps of Missolonghi proved too much for his weakened constitution, and he died there on April 19, 1824. Throughout all Greece he was mourned as a benefactor and a true friend of the country.

His body was embalmed and for two days an unceasing stream of people passed through the church at Missolonghi to pay a last tribute. Byron had wished to be buried in England, and his remains were embarked on the Florida under a salute from the fortress guns, the guns which had welcomed him to Greece a few months before. In July the Florida anchored near London Bridge. Here the body was transferred to a lead coffin, and the heart and brain to an urn, to lie in state at Sir Edward Knatchbull's house at Westminster for two days before the hearse began its slow journey to Nottingham.

It was on this journey that by some dramatic chance Lady Caroline Lamb, the wife of Lord Melbourne, was suddenly confronted with the coffin of her old lover. She had been infatuated with him, though she wrote in her diary that he was mad, bad, and dangerous to know. After their quarrel her temper was so unmanageable that Lord Melbourne determined on a separation, but while the deed was waiting to be signed the two were reconciled and she met Byron no more. Now, ten years after, she turned her head on this summer's day and saw the funeral procession on its way to Newstead. It was a shock from which she never recovered. She was separated from her husband the next year, and died a few years later.

It was on July 16, three months after the poet's death, that the funeral procession left Nottingham for Hucknall, and one more remarkable incident is recorded of the funeral. We read that a man in the crowd was knocked into the mud and the only good clothes he had were spoiled; he was a minor poet whose name may be remembered perhaps as long as Byron's, *poor John Clare*.

Lord Broughton, Byron's friend and executor, and the last person to shake hands with him when he left England in 1816, described how the procession, a quarter of a mile long, wound its way through Papplewick and Linby, passing under Annesley Hill "crowned with the peculiar diadem of trees" immortalised by Byron, to reach this village church. The churchyard and the little church were so crowded that it was with difficulty that the mourners could follow the coffin up the aisle.

So the wayward genius was laid to his rest in the vault where his mother had been brought in 1811, and where he was followed in 1852 by his daughter, Augusta Ada, who is buried by his side.

A Masterpiece of Sargeant Jagger

KELHAM. Attractive with winding ways and lovely trees, and the Trent flowing swiftly through spacious meadows, Kelham has memories of a famous family, and of a king who gave himself up to the Scots near by; and it has something of today which is one of the surprises of this countryside.

Some of its old things are gone. A five-arched brick bridge spans the river where an older bridge was cut in two by a sheet of ice last century; and a great brick house built by Sir Gilbert Scott has taken the place of the hall burned down in 1857, which itself had followed a Stuart house destroyed by fire at the close of the 17th century. In the old house Charles Stuart is said to have been held captive after surrendering to the Scottish army encamped near the village.

Now the great house is a Theological College, which has built for itself a chapel like no other church we have seen. It was still an unfinished building when we called, though completed for the time being, and in use. Its unsuspected beauty is inside, strikingly impressive with many round arches, soft light from round-headed windows, and a simple but charming colour scheme. A great grey dome looks down on walls of yellowy red brick as the builders left them, and an apse of deep amethyst is a fine background for a great bronze Crucifixion scene, a masterpiece of Charles Sargeant Jagger; Mary and John are below the Cross, both of them fine, and Mary a dramatic figure. The lamps, the altar, and the beautiful plate are all the work of Alexander Fisher.

The old church of St Wilfrid is close to the college, in company with fine trees and playing-fields. A splendid elm overtops the tower, and a good old yew is near the porch, which shelters an ancient studded door; on the hood of the doorway are two quaint heads, inside the church.

Coming chiefly from the last years of the 15th century, the church is pleasing and light, with aisles, a lofty tower arch with embattled capitals, an old font, a few old glass fragments, a fine old roof in the north aisle, and stone corbels at the ends of the chancel beams, carved with flowers, heads of women, angels, and grotesque smiling animals. The traceried screens across the chancel arch and the south chapel are 15th century.

Here in the church we are reminded of the Manners and the Manners-Suttons who lived for a time at Kelham Hall. Robert Sutton was made Baron Lexington for his loyalty in the Civil War, and took his title from the name of his ancestors, three Lexington brothers famous in the 13th century. Robert Sutton, the second and last Lord Lexington, was a diplomat who, while ambassador at Madrid, lost his only son at 15: the boy's body was brought to England in a bale of cloth and buried here at Kelham. We read of him on the ponderous marble monument of his parents, where the more than lifesize figures of Lord Lexington and his wife are reclining on a mattress, both in richly ornamented robes and sandals, Lord Lexington holds his coronet, and a long inscription tells of his family and his career.

The Lexington Papers, comprising the correspondence of the second Lord Lexington with various public men, were discovered at Kelham Hall, and were published in 1851.

The Beacon Beautiful

KEYWORTH. Its two things to see are the fine views of the Wolds and the wooded countryside, and the charming little church in a halo of trees, covered with creeper when we called. On the edge of the village is a forlorn old windmill.

Though much restored, the church has an ancient story, told by a Norman font nearly three yards round, and a beacon tower of rare design and exceptional beauty. Built about the end of the 14th century, and conspicuous for miles, the tower was used to guide travellers over the Wolds, and in times of danger as a signal station communicating with Nottingham, Belvoir Castle, and Charnwood Forest. Beautiful buttresses, stepped and gabled, strengthen it at the angles, and crowning it all is an embattled stone lantern with eight sides, little windows, and a tiny spire.

Charming as it is outside, the tower is no less pleasing within, where its lofty arch opens to the nave, and a small arch in its north and south walls lead to the extended aisles. This unusual arrangement made it possible to hold the village school here last century.

The 13th century chancel has a 14th century window with a sill forming stone seats, but the east window and the arch are modern. The old arcade still divides the 14th century nave and aisle.

KILVINGTON. It is only a few dwellings and a tiny church on a border hilltop, but it has a glorious prospect over the Vale of Belvoir and into Lincolnshire.

The church comes from the middle of last century, after the death of a rector who had allowed the old building to fall into ruin. With Staunton half a mile away, he thought Kilvington had no need of its own church, which was used for a time as a sheep-fold, and was actually offered for sale as building material. Its one ancient relic is a worn chalice and paten of thin pewter, dug up 40 years ago after having been buried with a priest before the Reformation.

The Babes in the Barrels

KINGSTON-ON-SOAR. It is a place of lovely trees. Firs and pines and cedars line the road by Kingston Park, and from the fine gates to the hall is a charming view of spinneys and wooded hills. Stately giants completely embower the three-cornered green, round which are gathered the old village pump, a crescent of cottages with mullioned windows and pointed eaves, and the charming little church, its lychgate set in a wall which makes another crescent and ends in a stone bridge spanning a stream from the Wolds. A long row of old dwellings and the beginning of the great park complete this scene of rural peace.

For the last hundred years Kingston has owed much to the Belpers. The first Lord Belper, a grandson of Jedediah Strutt of hosiery fame, built the stately hall, setting it on an eminence in the park with lovely grounds and a lake filled by the stream. Its entrance hall is famed for its alabaster columns, made from gypsum mined on the estate. After a long life devoted to business, science, and public service, Lord Belper was laid to rest in the churchyard in 1880, and we read on his memorial in the church:

> *Keep innocency, and take heed to the*
> *thing that is right, for that shall*
> *bring a man peace at the last.*

One of his sons was Frederick Strutt, a naturalist and archaeologist who has been sleeping in the churchyard since 1909. He was mayor of Derby, and left a valuable collection of local books, maps, and prints. His brother, second Lord Belper, refashioned the church, giving it the dainty embattled tower, and its nave and aisle, divided by arches on clustered pillars. He restored the chancel with its fine medieval sedilia, and rich glass glows in the east window in his memory. He rebuilt the Gothic chapel with the old material, stone by stone as far as was possible.

It is in this chapel that the fame of the church lies. Built by the Babingtons 400 years ago, it has an unusual bow window adorned with arms and badges of Babingtons, Ferrers, Stanhopes, and Belpers. Its great possession, unique in the county for the richness of its decoration, is a pillared canopy like an archway, through which we can walk from the chapel to the chancel. It was probably meant to stand over a tomb. In its extraordinary mass of fine carving, of wonderful variety, are shields and trailing vines, and about 200 tiny figures of babes in tuns, representing the family name in sculpture. Among them are 28 boys and girls forming a kind of ring-of-roses round each of two capitals, all in playful spirit. On the other two capitals the babes are sitting sedately with their barrels. Other quaint figures and heads peep from the magnificent panelling of the pillars, and on the wall is a fine carving of the Last Judgment, with the battered figure of Our Lord, Michael and Gabriel with trumpets, coffins giving up their dead, the saved climbing to the gates of heaven and the lost falling into the jaws of a fearful monster.

Sir Anthony Babington of 1544 is said to have erected this monument, but it is another Anthony of whom we think as we stand before it. Young, rich, and handsome, an ardent Roman Catholic, he is said to have hidden for a time on the top of this canopy after the discovery of the plot which cost him his life. Born at Dethick in Derbyshire in 1561, he was beheaded when he was only 25 for his share in the conspiracy to put Mary Queen of Scots on the throne.

At a farm here was born in 1716 a man who was to become famous and to live through most of the century. He was John Berridge, a wealthy farmer's son who studied hard at Cambridge (often working 15 hours a day) and became an evangelist, preaching to people on village greens and in barns. We read that he sent out preaching " gardeners, collar-makers, and shopkeepers." He came in touch with Wesley and Whitefield, and John Wesley called him "one of the most simple as well as the most sensible men." Tall, kindly, and witty, he drew immense crowds to listen to him. He lies in the shadow of the church at which he was vicar when he died at Everton in Bedfordshire.

On the edge of the village are the fine buildings of the Midland Agricultural College which were used during the war as prison camps for German officers. One of them was the famous Von Muller, Commander of the Emden, whose story was among the first exciting chapters of the war.

Two Men on a Sinking Ship

ONE of the wonderful letters of the Great War is that of an officer who left the British ship Sydney after she had disabled the Emden, and boarded the enemy cruiser as she was sinking. He wrote his father a full account of the sinking, and what follows is this officer's last chapter in the story of a brave enemy ship.

The rollers were very big, and the surging to and fro, and so on, made getting aboard fairly difficult. However, the Germans standing aft gave me a hand up, and I was received by the captain of the Emden. I told him from our captain that if he would give his parole the captain was prepared to take all his crew on board the Sydney and take them straight up to Colombo. He stuck a little over the word parole, but readily agreed when I explained the exact scope of it. I took an early opportunity of saluting the captain of the Emden and saying, "You fought very well, sir." He seemed taken aback, and said, "No." I went away, but presently he came up to me and said, "Thank you very much for saying that, but I was not satisfied. We should have done better. You were very lucky in shooting away all my voice-pipes at the beginning."

There are lots of redeeming points in the whole show. Best of all was to see the gun's crew fighting their guns quite unconcerned. One little slip of a boy did not turn a hair, and worked splendidly. Another boy, a very sturdy youngster, carried projectiles from the hoist to his gun throughout the action without so much as thinking of cover. I do think for two boys absolutely new to their work they were splendid.

It was very interesting talking to some of the German officers afterwards. On the first day they were on board one said to me, "You fire on the white flag." I at once took the matter up, and the torpedo lieutenant and an engineer both said emphatically, "No, that is not so; we did not fire on the white flag." But we did not leave it at that. One of us went to the captain, and he got from Captain von Muller an assurance that we had done nothing of the kind, and that he intended to assemble his officers and tell them so.

The day Captain von Muller was leaving the ship at Colombo, he came up to me on the quarter-deck and thanked me in connection with the rescue of the wounded, shook hands and saluted, which was very nice and polite of him. We seemed to agree that it was our job to knock each other out, but there was no malice.

KINOULTON. Its claim to remembrance is the glorious prospect from its hill of the great Vale of Belvoir, with the castle on the horizon. The Grantham Canal goes under the road to wander through the fields, and opposite the forge is the plain brick church, built in 1793 after the old one near the Fosse Way was pulled down.

Tale of a Pulpit

KIRKLINGTON. At one end of this pleasant patch in the green countryside between Newark and Mansfield is a charming scene where the little River Greet comes under the road from the fine millpool; at the other, lofty trees shade a lovely bit of road climbing toward Hockerton. The great house, an 18th century building modernised, stands in a park with a fine lake.

The Impressive Crucifixion Figures in the Chapel of the Theological
College at Kelham, sculptured by Charles Sargeant Jagger

Lenton　　　　**The Finest Norman Font in the Midlands**

Screveton　　　　**Arcaded Norman Font**

Though the church has small claim to beauty, it has a few old remains, two treasures, and a story. Some of the old stone is left in the brick tower, the hood of the south porch has heads of a king and a queen, and at the north door are two old faces amusing for their contrast, one a very fat man and one very lean. A lovely window in the chancel has most of its original 14th century work.

One of the church's two treasures is the fine 12th century font, carved with a band of four-leaved ornament and interlaced arcading; the other is an ancient stone built into an outside wall, four feet long and perhaps as old as the font. Within a border are stars, zigzag, and nine round bosses in a block, and on one end of the stone is a sundial.

The village story here is of a wooden pulpit we do not see, for it has been carried out of the church for the last time. The story is that early last century the vicar used to take the pulpit from its base and carry it to a swamp, where he used it as a screen for wild duck shooting. The holes through which he fired were filled up and the pulpit continued in use, but there have been no more vandal parsons of Kirklington, shooting ducks on Monday from the pulpit they preached from on Sunday. Now there is a stone pulpit.

KIRTON. It has little to show but a neat old church high above the road, looking over the housetops to a landscape bounded by the green depths of the Forest. Steps climb up to the churchyard, which goes on climbing higher still among fine trees.

The 500-year-old tower has a pyramid cap. From the 13th century come the north doorway with two worn heads, a window close by with two smiling faces, the chancel arch, and the fine little nave arcade of three bays, with stone seats round the pillars. Several windows come from the next two centuries, and there are a few old glass fragments.

Two treasures of the church are a splendid 14th century chest and a slender 16th century pillar almsbox stoutly bound with ironwork. The oldest relic is the small round bowl of a Norman font, long in the churchyard and now sheltered in the porch.

The Thirteen Chestnut Trees

KNEESALL. Set high on a little ridge, with winding ways and lovely trees, it looks out on a green and pleasant land.

A fine array of 13 great horse-chestnuts in the churchyard overhang the road, their beauty seen inside the church through the plain glass windows. The splendid 15th century tower has a striking parapet of pointed battlements and pinnacles like a crown, and between grotesque gargoyles at the corners is an angel on every side. Two smiling faces adorn the west window. The most remarkable of the huge gargoyles outside the nave has two figures with tiny bodies and huge heads, one sitting and one kneeling as they crouch close together. Their heads are touching, and they are looking out with wide eyes and eager expression, as if singing.

The south doorway comes from the close of the 13th century, when the tower arch was shaped; the nave arcades (with stone seats round the pillars and heads of human folk on the arches) are about 1400, as are the clerestory windows above them. Old lancets and fine 15th century windows light the chancel. A small old oak chest was given by the parents of two brothers who did not come back from the war. Eleven oak benches with traceried ends and worn poppyheads are 500 years old (with seats restored) an altar table is Jacobean, the font is old, and old woodwork remains in the roofs. A much-valued possession is a fragment of an 11th century cross, 20 inches high and carved with knotwork. It was found in the tower wall.

The Watcher on the Hill

KNEETON. On the top of a steep wooded cliff overhanging the Trent, braving all the winds that blow, is its little gathering of houses and farms with a tiny church.

Thousands know the red-roofed barns and the grey church that stands like a watcher on the hill when seen from Hoveringham across the river. Not so many know it for itself perhaps, for its magnificent view of the river winding like a serpent, and of the valley beyond, where trains look like toys as they pass. From the ravine going down to the river there are lovely walks among the trees, with delightful glimpses of the stream.

Four ugly gargoyles, half human, have been looking out from the battlemented tower for five centuries. The font is 13th century. A medieval arcade is seen in the nave wall outside.

The First Budget

LAMBLEY. It lies in a hollow of the hills, one of a group of villages where the stocking frame once rattled all day long, with the home of its inventor not far away. It has long been loved for its pretty Dumbles, watered by the little Cocker Beck, but its lasting claim to remembrance is that it was the birthplace of a famous man.

Here for a time lived some of the old family of Cromwell, and here the great Ralph Lord Cromwell was born about 1394, perhaps in the manor house which stood where the rectory is now; we may still trace something of its moat. He was the last of ten generations to bear the name of Ralph, was a great statesman and financier, and as High Treasurer of England in 1433 may be said to have prepared our first Budget in his masterly statement of the national accounts.

One of the wealthiest nobles of his time, he was able to gratify his passion for building. He built himself a manor house at South Wingfield, Derbyshire, now a splendid ruin. He built the castle and enriched the church of Tattershall in Lincolnshire, where he lies. He left a lasting memorial in his birthplace, for he refashioned the beautiful church except for the tower and part of the chancel. His badge of office, a purse, is carved on stone panels by the east window outside, and worn stones in the chancel floor keep green the memory of his family.

Other old coffin stones are in the stone seats of the porch, and its inner walls (like other walls of the church) are scored with marks which seem to have been made by bowmen sharpening their arrows. Most of the tower is 13th century; the top is 14th, but the arch opening into the nave is Norman. The north wall of the chancel was built in 1340 when the sixth Ralph Cromwell founded a two-storeyed chantry here. It has gone, but there is still the peephole from its upper room.

We come into the chancel through an old oak screen which has been here since 1377; it rises 11 feet high, and over it hangs a great wooden Crucifix in memory of an old lady of Lambley who died at 95 during the war. The canopied pulpit is a thankoffering for peace and the parson enters it by the old winding stairway in the wall. The altar table is Jacobean, and there is Jacobean carving in the lectern, the reading desk, and the stalls. The font is 500 years old. The east window has fragments of ancient glass with a Crucifixion, a crowned Madonna, and a saint in blue and gold.

A Norman Door

LANEHAM. There is high tide and low tide at Laneham, though its fine reach of the Trent is miles from the sea.

What is known as Church Laneham nestles close to the bank, which is like a seaside beach when the tide is out, and always picturesque with pleasure boats, barges passing to and fro, and the ferryboat crossing to Lincolnshire. From the riverside we see Lincoln's tower when the day is clear, and a delightful picture of Laneham's farms gathered round an old church on a little knoll, all mantled in trees.

Full of years and interest, the church stands where great chestnuts overhang the road. Its 13th century tower has an 11th century square-headed doorway, and a crude round arch of the same time in the walling above. There is early herringbone masonry in the walls, and a lovely Norman doorway through which we enter has two detached pillars on each side supporting an arch with a handsome array of zigzag enriched with sunflower pattern. Rarer still is the fine old door it frames, for it is one of the oldest in the land, one of the very few Norman doors we have opened and shut on our journeyings, perhaps a dozen in all England. As old as the doorway itself, its plain weatherworn boards are still good, and it is swinging today on the hinges made for it eight centuries ago.

The Norman chancel arch has a shaft on each side. Between the nave and its aisle is a beautiful 13th century arcade of three graceful bays: at the foot of one of the clustered pillars is a great stone seat, and the base of the other is continued to make two steps for the massive Norman font. Almost the only coloured glass in the medieval windows are 14th century fragments of amber and red, showing a crowned queen with a kneeling winged figure at her side.

The church has two old chests, one 16th century, another an exceptionally fine one of the 13th, bound with iron and adorned with roundels carved with sunflowers. Another rare possession of the 13th century are 14 sturdy seats of oak shaped with the adze, their plain ends chamfered at the top. One or two have restored seats, but the rest are entirely original and remarkable, for very few churches in England have any like them. Three are nearly 12 feet long and the others 8. The registers are another treasure, for they are continuous from 1538.

From the old pulpit here preached Samuel Slinn Skene while he was vicar from 1904 till 1919. He had the remarkable experience of living to see seven sons ordained in the ministry.

Kneeling on cushions on an elaborate 17th century monument in the chancel are Ellis Markham, a judge, and his son Jervase, a soldier who died in 1636. Both have lost their hands. The judge, with a beard and long hair, wears a ruff, a tunic, and a mantle trimmed with straps and buttons. Jervase is in armour; his hair curls on to his shoulders, and an extraordinary long plait from one side of his head is tucked under his sash. He is said to be the Markham Queen Elizabeth mentioned in the couplet:

> *Gervase the Gentle, Stanhope the Stout,*
> *Markham the Lion, and Sutton the Lout.*

A farmhouse on the river bank is on the site of their old home, but its cellars are said to have belonged to the still older palace of the Archbishops of York on this spot, in which Thomas de Corbridge died in 1304.

A good gift of this 20th century is the charming timbered porch which shelters the Norman doorway. It comes from a restoration which followed the 14th century design, and keeps the original timbered entrance arch to link the old with the new. It was the work of local craftsmen; the village joiner and his son did the timbering, the village builder set up the stone and brick and tile work, and the rich bargeboard was carved in the Laneham joiner's shop, so that all the work was done in the village. The joiner's son who helped to build it was the first to be carried through the porch to his last rest.

Cathedral of the Vale

LANGAR. A quiet little red and green village which we remember for its many fine trees, it was the birthplace of a famous philosopher and is the sleeping-place of a famous admiral, and it was long the home of a family that comes into a pathetic scene in Shakespeare.

Its beautiful church stands by an open field looking over the Vale of Belvoir. The churchyard gate opens under a yew arch to a peace memorial cross, and next door to the church is the ivied hall, its lawn coming up to the west wall. It is a modern house on the site of the old home of the Howes. Within a stone's throw are the 19th century gabled school and the spacious rectory where Samuel Butler was born just before the Victorian Era began. He was brought up rather unhappily in an extremely Puritan home, and he brings the village into the philosophical book that is really his autobiography, The Way of All Flesh. Langar in this book is called Battersby-on-the-Hill. The Way of All Flesh is one of his two famous books, the other bearing the curious title of Erewhon, which he made by transposing the letters of the word Nowhere. It is a satirical Utopia, in which Butler imagines a race that has evolved beyond the use of machinery, and has got rid very largely of the weaknesses of human nature and the failures of our imperfect civilisation. Butler, first meant for the Church, wished to be an artist, but was driven at 24 to sail for New Zealand to try his fortune as a sheep farmer. There he wrote for a local newspaper the first of two articles out of which his novel Erewhon was to grow. After five years he was able to sell his sheep farm at a handsome profit, come home again, and begin to study art, but in the end he turned to literature, and Erewhon appeared in 1872.

Well deserving its name of the Cathedral of the Vale, the church has the shape of a cross with a noble central tower. Though it looks almost new outside with its 19th century dress of rich amber stone, it was built in the 13th century, when it may have accommodated the pilgrims to the ancient church of St Ethelburga, whose site has lately been found again in a field.

The tower has a band of medieval lancets under a corbel table with worn heads. For over 500 years the porch has sheltered a panelled door with a small wicket, opening to the charming interior with many new windows and a great clerestory coming from the end of the 15th century. The 13th century arches of the tower rest on clustered pillars and carved capitals. The splendid nave arcades, enriched with ornament and faces, are of the time of Edward the First. There is an old font.

The effect of the old screenwork across the three bays of the tower is charming, one screen so open that none of the chancel is hidden, the others with beautiful cornices of vine and grape and open bays through which we see the splendid tombs in the transepts, for which Langar is famed. The traceried panels and vine trail now in a pew were once part of the old chancel screen; there is old tracery in a screen of the north aisle, and some old timber remains in the roofs. The massive altar rails are 17th century, and the delightful Jacobean pulpit is adorned with arcading and paintings of two angels. Holding its own with the old is a modern eagle lectern of beautiful craftsmanship in oak. The only coloured window shines with lovely glass showing the Crucifixion, Abel and his sacrifice, and an angel descending to see the rending of the Temple Veil; it is in memory of Thomas Bayley of Langar and Lenton Abbey, a kindly man and an MP, who died in 1906.

Splendid in themselves, the monuments are rich in story. In the north transept are tombs of three generations of the Chaworths of Wiverton, a family famous in Notts. The present Wiverton Hall, with battlements and turrets, seen from the road to Bingham with a background of trees, comes from 1814, but there is still at the back the turreted gatehouse of the dwelling built in the 15th century by Sir Thomas Chaworth. The old house was garrisoned for Charles Stuart by the Chaworths (who by this time had made Annesley their chief home), and Henrietta Maria slept there on her way to Ashby-de-la-Zouch. Prince Rupert and his brother Maurice stayed there after quarrelling with the king at Newark. It was surrendered in 1645, and all but the gatehouse was pulled down. Mary Chaworth, the last of her name and the first love of Lord Byron, brought the Wiverton estate to the Musters when she married the squire of Colwick Hall. Here in 1832 she died.

The oldest of the three tombs has an inscription to George Chaworth of 1521 and his first wife. Sir John Chaworth of 1558 lies with his wife on a lovely tomb enriched with tiny figures of 14 sons and daughters, six in shrouds. Sir John is a splendid knight in richly chased armour with dagger and sword, wearing a chain with a cross; his head rests on a crested helmet, and a lion is at his feet. His wife has a long mantle over her gown, her triple chain has a pendant, and her girdle (with a locket) hangs nearly to her feet. Both wear tiny ruffs and both have six rings on their fingers. On another rich tomb lies Sir George of the next generation, wearing plain armour with a ruff and a triple chain. With these tombs are a sword and a crested helmet.

In the other transept are the monuments of the Scropes and the Howes, the Howe vault spoiling the south aisle of the church. Both families have given famous men to England. Admiral Howe was one of three brothers, he himself famous for his relief of Gibraltar and his victory off Ushant on the glorious First of June. He has a monument in St Paul's but sleeps in this village church. One of the other two brothers fell on the field of battle, and the other won fame by leading a party of men up the goat path to scale the Heights of Abraham at the taking of Quebec.

Langar has in its safe keeping a precious relic of the admiral's First of June. From one of the seven ships he captured on that day he brought a cloth of rich Italian embroidery in gold thread and many colours on a purple ground, heavily embossed with pictures and patterns in a great medallion and in the arcaded border, all beautiful 16th century work. It is wonderful to remember that it was in the historic sea fight of the 18th century.

As for the Scropes, they too have given their country men of imperishable fame. A Scrope was a chancellor in the 14th century, and another an archbishop in the 15th; he lost his head as a traitor. His nephew comes into Shakespeare as a traitor, one of the three pitiful figures at Southampton as Henry leaves for Agincourt. None who has ever read it can forget:

> *What shall I say to thee, Lord Scrope? thou cruel,*
> *Ingrateful, savage, and inhuman creature!*
> *Thou that didst bear the key of all my counsels,*
> *That knew'st the very bottom of my soul,*
> *That almost mightst have coined me into gold*
> *Wouldst thou have practised on me for thy use!*
> *O, how hast thou with jealousy infected*
> *The sweetness of affiance! Show men dutiful?*
> *Why, so didst thou: seem they grave and learned?*
> *Why, so didst thou: come they of noble family?*
> *Why, so didst thou: seem they religious?*
> *Why, so didst thou: or are they spare in diet,*
> *Free from gross passion or of mirth or anger,*
> *Constant in spirit? . . .*
> *Such and so finely bolted didst thou seem:*
> *And thus thy fall hath left a kind of blot . . .*
> > *I will weep for thee,*
> *For this revolt of thine, methinks, is like*
> *Another fall of man.*

The magnificent tomb of Lord Scrope of 1609 and his wife Philadelphia has pride of place in the middle of the transept. It is said to be one of the finest of its kind, and has their white figures lying under a pillared canopy with coloured arms. Lord Scrope lies in the full regalia of the Order of the Garter, and wears ear-rings; his wife has a long mantle over a gown with a full skirt and tight bodice, and has her hair drawn straight from her forehead and rolled over a band. Kneeling at their feet, holding a book as he looks at his father, is the small bearded figure of their son Emanuel, who erected this monument.

One of the Scropes, who linked his family with the Howes by marriage, was with the party which rode into Nottingham market-place to proclaim the Glorious Revolution when James the Second ran away. Groom of the Bedchamber to William the Third, he became Viscount Howe in 1701 and has been sleeping in this church since 1712. His white bust is on a pedestal, and near it is another bust showing the Viscount Howe who was Governor of Barbados.

The Lonely Knight

LANGFORD. Its stone dwellings are on the highway, from which the big house is set back in lovely gardens and trees. Down a shaded lane leading to Holme the small church stands in company with the vicarage, with the Tudor manor house, now a farm, near by.

In this great seclusion a lonely knight, carved in stone, lies within the altar rails of the church. The arms of the Pierreponts are on his armour, his helmet is on his head, his hands are at prayer, and though his legs are broken there is something of the little dog on which his feet rested. He comes from the closing years of the 14th century, and would know the 13th century tower which still stands looking out over the pleasant meadows.

The chancel arch and the south arcade of the nave are about 1400; traces of an arcade which led to a vanished north aisle are in the nave wall outside. A beautiful archway which once opened to a chapel is enriched with flower medallions, embattled capitals, and a hood ending in heads. Medieval windows fill the place with light, and the fine old roof of the nave has curious bosses and faces pleasing and ferocious. The piscina is old; the splendid font of Sicilian marble is modern.

Close by the church the little stream known as the Fleet meanders among the willows in what was once the bed of the Trent. It is over three centuries since a great flood left the River Trent in its present channel on the other side of Holme, leaving the tiny Fleet to mark its old course.

Life as in Feudal Days

LAXTON. With houses dotted among a wealth of trees, on a ridge of land dropping sharply down to a stream, quiet old-world Laxton has a unique interest as the last stronghold of the open field system of cultivation evolved in medieval England. The plough land is divided into three great open fields of some 300 acres each, over which lie the scattered holdings of the tenants, and the old three-course rotation (winter corn, spring corn, and fallow) is still preserved. Stubbles and the fallow field are still grazed in common by the livestock of the tenants, and everything is carried on under the jurisdiction of the same Manorial Court. Laxton has a place for all time in the Medieval Village, the film record of feudal survivals which has been presented to the National Film Library.

It happened that as this book was passing through the press it was election day in Laxton, but the election was a kind that no other Nottinghamshire village, nor indeed any English village, holds, though in medieval days such elections were common enough. The inhabitants were choosing and swearing-in the jury which was to decide the portions of the neighbouring fields each local farmer was to own during the next twelve months.

Every year two of the three fields known as West Field, Mill Field, and South Field are cultivated, while the third remains fallow. The tenants hold their land under the lord of the manor, and his bailiff summons them to the court by ringing a bell, fining those who fail to attend *twopence*.

Every tenant is allotted ten strips, which may be scattered in any part of the two fields, each strip being separated from its neighbour by a grass track which may not be ploughed up even if a tenant has strips which lie side by side. The original idea of allotting the fields in this way was to ensure that each tenant shared the poor land as well as the good, and each had his fair share in keeping the hedges and ditches on their boundaries in good repair. It is the duty of the jury to see that these duties are performed, and to demand fines on court day from any who do not do their duty.

NOTTINGHAMSHIRE

At hay harvest the grass on the tracks is mown and sold by auction, and as soon as the corn crops have been gathered the jury fix a day on which the whole stock of the village can be turned loose among the stubbles. In normal times the village cattle have grazing rights on a common field. Should they be allowed to stray and damage the growing crops on the open fields an official called the Pinder collects them into the Village Pound and informs the jury, which duly fines the owner. Such was communal village life in the olden days.

This interesting village has memories of great days when it knew the Everinghams and the Lexingtons. Three Lexington brothers who won fame in the 13th century were Robert, judge and soldier, John, Lord Keeper of the Great Seal, and Henry, Bishop of Lincoln.

Only the sites are left of its great houses. One of them stood south of the church, and traces of its fishponds are seen among the trees at the foot of a field by the old vicarage. At the end of a green lane facing the church is a big field known as the Old Hall grounds, where stood a Norman castle which became the home of the Everinghams. Since their day the land has been quarried for the buried stone, but a green mound, two courts, and a dry moat are still seen. From this site there is a fine prospect of the countryside, and a delightful view of the village.

With walls of mottled grey and amber stone the church is a charming picture by the wayside, in a churchyard with trim yew hedges, a bower of slender yews, and a draped column in memory of nine men who did not come back. Attractive as it is now, the church was robbed of much of its glory when it lost some of its length and width in the rebuilding of 1860. Then the sturdy, picturesque tower (with a pyramid cap on its crown of battlements and pinnacles) was rebuilt a bay farther east. The base of the tower comes from the close of the 12th century, with a doorway and arch of the 13th, and among its gargoyles are grotesque animals, a cross-legged satyr with cloven feet, an animal ready to leap down, another with pointed ears climbing on the parapet, and a crouching man.

Beautiful outside and in is the clerestory of six windows on each side of the nave, two long lines of light in a place already ablaze with light from the plain glass. Fine pinnacles crown its splendid embattled parapet enriched with a band of quatrefoils, shields, and flowers, and in the gallery of gargoyle heads are demons with bared teeth, a bear, a laughing grotesque, and two faces close together, one showing its tongue. This clerestory was built about 1490 by Archbishop Rotherham, whose fine sculptured figure with two roebucks at his feet is in a niche on the battlement. The lofty chancel screen may be his gift, though it is much restored.

The nave arcades (of about 1200) have slightly pointed arches on tall round pillars. The chancel has beautiful medieval craftsmanship in the sedilia (adorned with angels and a canopy with tiny bosses in the vaulted roof), the double piscina with a quatrefoil between the arches, and the Easter Sepulchre with flowing tracery. In the back of the Sepulchre is an aumbry with a lovely arch. In the south wall of the chancel (at its east end) is a tiny low window less than four inches wide and 20 inches long. The font is 14th century, and from its close come the clerestory of the chancel and some of the aisle windows.

In the north aisle are remains of a fine screen set up in 1532 by Robert de Trafford, a vicar whose name is on the rail. Massive old beams are in the chancel roof, and with the lovely old work in the nave roof are bosses of shields and flowers, and four figures at the ends of the spandrels. At the foot of the stone pilasters climbing between the clerestory windows in the nave are 14 small figures, some with books, a staff, or a chalice, others playing instruments, while some are animals.

The choir seats, the screenwork in the chancel, and the lectern with St George are in memory of a vicar for 40 years of last century; the prayer desk is to a schoolmaster and organist for 40 years till 1927; the reredos and panelling of the east wall are in memory of the third Earl Manvers, lord of the manor. But it is in the monuments of bygone days that the chief interest lies.

The chapel on the north side of the chancel belonged to the Lexingtons, and the one on the south (now gone) to the Everinghams. All the figures which remain, all more or less battered, belong to the Everinghams, three actually resting on an open table tomb of the Lexingtons. The angels adorning this tomb are said to resemble those in the Angel Choir at Lincoln, which was begun when Henry de Lexington was its bishop. The three figures lying on the tomb are of Adam de Everingham the Elder (who died about 1336) and his two wives. Adam is a knight in chain mail with a belted cloak and sword, his legs crossed, his feet on a lion, and his hands at prayer. His wives are in similar dress, but it is Margaret, the second wife, who arrests attention, for she lies carved in oak, and is the only wooden figure left in the county. So well does the oak blend with the stone of the other figures that its nature is not easily seen at a casual glance. Over her long gown she wears a mantle of many folds, the drapery caught up under her arm. Her hands are gone, her features are still discernible, traces of her wimple are seen, and her headdress, held by a band, falls on to her shoulders. Her head rests on two cushions, and a dog is at her feet.

Three knights of the family lie on the south side of the chancel. Two are of stone, with crossed legs; the other is a headless trunk with one arm but no hand, all that is left of Baron Reginald Everingham, the last of his race, who died in 1399. The middle one of the three is Robert de Everingham of 1287, the oldest of all the figures, and the last of the Chief Lords and Keepers of the Royal Forests. The third is a 14th century Adam de Everingham, perhaps the son of Adam who lies here with his wives.

The Wonderful Font

LENTON. Nottingham, in making itself a splendid city, has swallowed up Lenton, but the village has kept its own identity, and has at least one treasure that brings the pilgrim here. Its ancient monastery, founded in the first years of the 12th century by William Peverel, rose proudly in the meadows where the little River Leen ran on its way to the Trent, and the monks would look up on one side to Peverel's castle on its high rock, and on the other to the green hills of Clifton. No man for miles around was so powerful as William Peverel. His priory was one of the richest, but it shared the fate of the religious houses seized by Henry the Eighth and its last prior was hanged with some of his monks.

Sir William Babington was buried here in 1455 when he was 99; he was Chief Justice and Baron of the Exchequer. Of all the ancient splendour, only a few fragments remain. The bases of two Norman pillars are in a back garden in Old Church Street. In the Abbey Church close by is Norman carving on an altar step, and part of a medieval gravestone showing a chalice and a book by the stem of a cross is near the west doorway.

This small church, with great chestnut trees for company, is on the site of a chapel of St Anthony which was attached as a hospital to the priory. The chancel and the vestry are part of the 16th century church built for the people when the monastery was destroyed, but the nave was made new half a century ago, after being in ruins for forty years.

The remarkable relic of the priory is the font, which was found at the close of the 18th century when foundations for a house were being dug. Then it was used for a time as a garden ornament; now it is in the spacious parish church, full of years and honour. It is indeed a wonder. It is almost square, and its sides are so richly carved that it is famed as the finest Norman font in the Midlands, and one of the best in the kingdom. On one side is the Crucifixion with the two thieves; on another a floriated cross; on the third two rows of rich arcading with angels, and the Baptism in Jordan; while panels on the fourth side may represent the Ascension, the Resurrection, the Church of the Sepulchre, and the three Marys. This noble font is the chief possession of Lenton's 19th century church, which has a lofty pinnacled tower, and a beautiful oak screen with a canopy rising from the middle of its single span.

Here is remembered one of the famous heroes of the Great War; it is thrilling to see his Victoria Cross engraved on his brass, with his other medals in the four corners of the plate. This rich brass, with a border of oak leaves, is a memorial to Albert Ball, the Nottingham airman who fell in France in 1917, a youth of 20 who won the VC, the DSO three times, the French Legion of Honour, and the Russian Order of St George. There is a fine bronze of him in the grounds at Nottingham Castle, and Lenton has a group of eight almshouses in his memory. They are in a charming setting, and have an aeroplane as a weathervane. In them live the widows of the Lenton men who never came home again; their peace memorial stands in front of the garden.

At the back of the White Hart Inn are the barred rooms of the old Peverel Gaol, founded in 1113 for the imprisonment of debtors and left standing when the Court was abolished in the middle of last century. Other relics of the past are the mounting blocks at the front door of the inn.

The Bayard of the Skies

ALBERT BALL, whose name should be written in gold in the annals of heroism, was born at Lenton in 1896. He was only 20 when the Germans laid him to rest in the cemetery at Annoeullin, near Lille. In that short span of life he won the love of all who knew him, and in his career as an airman he reached the highest pinnacle of success. From early boyhood he had shown great interest in mechanics, and, although when the war came he immediately joined the colours as a private of the Sherwood Foresters, he was already looking to the skies, and was soon transferred to the Royal Flying Corps.

As a flying man young Albert Ball, fit in mind and body as a man can hope to be, found himself borne on wings of joy. "I always sing up in the clouds," he wrote. As a fighting man, though he hated killing ("I only scrap because it is my duty"), he showed remarkable skill, and brought down at least 47 enemy planes. His last flight was in May 1917, when, after bringing down two German planes, his own machine was brought down by anti-aircraft guns.

In his lifetime the highest honours were given him, but he remained unspoiled. At his death enemy and comrade alike paid tribute to his sterling qualities, and on his grave the Germans set a wooden cross, carved with a laurel wreath and the words, "He gave his life for the Fatherland." That was Captain Albert Ball, without fear and beyond reproach, the Bayard of the Skies, a youth with the divine spark shining bright within him.

The Wonderful Water Wheel

LINBY. Its collieries have not robbed the heart of the village of its old charm, for here are stone cottages with red roofs, an ancient church, and two fine crosses on flights of steps, with a stream flowing on each side of the spacious road between them. It is uncertain what the crosses were, but it is probable that both marked the boundary of Sherwood Forest. The older cross has a restored shaft on its original seven-sided steps; the other, coming from about 1660, is a charming picture spanning the stream, backed by tall trees and a flower-bordered drive.

The church was in Domesday Book, and there is much Norman masonry in the north wall. The Norman arch of the north doorway is over one of later time, and is sheltered by a pretty 16th century porch. A Norman doorway and the head of a Norman window are built up in the south wall of the 13th century chancel, entered by a lofty arch only a little younger. At one side of the arch is a peephole. The nave arcade, a piscina, and the corbelled arch of the 15th century tower are 700 years old. One of two old glass fragments in a 600-year-old window shows a crowned head.

On the outskirts of the village is Castle Mill, with battlements to justify its name. Though much of it is 18th century, it keeps up the tradition of a Linby mill in Domesday Book, and is still grinding corn where corn was ground for the monks at Newstead centuries ago. Its magnificent water-wheel, over 100 feet round and one of the biggest in England, is turned by the water from a great lake on the other side of the road. The lake is filled by a stream which rises beyond Newstead and, after turning the mill wheel, goes on through the meadows as the little River Leen.

The great days of the Leen were in the 18th century, when it turned many a mill which had been converted for the spinning of cotton and flax. One of them was this Castle Mill, which will always be famous because here James Watt set up his first engine for a cotton mill in 1785. But the great days of the river were cruel days for the pauper apprentices who provided the labour for the mills, and the Linby registers tell of too many poor London boys buried in this churchyard.

A Roman Lady Turns to Dust

LITTLEBOROUGH. In this tiny village, looking across the fine sweep of the Trent to Lincolnshire's green fields and wooded hills, there may still be old folk who remember a solemn sight once seen in the churchyard.

Where the Normans built the church the Romans had been before them, for here they brought their road from Lincoln to Doncaster across the river, and founded their station known as Segelocum. Altars, urns, pottery, and coins have been found and one discovery here is famous. In 1860, while digging a grave, the sexton came upon a stone coffin, and on the raising of the lid there was revealed the perfect body of a young woman, wearing a garment fastened by a Roman brooch. It was a dramatic spectacle of a moment, for in the twinkling of an eye this Roman lady crumbled into dust.

Retford   **St Swithun's Church**

Markham Clinton   **The Medieval Church**

The Fine View Across the Lawn

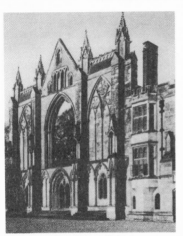

The West Front

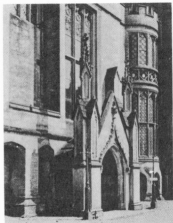

The Main Doorway

The Memorial to the Poet's Dog, Boatswain

NEWSTEAD ABBEY, HOME OF LORD BYRON

The time moves on two generations, and in the summer of 1933, when a great drought brought the river to a very low level, there was revealed the ford made here in the time of Hadrian. For many years it carried traffic between the north and south. Here Harold and his Saxons crossed on their way to Hastings. Here, while Harold lay in his grave at Waltham Abbey, the Conqueror himself may have come on his way from York to capture Lincoln.

The famous old highroad is quiet now. The Till Bridge Lane (as it is known on the Lincolnshire side) is only a grassy track, for the ferry (said to be the oldest in the land and to have been used since Roman days without a break) is almost abandoned. But still there is something important about the river here, for under it lie the trunk telegraph cables carrying our communications between north and south. Here, too, the Trent has a natural interest, for its waters rise and fall as the tides ebb and flow; and at the spring tides it experiences something of the famous Aegir, which rushes up the river at Gainsborough like a six-feet wall of water, caused by the meeting of the incoming tide and the downward rush of the river in its narrow channel.

A lofty elm and a sycamore shade the small lychgate into the churchyard. The quaint Norman church, with a bell turret, is one of the smallest in the county, with a chancel barely 13 feet long and a nave only 24. The walls have an abundance of herringbone masonry inside and out, and rarer still are the Roman tiles built into them.

We come into the nave through a lofty Norman doorway, and into the chancel by a recessed Norman arch on carved capitals crowning detached pillars. The round Norman font has been altered so that it has now eight sides at the top. There is a medieval piscina, an Elizabethan chalice, and a carving of the last Supper.

Good News from the Grange

LOWDHAM. We should come to Lowdham in springtime for the glory of the orchard blossom on the hillside, when the wayside nurseries are ablaze with all the colours of the rainbow, when the churchyard (trim and peaceful in a lovely hollow) is spangled with primroses and the lime avenue leading to the old Hall is aglow with daffodils.

M

The loveliest corner of the village, growing round its busy cross-roads, is where the church stands at the end of a little-frequented byway. With a brook flowing through the quiet dingle, and a background of woods, it is a beautiful picture outside, its 15th century spire crowning a sturdy tower built when the Norman style was passing. Inside it is full of light streaming through charming windows which are for the most part renewed, though the clerestory is 15th century.

The 13th century arcades have stone seats at the foot of their slender clustered pillars. The two bays between the chancel and its chapel are from the time of King John. The fine font is 14th century, a small altar table is Jacobean, and a studded oak door made in 1641 swings in the south doorway, which has a small consecration cross.

Lying in the chancel he founded in the 14th century is a cross-legged knight, Sir John de Lowdham, wearing chain mail and with a shield. The chancel was made new last century; on its south wall is a stone with the fine engraved figure of a 15th century priest in his robes.

Two interesting things we learn about Lowdham. One is that Cornelius Brown, a county historian, was born here in the middle of last century; the other is that Lowdham Grange has become the scene of an experiment for making bad lads into good citizens. It was about 1930 when a group of boys was marching from a Borstal Institution in Kent to this farmhouse in Notts, some of them thieves, some burglars, some violent young ruffians, but all on their honour to march to Lowdham Grange. They arrived here after nine days, living first in tents on the lawn, then in huts, and now in fine school buildings, built round the old farm. Neither by night nor day does the lock turn on them. Of 500 boys chosen at Wormwood Scrubs to come here only 52 have run away, and 50 came back. Of about 300 who had left Lowdham when we called fewer than 20 had been at their old tricks again, and it may be said that Lowdham Grange has become a notable landmark in the transformation of bad humanity into good.

Schools and Scholars

MANSFIELD. This market town of about 45,000 people, busy with industries and mining, takes its name perhaps from the little River Maun flowing through it. It has a roll-call of notable men of which many a bigger place might well be proud, and though there is little that is old in its streets, Sherwood Forest is near enough to lend it some of the glamour of days gone by.

There are old cave dwellings at Rock Hill. The Romans are said to have encamped here, and coins of Vespasian, Constantine, and Marcus Aurelius have been found. It was a residence of Mercian kings, and was for centuries a royal manor, Norman and later kings finding it a pleasant resort when hunting in the Forest.

It has great civic pride, and its mayor wears a chain worth £2000. It has a link with London and the very heart of the Empire, for stone from its quarries is in the Houses of Parliament. In the marketplace is a great stone monument with a canopied turret, elaborate with lions and heraldry, in memory of Lord George Bentinck, who died suddenly in 1848 when walking in Sherwood Forest. Disraeli wrote his biography.

Mansfield is proud of its schools. Brunt's School has modern buildings now, and is endowed partly by the bequest of Samuel Brunt of 1709, and partly by Charles Thompson, who was born here and became rich in his business career in Europe and the East. He settled down here after seeing Lisbon destroyed by earth-quake in 1755, and became a local celebrity; and he has been sleeping since 1784 on a hilltop a mile away on the road to Southwell, a spot he chose himself because it reminded him of the place from where he witnessed one of the most appalling spectacles in history. He lies with trees about his grave in a stone-walled enclosure.

The scholars of Queen Elizabeth's Grammar School have a fine modern building on a new site, but the 16th century one still stands in St Peter's churchyard. A tablet over the doorway tells of its foundation in 1561, and it has links with not a few of the men Mansfield delights to honour. Two of its boys became bishops and another was the Earl of Chesterfield who wrote the famous letters to his son. One boy who trudged to this school was Richard Sterne Archbishop of York and grandfather of the Laurence Sterne who gave us Tristram Shandy. Richard was one of Laud's chaplains and attended him on the scaffold. He founded four scholarships at Cambridge and two for natives of York and Mansfield, sometimes held by boys from his old school. He sleeps in York Minster.

The Archbishop was a son of Mansfield, as were also Hayman

Rooke, the antiquary who greatly loved his own corner of Notts; James Collinson, the artist who was a fellow student with Rosetti and Holman Hunt; and James Murray, inventor of the circular saw, whose father was " old Joe Murray," Lord Byron's servant. An old friar and a young footman are among Mansfield's most distinguished sons. The friar was William de Mansfield, famed in the 14th century for his knowledge of logic, ethics, and physics; the footman was Robert Dodsley who made a name as poet, publisher, and bookseller. Born in 1703, son of a master of the grammar school, he was apprenticed to a stocking weaver, but ran away to London and took a post as footman. While thus engaged he wrote a book of poems and a friend of Pope took him into his service. Later he started a bookshop and publishing business. A very delightful man, Dodsley was as modest as he was popular. Tristram Shandy and Young's Night Thoughts were two of the books he published. Dr Johnson called him Doddy, and Doddy suggested to the Doctor the scheme of an English Dictionary. The Annual Register owes its origin to him.

George Whitefield came here to preach, and George Fox spent the first four years of his mission work in the neighbourhood; he was imprisoned here for interrupting service in the church. In the cemetery on the edge of the town lies William Whysall, who played brilliant cricket for Notts and for England, and was bowled out of life in 1930. A tall granite cross marks his grave, and on a granite shield are carved a bat and a ball, and a wicket with one bail off.

The only old church among a number of modern ones is the parish church of St Peter, standing in the middle of the town on a site where one of Mansfield's two churches may have stood when Domesday Book was made. The outside is embattled, the inside spacious and pleasing. The two lower stages of the tower come from the end of the 11th century, and a wide Norman arch opens to the nave; the top stage is 14th century, and the short spire with dormers is 1669. There seems to have been an earlier wooden spire covered with lead, for the repair of which the steward of the manor gave eight trees in Elizabeth's time. There is a fragment of Norman zigzag in a wall.

From a rebuilding of the church when the 13th century style was passing to the 14th come the lofty nave arcades and the chancel arch. The chancel chapels are 15th century, and the clerestory is about 1500.

In each of the two porches are two big and two small tapering coffin stones, all engraved with crosses. Against the wall of the south chapel is a great stone with remains of a Norman inscription, and the figure of a priest under a canopy; he was perhaps Henry de Mansfield, a 14th century vicar. In a recess of the south aisle a 14th century civilian lies sculptured in stone, wearing a long-sleeved gown, belted and buttoned. He has clear features and flowing hair, angels support his head, and his praying hands are broken. He may belong to the Pierrepont family. One of many brass tablets is to Johannes Farrer of 1716, the Latin inscription telling us that he was skilful, prudent, and faithful. Another is to John Firth, vicar here for 45 years of the 17th century. He was followed by George Mompesson, son of the heroic William Mompesson who won immortality at Eyam during the Plague.

Standing in a fine situation just outside the town, at Harlow Wood, is a splendid modern hospital for cripples.

Fine Carving in Wood and Stone

MANSFIELD WOODHOUSE. Mining, quarrying, and building have made their mark on this village on the border of the Forest, where land was held six centuries ago for the service of blowing a horn to drive the wolves away; but something of the old days is left in the church, and in the great steps and base of the cross on the road leading to it.

Except for its 13th century base (with a modern west doorway and a window adorned with two fine crowned heads) the beautiful tower and its sturdy spire are 14th century, the spire unusual for its great dormer windows and the tiny ones at the top. The rest of the church was made new last century, and is interesting for its carving in wood and stone. Fine corbel heads of men and women, many of them crowned, adorn the windows and the porch; and among the great gargoyles are grotesques, a lion, and a dragon. On the fine sedilia are small scenes of the Sermon on the Mount, the Resurrection, and the Ascension; and in the arcade capitals of the chancel are flowers and angels. The big stone pulpit is of more interest than its plainness suggests, for it rests on a splendid corbel of Eve holding an apple, the serpent coiled round her arms.

There is abundant entertainment in the poppyheads of the bench-ends, which hide from the casual eye a host of tiny figures of animals and humans, full of humour. Among them are two-headed grotesques, an alligator, an eagle killing an adder, a fox jumping up at acorns, and a grotesque face with ears at the top of its head. One has the tiny head of a fox on one side and its tail on the other, as if it is creeping through the poppyhead; another is very quaint with a man at the top, a monkey at one side, and a grotesque animal creeping out from the other side.

Two relics of the 17th century are a shield of arms in a window, and a great stone monument with extraordinary standing figures of John Digby and his wife. John has flowing hair and is in armour with a sword, a thick sash of cord hanging from one shoulder; his wife has a quaint contented smile on her pursed lips, and wears a gown with puffed sleeves, flowing headdress, and a handkerchief tied under her chin.

In the churchyard, which is like a lawn, is an ancient stone showing the heads of a man with curled hair and a woman in a wimple, each recessed in part of a quatrefoil. It seems to be the upper part of a double coffin stone, and is set on a great stone block.

The Thankful Village

MAPLEBECK. It is one of the Thankful Villages, with a grateful pride it shares with two other villages in the county and with only 30 others in all England. It sent its share of men to the war and they came back. This little group of homes at the foot of a hill, hidden from the world among trees and orchards, gave two of its sons to the war; both came through.

One was William Henfrey, a farmer's son who joined up in 1914, went through the war unscathed, and is now a village innkeeper. The other was Reuben Percy Whitworth, who left his farming and his widowed mother in 1916 and went to France. He was wounded twice. The first time the bullet hit his cigarette case, which saved him; the second time he was wounded by shrapnel in the German advance of 1918 and left lying on the battlefield for five days, when the Germans picked him up and took him prisoner. He came home to do a little farming and keep the cottage inn, one of the smallest inns we have seen. In this little place, with low ceilings and great beams, the most interesting thing we saw was the bullet that nearly cost him his life. There is a written roll of honour in the church on which are the two names, with the names of other men who did not go from here; but there is no peace memorial.

Picturesque with its grey walls and red roofs, the pleasing church is high above the road in a setting of fine beeches, limes, sycamores, and chestnuts, with a splendid old yew 20 feet round its hollow trunk. On the slope toward the old vicarage are two great cedars.

It is a medieval church restored. From the 14th century come the tower with its low spire, and the nave arcade. The 13th century chancel has two of its original lancets, and a 13th century doorway is in the aisle. The head of an aisle window is formed by part of an ancient coffin stone, and part of another is built into the aisle wall. Here, too, are four small pillars set in the wall, believed to have supported the 13th century stone altar. The fine old font bowl has been partly made new.

Most of the woodwork is Jacobean—the altar rails, the canopied pulpit, the neat oak benches with many of the seats renewed, and the chancel screen with balustrades to which has been added a 15th century beam. Fine 14th century timbers, grey with age, support the roof of the porch, and on one of the beams a wooden face near the door has been greeting all who have come this way for 600 years.

The Tyrant Lord

MARKHAM CLINTON. (We may call it West Markham.) It lies near the Great North Road, in sight of three windmills in rather sorry plight.

Here in stone and marble is the sequel to one of the strangest chapters in 19th century social history, a chapter based on the text: Is it not lawful for me to do what I please with mine own? To do as it seemed lawful to him the fourth Duke of Newcastle, last of the feudal autocrats, caused an ancient church to be deserted and fall into decay, transferring the worshippers to a church of his own, which he summoned Sir Robert Smirke, architect of the British Museum, to build for him half a mile away.

The old church was being slowly restored at the time we called, to be a more fitting shrine for its treasures. In a churchyard with fine chestnut trees, its grey walls and red roof, with Elizabethan timbering in the bell-turret and the porch, rise in simple dignity above the wayside. It is said to have been founded by Roger de Builly, and some of the Norman work is still here. In the Norman doorway hangs an old oak door on its old hinges. There is a Norman shaft piscina, and joyous work of these master carvers remains on the fine Norman font, in whose arcading are seven happy figures, one a priest with a chalice, two holding books, some in cloaks, and some in belted gowns.

A few windows are medieval, and a piscina is 16th century. The roofs have new beams and three old carved bosses, one with a crowned man, one with a grotesque showing his tongue. There are six very high old oak benches, altar rails and a chest of the 17th century, and an old pillar almsbox. The old altar stone, more than seven feet long, is still here, and a venerable ladder which may even be Saxon has new rungs 19 inches apart.

With her cushioned head guarded by battered angels, and a grotesque figure at her feet, a lady lies here carved in stone; she was perhaps one of the Lascelles who were lords of the manor till the time of Henry the Eighth. Signs of their moated house are in the Old Hall Field south of the church.

The church built by the fourth duke in 1831 as a resting-place for the Clintons has nothing so beautiful as the road bringing us to it, a fine avenue of limes shading the way to the hamlet of Milton. Like a classical temple outside, with four columns supporting a pediment, it is depressing inside, and apart from the monuments in a chamber at the east end its only interest is in an Elizabethan pulpit and an old altar table.

The duke's wife, Georgiana Elizabeth, a great heiress who died in 1822 when only 33, has a marble monument by Westmacott showing her reclining on a mattress with the two babes for whom she sacrificed her life, though they were buried with her. She gazes, as if anxious to follow, at a figure in gossamer drapery carved above the tomb; it is the figure of one of her many children (Anna Maria) who had died not long before her. Here, with a wall monument, sleeps her tyrant lord, the fourth duke, who throughout his life fiercely opposed civil and religious reform, and never more angrily than when the Reform Bill took from him the right to return members for six pocket boroughs. In 1829, with a friend, he evicted 40 Newark burgesses for voting against his nominee; but three years afterwards he brought Mr Gladstone into Parliament for the same borough (Gladstone's first election, of which we may see many relics in the Newark Museum), only to turn him out later because he was angry with Free Trade. His treatment of his tenants was raised in the House of Lords, where he haughtily answered that he would do as he liked with his own. Nottingham Castle, which he owned, was burned down by the Reform Bill rioters. He fortified Clumber and his London house, but in 1839 he was dismissed from the lord-lieutenancy of the county and informed that the Queen had no further use for him.

Dying in 1851 at 68, he was succeeded by his more liberal son, a statesmen who held office under Peel, Aberdeen, and Palmerston, and was buried here in 1864 after dying suddenly at Clumber. His inscription, with that of the sixth duke who followed him to the grave 11 years later, is on the fourth duke's monument, the three inscriptions flanked by lifesize figures with bowed heads crowned, one with a peacock, the other with five feathers.

The Wonderful Cartwrights

MARNHAM. It is quiet and pleasant, with High Marnham's few houses and many trees up a pretty lane near the Trent, and Low Marnham with a lovely church of 700 years.

Quaint gargoyles keep watch outside, where much that we see, including the tower, is 15th century. A 13th century doorway has deep mouldings all round, and a hood adorned with heads of a bishop and a queen with charming ringlets. The open doorway frames a delightful view of the interior, filled with light, its modern roofs looking down on 13th century arcades in nave and chancel. Very beautiful is the south arcade of the nave, with detached shafts and carved capitals. A similar pillar is in the chancel, which is entered by a 13th century arch.

The south aisle has a medieval piscina and a holy water stoup by the door. There is a Jacobean altar table and a 17th century chest. The old stone face of a man with a frightened expression peeps from a corner of the nave.

Wilfrid, the patron saint, is in old glass in the north aisle; and it is odd to note that he has two right hands, owing to the remains of the original figure having been made up with fragments. There is also an ancient roundel.

Above her floorstone in the nave is a testimonial to Mary Outram, who "resigned her breath" in 1778 in the family of William and Anna Cartwright, where she was housekeeper for 45 years. She was a wonderful servant to a wonderful family. Their old home was pulled down at the end of the 18th century, but their memorials are in the church. One is a floorstone in the chancel to William Cartwright of 1781, who had something to do with the raising of the road from Newark to Muskham above flood level, but is best remembered as the father of a group of remarkable sons.

We owe a debt to the whole generation of Cartwrights—John, Edmund, Charles, George, and their father too; a kindly soul was he who felt he was doing a work of national importance when he began a movement to abolish tips to servants, a system that had become such an evil, he said, that only the rich could afford to go visiting.

John was the father of parliamentary reform, the self-sacrificing begetter of many of the liberties of our common life, a man who gave up his chance of promotion in the Navy because he would not fight against our American colonists. He could fight and he could talk; he could write and he could farm; he had the gifts of the architect; he could plan national defences and, fortunately, when his pleas for human rights for British citizens led him to the dock and a £100 fine, he could pay. They put up a statue of him in Cartwright Gardens, London, where he died and which they named after him.

Brother Charles, who also served in the Navy, had the rare family spirit, and when £1000 was allotted to him as prize money for a successful sea fight he made it over to his sailors.

Brother George, an army officer of far-ranging activities, published a massive work on his 16 years of life in Labrador, a volume which gave the world perhaps its first detailed description of Eskimo life and habits.

We have still to meet brother Edmund, the prince of them all, who was born in this village and so won for it a high renown. Need it be explained that he was the inventor of the power-loom, and the man who, in his quiet old parsonage, afforded England the means of becoming the richest and most powerful nation in the world? To forget that is an injustice to one of the most delightful characters who ever adorned our green and pleasant land, and one of the most remarkable intellects of all time. We come upon him at Battle in Sussex where he lies near the old Abbey; and there we tell his story.

In this splendid generation of Cartwright boys a fine old Nottinghamshire family burst into flower from stock which had been for generations slowly coming to intellectual maturity.

With the Idle Passing By

MATTERSEY. It looks its loveliest from the fine little bridge carrying the road over the Idle, a picture of red and grey walls gathered round a venerable church.

The narrow bridge of three round arches, still showing mason's marks, is said to have been built by the monks of Mattersey Priory, founded in 1185. The only house of the Gilbertine order in the county, its ruins are at the end of a mile-long lane, in a delightful spot where the river swings sharply round in the meadows. In picturesque company with a farmhouse built partly with the stone of the monastery, the whole of the ground plan is laid bare, showing the buildings outlined in grey stone round the four sides of the cloister. There are parts of two walls of the refectory, a corner of a medieval tower or chapel which stood north of the small church, the bases of two altars, and several coffin stones.

Mattersey church was given to the priory in 1280. Its 15th century tower, with eight gargoyles of ugly little men, stands partly in the nave, and its narrow arch rests on the heads of a boy and a girl. In the sculpture gallery adorning the north wall of the church outside are three gorilla-like gargoyles on brackets, and heads of human folk, grotesques, and a dog with long ears are on the hoods of the windows and the old doorway.

The nave arcades, with deep-pointed arches on short pillars, come from the end of the 14th century. Older still is the fine little chancel arcade of two bays with nail-head on the capitals and the letter A on a pillar; it is the initial of John Acklom, who repaired the chancel. The lovely 15th century east window of the chapel has blue and yellow fragments of old glass. A window showing five soldiers looking up to Our Lord holding a jewelled crown is to

19 men who did not come back, three of them brothers. The south aisle has a founder's recess; the modern font, with elaborate carving of foliage, has an extraordinarily high cover, like a hollow steeple resting on open arcading, crowned by a dove.

Two stone panels set in the walls of the vestry, elaborately carved with figures under canopies, were found under the chancel floor, and are rather battered. In one we see St Martin on horseback sharing his cloak with a beggar, in the other St Helena finding the Cross.

The Wandering Village

MISTERTON. A big, wandering village within two miles of the Trent, it has a fine view of the flat lands known as the Cars, and treasures lovely old work in its church.

It was lightning in the middle of last century that brought about the church's restoration and rebuilding. The tower was made new in its original 13th century style, and the actual stonework of its windows (with carved hoods) was replaced; the broached spire was added at the same time. Its 13th century arch still opens to the nave, but the glory of the tower is in another arch of that time leading to an aisle. Resting on two splendid corbel brackets carved with flowers and foliage growing from stalks, and framed by a fine hood, it is arresting as we enter the church through a lovely old doorway.

Three fine arcades add to the old array. The 14th century north arcade of the nave has foliage capitals, and two great heads supporting its end arches; one has curled hair, the other has grotesque ears and a beard all round a smiling face. The south arcade comes from the close of the 15th century, the time of the clerestory windows, the chancel arch, and the pillars of the arcade leading to the chancel chapel. These support three horseshoe arches of about 1200, the oldest remains in the church.

The east window with unusual tracery, a piscina with two drains, and the base of the font are medieval. A bell in the tower has an inscription older than the Reformation, saying "Let Gabriel's sweetest voice sound forth Jesus."

An old glass fragment showing a bishop in a blue robe and golden mitre (perhaps St Hugh) may have come from Lincoln. Rich modern glass has the Evangelists, the Annunciation, the Nativity, and the Temple scene with Simeon, Jesus, and Mary, and Joseph. Oswald with a crown, Stephen with stones, and Alban with a sword are in a lovely window to those who died for peace. The names of 22 men and a nurse who gave up their lives are on a cross outside the churchyard. Among seven striking gargoyles looking out from the north wall are grotesque animals with manes, a griffin, and a creature with a bearded face, the body of a bird, and arms ending in claws.

MORTON. Quiet little Morton has an ivied brick church of 1756 where the Fiskerton folk come to service, and at the end of a lane, where a stream skirts the village, we have a charming glimpse of the dovecot belonging to the manor house, in a setting of lawns and brilliant flower borders.

In This Castle Died King John

NEWARK. A busy little Trent town still wearing its medieval dress, it is Newark because it was new work nine centuries ago, but it was probably a Roman town nine centuries before that. The Fosse Way passes through on the road to Lincoln, and the Great North Road, crossing the river here, brings a stream of motor cars instead of the old stage coach. The sound of the horn is gone, but we hear the shriek of the Flying Scotsman racing through this home of 18,000 people, and see all round the sign of active industries.

The river which once carried wool from here to Boston on its way to Calais (bringing back cloth and wine) has also seen much change. The main stream flows today by Averham and Kelham, and a branch of it still flowing in its older channel is joined by the River Devon before being canalised under the ruined castle walls. The Castle stands magnificent, one of our chief relics of antiquity.

In the days of the first King of All England the Castle was the Key to the North. In Norman days it was rebuilt by the Bishop of Lincoln. In 1216 the wretched King John came here to die after being taken ill at Swineshead Abbey. It was made a ruin in the Civil War, when Newark made its greatest contribution to the story of our land, remaining steadfastly loyal to Charles. It withstood three sieges. South of the town are the Sconce Hills, the surviving fortification of the Royalists, and one of the most perfect examples of military engineering of the Civil War.

Dominating the entrance of the town from the north, the Castle rises between the canal and a garden of green lawn with flowers and trees. The north and west walls are more or less intact, with three corner towers; another tower is in the middle of the west wall, in whose great length are many arches and windows of Norman, Gothic, and Tudor styles. Three windows here belonged to the Great Hall (altered in the 15th century when the castle was a dwelling), and the lovely oriel here has the arms of Thomas Scot, who was Bishop of Lincoln till 1480. Other remains of the Norman Castle are the splendid north-east tower with its three-arched gateway, the south-west tower in which tradition says King John died, and the crypt. In the 13th century the west wall was completed and the six-sided north-west tower was built.

It was fine, when we called, to see the red sail of a barge as we stood under the Gateway Tower. From the top of its splendid spiral stairway (which has its original roof), it was thrilling to see the pigeons wheel into the air from nooks and crannies of the ancient walls which give them shelter.

Built into the walls of the room where John is believed to have died is an ancient beam. If this were indeed his room, and if beams could hear, this might have heard him say to Faulconbridge:

> *The tackle of my heart is cracked and burnt,*
> *And all the shrouds wherewith my life should sail*
> *Are turned to one thread, one little hair:*
> *My heart hath one poor string to stay it by.*

From the Terrace Walk we go down to the fine crypt with a vaulted roof springing from a row of pillars. Here is a big collection of ancient stones (some carved with zigzag and key pattern) which once adorned the castle walls and have been rescued from the canal. Here too is a slit in a wall nearly eight feet thick, and at the end of the crypt is a passage where the sentry could keep watch on the Great North Road. Close by we can see the groove for the portcullis, for here was the watergate and a drawbridge over the moat.

The ground floor of the 13th century north-west tower was the guard room, and in its walls are fragments of zigzag and beak-heads. Down in the dungeon below it, shaped like a commodious beehive, we could feel something of the terror of the reign of King John. In that deep stone cell beyond all human hope men were chained to the walls and left to die; we can see where their hands were chained, and can peep through the narrow slot 14 feet deep through which came the last air they breathed. We climbed out by the hole through which men dragged the dead bodies.

It is pleasanter to remember the great days of the castle, when Edward the First and Henry the Sixth came here; when Elizabeth walked through these great rooms, and Cardinal Wolsey called, a tragic figure, on his way to Southwell. Much that he saw we see still, for Newark has many witnesses of those spacious days. We may wonder if any other town so small can be more rich in ancient peeps. We look through gateway after gateway, along passage after passage, and think ourselves back in the corridors of time. At the entrance to Stodman Street is the house where Governors of the Castle lived during the Civil War, with three tiers of vaulted timber overhanging the street, and black and white walls at the back. At the corner of the marketplace, by the 18th century town hall, is a glorious peep of Tudor Newark; and at another corner is what many will think the best front Newark has, with overhanging storeys and a charming gallery of 24 painted figures under canopies—gems of antiquity which were looking out across the marketplace long before the first Stuart king passed this way. Once part of the White Hart Inn but now a draper's shop, it is 14th century, one of the oldest domestic buildings in the country.

Near it is the Saracen's Head, where they say Charles Stuart slept, the inn which Scott made a resting-place for Jeanie Deans in his Heart of Midlothian. Next door is the Clinton Arms, where Byron stayed to see his first volume of poems through the press; and through its windows Mr Gladstone must have made one of his first political speeches to Newark men. Here he started that career in politics which was without a parallel for magnitude of power and length of days. Near the castle is the old Ram Inn where George Eliot stayed in 1868, and the attractive Ossington Coffee Tavern in 16th century style, built by his wife in memory of Viscount Ossington, Speaker of the House of Commons. Two old houses facing the post office in Kirk Gate, now shops under the projecting timbered storey, belonged to St Leonard's Hospital, a 12th century institution which has become one of the many charities of the town; it is thought that Henrietta Maria stayed here in 1643.

There are gabled houses of the 18th century, and a fine cross with a group of figures in niches round the top. Known as the Beaumond

Cross, it is perhaps old enough to be one of the Eleanor crosses which marked the funeral procession of King Edward's queen from Harby to Charing Cross. In Carter Gate near by Dr Warburton, Bishop of Gloucester, is believed to have been born in 1698, son of the town clerk. Like the musician John Blow (born here and remembered as the organist of Westminster Abbey), Richard Foster Sketchley (another native and a poet on the staff of Punch), Dean Hole of Rochester, and Dr Stukely the antiquarian, Dr Warburton was educated at the grammar school founded here by Thomas Magnus, a poor boy who attracted the attention of Cardinal Wolsey and became an ambassador. Now the scholars are in new buildings, but the old school still stands facing the east end of the church, set back from the road and partly hidden by a 19th century front. It has still its fine stepped chimney stack. We enter by the old door-way, and find the Tudor schoolroom restored as it was for the Education Department, with three walls of stone and one timbered.

By it is Newark's admirably arranged museum and art gallery, with collections of local pictures forming a graphic record of the town, rubbings of the brasses in the church, pictures and notes on the association of Dean Hole and Mr Gladstone with the town, pencil sketches of Newark by William Nicholson, an original painting by Old Crome, A Woman Smoking by Gerald Dou, and a portrait of Anne Bellamy by Hoppner. Last but not least are the Roman relics from Littleborough. Concerning Mr Gladstone, there is probably no better collection anywhere illustrating his early days.

The marketplace has still visible the stone to which bulls were fastened in the days of bull-baiting. Surmounting the town hall front are figure of Justice, a lion, and a unicorn. Rising behind another side of the market square are the tower and spire of the old parish church, second to none in the county. Beautiful indeed is this spire, climbing 252 feet (as high as the church is wide) and making a charming end to a view along the narrow Kirk Gate.

There was a Saxon church here, and of the Norman church which followed there remain the vaulted crypt below the sanctuary and the piers of the central crossing, perhaps meant to support a tower which was never built. The lower part of the west tower is 13th century; the rest of it, and the spire, are early 14th, the time of the south aisle of the nave, with beautiful tracery in its great

THE CHURCH OF ST MARY'S, NEWARK

THE SPLENDID RUINS OF NEWARK CASTLE

windows and fine heads on the hoods. After the Black Death there was a long pause in the building; the nave, the north aisle, and the chancel are 15th century, and the transepts were added in 1539. Thomas Mering's chantry chapel was founded in 1500; Robert Markham's is six years later, with a small peephole, and with paintings on two stone panels representing the Dance of Death. One painting shows a young man gaily dressed, a feather in his cap; the other is his lordly skeleton, holding a rose.

Looking at the church outside, we do not know whether to be more astonished at the wonderful detail or at its massed effect. The walls have a marvellous gallery of sculpture, with hundreds of gargoyles and figures and shields. Parts of the battlemented parapet are impressive with them, and the traveller will stand long by the peace memorial on the green, looking at the tremendous east window with Mary Magdalene in the niche above it, the quaint figures ending the window arches, and a host of curious faces centred in the parapet's panelled tracery.

All the buttresses have gargoyles, all the pinnacles are charming, and the sculpture is remarkably varied. On one east-end buttress are two men in a boat with another man pushing them off; another has two men quarrelling, one pulling the other by the hair. There is another man evidently in distress. Two odd figures at the east window have their hands on their knees. All round the walls are these faces, many worn with time but their expressions still left; it is queer to see the stones still laughing though the face has disappeared. There is a fine corbel table round the walls. The tower has a parapet walk round the spire, statues of the Apostles in niches, and a lovely west doorway with carving in its mouldings and in the niche at each side. Indoors we find similar ornament adorning the massive 13th century arch of the tower, which has smaller arches opening to the aisles. Angels adorn the nave arcades, the arches resting on lofty clustered pillars with capitals carved with foliage and faces and symbols of the Four Evangelists. The splendid clerestory runs above the arcades in the chancel.

The west window of the tower has ten stately figures of familiar saints, the north aisle has a dozen figures from the Old Testament and little scenes from their lives, and in two Kempe windows of the south aisle are the Four Evangelists and Old Testament characters.

The most precious window here is the east of the south chancel aisle, filled with a medley of old glass in red, blue, and silver; in the thousands of small fragments about 200 faces can be recognised, one piece showing two people whispering.

One thing stands out grandly in this place, the lovely screen carved in oak as the 15th century was closing. It crosses the face of the chancel and turns east to enclose the 26 stalls; black with age, it is enriched with tracery under a vaulted canopy with a cornice of vines. The stalls are fit to keep it company. They have arm-rests neatly carved with heads, quaint animals, and grotesques, and misereres among the best of their day, showing the humour and philosophy of the 15th century craftsmen. One has an owl carrying off a rat, dragons on another have crowns round their necks, a man on a monster is fighting a cockatrice, there are two lizards, and two birds are pecking grapes. In the fine poppyheads we see heads and grotesques, a bird in an oak tree, and lions and a dragon which seem to be fighting. At the end of the stalls on each side is a 19th century oak and brass screen, and there are old benches with carved ends in the chancel aisles.

Behind the high altar is a row of 13 stone seats in the lady chapel, their canopies enriched with tiny heads of animals and people. Running along the top are queer creatures, and above is a modern mosaic with 16 angels; it is a copy of Van Eyck's triptych of the Adoration of the Lamb at Ghent.

Enclosed by good modern screenwork at the east end of the north chancel aisle is the memorial chapel for those who never came back, with a tin hat worn in France, and a book of names on a bracket carved with a crouching hooded man.

The font was broken up in the Civil War, and repaired with a new bowl in 1660. The lower part of the stem is 15th century, and it is curious that each of the 16 figures round it is partly medieval and partly of the later time. Its fine lofty cover is 19th century. The pulpit was made to match the screen. The big painting of the Raising of Lazarus was once the altarpiece. There is an old pillar almsbox, and in the upper room of the south porch is part of a library left by a 17th century vicar. Modern stone figures of Mary and Gabriel are in niches by the east window of the lady chapel.

Two painted wall monuments have figures of 17th century men:

Robert Ramsey, a servant of Charles Stuart in his early days (with a moustache and pointed beard) and Thomas Atkinson, who lived to see the second Charles enthroned; very miserable he looks, with a cherub and a skull to keep him company. At the back of the screen in the north aisle is tucked away the painted bust of a man like Shakespeare, a mayor of Newark in Cromwell's day. Robert Browne's tomb in the lady chapel has shields of arms; he was a 16th century benefactor of Newark, and the glass in the clerestory windows of the church was paid for out of the rents of his charity for ten years of last century. A wall memorial in the south chancel aisle is to Hercules Clay, who gave money for an annual sermon and a dole of bread. A 16th century brass of an unknown civilian is in the north transept, and at the west end is the brass portrait of William Phyllypot, who died in the same century. Let in the wall at this end of the church are two very queer faces, one with three mouths, two noses, and three eyes, the quaint fancy of a medieval mason.

An extraordinary work of art that has survived the centuries is a colossal brass, one of the four biggest Flemish brasses left in England. It is much worn, but a tracing below enables us to see Alan Fleming, who founded a chantry here in 1349 for a priest to pray daily for his household. He stands with his hands at prayer, curls on his head, his cloak richly embroidered, and all about him traceried canopies and 50 small figures.

The new reredos in the chancel, blazing with gold and reflecting the sunlight, is the work of J. N. Comper. In the centre is Our Risen Lord, and below and at each side are painted scenes and figures. We see the angels at the empty tomb, Mary Magdalene kneeling, the Raising of Lazarus, the anointing of Christ's feet at Bethany, the Entombment, Mary Magdalene announcing the Resurrection to the Apostles, and Gabriel and Mary with 14 other saints. It is the newest addition to this famous old church, a shrine to which the pilgrim in search of beauty must always find his way in Notts.

A Marvellous Man Forgotten for Centuries

WHO knows John Arderne of Newark? Yet five centuries ago he burst upon the darkened sky of England like a comet of learning and healing, then sank and left medicine and surgery to quacks and wizards. He was our first real doctor.

Where and when he was born is beyond discovery, but this fact we have in his own writings: "From the first pestilence which was in the year our Lord 1349 till the year 1370, I lived at Newark in the county of Nottingham."

Arderne was a genius of the first magnitude two centuries before Harvey. He came to London from Newark in the plentitude of his powers, and seems to have taken all our princes and potentates under his care. His patients included the Black Prince, whom he appears to have accompanied at the Battle of Crecy; Henry of Lancaster and other warriors whose names blaze in the warlike annals of the age; and preachers, merchants, and others who formed the background of that warring era. All these he cites among the cases he had treated. He wrote books in Latin, but was not of the order of twaddling schoolmen. He seems to have known only one book of Galen and nothing of his French and Italian contemporaries. How he got his skill and knowledge is a perfect mystery, but in an age which knew almost nothing of science, and appealed to magic and the moon for cures, he towers ahead of the rest of the world.

He was a brilliant operating surgeon, with a knowledge of anatomy astonishing for the period, and he taught by his books as gladly as he cured. He withheld nothing that study and practice had enabled him to perform.

There were no anaesthetics in Arderne's day, yet he insisted that the patient should be rendered unconscious before an operation, and then, "If you must cut, do so boldly; loss of blood is less, and shock minimised." Five hundred years before Pasteur and Lister he proclaimed the necessity of aseptic surgery. "Keep wounds clean (he said); they should heal without suppuration; but where this does occur assist the process by washing, that the wound may heal from the bottom upwards; otherwise do not dress too frequently."

Yet the teachings of this old seer, a miraculous man of his age with his miracles based on reason, was forgotten and lost for ages, and his work gave place to methods of gross superstition. It has remained for our own day to realise what a genius came out of Newark to offer health and healing to a disease-ridden realm.

The Home of Lord Byron

NEWSTEAD. For long its name has conjured up a strange and haunting picture in the story of the county, coloured with the charm of medieval ruins, and the tragedy and romance of later days. Now Newstead has become a reality for us all, for the lonely forest shrine which began life anew in the 16th century as part of a great country house, rich in association with monks and famous men, shares in the good fortune which has lately come to the City of Nottingham.

The historic part of the abbey (we must call it so, though it was a priory and never an abbey), with the Byron rooms and the wonderful gardens and lakes, are the magnificent gifts to Nottingham of Sir Julian Cahn; the Byron relics, including his furniture and his portrait by Philips, are the gifts of Charles Ian Fraser, who also gave to Nottingham the wood known as the Poet's Corner, 75 acres of parkland, the entrance lodge, and the land on which stands the famous Pilgrim Oak. The rest of the house is now turned into flats, owned by the people who live in them.

To show the admiration which the people of Greece have for the last of the Byrons to own Newstead (the poet) Venizelos came to Nottingham and handed over the deeds of this gift to the city in the names of the two donors. It is not likely that Greece will ever forget how Byron died in defence of her liberties.

They say it was out of a black deed that the beauty of Newstead Abbey came, for it was because of his sorrow for the murder of Becket that Henry the Second founded a monastery for Black Canons in this region of Sherwood Forest. When the monks were scattered by the heavy hand of Henry the Eighth, the abbey was granted for the sum of about £800 to Sir John Byron of Colwick, and this little Sir John with the great beard, as he was called, fashioned a house out of the monastic buildings which was the home of the family till the poet's day. They had come from Normandy with the Conqueror, and had held many manors in Notts and Derbyshire, living at Colwick till coming here. They were Royalists in the Civil War, half a dozen brothers fighting at Edgehill. Sir John was given a peerage in 1643 but died in poverty in Paris; Sir Richard, who inherited Newstead and entertained Charles the Second here, was a gallant defender of Newark and had Newstead given back to him in 1660; he fortified the old church of the priory.

Evil days fell on Newstead after the fifth Lord Byron killed his cousin, William Chaworth of Annesley, in a duel fought in a tavern in Pall Mall. He was found guilty of manslaughter and acquitted on payment of a fee, and after quarrelling with his son and heir about his marriage, this Lord Byron (the Wicked Lord) retired to Newstead, living in seclusion and allowing the place to fall into dilapidation. He cut down the timber round the house, killed the deer, ill-treated his wife and bullied his tenants, and died in the only room in the house left weatherproof. He was succeeded by his great-nephew, a boy of ten living at Aberdeen with his mother, who claimed royal descent from the daughter of James the First. She was the widow of Mad Jack Byron, a scoundrel who spent her fortune; and mother of the poet whose meteoric fame was a wonder of the 19th century.

It was in 1798 that George Gordon Noel Byron first saw Newstead, then in so deplorable a condition that he wrote of it later:

> *Through thy battlements, Newstead, the hollow winds whistle;*
> *Thou, the hall of my fathers, art gone to decay:*
> *In thy once smiling garden the hemlock and thistle*
> *Have choked up the rose which late bloomed in the way.*

Mrs Byron and her son were too poor to live at the abbey, which was let while they lived at Southwell. But in 1808, when Lord Byron had left Cambridge, heavily in debt, he came here to live, and formed a deep attachment for the home of his fathers. But, in spite of his determination never to part with Newstead, Byron was compelled to do so through financial distress. He saw it for the last time in 1814, and a few years later it was sold for £100,000 to Colonel Wildman, his schoolfellow at Harrow, who spent a quarter of a million pounds on its restoration. He remodelled the house and built the Sussex Tower at the south end of the front (named after the Duke of Sussex to whom he was equerry), and he planted most of the beautiful woods. The money he spent here, and the loss of his income from the slave trade of the West Indies, brought about the sale of Newstead on his death to William Frederick Webb, who carried on the work of restoration and remodelled the gardens, which owe their fascination largely to him and his daughters. He built the handsome stables with the clock tower.

This remarkable man, who stood six-feet-four and was one of the best swimmers Eton ever had, was a great traveller, and a delightful story is told of him when returning once from Africa. He was horrified to find that the captain would not stop to pick up two

Lascar seamen who had fallen overboard, "We don't stop the boat for Lascars," he was told. "Then perhaps the captain will stop for a white passenger," he exclaimed, leaping into the sea. In the wilds of Africa he met Livingstone, whom he entertained for eight months at Newstead, where Livingstone wrote his book on the Zambesi and its Tributaries. He often referred in later years to the restful time he spent here, and trees planted by him and H. M. Stanley (who also visited Newstead) are now growing by one of the lakes. The table Livingstone used is treasured here.

A charming drive of over a mile from the Mansfield road, banked at first with rhododendrons, then shaded by lovely trees of many kinds, opens out to a little heath with bracken and heather, bringing us to the lovely west front of the Gothic pile, which comes from the close of the 13th century, and is set off by lawn and a lake with waterfalls and a cascade. Here is still the empty frame of the great window which lives in the lines:

> *A mighty window, hollow in the centre,*
> *Shorn of its glass of a thousand colourings,*
> *Through which the deepened glories once could enter,*
> *Streaming from the sun like seraph's wings,*
> *Now yawns all desolate.*

In the gable above it is a smaller window, and a niche with the Madonna. At each side are great windows which have never been pierced, carved with geometrical tracery, while open parapets and buttresses with niches and pinnacles add beauty to the whole.

The two bay windows next to the ruined front belong to Byron's bedroom and the abbot's parlour which was his drawing-room. The parlour has a fine 16th century mantelpiece with carving of heads and heraldry. The three tall windows light the dining-hall (which was the refectory), 64 feet long and about 30 feet high, with oak panelling and a Gothic screen set up by Colonel Wildman; over the screen is the Minstrels Gallery. The Grand Saloon is 75 feet long, with a roof of plaster and oak of the time of Charles the Second, no two of its panels alike; its marble mantelpiece has busts of Socrates and Demosthenes, and a sculpture of Androcles taking the thorn from the lion's foot. Among the pictures in this room is Philips's portrait of Byron.

His bedroom and dressing-room are much as the poet left them, with the original paper on the walls; here is his great four-poster bed with its hangings, his washstand with its jug and basin, the table on which he wrote part of Childe Harold, and portraits of his friends.

The lovely chapter house comes from the middle of the 13th century, its vaulted roof supported by two graceful clustered columns; it has a fine doorway, two richly carved windows, and is 24 feet square inside. In the middle of the quiet cloister garth is the fountain adorned with quaint animals and dancing figures; its upper part is 13th century but the rest is modern. Byron writes of it:

> *Amidst the court a Gothic fountain played*
> *Symmetrical, but decked with carvings quaint,*
> *Strange faces, like of men in masquerade,*
> *And here perhaps a monster, there a saint.*

Housed in the long drawing-room is what is believed to be one of the finest collections of Byron relics in the country, bequeathed to the City of Nottingham by Mr Herbert Roe, and known as the Roe–Byron Collection. The collection is in eleven sections, arranged mainly in chronological order, and includes a mass of documents and manuscripts; busts, paintings, and miniatures of the poet; pictures and prints, and rare editions of his works. A few of the interesting things are a small portrait of Byron in Leeds pottery, surmounted by a cornucopia design and a ship; a seal ring with his head; and a letter written by Byron's valet from Missolonghi giving an account of Byron's death. Here also, written in Byron's own hand, are verses he wrote on leaving Annesley when he was about 15:

> *Adieu to sweet Mary for ever;*
> *From her I must quickly depart.*
> *Though the fates us from each other sever,*
> *Still her image will dwell in my heart.*

Byron's boxing gloves, a lock of his hair, the collar of his dog, his fencing sticks, two helmets he wore in Greece, and an early edition of his poems, are among the treasures of Newstead. There is a wonderful table of Florentine work in mosaic of valuable stones, showing butterflies, beetles, and caterpillars in gorgeous colours on a blue ground. It was once in an Italian palace. The portrait of Byron's servant, Joe Murray, shows him with the long church-warden pipe which was added after the painting was finished, because Joe said he felt uncomfortable without his pipe. There are flags of Waterloo and Corunna, and the portrait of Gerald Little-hales Goodlake who was one of the first to win the VC in the Crimea. His uniform is in a case.

Here, too, are the old deeds of the abbey which have had a strange adventure. Before the Dissolution the monks threw their brass lectern into one of the lakes, and when the lake was dredged about 200 years later the documents were found in the pedestal. The brass eagle of Newstead is in exile in Southwell Minster. The lake, known now as the Eagle Pond, is a sheet of water 100 yards long and half as wide, framed by lawn like a mirror reflecting a picture of the abbey. Near this spot is the striking marble monument which Byron raised to his dog Boatswain; it stands on a flight of six steps and is crowned by an urn, and has a long epitaph. Boatswain was born in Newfoundland in 1803, and died late in the year his master came to live at Newstead. According to Byron he had "beauty without vanity, strength without insolence, courage without ferocity, and all the virtues of man without his vices." In a will of 1811 Byron directed that he should be buried in the vault below this monument, near his dog; the site is supposed to be that of the high altar of the ancient church.

Wherever we turn there is beauty at Newstead. Nature and the landscape gardener have made a paradise of the grounds. There are many varieties of scenery, romantic and formal, with the silver lakes, wooded slopes, fountains among the bushes, flower borders and lawns with beds ablaze with colour. There are bowered arches, herbaceous borders, an old-world garden, and goldfish swimming in pools fringed with blue flowers; there are bamboos and tropical plants, and a fernery. Of the Japanese garden (made early this century by Miss Webb) the tale is told that it was the only thing which made a Japanese visitor feel homesick. At one end of the long terrace on the east front of the house a flight of 20 steps leads to a pool with an aisle of yews at its side.

Truly we may feel that Newstead is still a poet's place; a paradise for lovers of Nature in her quiet beauty.

Delight by the River

NORMANTON-ON-SOAR. It lines the bank of the Soar where it is for a long placid stretch the delight of river lovers. Some of the gardens run down to the water, and from the churchyard high above it is a fine peep into Leicestershire, with a little white windmill by Beacon Hill, and a lovely glimpse of the winding river through an archway of roses on the rectory lawn. The treasure of the village is the aisleless church, almost wholly 13th century, with one of the county's two central towers crowned with a spire. The spire springs from a corbel table of heads much worn by time, and is lofty and beautiful. The transept forming the north arm of the cross is 19th century; the timbered porch is made new, but it shelters a lovely 13th century doorway letting us in.

Among the charming old windows are many lancets, one with a hood of four-leaved flowers. The great west window is a group of five. The east window, with quatrefoils in the tracery, is 14th century. The font was cut from a single stone and richly carved 600 years ago. The old altar stone in the lady chapel has still five consecration crosses, but the epitaphs on three old gravestones are worn with the feet of many generations. The panelled roof of the chancel has carved medallions, and five old tie-beams in the nave roof have carved bosses. Seven splendid oak benches are over 400 years old, there is an old chest, and the arms of Charles the Second are handsomely fashioned in plaster.

For over 300 years three people have been kneeling at prayer on the chancel wall, William Willoughby and his wife Susannah, and Frances Walkden, who married first a Willoughby and then Peter Columbell of Darley Dale. She wears a ruff and a hooded mantle over her gown.

NORMANTON-ON-TRENT. It has on each side of it a stream flowing to the Trent, gay gardens, and a neat little church. On one side of the churchyard is a fine row of yews and beeches, through which we have a peep of the trim lawn and trees of the great house.

Though the church is much restored, some of it stands as it stood in medieval England, the nave arcades and the chancel arch 14th century, the tower and the clerestory 15th. The altar table is Jacobean, a stout ironbound chest is two centuries older, tracery from old bench-ends enriches new seats in the chancel, and there is old work left in the roof. The shallow bowl of a Norman font is set up in the churchyard.

By the Fleet in the Willows

NORTH COLLINGHAM. It shares some things with South Collingham, its close neighbour. Both line a stretch of the road between Newark and Gainsborough, and each has a lovely old church set in its most charming spot, built of the limestone quarried on this eastern bank of the Trent.

Both belong to a neighbourhood of ancient story. South-east is Brough, the site of a Roman station on the Fosse Way. East of the villages, still on the Fosse Way, is the grassy slope of Potter's Hill with a tumulus, and just below the Hill between 60 and 70 skeletons were found a century ago.

Hobnobbing with the gawky symbol of the Petrol Age are the remains of North Collingham's 14th century cross, so enormous that it dwarfs the window of the garage that has crept up to it. Its three feet of shaft with traces of carving rests on a huge stone and a flight of three great steps, each 14 inches deep, the bottom one nearly three yards square.

High above a quiet wayside is the church, looking down through a fine screen of elms, taller than the tower, to a pretty lane crossing the Fleet in the willows. This delightful spot has more than once been a scene of desolation, for in the churchyard wall are stones showing the height of floods which made this countryside a sea. One near the churchyard gate is the base stone of an old cross, still with its socket, and it marks the height reached by the river in the devastating flood of 1795, when the Trent and the Witham joined owing to a sudden thaw after a seven-weeks' frost; it was about five feet above the level of the road. The other stone marks the flood height of 1875, which was 21 inches lower than in 1795.

The 15th century tower has a huge buttress at one corner, and the outer moulding of its fine arch to the nave rests on two heads, one with a tranquil expression, and the other grotesque with a toothless grin. The north side of this tower arch is the oldest part of the building, coming from the end of the 12th century.

In the 15th century north porch (with a stone roof) are two 14th century coffin stones carved with praying figures. The south porch is a little younger than the north; both shelter fine original doors, and another old door opens to the vestry. The glory of the church is in the 13th century nave arcades with clustered pillars: the north, the older of the two, has capitals carved with leaf and scroll, and one with two corbel heads.

Above the 15th century chancel arch is a row of seven heraldic misereres reaching from wall to wall; they are over 400 years old, and were placed here when the stalls were destroyed last century. Some old beams are in the chancel roof, and the beautiful modern roof of the nave has floral bosses. There are two old piscinas, and the massive 700-year-old font has a 17th century pyramid cover with a mass of carving.

One of the windows has a choir of red-winged angels hovering above, while Our Lord in a gleaming gown of rose and gold appears to Mary kneeling in a rich blue robe. The window is in memory of Thomas Berry, the first man of the village to offer himself for the war and the first to fall. A window showing the Good Samaritan is to a doctor who died in 1915, and there is a charming group in dainty colouring of Jesus with a baby on His knee, a little maid with plaited hair standing at His side.

A lovely thing in the churchyard is a slender column with a crucifix to those who died for peace, one a nurse who lies by the gate.

Glorious Home

NORTH LEVERTON. Gay with orchard blossom in springtime, it gathers pleasantly round the cross roads. At one end of the village is a fine windmill with sails that turned proudly as we watched the miller grind his corn, and at the other end is an obelisk to seven men who died for peace. Between them is a small church with a charming approach along an avenue of lofty chestnuts which appears unexpectedly between the houses and crosses a stream from Caddow Wood.

The church is more attractive outside than in, and tells its oldest story in Norman masonry in the north wall of the chancel. Only a little later is the handsome doorway through which we enter, built when the Norman style was passing, the shafts on each side with capitals of stiff foliage. Among some fine 14th century windows still remaining are five in the chancel with flowing tracery. The embattled tower is 15th century, and the nave arcade comes from about 1300. There are two old piscinas, an image bracket, and buttresses with canopied niches.

With the inscription round the grave of Walter Steedman, who died in 1929, are a few bars of music engraved in gold. He kept the local post office, and loved teaching the children hymns at Sunday school. The last one he taught them was Glorious Home, and it is a line of this which is on his grave in the churchyard.

Beauty Off the Great North Road

NORTH MUSKHAM. We leave the Great North Road for this long village on a bank of the Trent. It has the shaft of the old wayside cross, a veteran windmill with battered sails, and a lovely 15th century church, its fine tower facing the road, and its east end looking across a sweeping bend of the river to Holme church mantled in trees. A ferry links these villages which were side by side till the time of Elizabeth, when the Trent changed its course in a flood and flowed between them.

The embattled grey walls of the church are adorned with many corbels, and gargoyles of grinning figures and grotesque heads. Two crowned women smile from a window, a winged grotesque shows two teeth, and a staring jester is holding his knee.

The lowest stages of the tower are 13th century, its small west window is a century younger, and the rest is 500 years old. A splendid door of studded oak opens to a delightful interior, where bright light streaming through plain glass in most of the windows falls on white walls and stone arcades, and on a wealth of lovely woodwork old and new. The south arcade is a little earlier in the 15th century than the north, which has fragments of a Norman arcade.

The shallow 15th century bowl of the font is on a tall Jacobean shaft; its fine cover of gilded oak is new, with winged grotesques, and a charming figure of John the Baptist. The bowl of an ancient font lies in the nave, and the chancel has its old piscina.

Among old glass fragments is the tun with a bar across the head, the picture name of the Bartons, who lived at Holme in the 15th century and were good friends to the church. They built this north aisle, which has a window with 28 of their small barrels, and three buttresses showing their initials and arms in panels carved with oak leaves and acorns; there are the three bucks' heads of their shield, and their badge of a chained bear sniffing at a barrel. In the aisle hangs a copy of the will of John Barton, who lies in Holme church, his original will being in Nottingham Castle.

The east window has beautiful modern glass showing Our Lord, Paulinus, Mary, Wilfrid the patron saint, and Mary Magdalene. In the array of old woodwork are two carved chests, an armchair, the baluster altar rails, the pulpit, a Jacobean table, the door to the rood stairway with its original hinges, traceried panelling from old seats now in a screen, and the lovely roof of the nave which has nearly all its old rafters, beams with floral bosses, and figures along the sides in cloaks of leaves. One (perhaps modern) has his locks curling up instead of down and seems to be wearing a collar and tie. The chancel screen is a beautiful blending of old and new; its gates, fan-vaulted loft, and painted figures of Our Lord, Mary, and John were added to the medieval remains. The chancel roof with floral bosses is part of the modern woodwork completing the scheme.

A Crucifix shrine to eight men who died for peace was made from the wood of the old training ship Britannia. A curious memorial is an alabaster pyramid to Jhon Smith of 1591, three of its sides filled with the terms of his will.

The Wonderful Stairs

NORTH WHEATLEY. Its red houses, grey church, and gaunt old windmill without sails climb a gentle hill between the River Idle and the Trent. Orchards and trees add to its charm, and in the heart of the village is the handsome Old Hall of 1673, a farmhouse now, with the arms of the Cartwrights over the entrance, and a pretty display of ornamental brickwork.

Set among limes and elms and a fine beech is the small aisleless church, which has a 15th century tower, a chancel made new last century, a new timbered porch, and a story as old as the huge Norman font. A curious relic projecting from the wall, looking like a stoup, is really a mortar with stone bands. The nave has a medieval piscina and old tie-beams in its roof; the 17th century pulpit and the old rood beam across the tower arch are partly restored, and 25 traceried bench-ends come from about 1500.

A wonderful oak stairway to the platform where the bellringers stand is a fascinating possession; grey with age, it has 28 steps of roughly trimmed and quartered logs secured with wooden pegs to two stout beams, each of which is over a yard round near the top.

A brass inscription to a London wine dealer of 1445 is a memorial for a second time, for on the other side is an epitaph to Joan Cokesay. Adam Haket's 15th century floorstone has a cross and coats-of-arms. There are three Elizabethan chalices and three small Jacobean altar tables. Two 13th century shafts support stone tables under the tower and in the vestry.

There is a delightful view of the village from South Wheatley half a mile away, the home of a few folk who lost their church half a century ago. Its chalice and altar table are with those at North Wheatley, and its ancient font is in a Nottingham church. In the old churchyard stands the tiny Norman chancel arch, looking across what was once the nave to the 15th century tower, with its arch built up and two of its pinnacles gone.

Northwell No More

NORWELL. It was once important with a market and a fair, three prebends of Southwell Minster, and six moated houses; the old water moat of one of them is by the churchyard where meadows go down to the Beck. Now it is content with its farming. Even its name has changed, though the old Northwell (distinct from Southwell) is still seen on the church plate.

The church stands in a churchyard with fine elms and chestnuts, and a sundial 200 years old. It came into Domesday Book, and there are remains of Norman days in the fine grey pile. With transepts and a splendid western tower with a domed cap, it is beautiful indoors and out. Except that it was topped and pinnacled in the 15th century, the tower is 13th century. The 600-year-old porch, with a modern St Lawrence over the entrance, shelters a splendid Norman doorway with detached pillars. The north arcade is as old as the porch, but the south, with round pillars and scalloped capitals, comes from about 1190. Each arcade has a smaller arch at the west end, resting on 13th century corbels.

The village is proud of its church's medieval windows. The long lines of the clerestory on each side show quatrefoils in diamond-shaped tracery. The 700-year-old arch frames a lovely picture of the chancel with some lancets, and a 14th century east window with modern glass in delicate colours, showing the Crucifixion with Mary and John, St Lawrence, and Hugh of Lincoln. In striking contrast are Bible scenes making a vivid splash of colour in an aisle, and Faith, Hope, and Charity glowing in a transept.

The fine old roof of the north transept has moulded beams and carved bosses. On the arch from this transept to the aisle is the great head of a grotesque with pointed ears and a mouth showing three huge teeth. Two little heads adorn an aumbry, and lining its wall is part of a Norman coffin stone. A pretty effect is given by three steps leading to the narrow doorway of the old rood stairway. A handsome piscina in the south transept is carved with foliage and faces.

In three recesses are memorials of forgotten folk. One is a loose stone carving of a head with wavy locks; another is a 14th century cross-legged knight with his sword and shield; the third is a woman in a wimple, with a charming face, her hands at prayer, and a dog at her feet. Outside the porch lies an old stone with a beautiful cross.

The Stately Queen of the Midlands

NOTTINGHAM. She is the Queen of the Midlands, and is making herself more beautiful than ever. She is a great industrial city and will soon have 300,000 people living on her industries; yet it may be said of her that she is renewing her youth like the eagle, and even in these years of transition and transformation Nottingham is a beautiful place.

It will soon be eight centuries since Nottingham received its charter, but not half a century has passed since it was made a city, and in these 50 years those who have been looking on at Nottingham have witnessed a great tragedy and a great triumph. They have seen the long, slow breaking-up of an industry that made this city famous through the world. Nottingham lace was everywhere, in cottages and palaces and in every land. Its lace factories hummed with prosperity; the lace market was the throbbing hive of the town. The lace machines were wonderful to behold.

It was fashion that struck a bitter blow at the heart of this great scene. Nottingham lace has had its day.

But, though beauty passes, cities do not perish, and Nottingham

The Council House in the Heart of the City

Jasmine Cottages, a few minutes walk from the Council House

THE FASCINATION OF OLD AND NEW AT NOTTINGHAM

NOTTINGHAM'S LOVELY PEACE MEMORIAL

has faced adversity with a spirit that has known no bounds. It has made its power felt in English education and established a University College which is not to be beaten as a spectacle in any English city, and for efficiency and progress is second to none in the provinces. It has laid out nine miles of boulevards, and preserved the old Forest. It has bought a great Tudor hall which in itself would give distinction to any town. It has added Lord Byron's home to the possessions of the city. It has built a new bridge over the Trent, and has beside it one of the finest memorials any city has set up to its heroes. It has used its noble castle in the noblest way. It has swept away the biggest open marketplace in England and made it into a public square, with a city hall of great magnificence rising at the end of it. It has become the centre of a new railway linking London with Manchester, and has taken to itself village after village from the country round. In one of the streets began two mighty enterprises: a business which has grown until it has about a thousand shops, and a work which is now world-wide, world-needed, and world-honoured, the Salvation Army. The founder of the shops was Jesse Boot, the founder of the Army was William Booth, and both began in Hockley, two streets away from Nottingham's City Centre.

More than all this, Nottingham has turned itself in half a generation into England's most inland river port, building dams with locks and weirs as far as Newark, so that the Trent has a permanent channel to the sea. It has made itself an important airport with an aerodrome of 140 acres at Tollerton, three miles away.

It is not a bad record for a city faced with bitter adversity, and all this time this stronghold of our industrial Midlands has been sweeping its slums away, making itself worthy of its great future in the spirit of its historic past.

Nottingham has a prehistoric past of which little is known, for it has a remarkable group of rock-hewn chambers, of holes and caves and underground passages hollowed out in the soft sandstone rock; and in these it is believed that tribes of Ancient Britons lived before the Romans came, finding their food in the river and in the forest where bears and wolves abounded and timber could be had for fueling and building. It is known that for centuries the caves of Nottingham were used as dwellings. We see some of them still cut out of the castle rock, one a chamber with three windows and doorway; and there are hollowed-out dwellings in the picturesque Rock Cemetery looking down on the Forest. Every schoolboy in Nottingham knows that Robin Hood and his Merry Men lived in them, and every historian knows that they were the home of ancient tribes who formed the nucleus of the great community that has now grown up in Nottingham till it is 280,000 strong, in homes spread over 16,000 acres.

The Romans were hereabouts, but the town has no trace of them; it was the Saxons who made it a place of importance, and the Normans who gave it the name we know. The Saxons are said to have built a tower on the summit of the great rock which rose above the marshes on the edge of the dense forest, and not long after Egbert had consolidated England the Danes came down the Trent and planted their standard on the Rock. King Alfred, after a long struggle, compelled them to come to terms, and in the division of the country which followed Nottingham became the chief of the five Danish Burghs. Alfred's son began the reconquest of Danish England, and recovered the old kingdom, his success in the Midlands culminating in the capture of Nottingham. He fortified it with a wall and a ditch, giving the wall towers and gateways, and cutting most of the ditch from the solid rock. He threw a bridge across the Trent and built Bridgford. Athelstan, first king crowned for all England, set up a mint here, and his coins have the mark of the town.

In the days of the Normans the story of the town became closely linked with that of the castle, which the Conqueror ordered William Peverel to build on the precipitous Rock. The Normans settled about the castle and left the people undisturbed, so that for a time there were two races in Norman Nottingham, the Saxons in the English borough on St Mary's Hill, the Normans in the French borough, each borough having its own laws and customs, its town hall, and its mint. Henry the First rebuilt William Peverel's wooden fortress in stone, but his castle was burned down, and was rebuilt by Henry the Second, whose energy and goodwill Nottingham has reason to remember. He gave it its first charter in 1155, and in 1177 held in the town a council for establishing judicial circuits throughout the land. He helped the people to rebuild the town and closed it with more extensive fortifications, and encouraged the dyed-cloth industry which was growing. He held Nottingham Castle as a royal fortress and rebuilt it on a grander scale, and he loved to hunt in the neighbouring Sherwood Forest. He gave the castle to his terrible son John, to whom, in spite of his cruelty, Nottingham was always loyal. Yet the town has witnessed no more ghastly scene than that enacted on the castle ramparts in 1212, when John, furious at the news of another Welsh rebellion, ordered the hanging of 28 youths who were held as hostages for the good conduct of their fathers.

The son of the Norman founder of our Parliament, Simon de Montfort, became Governor of the castle in due course, and in the reign of Edward the First the town elected its own mayor. Edward the Second lived at the castle, and in the early years of Edward the Third his mother, Queen Isabella, and her favourite Roger Mortimer, established themselves here. In 1330 they were captured by the young king and his followers, who secretly entered the castle by the passage through the rock known as Mortimer's Hole. We may go down it today. Edward held several Parliaments here where laws were passed which were to have a great influence on the growing trade of the town, the manufacture of wool into cloth. Richard the Second sat here in conference with his judges, and sought in vain to encroach on the liberties of the people. Henry the Fourth found refuge here during rebellions and here he imprisoned Owen Glendower. Edward the Fourth proclaimed himself king from the castle and here denounced Warwick the Kingmaker as a traitor. He lived here in sumptuous style and made many improvements in the castle which were completed by his bloodstained successor Richard the Third. We may still see part of a tower built by Richard; it is in a garden near by.

It was from Nottingham that Richard set out for Bosworth Field, there to end the Plantagenet dynasty and to bring in the reign of the Tudors; and it was at Nottingham, when the Tudor dynasty was over, that Charles Stuart raised his standard on Standard Hill, at a spot marked by a tablet in the roadway looking down to the castle grounds; it is near the entrance to the hospital. It was during the Civil War that the heroic Colonel Hutchinson held the castle for the Parliament, refusing the Duke of Newcastle's offer of £10,000 and the gift of the castle if he would join the king's side. His answer was that if the duke wanted the castle he must wade to it through blood, and the story of the colonel's courage in holding the town is nobly told by Lucy Hutchinson in her memoirs of her husband's life. When the war was over Parliament gave the garrison a thousand pounds, and the castle itself was dismantled and mostly demolished. The first Duke of Newcastle cleared away the ruins, and he and his son transformed the walls into a ducal palace. Part of the duke's statue on horseback, cut from a single block of stone, is still in its original place over the north doorway.

In the days of the Industrial Revolution, when the poor stockingers were driven by hunger to smash the machines they blamed for their plight, Nottingham was the scene of much rioting, which was re-newed when the Reform Bill was rejected by the House of Lords. The castle was burned by the mob and remained a blackened and roofless shell for over 40 years. Its long place in the political history of England was over, and its new life as an art museum was begun.

The River Trent and the great Castle Rock are Nature's spec-tacular gifts to Nottingham, but many other splendid possessions the town has given itself or acquired. It stands on the edge of the romantic old Forest of Sherwood, which still survives in the Dukeries. It is from this forest that the city shares with the county in the rich lore of Robin Hood and his Merry Men. The story goes that Robin himself was a porter at the castle, and that Little John disguised himself as a servant so that he could carry off the sheriff's silver plate.

In these go-ahead days the city has developed as much as any place in England; it has got rid of many of its slums and claims to have built more houses than any other town of its size. It has made Nottingham one of the most wonderfully equipped cities in the kingdom by adding to itself wide roads and boulevards, parks and spaces and playing-fields. It has a fine group of hospitals (one going back to the 18th century), a dozen sets of almshouses and many charities, a high school for boys founded in 1513 and a high school for girls founded last century, and three secondary schools with accommodation for nearly 2000 scholars. It will be seen that Nottingham is a city on a fine scale.

We have only to see what it has done with its shabby old market to realise that the Queen of the Midlands has a great imagination. The marketplace was the biggest open-air buying and selling place in England, but it was much too shabby on market days, and the new Nottingham has put the market under cover and laid out this wide space in the centre of the town in a stately way. Where the old stalls stood there are now lawns and flowers and trees and marble walks, and looking down on the square is the Council House, opened in 1929 with a golden key which hangs inside. It is a magnificent building of which any city might be proud, crowned by a striking dome. Some of the facing stone is said to have been marked for St Paul's by Sir Christopher Wren, who had it cut and dressed but did not use it, so that it was left in the quarry.

This great white block which strikes the keynote of 20th century Nottingham was designed by Cecil Howitt. Built at a cost of £500,000, it is stately outside and in, furnished in every detail from floorstep to roof with dignity and great variety.

The splendid two-storeyed dome is impressive by day and by night, for at night it is floodlit. The plain lower storey has openings on four of its eight sides; the second storey is adorned with four groups of sculpture by old students of the College of Art, the sculptures representing Law, Prosperity, Knowledge, and Commerce. We may climb up 70 steps to this colonnaded storey where we are rewarded with the sight of the bells and the spectacle of the Queen of the Midlands with the country round about her. It is an aerial view of towers and spires and chimneys. On the one hand are the Mapperley Plains, on the other we look over the Trent Valley to Wilford Hill— the height from which we may see one of the fairest views of Nottingham set on its three chief hills, St Mary's, Sneinton, and the Castle Rock. Eastward are Colwick Woods, Sneinton church and Sneinton Mill. By the castle on its mighty rock are the fine houses of the Park, the buildings of the general hospital, and, beyond these, the Elizabethan Wollaton Hall and the 20th century University College. There are five bells in this great dome, weighing over 16 tons, one of them (Little John), said to be the biggest of all tuned bells, weighing 10 tons. Except for great Peter of York, it is the heaviest bell in the provinces, and the hammer for striking the hours on it weighs a quarter of a ton.

The dome looks down from its 200-feet height to the floor of a spacious arcade of shops and offices, approached by great arches from the streets. Round the bottom of the dome we read that the Corporation of Nottingham erected this building for Counsel and Welcome, and to show Merchandise and Crafts. The spandrels of the dome are enriched with frescoes by a Nottingham artist (Noel Denholm

Davis), showing in unfading colour four scenes in the city's story: the coming of the Danes, the Conqueror ordering the building of the Castle, Robin Hood and his band, and Charles Stuart raising his standard.

On the ground floor of the Council House front, looking down on the great square, an arcaded portico guarded by two lions leads to the loggia. Above the arcade are eight columns supporting a pediment with sculpture representing the activities of the city. There are about 20 figures and a group of animals sculptured by Joseph Else, principal of the College of Art. In the middle is Justice with scales and a golden sword, her eyes open; Education and Law stand beside her; Labour has a team of horses, and Agriculture has sheep and oxen. Another group represents Motherhood. A mason is erecting a column, a sculptor is carving figures of a woman and a child, there is an artist with his palette and a woman with musical instruments, and a reclining figure is bearing a model of the domed Council House.

Above the great windows of the reception hall, which look on to the square from behind the eight columns, runs a charming frieze with a procession of sturdy children engaged in the arts and crafts and industries in which Nottingham is or has been renowned. There are reapers, weavers, spinners, and iron workers with anvil and forge. Eight children carry a great bell, reminding us of the bell-founders famous here from the 16th to the 18th century; and eight little coal miners are hacking and drawing tubs of coal, reminding us of the days when such children worked in the mines. Children working on the tomb of a knight recall the alabaster carvers famous in medieval centuries, and leather workers represent an industry that is thriving still, 60,000 sheepskins being dressed every week in the city.

In the floor of the entrance hall is a mosaic of the city arms made up of 700 pieces. The balustraded staircase is lit by a beautiful dome of 144 panels of amber-tinted glass. At the top of the first flight of steps stands William Reid Dick's bronze figure of a woman holding out her arms in welcome, above her a fine wall painting by Noel Denholm Davis, representing Merchandise, Counsel, Welcome and Crafts. All the floors have panelled rooms with lovely ceilings and hidden lights, or light shining from beautiful electroliers of bronze or crystal. The woodwork is walnut and oak. The reception hall has 20 fine columns and a panelled ceiling, decorated in cream relieved with pink and blue and gold. Its floor is oak, walnut, and pearwood, and at one end is a mirrored wall adding to the charm, while looking down from above are galleries for minstrels and guests. The Lord Mayor's Parlour has on each side of the fireplace and the door exquisite carving in limewood of flowers, fruit, and wheat, and some panelling from Aston Hall in Derbyshire. The handsome dining hall has walnut walls with a striking figured panel over the fireplace, and the room of the lady mayoress is in Adam style with green and gold walls. In the Member's Room the ceiling is enriched with vines, and on the table is the telephone which we are told was the 100,000th instrument installed in the North Midlands. The Council Chamber forms a semi-circle, where every member sits within 26 feet of the lord mayor's chair. The walls are panelled with walnut, with loose tapestry panels over a lining of seaweed, an ingenious device for helping the acoustics of the Chamber. One of the mottoes here is, "Laws are made for the good and safety of the State." There is a small mallet (for the chairman's use) made of oak from a pier of old Trent Bridge, and there are pictures of Old Nottingham by Tom Hammond on the walls of the corridors.

We may wish it had been possible, in the replanning of this heart of the town, to open up the view of the castle on the rock from the great square. It would have been one of the finest spectacles in the heart of any city. As it is, the castle is but a stone's throw or two up a street off the square, so that we step from the City Centre to the Castle Rock in a very few minutes. One of Nottingham's rare sights is at the entrance gateway to the castle, with banked lawns like velvet, rockeries and trees climbing to the terrace, and delightful flower beds.

The magnificent view from the terrace is like the view from the Council House, save that the dome is in the foreground of the castle's picture of the city rising to the hills. On one of the lawns beyond the medieval gatehouse (looking almost new with restoration) is Nottingham's memorial to Albert Ball, VC, the gallant airman who accounted for about 50 enemy aircraft, and was killed in action three months after receiving the freedom of Nottingham when he was only 20. His bronze figure stands on a stone pedestal, dressed in flying kit and looking upwards, while the bronze figure of a woman, gracefully poised behind him, is pointing to the sky. On another lawn stands an obelisk in memory of men who fell in the Afghan War, and there is a bronze bust of Jonathan White, a Nottingham soldier who won distinction in India. By a broad path is part of an old bastion of the old castle wall, and here also is a lead cistern of 1681. At the end of a path leading to the inner moat is a square block, built up with original stones of the town wall which came to light when the Great Central railway was being laid through Nottingham, and facing it stands a Georgian doorway. An old stone archway leads into the moat, now a charming walk and bowered with trees, from which rustic paths wind up the steep bank to the castle. An interesting relic in the moat is a great oak beam taken from a pier of a 17th century bridge over the Trent at Cromwell near Newark. It was found in the river bed some years ago.

Down a 17th century brick stairway from the terrace we may reach the medieval dungeons which the Duke of Newcastle used as his wine cellar, and there is a vivid reminder of olden days in Mortimer's Hole, a passage with golden walls which winds through the rock from the height of the terrace down to Castle Boulevard; it is lit up for us today and has been made more roomy, but we may see the original spiral stairs at the top. It is thrilling to stand on Castle Boulevard and see the massive side of the rock through which this passage runs.

We enter the castle under a crescent colonnade, where is an array of bronze memorials of renowned poets. Here is Albert Toft's bust of Philip James Bailey, with a plaque on the pedestal showing Festus. Oliver Sheppard's bust of Henry Kirke White has on the pedestal a bowed woman holding a spray of laurel. George Frampton's busts of William and Mary Howitt are delightful; Mary's cap is tied under her chin, and her arm is round William's shoulder, both looking at an open book. Byron's bust is by Alfred Drury. There are two sculptured panels by Ernest Gillick, one showing Thomas Miller, the basket-maker's apprentice who wrote Songs of the Sea-nymphs, the other showing Robert Millhouse with his quill pen; he was the weaver-poet who worked a stocking-frame when he was ten, sang in the choir of St Peter's Church, and lies in the General Cemetery here.

In the castle is one of the rarest miscellaneous art collections in

The Noble Buildings from the River

The Magnificent Entrance
NOTTINGHAM UNIVERSITY

BY THE TRENT AT NOTTINGHAM

St Mary's Church

The School of Art

Long Row in the Council Square

Council House Reception Hall

The Long Gallery at the Castle

FAMOUS SIGHTS OF NOTTINGHAM

On the Rocky Height above the Trent

The Gateway and the Grounds

NOTTINGHAM CASTLE

the kingdom. Nottingham's own group of poets and artists and historic folk is well represented. We see Colonel Hutchinson in his wig and armour, Charles Stuart, Albert Ball, William Booth, Richard Arkwright, Philip James Bailey, William Howitt, and Dr Thoroton, the county historian, by Sir Godfrey Kneller. There is a portrait of Kirke White by Hoppner, a portrait of Richard Parkes Bonington by himself and another by Thomas Philips, and a portrait of Samuel William Oscroft, a local painter and collector who bequeathed much of his collection to this museum. Three of Richard Bonington's pictures here are his famous Fisher Folk on the Coast of Normandy, the Coast Scene, and the Undercliff, a dainty little picture covering only 40 inches. On the back of it is written : " The last drawing made by our dear son prior to his fatal dissolution; never to be parted with." He was born in the beginning of last century and lived barely 27 years, bequeathing the rich treasure which Nottingham shares with the Wallace Collection. There are some of his fine pencil sketches in this museum.

Other notable pictures here are Laura Knight's On the Sands, and Motherhood; Arnesby Brown's Full Summer, and Tom Browne's Old Cronies, all these being Nottingham artists. Thomas Sandby and his brother Paul, founder members of the Royal Academy, were also Nottingham artists, and here hang two of Thomas Sandby's works, one of the Colonnade at Covent Garden. Here is Richard Wilson's picture of Snowdon, George Morland's portrait of himself and his man cooking a sausage, the Major Oak of Sherwood Forest by MacCallum, and John Laslett Pott's picture of Mary Queen of Scots being led to execution.

On loan for an indefinite period at the Castle is the priceless Clumber Collection of old masters, among them Rubens, Reynolds, Vandyke, Rembrandt, Hogarth, Holbein, Kneller, Teniers, and Snyders. Lely is represented by his Prince Rupert, and Gainsborough by his Beggar Boys.

The rare examples of alabaster sculpture here are attributed to the Nottingham carvers who made this work famous in medieval days, when most of the alabaster came from Chellaston, being fashioned by them for churches and great houses throughout the land and on the continent. The quarries they used are busy again today yielding gypsum for plaster of paris. One of the alabasters here is the

Crucifixion, with the two thieves; on it are 20 figures and two horses. Another is the Entombment, and there is a quaint Resurrection scene with three soldiers asleep and one watching Christ rising from the tomb. In a fine piece about 20 inches high the patron saint of metal workers is shoeing a horse said to be possessed of the devil, and has taken off the horse's leg in order to do the work more easily. Three beautifully draped figures have won more than local fame since they were found in 1779 on the site of the destroyed church of the lost village of Flawforth, between Edwalton and Ruddington. Known as the Flawforth figures, they are a smiling Madonna, wearing a crown, Peter holding a church, and a bishop giving blessing.

The museum has much beautiful Nottingham ironwork. There are the lovely gates from Colwick Hall, the garden screen from old Plumptre House, the railings from Bramcote Manor House, and an old sign with the date 1752 cleverly worked in with the hammer, horseshoe, and pincers of a smithy. One of Nottingham's famous smiths was Huntingdon Shaw. Here also are shown such things as an iron-studded doorway from an old lane in Nottingham, some ornamental leadwork, and carved oak pillars from an Elizabethan colonnade round the old marketplace.

In the collection of old porcelain are examples of most of the famous wares, and there are two cups, a saucer, and a plate of the now rare Pinxton porcelain, in apple green and amethyst. A jug in Derby china of 1782 has the head of Admiral Rodney for its spout. The collection of Wedgwood left to the city by Mr Felix Joseph is a rare possession in which are cups and saucers, teapots, plaques, medallions, vases, dainty little figures and black busts of Byron, Addison, Ben Jonson, Milton, and Rousseau. There is a famous vase of the Apotheosis of Homer designed by Flaxman, and a copy of the famous Portland Vase. With the local pottery of salt-glazed ware is a stout 15th century jug found during excavations, and a great jug of Chesterfield ware decorated with hunting scenes and classical subjects, the neck being fashioned of vines and the spout shaped into the head of Bacchus.

There is a splendid collection of coins of all ages, among them medieval medals and tokens of Nottingham merchants. There is the mummy of a baby among the Egyptian antiquities, and among the Roman relics a head of Julius Caesar, a bust of Jupiter, and the portrait bust of a Roman lady said to be among the finest of its kind; she has her hair bunched up in a quaint plait at the top of her head.

The old kitchen of the castle, where we can still see the ovens in which bread and cakes were baked in the 17th century, are now the textile gallery, packed with interesting and beautiful things. Chinese and Persian embroideries arrest us on the stairs as we go down. There is a Chinese banner of gold thread and pearls, and a fine reproduction of the famous Bayeux tapestry, with its 72 scenes and 623 people, 202 horses, 55 dogs, 505 other animals, 37 buildings, 41 vessels, and 49 trees. But perhaps the most arresting thing here is a wonderful collection of laces and embroideries, handmade and machine-made, with bobbins and spinning wheels and machinery to tell their story. The handmade lace is so exquisite and delicate that it almost shames the spider. There is one of the old lacemaking frames here for us to see, and a model of Heathcote's lace machine of 1809. A remarkable portrait woven in silk of Joseph Marie Jacquard, sitting with his compasses and a model of the mechanism of the loom which bears his name. He was a French mathematician, who invented the device for controlling threads in weaving.

Among the host of miscellaneous treasures here we remember a 14th century cross, the castle alarm bell of 1684, a plaster cast from the death-mask of Cromwell, an inscribed brick from Babylon, a copy of the Standard of Charles Stuart with its motto Give to Caesar his due, the original of Lucy Hutchinson's Life of Colonel Hutchinson (open in a glass case), two Pompeian bronzes (Narcissus listening to Echo and Winged Victory), exquisite fans of whalebone set with jewels and of Chinese ivory (both looking like lace), and a lovely set of ivory chessman on pedestals of concentric balls. The pawns in this set are soldiers on horseback with bows and arrows, the knights are in armour with shields, the mitred bishops and the kings and queens are in fine robes, and the castles are elephants with men and castles on their backs.

Keeping company with the great Council House and the historic castle is Nottingham's beautiful University college, rising on a green hill by the Boulevard named after it. It has one of the loveliest towers in the Midlands, crowning a building of great beauty, which was one of the life-dreams of a poor Nottingham boy who became a prince of commerce. The story goes far back, and has in it something of pride and pathos and tragedy.

About the middle of last century a little boy named Jesse Boot stood behind the counter with his mother in a herbalist's shop started by his father, in a street leading into Nottingham from Sneinton. And about the same time two of Nottingham's leading citizens, Dr J. B. Paton and Richard Enfield, had the bold idea that Oxford and Cambridge could throw out their arms to reach beyond the bounds of their walls, and it was to Nottingham that Cambridge sent out the first lecturers in connection with the University Extension Movement. Nottingham was the first town in England to maintain a University College out of the rates, and it was fitting that it should start this great development of university life. This seed was being sown when Jesse Boot and his widowed mother were working hard in their little shop in Hockley. He was building up his business; the educators were opening the way he was to go when he had done with his 800 shops and wanted something more to build.

The idea behind the education movement in Nottingham was to build up an East Midland University, and it began with University College, the old buildings of which are still used for textile and mining and law departments, and for all the evening classes. They stand near the heart of the town, and have done fine work for half a century, but it was not enough. Then, to make every struggle in this world a little harder, came the Great War, and it seemed that the dream was broken.

But it was with the Great Peace that Sir Jesse Boot came on the scene. He had grown rich and famous, but all his wealth and all his fame he would have given for good health. Rheumatoid arthritis had him in its grip; his body failed him more and more. He lay on his back day and night, unable to move alone, but with a mind alert and dreaming of doing some great new thing. What he did was to build this University College, one of the finest monuments learning has. It rises from its mantle of trees at Highfields with the graciousness and elegance of a beautiful white lady. The south front, impressive by its very simplicity, is 400 feet long, its great masses well balanced in the curves of the hillside. The boulevard laid out in front of it with lawns and banks and lime trees is nearly a mile long. On one side are playing fields, on the other the lovely grounds with masses of rhododendrons, shrubs and trees, rock gardens and waterfall, a lake for boating, and the biggest open-air swimming pool in England, 330 feet long and 75 wide. It is filled by electric pumps, and though it holds 772,000 gallons of water it can be filled at a cost of less than a pound. There are scores of cricket pitches, football grounds, tennis courts, bowling greens, hockey fields, and croquet lawns, and rising in the midst of them is Mr Morley Horder's lovely College, crowned by the elegant tower Giotto himself would have loved to see.

On the day when the dream of Sir Jesse Boot was coming true, when the King was coming to open the door with a golden key, we drove past the great university building through streets alive with joy and sunshine, and gay like the rainbow with colours flying in the breeze, and found the giver of all this good lying alone in a small room near the banks of the Trent. The people were waiting for the King and Queen, thinking how beautiful their city looked, and thrilling with pride on this great day, and the founder of all this happiness lay there on his plain bed physically helpless, with two or three men within call if he should need to be moved, and the two or three secretaries he was always needing. He was cheerful and uncomplaining, a poor boy grown rich and sharing his riches with the town that had helped him, a strong man grown weak, yet fashioning his life into things that are better than gold. His face looks out in bronze at the entrance gates on the boulevard, and in front of him his work and his works go on, for he faces the great glass factory which sends out the thousand products of his firm. It is one of the industrial spectacles of the city, with Sir Jesse Boot's son, Lord Trent, at the head of it.

The new University has a fine possession in the collection of Roman remains discovered by Dr Felix Oswald when excavating at East Bridgford. The remains tell the story of a camp from its prehistoric days to the days when it came into history—from the days of the Early Britons to the days of its Roman occupation and its lapse into oblivion. It lies on the Fosse Way, the straightest road in England, midway between Leicester and Lincoln, and the camp covered about seven acres, enough to accommodate a thousand men and some cavalry. Here were found Roman coins from the first century to the fourth, a fine little sepulchral stone carved with two figures, one with a staff and one with a basket of fruit; great jars and cooking pots, and vessels moulded with human faces; fragments of glass, ladles, bucket handles, bone and bronze pins, and horse trappings (one engraved with a dragon); and many flint arrow heads, scrapers, and axes of the Bronze Age. But most remarkable of all these treasures is what we may be allowed to describe as a piece of Roman oak panelling, for it is nothing less than a complete section of the oak lining of a well of the time of Claudius. It is shaped like a square cage, and the roughly-cut oak planks still show the marks of the saw and the adze used by the carpenter 19 centuries ago. Such are the remains of the Roman Margidnum.

Nottingham has been an industrial city for many generations. It was mining coal in medieval days. It has been linked with the hosiery and lace trades from their birth, for both owe their beginning to the genius of William Lee, a curate a few miles away, whose hand-frame for knitted stockings, invented in the time of Queen Elizabeth, was the first machine ever known to make a looped or knitted fabric. Some of the old houses with the long windows where the old frames were worked are still to be seen in Sherwood Street. The first of many improvements in the stocking-frame came in 1758 in Jedediah Strutt's invention for making a ribbed frame, and the next advance was the introduction of the "circular looped wheel" frame. Two centuries after its invention by Lee the stocking-frame was adapted for producing lace. John Heathcote's twist lace machine came in 1809, and the net-weaving machines of John Levers a little later. The coming of Hargreaves with his jenny and Arkwright with his spinning-frame had given a great impetus to the town's industrial activity, and Nottingham saw the first cotton mill built in England, in the year 1769.

Today the trades of the city have an almost endless variety, and there are other firms besides Boots that have won for themselves a national or worldwide reputation. At a splendid factory covering five acres, Thomas Formans produce art calendars and printing that most people handle whether they know it or not. On Radford Boulevard are the palatial factories of John Player and Sons and the Raleigh Cycle Company, two vast concerns known the world over, each with a romantic story. In the last quarter of last century John Player bought a small tobacco factory in Broad Marsh and moved it to Radford, where it has now grown to 45 acres, half of which is used for the recreation of its 7000 people. It is said to be the biggest tobacco factory under one roof in the world, and turns out cigarettes in tens of millions every day. Also in the last quarter of last century a small factory in Raleigh Street was making two or three bicycles a week. Mr Frank Bowden, coming home a sick man from Hong Kong, bought one of them, rode it for six months in the Pyrenees, and came home strong and well, and with such faith in his bicycle that he started making cycles and has built up a firm which is second to none in the cycle world.

These are Nottingham's great trades today, though the city has fifty or a hundred more—building machinery and rolling stock for railways, bleaching, dyeing, brewing, electroplating, box making, leather dressing, making typewriters and perambulators and thermometers, producing fine chemicals, surgical appliances, soap and glue, glove fabrics, furniture, and bricks. Everywhere in its street names we are reminded of the old trades of the city. The wheelwrights lived in Wheeler Gate; Bridlesmith Gate and Smithy Row echoed with the clang of hammer and anvil. The tanners were in Barker Gate and the fur workers in Pilcher Gate.

Nottingham is rich in the opportunities it gives its people to enjoy their leisure, and to educate themselves in noble things. It has not only developed its castle on the lines we have seen, but has taken to itself the Elizabethan Wollaton Hall and the home of Lord Byron at Newstead. Wollaton Hall is a mile or so from the City Centre; Newstead is nine miles away.

The great Natural History Museum of the town has been moved to Wollaton, so that this collection is as splendidly housed as any collection in the country. The Wollaton estate was sold to the city in 1924, thus bringing to an end an association between Wollaton village and the Willoughbys that had lasted 600 years. The Hall, which took eight years to build and cost £80,000 in Queen Elizabeth's coinage, was completed in Armada year, all the stone carried from Ancaster by donkey or packhorse and paid for with Wollaton coal. It is believed to have been designed by John Thorpe.

This great pile of ornamented stone, an impressive spectacle, has a variety of Gothic, Tudor, and classical styles, and is striking for its countless windows, pilasters, cornices, balustrades, and niches, in which are busts of Plato, Virgil, Aristotle, and Diana. A fine Prospect Room with projecting turrets crowns the centre block, and there are four square pavilions at the corners with Dutch gables and pinnacles. The great hall has a handsome stone screen and a hammerbeam roof. The museum housed here includes a collection of butterflies from China and Hong Kong, the Fowler collection of British beetles, and the Crauford collection of 25,000 insects.

The glory of Wollaton has always been its magnificent park, with 800 acres of plantations and groves and wonderful gardens. Here is said to have been built the first glasshouse in England for protecting plants. The park was enclosed by a brick wall seven miles long, on which a boy served a seven-years' apprenticeship. The wall has been disturbed and the builder has been at work within it, but the deer still browse by the great lake in the woodland hollow, the gardens are still lovely to see, there is a cedar grove by a splendid flight of steps, a lime grove three-quarters of a mile long leading from the great stone gateway to the hall, and a marvellous house which is unforgettable when the camelias are in bloom; it is said that this house cost £10,000 to build. Looking out over all this from the fine leaded roof of the Prospect Room, we see Belvoir Castle 20 miles away.

Newstead Abbey, home of Lord Byron, once stood in the heart of Sherwood Forest, having been founded about 1170 by Henry the Second in his remorse for the death of Thomas Becket. After the Reformation it became one of England's great country houses, and Byron was the last of his line to possess it. It has an association with two men whose dramatic meeting in the Dark Continent was one of the immortal moments of the 19th century, for here David Livingstone stayed for a year, writing a book, and here came Sir Henry Stanley several times. Now it belongs to the city, the gift of Sir Julian Cahn, and it is one of the most enjoyable experiences a Nottingham citizen can give himself to walk through the acres of these enchanting gardens, and to wander through these rooms. One of the earlier owners, Mr Charles Ian Fraser, has given the city the Byron relics, the entrance lodge, the land on which stands the famous Pilgrim Oak, over 70 acres of the park, and the six-acre wood known as Poet's Corner. When the Abbey was dedicated to the city in 1931, Prime Minister Venizelos of Greece was present to pay tribute to the memory of the poet who died fighting for the liberty of Greece.

Next door to the old University College is Nottingham's central library, controlling the issuing of about a million volumes a year through its branches. It has on its stairway an oil painting of Homer singing at the gate of Athens, and on the landing is a framed facsimile of the death-warrant of Charles Stuart, with a print showing the king dictating his proclamation at the raising of the standard. The reading room has a collection of water-colours showing scenes in bygone Nottingham, including the Windmills on the Forest, the old Postern Gate in Middle Pavement, Wilford Ferry, and the old Trent Bridge. There is a portrait of James Prior Kirk (of Forest Folk fame) and one of William Booth by Denholm Davis. The library has a special lending department for the blind, and it has an interesting collection of rare books, among them the unpublished letters of Byron which were suppressed before publication and of which only ten copies were distributed, and the original manuscript of Robert Thoroton's Antiquities of Notts.

Close by is the Guildhall, an imposing block now planned for reconstruction, its entrance hall with classical columns and a rich ceiling. Not far away, in Goldsmith Street, is the Masonic Hall, a handsome new building with a frontage of 450 feet, and housed in an attractive building near by is the College of Art, the development of the School of Art, to which Dame Laura Knight, the second woman to be elected ARA, came as a schoolgirl of 13. Her first picture accepted by the Royal Academy now hangs at the castle. Her artist husband is a Nottingham man. So too were Paul and Thomas Sandby and Arnesby Brown. In the grounds of the College of Art is a statue of Richard Parkes Bonington, born on the outskirts of the city.

Near to this notable College of Art is the Arboretum, a charming park of 19 acres of grassy banks, shady walks, and beds of flowers. Swans and water fowl swim on the bowery lake, and the gorgeous plumage of some of the birds make the aviaries an unfailing attraction. In a riot of flowers on a small hilltop stands a copy of a Chinese pagoda sheltering a bell captured at Canton by the Notts

Regiment, and at the corners of the Pagoda are guns captured at Sebastopol. Along the paths close by is a statue of Feargus O'Connor, holding a scroll. He was local leader of the Chartists in the agitation for the Reform Bill, and sat for Nottingham in Parliament. In the middle of a stone seat near one of the gates is the fine bronze bust of Samuel Morley, whose marble statue used to stand outside the Theatre Royal, looking down into the marketplace; the statue was being moved for traffic purposes when it fell and broke into pieces. He was of the great hosiery family associated with Nottingham so long, and is still remembered for his philanthropic interest in the city. The bust in the Arboretum is by Mr Else, Principal of the College of Art.

Only a few hundred yards from the beautiful Arboretum is the great open space of the Forest. It is the city's oldest recreation ground, and its 70 acres were once part of Sherwood Forest. The old Goose Fair which used to be held in the marketplace is now held here.

Thousands of city folk seek their recreation by the river, a most attractive place which may be taken as a model by many towns which waste their river banks. From time immemorial the crossing of the Trent at Nottingham has been an important link between north and south, but the first bridge of which we know was built of wood a thousand years ago. The medieval stone bridge had a chapel, and a shallow arch of it still remains at the southern end of the present bridge, which was built in 1870 and widened in our own time. It has now three iron arches on stone piers, and is 80 feet wide between the parapets. From this bridge to Wilford Toll Bridge a magnificent promenade runs for over a mile, covering 28 acres, shaded first by fir trees and then by limes. On one hand is green lawn, a fine flight of steps, and the river gay with pleasure boats; on the other hand wide playing-fields, green spaces, lovely gardens, and a noble monument to the thousands of Nottingham men who fell in the war. It was designed by the City Engineer, Mr Wallis Gordon, and has a stately triple archway, with colonnaded wings embracing lawn and shrubs and balustraded terraces continuing across the boulevard to the river. The iron gates are enriched with scrolls of the city arms, and along the top of the gateway is the city's motto, Virtue is Immortal. There is a fine view of the city from the embankment, and through the memorial gateway we come to lawns and flowers, trees and shrubs and rockeries, set about a lily pool like an ornamental cross.

A little way off, on the West Bridgford side of the river, is the famous ground of the Notts County Cricket Club, where have been cradled so many players of renown; and here, too, is Sir Julian Cahn's cricket ground and a famous football ground.

Of Nottingham's great group of churches and chapels only a few are old. In the heart of the Lace Market, crowning the hill which rises 90 feet above the low land which was once green meadows, rises the stately church of St Mary's, its tower ten feet higher than the top of the castle to which it looks across the city roofs. It rises 126 feet, with eight pinnacles, and is as old as the Tudor dynasty. The church is a splendid example of 15th century work and has impressive walls richly adorned with buttresses and panelled battlements. The south porch, weatherworn but still beautiful, has a panelled gable and a vaulted roof, the inner doorway set between canopied niches with the great head of a lion above it. Its splendid double doors are faced with bronze scenes in the life of Our Lord and the Madonna, and over the doors is a Pieta, a sorrowing dove withdrawing behind a veil to appear again as a joyful dove, symbolising the weary soul finding new life; the doors are of our own time, in memory of a vicar, Francis Morse, "Father, pastor, friend." Angels and flowers enrich the west doorway, which was put here when Sir Gilbert Scott restored the west end to its original style. Kings, bishops, and animals guard the windows on the north side. The fine panelled chimney of the old vestry is probably 17th century.

Except for the dim chancel, plainer than the rest of the building, the interior is full of light, the clerestory like a lantern with 12 great windows on each side. The lofty nave arcades have no capitals. Transepts open from the tower, whose massive pillars, 24 feet round, were twice rebuilt last century. The south transept is one of the oldest parts of the church; so, too, is the doorway in the north aisle, with crowned heads, probably those of Richard the Second and his queen; the old studded door still hanging in its original iron fastening led to a chantry. In the stone seats along the aisle walls are stones from the earlier church, and there is part of a very old pillar covered by a movable board in the floor by the north arcade. Round the 15th century font is the familiar Greek inscription which reads the same both ways, meaning: Wash thy sins and not thy face only. There are fragments of 16th century glass in the north transept, where is also a carved Jacobean altar table, and kept under glass in the south chapel is a beautiful fragment of alabaster of much interest. It shows a pope sitting under a canopy attended by two cardinals, and a kneeling bishop with his chaplains, and is said to represent Thomas Becket resigning the see of Canterbury. It was probably part of a medieval reredos. A rare treasure is a lovely Madonna and Child painted by Fra Bartolomeo, pupil of Raphael and friend of Savonarola.

Over 500 years ago John Samon left six-and-eightpence for a light to be kept burning for ever in a chapel here. He was four times Mayor of Nottingham and lies on his canopied tomb in the south transept, a civilian in a loose-sleeved coat buttoned from his collar to his feet. His pointed shoes rest on a dog, and battered angels support the cushion for his head. His son Richard, who died in 1427, has a battered floorstone near the north-west door, with his arms on the stem of a cross. In the north transept is a handsome canopied tomb seeming to have belonged to three memorials. The canopy, which has rich niches in its gable, covered the 15th century tomb of Thomas Thurland, who was nine times mayor and four times MP, and is remembered in Thurland Street. The alabaster tomb below the canopy, with carvings of the Madonna, Gabriel, Peter, and John the Baptist, and with a lily carved with a crucifix on its stem may be that of John Tannersley, another medieval mayor. The marble stone on the top of the tomb, which has lost its brasses, may be that of William Amyas, a wool merchant. On this triple tomb we found resting the memorial of still another mayor, Robert English, an alabaster fragment with a mitred figure on it. The battered figure in the north aisle may be his.

One of the memorials in the north transept to the Plumptres is an 18th century alabaster medallion to a boy of ten who was greatly learned in history and mythology, Latin and French, and has on his memorial these words from Virgil's Lament for Marcellus:

> *Over the shade of him who was my son*
> *Heap I these gifts, and now my task is done.*

There is another delightful epitaph in the north aisle on a tablet to Ann Hollings of 1770:

> *Rest, gentle shade, and wait thy Maker's will,*
> *Then rise unchanged, and be an angel still.*

Two great alabaster shields and an inscription now in the South transept are all that remain of the tomb of John Holles, the Earl of Clare, who fought against the Armada.

Near the pulpit is a floorstone to John Whitlock, who was in charge of St Mary's during the Commonwealth, and helped to found the Unitarian chapel on High Pavement. The great west window with 42 panels telling the story of Our Lord from the Manger to the Cross, is in memory of one of Nottingham's most famous citizens, the 19th century lace merchant, Thomas Adams; and the 19th century glass in the south transept, with the parables in 48 panels, is in memory of the founder of modern banking, Thomas Smith, who was buried here in 1699. An 18th century monument with an elephant's head is to another of the Smiths. In a north transept window are 16 panels of the Miracles. A pathetic window in the south chapel is in memory of Catherine Monica Dalton, who was baptised here in 1899 and died a week after her marriage here in 1918; we see her in the bridal gown and lace veil in which she was married and buried; she kneels before the Madonna, with St Catharine and St Monica standing by.

In the south aisle is the best glass in the church, a modern gallery of 24 saints, bishops, and kings, by Kempe; it keeps green the memory of the men of the Notts Regiment who fell in South Africa. A Scout window shows Scout badges, a knight in armour typifying courage, Christ with his arm on the shoulder of a path-finder, a Scout setting out from home, and a camp-fire group in a field of bluebells. A window to the Notts veterans of the Crimean War and Indian Mutiny has for its theme: Young men shall see visions and old men shall dream dreams. The dull window in the chancel of Gethsemane, the Last Supper, and the Road to Calvary, is said to be designed by Sir George Frampton (though it does not look like it).

In the tower hangs a peal of ten bells, all having been recast except one, which comes from 1595; the last of the great Nottingham firm which cast it, and which sent so many bells round England, lies in the churchyard near the vestry, George Oldfield.

We may wonder if anywhere else in England is anything quite like the way in which Nottingham has remembered the men who did not come back from the war. It is one of two peace memorials at St Mary's, the other being a bronze panel in the chancel showing an officer leading his men up the line, with the Book of Remembrance below. What we believe to be a unique memorial is at one of the entrance gates to St Mary's, where, in the middle of a flight of steps, is a cross carved with furled flags round a shaft, and on the pedestal the name of every parish in the city and the number of men the parish lost; there are 5400. At each side of the steps are tablets with the names of the villages in the county and the number of men each village lost. There are 204 villages and towns and they lost 6912 men. Eight villages lost one man, ten lost two men, and eleven lost three. It is an admirable record in stone that the city has made for the county.

St Peter's, a stone's throw from the Council House, is Nottingham's oldest church, with ten bells ringing in its 15th century tower, crowned by a lofty spire. One bell was given in 1544 by Margery Doubleday, a washerwoman, with 20 shillings a year to pay the sexton to ring it at four every morning to wake up the washerwomen of the future. The tower has a vaulted roof, and its slender arch frames a charming patch of colour in the west window with figures of Moses, Christ, Elias, Peter, James, and John.

The interior is spacious, stately, and light, with aisles divided from the nave by arches on clustered pillars. The south arcade is mostly 13th century, with foliage and heads enriching some of the capitals. Some of the masonry in the wall of this arcade is said to have been part of a church built soon after the Conquest. The north arcade is 15th century, with loftier bays and embattled capitals, and faces between the arches. Some of the 15th century timbering is left in the roofs; in the nave the roof rests on stone angels and grotesques. At the top of the roodstairs is an old altar stone set up on end. The stone reredos has an angel setting Peter free from his chains, by Albert Toft.

On one of the pillars, under a rich golden canopy, is the lovely alabaster figure of St George, in armour with golden trappings and helmet, killing the dragon; it is the peace memorial. Three beautiful memorials brought here from St James's Church (lately pulled down) are a marble plaque to 16 men of the war, showing a youth in his last sleep, with winged angels watching; a bronze figure by Albert Toft of a woman with outstretched arms, in memory of a daughter; and a bronze plaque by Sir George Frampton to a vicar, Lawrence Wilkins. The modern oak screen, vaulted both sides, has 18 angels playing instruments and 12 cherubs singing in the tracery. A rare old treasure is the Guild Book of St George, with its beautifu handwriting of 500 years ago.

Though the red brick church of St Nicholas has little claim to beauty, it has an interesting story. It was built in 1682 and enlarged in the next century, but it stands on a site where stood a Norman church. It was after the Royalists had bombarded the castle garrison from its tower that Colonel Hutchinson had the old building demolished. On the battlements is a great stone sundial.

St Andrew's 19th century stone church, standing well at the top of Mansfield Road by the Rock Cemetery and overlooking the Forest, has a tower with lantern and spire, and some fine modern craftsmanship inside. Two beautiful oak screens, one with fan-vaulting, are in memory of only sons lost in the war. Notable wood-work furnishes the chapel, where an alabaster tablet with two figures in niches keeps green the memory of others who did not come back. The rich panelling of the sanctuary and the lovely alabaster reredos were the gift of John and Margaret Player in 1918, "for 25 years of happy married life," the reredos showing in high relief Christ enthroned, a charming Nativity in which the ass and the ox peep over the stall, Christ walking with two disciples, the Baptism, Gethsemane, and the Resurrection with an angel and two sleeping soldiers.

Holy Trinity Church in Milton Street, about a century old, is in 13th century style. It has lost much of the beauty it once had on its island site near the centre of the town, and is plain inside with galleries, but its needle-like spire, rising from the pinnacled lantern crowning the tower, is conspicuous in views of the city. All Saints in Raleigh Street comes from 1864, its tower surmounted by a sturdy broached spire, its apsidal chancel gabled on every face. The Roman Catholic Cathedral of St Barnabas on Derby Road, designed by Pugin in 13th century style, comes from 1842, its tower and spire rising to 170 feet from the middle of a cross. Opposite is the Albert Hall, the headquarters of the Wesleyan Mission; built in 1909, it has room for 2600 people, and has a magnificent organ given by the first Lord Trent.

St Catharine's Church stands in a workaday part of the city on St Ann's Well Road, and was built of stone in 1896 in place of an iron church whose length led local people to call it the " shooting gallery." One of its treasures is the font, with a rough-hewn bowl coming from Norman days, set on a medieval base. It belonged to the ruined church of South Wheatley near Retford, and while here it has served at over 3000 baptisms. The lectern is a pelican, its long legs hidden in the wooden pedestal. The crucifix in the lady chapel was carved by the peasants of Oberammergau. In the Children's Corner we come upon the memory of a family which has done much for this church. When he died in 1926 John Sargent had been St Catharine's only verger, and here is his grandfather clock and his table. The old sexton, his wife, and his daughter all died in one week. The daughter had for many years helped him to clean the church, and she left £20 to the hospital, and to the church £50, to be spent on a window to the patron saint. Here it is in the Children's Corner, in the spot she chose for it. Below the figure of St Catharine we see Alice Sargent kneeling on her scrubbing mat, her bucket, soap, and brush beside her, a tribute to one who looked on work as a holy thing. Under the window is a prayer desk she used in her home. With part of the money John Sargent left, new hymn books, hangings, and many things needful were bought for the church.

High Pavement's Unitarian chapel is a pleasing stone building of 1876, with a tower and a lofty spire, and an arcaded interior. It was founded by John Whitlock (who lies in St Mary's), William Reynolds, and John Barnet, the first two joint-ministers of St Mary's during the Commonwealth. Three memories of the older chapel are of Samuel Taylor Coleridge preaching a charity sermon in 1796, of Byron coming here as a boy, and of the baptism of Richard Parkes Bonington in 1802. Its great interest is in its beautiful glass. The seven-light window facing south has a splendid gallery of 21 graceful figures in three rows by Burne-Jones, shining red, blue, green, and gold on a background of foliage. Row One shows Truth with a torch, Light, Faith, Love, Hope, Joy, Peace. Row Two has

Justice with the sword and scales, Courage staving off darts with a shield, Reverence beside a figure of Jesus with four children, Mercy with hands on a sword, Purity, and Humility carrying a lamb. Row Three has Science, Literature, Theology, Labour, Philanthropy, Art, and Theosophy. Another window full of light and colour, in memory of war heroes, shows a soldier and a sailor with bowed heads and arms reversed, knights in armour, a man with a plough, an angel above him putting away the sword; Joan of Arc with a Scout and a workman and women; St George with children, women, soldiers, and sailors; and a mother and her children mourning by a wooden cross. A Kempe window with St George and Sir Galahad is to two men who did not come back.

Another nonconformist church of note is Castle Gate Congregational, the oldest chapel in Nottingham, founded in Cromwell's day, and the first church in the city to be wired for broadcasting.

The quaint streets and old houses of Nottingham remain as a striking contrast in these days when Nottingham is putting on its 20th century dress. Hockley, leading into the heart of the town from the ancient village of Sneinton, has turned into a warehouse the 18th century chapel in which John Wesley preached his last Nottingham sermon, but it can never destroy the spot where William Booth used to stand and preach to passers-by who would stop and listen; it was the beginning of the Salvation Army. Friar Lane, leading from the Council House to the castle, has lost the little room in which William Carey preached the sermon which led to the founding of the Baptist Missionary Society, and has put the Theosophical Hall on its site; but across the road is the old Friends Meeting House, with a new outside dress, and opposite this, at the corner of Spaniel Row, is a tall gabled house where George Fox stayed with the sheriff when he was thrown into prison for interrupting the service at St Mary's. Henry Kirke White's birthplace in the old Shambles has been swallowed up by the Council House, but on a wall of the shopping arcade is a bronze plaque showing his father's little butcher's shop.

In the short walk from Lister Gate following the line of part of the old town walls along the three Pavements towards St Mary's we come upon many notable 18th century buildings. On Low Pavement is Willoughby House, with a stone doorway and iron rails; it stands on some of the best rock cellars in the town. Just above is Vault

Hall, used in the past for storing wool and as a secret meeting place of nonconformists; its arched gateway has perhaps the best old ironwork left in the town. The narrow thoroughfare at the corner of which it stands has been known as Drury Hill since Alderman Drury lived here in the 17th century. The four splendid fluted columns at Number Seven Low Pavement belong to the Old Assembly Rooms. Middle Pavement leads to Weekday Cross, where the Saxons held their market. Here was the town hall of the English borough in the time of the Normans; the Moot Hall Inn at the corner of Wheeler Gate and Friar Lane is on the site of the town hall of the French borough. On a wall in Weekday Cross a tablet marks the birthplace of Philip James Bailey, the Nottingham poet who wrote the forgotten poem of Festus, with the unforgettable lines:

> *We live in deeds, not years; in thoughts not breaths;*
> *In feelings, not in figures on a dial.*
> *We should count time by heart throbs: he most lives*
> *Who thinks most, feels the noblest, acts the best.*

On High Pavement is the Shire Hall, a stone building with pilastered entrance and balustraded parapet, where even till 1864 criminals were publicly hanged. Remains of the old prison can be seen at the back, and below are the cabins and dungeons used as condemned cells. The hall is unique among Nottingham buildings, for it is the smallest civil parish in all England, a bit of the county within the town, having been left under the old jurisdiction when Henry the Sixth separated the town from the county. Facing the Shire Hall is a fine house in which judges were lodged years ago, and in which the County Council now has offices. Much of it is still the old house where Lady Hutchinson lived while her famous stepson was governor of the castle; it is said that she was prosecuted for having music in this house on a Sunday. In the panelled hall, when we called, were two battered drums which beat the charge at the Battle of Culloden.

In Castle Gate, close by, stands the square many-windowed Newdigate House of the time of Charles the Second, fronted by rich old ironwork. In it was sheltered the illustrious Marshal Tallard, who was captured at the Battle of Blenheim. He was a great gardener, and it is said that we owe to him the cultivation of celery, which he found growing wild in the neighbouring marshes. Facing Newdigate

House is a house built by the master gunner of the Castle in the Civil War. Bromley House on Angel Row, facing the Council House, was built in 1725 by one of the banking Smiths. In Chapel Bar, a little way up the hill from the square, an early member of the Ingram family evolved the idea of the first illustrated paper. At the corner of Parliament Street and Newcastle Street, five minutes walk away, William and Mary Howitt had a chemist's shop, and in their parlour here Philip James Bailey read Festus to them, and a greater than all came to see them, William Wordsworth himself.

Hereabouts, at the bottom of Park Row, leading toward the General Hospital and the castle, is a shop with two ornamental windows which attract the eye of the passer-by. They are perhaps the only windows that are left of the Houses of Parliament burned down at the beginning of the Victorian Era. Leading to the hospital yard from Postern Street is a beautiful archway of weathered timber, made from four spandrels of the 14th century roof of Alfreton church. In a café in Wheeler Gate is a magnificent plaster ceiling moulded with fruit and flowers 300 years ago. The Walter Fountain in Carrington Street near here is a reminder that one of The Times proprietors was MP for Nottingham. In Bridlesmith Gate, one of the oldest streets in the heart of the town, are timber-framed shops with overhanging storeys, stone floors, and massive beams, and with caves behind them extending under neighbouring streets. Facing the castle from Castle Road is a group of modest 17th and 18th century dwellings with gabled roofs, and by them, partly hidden from the road, are the pleasant Jessamine cottages. But older than all these interesting things is the stone window built into the wall of an archway in the lace market. It is in Broadway, and as the window was made by Norman masons it is thought that it belonged to the Norman church which stood where St Mary's stands, close by.

One or two ancient inns remain in the city. The Trip to Jerusalem Inn is said to have been a calling-place for crusaders on their way to the Holy Land; it has rooms and cellars cut deep back into the castle rock, ventilating shafts climbing through the rock, a speaking tube bored through it, and a chimney climbing through the rock 47 feet above the chamber in which it begins. The Salutation Inn in Houndsgate, close by, has rock cellars which are believed to have been part of a Saxon cave settlement, and the inn itself has an over-hanging gabled storey, with a painted sign of two clasped hands, representing Gabriel bringing the good news to Mary. It is nearly all 15th century. There are rock cellars in the Lion Hotel in Clumber Street, an old coaching inn; and another coaching inn, which has been delightfully restored, is the Flying Horse in the Poultry, its gabled front a pleasant vista from the arcade of the Council House. In the castle museum is an old chair in which the night porter of the Flying Horse used to sit.

In the ancient little graveyard called Fox's Close, at the meeting of St Ann's Well Road in Bath Street, lies a man whose name was once known far and wide. He was born William Thompson, he grew up to be the famous pugilist Bendigo, and he has been made familiar by Sir Conan Doyle as the Pride of Nottingham. His resting-place is typical of the old fighter, who was converted and became a popular preacher, and on occasion borrowed five minutes from the Lord that he might deal in his own way with the troublesome front row of the congregation:

> But the roughs they kept on chaffin' and the uproar it was such
> That the preacher in the pulpit might be talking double Dutch,
> Till a working man he shouted out, a-jumpin' to his feet,
> "Give us a lead, your reverence, and heave 'em in the street."

> Then Bendy said, "Good Lord, since I first left my sinful ways,
> Thou knowest that to Thee alone I've given up my days,
> But now, dear Lord" (and here he laid his Bible on the shelf)
> "I'll take with your permission just five minutes for myself."

On Bendy's tomb of rough grey stone crouches a fine lion as if about to spring, and the inscription runs:

> In life always brave, fighting like a lion,
> In death like a lamb, tranquil in Zion.

Nottingham has drawn within itself villages which the last generation knew as separate and distinct: Arnold, Basford, Beeston, Bestwood, Bilborough, Bulwell, Carlton, Colwick, Daybrook, Lenton, and Wollaton. Most of them are completely in the city, and some partly, and some of them have enough village character left to belong to the countryside still. Others are as much a part of the city's life as the crowded district of Sneinton, where William Booth and Jesse Boot began their work.

Sneinton is within easy reach of the City Centre, near the bottom of Hockley, and it has two modern churches worth coming to see. St Stephen's is spacious and pleasing, with a central tower and lofty arches, a barrel roof to the nave, and good oak screens. The reredos in the chancel has canopied scenes in the Life of Our Lord. The oak reredos in the south transept chapel has canopied statues of the Madonna, Isaiah, and John the Baptist. The treasure here lies in the medieval seats in the chancel, which were cast out of St Mary's last century; the panelling on the walls has a cresting of shields and Tudor flower, and spandrels carved with two snarling dragons, grotesque heads with foliage coming from their mouths, a mermaid with her comb and mirror, and a quaint animal. In the rich carvings of eight of the miserere seats are heads, an animal with another animal on its back, a quaint creature like an ass, a chained monkey holding a pitcher, and an animal blowing a horn as it rides on a hound. The poppyheads have foliage and faces, human and grotesque. Tucked away in drab surroundings, a stone's throw from the turmoil of Sneinton market, is St Alban's Church of 1887. Inconspicuous outside with its brick walls and modest turret for one bell, its fine stone interior is all the more surprising and arresting in its spaciousness and stately height. It has fine arcades, pleasing glass, and a lofty oak screen.

In St Stephen's churchyard, east of the chancel, lies a little-known mathematical genius who inspired Lord Kelvin. He was George Green. On the flat stone marking his grave (with inscriptions to his parents and his son as well as his own) we found a wreath from the British Association, which had lately organised a pilgrimage to his grave and his old home. He was born at Sneinton Mill, a landmark at the top of a steep climb not far from his resting-place, its old red brick cone wearing a copper domed cap, its sails gone. On it a tablet tells of this man, who would climb to the top storey of the mill (when he could spare time from helping his father to grind corn) to study the scientific problems on which he was to throw so much light. He would see the wonderful panorama which rewards all who climb this hill.

The busy suburb of Basford has its old church dedicated to the little-known St Leodigarius, and the church has still Norman masonry in its walls, 13th century work in the chancel, the nave arcades, the font and the south doorway, and 15th century work in the south aisle and the south porch. The porch has a gallery of medieval heads. The west window with the Good Shepherd and the Light of the World is in memory of Henry Roger Pitman, who was vicar here for the whole of the second half of last century and two years of this. Built into the wall by the south doorway is an ancient Pax stone, which had some significance long ago in connection with the Apostolic injunction, "To greet one another with a holy kiss." Near the porch is the stone tomb of Henry Ward who is said to have died at 108, and close by the church is an old brick manor house in which Philip James Bailey lived.

Bulwell lost its old church when the new one was built last century, but it keeps its old 17th century grammar school founded by George Strelley, who wished that the pupils might be "used mildly and taught Latin and accounts." It is no longer a school, but has been taken over by the Association for Unemployed Workers as a recreation centre. Its diapered brick walls are among the oldest in this part of Nottingham and the building has curved gables and a two-storeyed porch.

Daybrook, on the fringe of the city, has built two fine things for all to see who pass along this busy stretch of the old North Road. Side by side, both of our own day, they are tributes in stone to the love of a man for his wife and the love of a father for his son.

One is the splendid block of almshouses with lawns and flowers and a fine gateway, given in memory of his son by Sir John Robinson. The other is the church, whose beauty has only to gain with the mellowing of time. Its great tower, with fine windows, pinnacles, and a lofty spire, stands at a corner and forms a south porch with a vaulted roof. The great west window is between buttresses adorned with figures in canopied niches, and above it is an array of eight more handsome niches.

Attractive as it is outside the church is equally so within, where arcades of four bays divide the nave and aisles. It is so spacious and lofty that 15 windows glowing with countless figures do not rob it of light. The great east window of seven lights has nearly 70 figures; and shining in the west are the twelve Disciples. The only plain glass is in the clerestory. A charming feature of the church is the stone, which seems to burst into life in a wonderful mass of carving—in the alabaster reredos with its vivid scene of the Last Supper, in the three sedilia and the piscina, in the pulpit with figures all round, and in the font, which has on its seven sides figures of Faith, Hope, Charity, Courage, Truth, Purity, and Industry.

Delicately beautiful is the ironwork on each side of the chancel, and on the gated chancel screen. The floor of the chancel is Italian mosaic in soft colours of cream and green and rose; but loveliest of all is Sir Thomas Brock's marble figure of a beautiful woman in the sanctuary, a gentle smile on her lips, and a lily beneath her folded hands. Her head is on an embroidered cushion, and a light wrap draped over her hair is knotted on her breast. We read that she was gentle and good, the friend and counsellor and delight of all who knew her. It is fitting that we should find her here, for she inspired the beauty all about her. She was the wife of Colonel Charles Seely and mother of Lord Mottistone; and the church, built by Mr J. L. Pearson RA, architect of Truro Cathedral, is her memorial. Colonel Seely was MP for Nottingham and gave £100,000 to its hospital.

The bringing of part of Bestwood Park into the city added to Nottingham more than a thousand acres, though the heart of the city is six miles from the Park. Charles the Second gave this estate to Nell Gwynn's son Charles Beauclerk, whom he made the first Duke of St Albans when Nell Gwynn threatened to throw the brat out of the window. The tenth duke built Bestwood Lodge last century, making it a handsome brick house with gables, and he also built the church in which he lies.

The Queen of the Midlands, by bringing more than 5000 acres into her area in 1932, increased her kingdom to 16,166 acres. She is the 12th great town in the provinces, and is making herself in every sense worthy of her central place in the industrial, commercial, and intellectual life of the nation.

The King With His Jewelled Belt

NUTHALL. It has lost a great house like an Italian villa, but has kept a yew tree venerable enough to have seen most of the happenings in this place, growing fast along a busy highway. The tree may be nearly as old as the church, by which it spreads its shapely arms in a garden of flowers and firs and evergreens, the gateway shaded by magnificent beeches. The sturdy tower was made new in the 18th century, except for its base which is mainly 12th century and the oldest part of the church, its pointed arch of a little later time resting on the original sides.

Like most of the old stonework, the lovely doorway letting us in (adorned with medallions and heads of a king and a queen) comes from the end of the 14th century, the time of the nave arcade and the windows with flowing tracery. The 15th century east window has old glass showing the Crucifixion and heraldic shields; other windows have old shields and fragments. The medieval chancel screen (with modern gates), and the old part of the screen hiding the organ, enclosed the east end of the aisle till half a century ago.

On a floorstone of 1558 are the engraved portraits of Edward Boun, his wife, and five children. A rector's stone has a cross, a book, and a chalice, and fragments of other coffin stones are in the wall outside. In a founder's recess in the aisle lies the alabaster figure of Sir Robert Cokefield, a 14th century lord of the manor. He wears plate armour and a jewelled sword-belt; his head is on a crested helmet, a lion is at his feet, and his hands are at prayer. His family were lords of Nuthall for about 200 years; he may have known the old yew when it was young.

The Wonderful Beeches

OLLERTON. New roads and a colliery are making their mark on this old village, but it still stands at the doorstep of the Dukeries and Robin Hood's Forest, and it has one of the finest natural monuments in England. The village is on the bank of the little River Maun, near its meeting with the Rainworth Water which has come a lovely journey through Rufford Park.

Where the road sets off to Bawtry, and the great stretch of Bilhagh begins, are the famous Ollerton Beeches, a superb bit of Sherwood Forest. It is like a nave and aisles not made with hands, the trees growing 50 feet apart, some with branches about 200 feet round. It was meant, we understand, to be the entrance to Thoresby, one of the three great houses of the Dukeries, but has come to have a glory of its own. We walked over a brown carpet of about 180,000 square feet, and we have seen few sights more impressive than these hundred giants so ancient and so still. From their dim twilight, their brown carpet, and their majestic trunks, we step into the loveliness and light of a thousand silver birches rising from a green carpet of ferns. On the brown carpet we look up to a roof like cathedral vaulting; on this green carpet it seemed to us, as once it seemed to Tom Hood, that birches with their slender tops were close against the sky.

Older than anything else in the village are the red bricks of the mill at the little bridge, by which is a garden of shrubs on an island made by the river as it turns the mill wheel; it is the Island of Remembrance, with a plain grey cross to 16 men who never came back.

It is sad that where Nature is so rich the church is so poor. It was made new in the 18th century, and has little except a stoutly bound oak chest with three tremendous old padlocks, and a modern screen made from the oaks of Sherwood Forest. There is a stone here to Thomas Markham who came home from battle in the Civil War to die in the Elizabethan house his father built where Ollerton Hall stands now. Thomas was the last of the men of this line of a famous Notts family.

One little story we heard which we shall not forget. In the ivy which was growing thickly round the dooway of the old inn when we called a rare spider lived for years. It lived and grew fat on thousands of flies, and it would allow itself to be seen without fear when it was the size of a small walnut. It was one of the minor sights of Ollerton until one day its friend the innkeeper, who had watched it for four years, showed it to a lady staying at the inn. It was the end of the Ollerton spider, for a little while afterwards the lady was seen to probe into the ivy, dash the spider to the ground, and crush it with her foot. Such things will some people do.

A Prime Minister's Window

ORDSALL. Straggling along a bank of the River Idle, Ordsall belongs to East Retford, but is old enough to have come into Domesday Book and has remains of three medieval centuries in its much restored church.

The two lower stages of the lofty tower are 14th century, with a modern west window; the two others, with a crown of battlements and pinnacles, are 15th. The 14th century nave arcades have a little

13th century work in a pillar with slender shafts, two half-pillars, and some ornament. The only old windows, apart from the tower, are two of the 15th century in the chancel, one showing Paulinus with the model of a cathedral, Mary with a book and lilies, and Hugh of Lincoln with a swan at his feet. The other, glowing richly with a scene of the marriage feast at Cana, was given by Sir John Hall, Prime Minister of New Zealand, in memory of Joseph and Catherine Hall who were married in this church in 1696, a century before the first Englishman set foot on the great southern island.

The massive oak screen across the tower arch comes from the close of the 15th century, but has been spoiled. A treasure of the church is a chalice of 1517. The bowl of an ancient font lies in the church-yard, near the base-stone of an old cross.

In a canopied wall monument a man kneels at a desk on which is an open book. He has short hair and a beard, wears rich Eliza-bethan dress and a ruff, and is thought to be Anthony Bevercotes of 1612. It is recorded that during the Commonwealth Marmaduke Moore was turned out of the living here for playing cards with his wife, and also that he lost his estate through treason.

The Lady of Long Ago

ORSTON. If we come from the hilltop we look down on its red roofs nestling in the trees. The low road, shaded by trees, brings us over two bridges, spanning the River Smite and a brook. The prettiest corner is by the stone church.

Made partly new, with a tower in the classical style of the 18th century, the church is charming inside with a clerestoried nave and wide aisles, many big medieval windows with tracery varied and beautiful, and lancets in the 13th century chancel which has its old piscina and a priest's doorway.

Except for two 13th century round pillars on the north side, the nave arcades are 600 years old. Much of the nave roof, with its bosses, is 500 years old, and fine timbering a hundred years older still is over two bays on the north aisle. There is a Tudor chest. The font of 1662 has winged heads of three cherubs, a nosegay of flowers, and three tulips in a pot set in the middle of a flower, per-haps representing the Trinity.

A lady who must have been very beautiful six centuries ago

lies here asleep, carved in stone. Her curly head rests on a cushion sheltered by a canopy, and in her folded hands she holds a heart. She was Margaret de Ros, daughter and heiress of Giles de Badlesmere.

The Ship of Good Fortune

OSSINGTON. The world seems far away in this delightful spot at the end of a charming ride from Kneesall. Its lanes are leafy glades; its few dwellings are trim with red walls and roofs. Not far from a group of stately larches, sheltering a bronze crucifix to men who died for peace, a fine lime avenue leads to the church and the gates of Ossington Hall.

From the road to Moorhouse we have a splendid view of the modern hall in its park, beyond a sheet of water formed by a stream flowing to the Trent. The house stands where stood an older dwelling destroyed in the Civil War. It was the home of the Cartwrights, who in 1780 sold the manor to William Denison, a wealthy wool merchant who rebuilt the church, setting it so close to the hall that we have a peep of its grounds from the churchyard.

Built in classical style, with a domed tower to which a Speaker of the House of Commons gave a clock, the church has rich glass filling its round-headed windows, and is interesting for monuments of Cartwrights and Denisons. Older than any of these are two brass portraits on a great tomb, one showing Reynold Peckham of Wrotham in Kent (who died in 1551) as a knight in armour, and the other his wife in a long gown and embroidered headdress. On a huge stone monument of 1602, adorned with arms, are William Cartwright (in armour) and his wife, both wearing ruffs. Under the projecting table on which they kneel are lifelike figures of six sons and six daughters, most of them holding books, and two of the girls with skulls. They are charming.

Very fine are two statues by Nollekens of William Denison and his brother Robert, both in dress of their day. It was an ill wind for Lisbon that blew William's ship to good fortune in 1755, for it is said he owed much of his wealth to the fact that one of his ships arrived there after the city had been nearly destroyed by an earthquake. Carved at the foot of his monument is a scene of the ship unloading in Lisbon harbour; a group of men on shore have bales of merchandise, and in one corner sheep are grazing.

John Evelyn Denison, first Viscount Ossington and Speaker of Parliament, has a memorial of stone and coloured marble. He was one of a family of 14 children, of whom many won distinction. A beautiful plaque has the head and shoulders of W. F. Evelyn Denison in his soldier's uniform; he died from wounds received in the Great War, and his khaki hat is in the chancel. The handsome panels of the oak pulpit were carved by Lady Elinor Denison, lady of the manor.

Colonel Hutchinson's Last Home

OWTHORPE. Remote in a hollow of the Wolds, with the beautiful Vale of Belvoir like a fairy frontier, it is a home of quiet which has echoed to the ring of hoofs and the tramp of marching soldiers, the setting of events enshrined in an immortal story of Stuart England. It has only a few cottages and farms, and an odd little church made almost new; its great house is gone, but there are still trees here planted three centuries ago by a man who sleeps in the church and sheds a lasting lustre on the scene.

We can still picture it as it was when generations of Hutchinsons lived here, when Colonel John Hutchinson, the Puritan Governor of Nottingham who kept open the way from north to south for the Commonwealth, brought here his young wife Lucy, who was to enrich literature with her delightful Memoirs. The bride was loth to come to the place she grew to love, for the north, she wrote, "was a formidable name among the London ladies," and she was a Londoner indeed, born in the Tower itself, where her father, Sir Allen Apsley, was governor, and a good friend to his prisoner Raleigh. It was Lucy's mother who paid for Sir Walter Raleigh's chemical experiments.

Here Hutchinson and Lucy wandered in the happy days before the Civil War, guardians of the poor. Up at the big house, while he was studying divinity and the problems which were soon to rend the nation asunder, she, versed in classical languages as well as in Greek and Hebrew, was translating Lucretius into verse.

The scene changes. War has come; he has prayed to God for guidance; has decided that justice is on the side of Parliament; and has gone to fight for his faith. A little troop of horse comes here stealthily by night to carry Lucy and the children through the Royalist lines to the safety of Nottingham Castle, where she is to be the

17th century Florence Nightingale, nursing and healing wounded Puritans and Cavaliers with equal tenderness.

Again and again Cavaliers come raiding and ravaging, and the old house is made a ruin. But the Civil War ends, and Colonel Hutchinson and his wife return to rebuild and restore in blissful peace. She tells us that "the colonel lived with all imaginable retiredness at home, and, because his active spirit could not be idle nor sordidly employed, took up his time in opening springs and planting trees and dressing his plantations. These were his recreations, wherein he relieved many poor labourers when they wanted work, which was a very comfortable charity to them and to their families. With these he entertained himself, giving them much encouragement in their honest labours, so that they were delighted to be employed by him."

Here still are some of his trees growing; here is the church in which he sleeps. They brought him here from Sandown Castle, where he died, in a hearse drawn by six horses in mourning, with a mourning coach and six horses to wait on it, having crossed England and returned after redeeming the body from an unworthy castle governor who held it to ransom, and fighting with broken heads through hostile villages.

So he came home, in peace at last, to lie with his kindred, and with the inscription (the bold indictment of his accusers and judges) that "he died after harsh and strict imprisonment without crime or accusation." On his memorial (which gives his death as in 1663 instead of 1664) are the lines believed to be written by his widow, from which we take these:

> *This monument doth not commemorate*
> *Vaine ayrie glorious titles, birth, and state ;*
> *But sacred is to free, illustrious grace,*
> *Conducting happily a mortal's race,*
> *To end in triumph over death and hell,*
> *When, like the prophet's cloake, the fraile flesh fell*
> *Forsaken as a dull impediment,*
> *Whilst love's swift fiery chariot climbed the ascent.*
> *Nor are the reliques lost, but only torn,*
> *To be made new, and in more lustre worn.*
> *Full of this joy he mounted, he lay downe,*
> *Threw off his ashes, and tooke up his crowne.*

The church is smaller now than then. In the middle of the 18th century it was rebuilt with the old stone, but part of the old north wall and some original windows are still here. The nave and chancel are under one roof supported by great beams and king-posts, and between them is an ugly painted screen. There is a fine Jacobean pulpit with a canopy, and the 15th century font has an embattled edge. The low west tower serves as a porch, and over the entrance is a finely carved medieval corbel with two angels holding a shield. A memorial to Colonel Richard Norton tells us that he entertained four kings of England at his house.

The Puritan Colonel

COLONEL HUTCHINSON was born at Nottingham in 1615, and passed from Cambridge University to the study of the law; but he preferred music and the arts, and followed no profession.

With all the graces of the age, he was a favourite in London Society, but his fine character preserved him from pitfalls, and at 23 his romantic love affair with Lucy Apsley ended in a marriage of unclouded happiness. He was, like his father, a member of the Long Parliament, but it was not without heart-searching that he denied the king's right to seize the county's store of gunpowder, and became Governor of Nottingham. There he played a heroic part, sustaining sieges and combating dissension in his own ranks, but remaining throughout triumphant. One of Charles Stuart's judges, he signed the death warrant.

He lived quietly here between the expulsion of the Long Parliament and its restoration six years later. He drifted apart from Cromwell, extended hospitality to oppressed Royalist relatives, and, becoming a member of the Convention which welcomed the return of Charles the Second, he was spared under the Act of Oblivion.

His enemies, however, falsely charged him with complicity in a petty plot, and in 1663 he was imprisoned in his wife's birthplace, the Tower of London, where he was subjected to cruelty and extortion. After six months he was transferred to certain death in a veritable pest-house, the ruinous and insanitary Sandown Castle, where he died.

When, following the Restoration, there was first a possibility of his falling prey to his foes, he had faltered, urged by his devoted wife to excuse his earlier actions, but on danger actually threatening him he longed to die with the victims of the cause for which he had fought; it is said that he submitted to his wife's pleadings and so saved his life. He lives rather as a serene character in literature than for his own courage in action.

Lucy Hutchinson's famous Memoirs were written for their children, to vindicate the memory of the husband she had idolised. The book is a unique record of the life of a happy Puritan family, a classic carrying to the ends of the earth the fame of this village that was their home, and of the Puritan squire whose figure, says John Richard Green, stands out from his wife's canvas with the tenderness of a portrait by Van Dyck. The manuscript (which is lost) lay unpublished for about 130 years, perhaps because it fell into Royalist hands; but since it was first published in 1806 it has had a high place among English biographies.

The Sherbrookes Through the Centuries

OXTON. There is an air of content in this old-world village, where the church and the houses line the road, great trees make arches of living green, and the lanes, with their gorse and bracken, remind us that Oxton lies on the fringe of the old Sherwood Forest. Round about are ancient earthworks, with Oldox Camp in a hollow of the hills. Its age is unknown, and it was used perhaps as a place of safety for women and children in times of danger.

The hall, a fine house refashioned last century, looks out on a broad stretch of parkland with a lake made by the damming of a stream which runs through a shady plantation; and not far away an ivied stone archway, and a flagged path shaded by a yew said to be over 600 years old, make a charming approach to the small restored church.

The squat 14th century tower has battlements a century younger, and 13th century buttresses strengthen the north side of the church where a doorway of the same time opens to the light interior with its benches and box-pews. Between the clerestoried nave and its aisles are 14th century arcades. The chancel of crazy stone has a fine Norman arch and Norman masonry in the wall close by, a beautiful 13th century lancet deeply splayed, and a 600-year-old east window with St George, St Nicholas, and a soldier at the foot of the Cross.

It is the peace memorial. The altar table is Elizabethan. In harmony with the rest of the church is the dark oak of the low chancel screen (with a quaint minstrel on each side of the entrance), and of the stalls with a Bible inscription carved round the top, all of our day.

Some of the possessions of Oxton have had their queer adventures. A rare relic is a Norman shaft piscina found in a wall in the village, and the 14th century font has been used as a pump trough. There is a 17th century font, and the round Norman bowl of a third is on the floor. In the nave lies a stone man in a long gown, who may have been a judge in the 14th century; his feet are on a dog, and two headless angels support his pillow.

There are many memorials of the Sherbrookes who have lived here for centuries and were succeeded on the death of the last of them in 1847 by their cousin Henry Porter Lowe, who took their name. His brother Robert Lowe became Lord Chancellor and was made Viscount Sherbrooke; their father Robert Lowe, lying in Oxton churchyard, was one of the originators of the Poor Law system, and a keen follower of hounds he comes in Philip Pierrepont's hunting song in this way:

> *Next little Bob Lowe, on his little brown mare,*
> *Comes nicking across with all possible care.*

In the chancel is a thrilling memory of the Great War, a wind-whipped flag which was the first to fly in Bagdad in 1917. It flew proudly at the mast-head of Henry Graham Sherbrooke's ship Tarantula during operations which resulted in the capture of Bagdad. Some of the treasures brought home by Commander Sherbrooke, DSO, are here under glass for us to see, a soldier-sailor's bag of souvenirs, including part of an inscribed brick from ancient Babylon. Another great soldier of the family was Sir John Coape Sherbrooke, who has been sleeping here since he died in 1830. He served in the Netherlands and the Mysore War, and was Governor-General of Canada in 1816.

Behind the wall, where the road goes to Southwell, is a stone tomb hobnobbing with the sheds of a farmyard. Under it lies Robert Sherbrooke who seems to have been an early nonconformist.

The Lord Treasurer

PAPPLEWICK. Here kings hunted when it was all wild forest, and every boy will tell you that here Robin Hood stabled his horses in a cave cut in the solid rock, now guarded by a gaunt old oak. The place is older still, for its name tells us that it was the home of a Saxon chieftain. Today it is delightful with pretty lanes and bright gardens, plantations, and a babbling brook.

The great house was planned by the Adam brothers for Frederick Montagu, Lord of the Treasury, who sleeps in this country churchyard under an unusual tomb like a stone table resting on six legs. In this charming forest-like retreat is a splendid old yew 14 feet round the trunk, its branches covering a patch of ground about 60 yards round. From here we see Papplewick Dam below the church, a sheet of water reminding us of the days when the little River Leen was busy working cotton mills.

The Lord Treasurer, who sought to abolish the fast day for King Charles 90 years before it was in fact abolished, and who helped to prepare the impeachment of Warren Hastings, loved nothing better than his home in this village where he lived about 13 years, making plantations and giving them names of commanders famous in the naval victories of the time. He was a great friend of authors and poets, among them Thomas Gray and William Mason, Mason writing part of his English Garden here.

Except for its 14th century tower, Montagu rebuilt the odd little church in the style of his day, and his initials are on the porch. There is a memorial to his father, Charles Montagu, and one to Lady Culladon, wife of Queen Anne's physician, whose daughter Charles married.

Over the doorway into the church is a small figure of St James with his pilgrim's staff; he is at any rate as old as Norman. The shallow battered bowl of the font, thought by some to be Saxon, was restored to the church a few years ago from the churchyard. Other interesting relics are a number of coffin stones showing the occupations of the men they commemorate. One in the nave floor has the bow and arrow, the belt and hunting horn of the forester; and another has a cross and billhook. Two in the porch are rare for having a pair of bellows, the symbol of the ironworker. They are perhaps 700 years old, and are believed to have marked the graves of officials who had charge of the mill erected by the monks of Newstead on the outskirts of Bulwell, which was used as a forest smithy. Known as the Forge Mill, this stone mill was still grinding corn in 1938.

Fragments of 15th century glass have figures of Peter and Stephen, a knight kneeling at a desk, and a procession of monks. Lovely figures of Faith and Hope in the east window are copied from Sir Joshua Reynolds's picture in a window of New College Chapel, Oxford. The squire's pew still has its old fireplace, and the story is told how Squire Walter, a proprietor of The Times who lived at Papplewick Hall for about 30 years, used to poke the fire noisily when he had had enough of the sermon.

The Forest Oaks

PERLETHORPE. It stands on the edge of Thoresby Park, where the glorious oaks and beeches make a wonderful setting for the fine modern house of Earl Manvers.

Just inside the park gates, a peace memorial lychgate carved with vines opens to a beautiful churchyard rich with shrubs and noble trees, two of them magnificent beeches and two splendid yews. We may wonder if any church has more natural beauty about it, and this church is worthy of it. It is not yet nearly a centenarian, having been built in 1876 by Earl Manvers. Its walls are adorned with battlements, pinnacles, and buttresses, corbel heads and gargoyles, and bands of quatrefoils; and rising to 128 feet from a lovely tower is a spire with two tiers of windows, like a needle in the sky seen from far around.

It is lovely inside and full of light, and in its enrichment the oaks of the Forest have a place, for the lovely stalls, the benches, and the pulpit have been shaped and carved from them by masters of their craft. The pulpit has a stone and marble base with handsome foliage capitals crowning the pillars. The bench-ends have exquisite carving of fruit, and medallions in which we found a bird on her nest, a pomegranate, a water-lily, and a passion flower. The stalls have a fine array of 16 crouching animals, and there is a fine door to the tower.

There is rich stone carving in the corbel heads of bearded men on the nave arcades, and in their foliage capitals; in the splendid font on pillars of coloured marble; and in the reredos, showing the Good Shepherd and the Four Evangelists. The Te Deum east window, with figures of St Martin, St John, St James, and St Margaret, is in memory of the 3rd Earl Manvers who built the church; he died in 1900. The 4th Earl has a small white monument with a figure of St George and the Dragon in a wreath of flowers, daintily carved and delicately coloured. A picture of St Peter's Denial hanging in the chancel is said to be by Benjamin West.

A rare treasure of the village is its register, for it is one of only three now known to go so far back as 1528. It is curious that one of the other two should be only three miles away at Carburton, the third being at Elsworth in Cambridgeshire.

Thoresby House in the deer park was built last century, a quarter of a mile from the site of the house where Lady Mary Montagu was born and where she spent much of her girlhood. Formed in 1683 with 2000 acres, the park is a world of its own, over 12 miles round, with a beautiful lake of 65 acres, filled by the River Meden. It is a magnificent fragment of the old Sherwood Forest.

Marvellous Mary Montagu

LADY MARY MONTAGU, born in this great park when it was new, was a queen among the wits and poets of 18th century England. Her father was the Duke of Kingston, and being left motherless at five she grew up in her father's library, a student, beautiful, and witty.

At 23 she defied her father by marrying Edward Wortley Montagu, with whom she went to Turkey, where she wrote the brilliant letters on which her fame rests. Adopting Turkish costume, she studied Turkish, and was the first to present in modern language and with modern ideas a picture of a land then veiled in mystery.

Next in importance to her letters was her introduction into England from the East of inoculation for smallpox, a fact recorded on her cenotaph in Lichfield Cathedral. For 20 years after her return to England she was a neighbour of Pope at Twickenham, but, her friendship with the poet ending in a quarrel, he savagely satirised her under the name of Sappho.

In 1739, her daughter having eloped with Lord Bute, and her millionaire husband being generally absent from her, she left England and did not return until after his death, living a strange and lonely life for 22 years in various parts of Italy. She reached England again in 1761, with spirit undimmed, but stricken with a fatal disease, and, dying a year later, was laid to rest in London.

The Old Bridge in the Church Walls

PLUMTREE. With its charming neighbour Normanton, this trim and pleasant village is on the edge of the Wolds, the busy road now passing them by. At one end is the white-walled smithy with its huge black horseshoe; at the other is the church, with part of Nottingham's old Trent Bridge and some Saxon masonry in its walls.

The churchyard is a garden, with great trees overhanging the road, and from its gate we have an impressive view of the massive tower; it is the finest part of the church, and has the oldest work, for in its Norman base is the Saxon walling which came to light when the tower was refashioned early this century. Its recessed Norman doorway has roll moulding in the arch resting on capitals which have lost their shafts; outside it there is a simple arch of radiating stones, and within it a later doorway has been built. Two round arches are blocked in its south wall, its buttresses are 13th century, and the top storey is a century later.

The stone of Old Trent Bridge supplied the fresh material needed in the restoration last century, when the porch was made new, most of the window tracery renewed, and the north aisle given a new arcade. The south arcade comes from the close of the 13th century. The nave has a 15th century clerestory, and is adorned with four crude gargoyle heads with hands in the mouths. Three lovely sedilia, their canopies enriched with pinnacles and finials, are much restored.

Though bright now with electricity, the old iron candelabra still hang in their places. There are some old timbers in the flat roofs, which are painted in medieval colours with gold stars. The best effect of the interior is seen from the dim chancel, the light walls contrasting with the dark wood, and a Norman arch leading to the tower.

Napoleon on Fire

RADCLIFFE-ON-TRENT. It has grown round a road all twists and turns. High up on the ridge of fine cliffs, and of woods overhanging beautiful reaches of the river, is a charming garden where the memory of the men who died for peace is kept green by the fragrance of flowers, the beauty of trees, and the song of birds. It was the gift of the father of one of them, and his own ashes have been scattered here.

The roomy church, with many arches and a saddleback tower over 100 feet high, is not yet nearly a centenarian. One relic of the old church it replaced is a brass engraved with the figure of a lady wearing a ruff and a long veil as she kneels at a desk; she was Anne Ballard who died in 1626, and her epitaph runs:

> Ask how she lived and thou shalt know her end,
> She died a saint to God, to the poor a friend.

An inscription to Stephen de Radcliffe of 1245 brings to mind the story of his oak figure, which lay in a recess of the old church. It is said that the villagers, in their great excitement at one of the victories over the French, fetched Stephen from the church, dressed him up to represent Napoleon, and committed him to the flames.

Next Door to Lincolnshire

RAGNALL. The Trent divides from Lincolnshire this small place looking from a gentle slope to the low hills across the valley. Its neat stone church, much restored, nestles among great trees—yews and sycamores, a splendid walnut, and an ash topping the embattled tower.

There are pleasing windows of the 14th and 15th century still here, and in the little gallery of sculptures adorning them are a woman in a wimple, a praying angel, a knight with a shield, and the bust of a lady in a headdress. The font has roses in quatrefoils. One of two elaborate 17th century wall monuments is to William Reason; the other is to William Mellish, a London merchant who was brought to this village to lie with his wife.

Families of Fame

RAMPTON. Over a mile from the Trent, beyond which is Lincolnshire, are its cheery red houses with bright pantile roofs, the old church with something of Saxon England, and the lovely old gateway reminding us that families famous in the county made this village their home. De Ramptons, Malovels, Stanhopes, Babingtons, Eyres—all have been here.

Nothing is left of the old hall to which the Eyres came in the 17th century, built in the time of Henry the Eighth and pulled down two centuries later when they went to live at Grove. But its fine Tudor gateway, adorned with the Stanhope and Babington arms, still stands at a corner of the churchyard. A 19th century gateway in similar style stands by the wayside, and from it a long avenue leads to the house they built when they came back to the village in the middle of last century. Here, too, the glory is gone; we found the house being turned into flats, and the grounds becoming a wilderness.

Fine limes and chestnuts and a great oak are about the church. Its high tower, looking all the taller for having no buttresses, is 14th century except for its west window, which is 15th, and under its battlements are ballflowers. The medieval porch has two charming windows, a sundial, and two worn figures said to represent an angel carrying a soul to paradise and a demon bearing away a soul lost. The old doorway into the church has heads of a king and queen.

The church's most venerable possession is a strangely crude piscina, a tiny recess formed by overlapping courses of the walling; it is in the north aisle, and is thought to be Saxon. A massive square pillar in this aisle, and some masonry in its north wall, are also believed to be Saxon. This ancient walling was taken from the original north wall of the church when it was pierced by the north arcade about 1290; the south arcade is a century later.

The bowl of the font is Norman, its splendid arcading re-worked at a later time, and it rests on a 15th century pedestal. There are two medieval piscinas, and the south aisle has a tiny peephole to the altar. A pillar almsbox may be 15th century, and the altar table in a chapel is Elizabethan, with a strip of the old chancel screen fixed on to it. The present screen is modern, with beautiful carving of roses, vine, and thistle, and gilded medallions with emblems. A shrine made of timber from HMS Britannia has the names of those who served in the war, and in memory of those who died the east window glows richly with the Crucifixion and figures of St George and St Nicholas. The only other colour in the old windows is the charming glass in memory of Inez Ellis, painted in 1924 by her artist friend; it shows Mary and Jesus, and two kneeling angel children with red, yellow, and gold wings, one with a bunch of lilies, the other with head bowed in prayer.

The chancel walls are lined with memorials of the Eyres, a soldier race who came here when Sir Gervase married the heiress of the Babingtons. He died at his post in the Civil War, defending Newark for Charles, and here he sleeps. We read of him on a monument to Gervase Eyre of 1703, elaborate with urns, cherubs, and heraldry.

Three inscriptions are to three generations; Admiral Sir George Eyre of 1839 who served in the French wars, Sir William Eyre who fought in the Crimea, and Anthony Hardolph Eyre, an only son killed in the Ashanti War. A small brass tablet, held by a child angel, is in memory of the wife of one of the Eyres.

Two floorstones with crosses may be 15th century, and over a doorway outside is a stone medallion to Jacobus Twist, a vicar of Shakespeare's day.

Four Stone Knights and their Ladies

RATCLIFFE-ON-SOAR. A lane winding with the river brings us to its neat cottages with hooded windows, and a brook flows under the road which ends at the church and the old manor house, now a farm. The churchyard is filled with the murmur of running water, and from a great ash tree we catch a glimpse of the river leaping the weir, and of Red Hill where it falls into the Trent.

It has a church in Domesday Book, but much of the church we see is 13th century. Its glory is in splendid tombs, in bright light streaming through medieval windows, and in the feeling of simplicity and age which restoration has not disturbed. Time seems to have stood still within these grey walls.

The tower is from the end of the 12th century, and the 13th century spire springs from a corbel table with corner pinnacles which are miniatures of the spire itself. The spacious chancel is remarkable for being longer than the nave; some of its walling and part of the south aisle is also 13th century. From the 14th come the porch with its old roof timbers, the doorway and the lovely windows of the south aisle, the arch and east window of the chancel, and the nave arcades. The chancel has its old sedilia and piscina and a founder's recess. The 600-year-old font bowl has a cover of about 1660. The medieval stone altar is still in use, and there is an unused Jacobean altar table. The altar rails are 17th century, and splendid old beams are left in the nave and chancel roofs.

The battered but still magnificent tombs of the Sacheverells are remarkable for the beauty of their detail. They are of four generations, and bring to an end the Ratcliffe branch of this famous family. On a handsome tomb with an elaborate canopy lies Ralph Sacheverell of 1539 and his first wife Cecilia, he in plate armour and SS collar, his head on a helmet and his feet on a lion; she wearing a cape, a lovely headdress, and round her neck a triple chain with a cross. On a splendid tomb between the chancel and the chapel, with figures of their 17 children, Sir Henry Sacheverell of 1558 lies with his wife, who wears a close-fitting gown with puffed sleeves, a cap, and a triple chain. Henry has tiny ruffs with his plate armour, and a double chain with a cross. His bearded head rests on a helmet with the crest of a goat, and his gauntlets are at his side.

Under the adjoining arch lies the next Henry Sacheverell with his wife, both in ruffs, with their six children carved on the side of the tomb. Henry's head is on a helmet and his gauntlets are at his feet; and his lady has a bit of lovely lace at the top of her gown. We see the last of them, Henry Sacheverell of 1625, lying in armour on the tomb of a monument in the chancel. Under the canopy above him kneel his three wives, their dress showing how fashion changed in the early part of the 17th century. On a panel are a son and two daughters. One of the daughters was grandmother of little Anne Columbell, who died when she was 15; her floorstone is in the chancel. A stone with the portrait of a priest of 1497 perhaps belongs to John Prescott; another shows Isabel, the wife of Sir John Babington.

St Peter in the Rushes

REMPSTONE. It lies at the end of a lovely road from Hathern, where we have magnificent views of the widespread countryside. Its name is its distinction, for here lived generations of the Rempstones, and here was born that Sir Thomas who helped to put Henry the Fourth on the throne; he lives in Shakespeare, and sleeps with his soldier son in the church at Bingham.

The plain but neat little church has a gallery adorned with carved panels, a beautiful peace memorial of bronze and alabaster, and a richly engraved brass plate in the floor to the Davys family; on it is mentioned George Davys, the Bishop of Peterborough who was tutor to Queen Victoria. The church was built in 1771, much of the material coming from the ancient church which stood in the fields not far from the white-walled hall. Known as St Peter in the Rushes, the site of the lost church is marked by a number of old gravestones and the railed-in tomb of Robert Marsden, who was rector here for 46 years of the 18th century. His charity still keeps his memory green.

Where East Meets West

RETFORD. East and West Retford are joined by an iron bridge over the River Idle, the old market town having gained much in importance when the Great North Road was diverted to it in 1766.

There is an ever-burning light in the turret of a fine stone monument in the middle of the market square, set up in memory of the men who died for peace. On one side of the square is the 18th century town hall, proud of its historical portraits, and the fine regalia given for the most part in the 17th century. In front of it stands the Broad Stone, said to be perhaps the base of a cross which stood on a little hill called Dominie Cross, and believed to be one of four similar boundary stones in the neighbourhood.

The glory of the town is the church of St Swithun near the marketplace, built like a cross with a central tower; the lovely exterior is adorned with battlements, lofty pinnacles, and panelled buttresses, and a splendid clerestory adds dignity and charm to the nave and chancel. The pinnacles are a study in themselves, for their lowest crockets make a fine gallery of about 254 heads of human folk and animals, with faces young and old, pleasant and grotesque. Other faces are on the hoods of the windows, and there are grotesque gargoyles here and there. In an outside recess is a modern figure, seated and crowned, said to represent Henry the Third.

Founded in 1258 by Roger, Archbishop of York, the church is for the most part 15th century in style, but is much rebuilt and restored. The tower collapsed in 1651, destroying most of the chancel, and both were made new. Two centuries later the chancel was enlarged, the north aisle rebuilt, and all the exterior re-faced.

The tower, 90 feet high, has its old base with four 13th century arches, and the nave arcades are chiefly 13th and 14th century. Very lovely are their capitals, carved with flowers and foliage—bluebells, thistles, berries, oak and acorns. One has vine and grapes growing from the mouth of a grotesque face, and two little figures are leaning on the branches. The middle pillar of two lovely bays dividing the north chapel has exquisite foliage.

Two chantries on the north side of the church are now a peace memorial chapel, and here is a charming little oak screen delicately carved with vines, trailing roses, and figures of Our Lord and angels. Leaves and berries enrich the dainty iron gates.

Among a few old glass fragments are three heads of bishops, and a curiosity in a window of the same transept is a penny set in the glass. St Swithun (whose great statue is over the door inside the church) is a pleasing figure in a lancet. Two beautiful windows facing each other from the ends of the transepts are in memory of the Sherwood Rangers who fell in the Boer War and the Great War; one has ten fine saints, the other has Our Lord enthroned, saints singing, and figures representing Faith, Fortitude, Patience, and Obedience. A pleasant story we heard of two north-west windows, the gift of an old man who lived in an almshouse near the church, who loved nothing better than showing people round and with the money he received paid for these windows. He had little to call his, but he had a great heart.

Roses and quatrefoils and a happy little face peeping out of leaves are carved on the font, which has a pyramid cover. The roof beams of the nave and aisles rest on 25 stone angels, some with books and shields, others praying or playing instruments. Supporting the arch at the east end of the north aisle is a quaint jester, and a figure with a face half-veiled is holding up the corresponding arch of the south aisle.

The beauty of West Retford's church of St Michael is outside, in its churchyard of lawn, and in its tower and spire. A "poem in stone" Pugin is said to have called this spire, and certainly both it and the tower are a high tribute to their 14th century builders. The tower (which becomes eight-sided at the top) has fine windows, and buttresses ending above the battlements in four lofty pinnacles. From these spring flying buttresses, and from the top of these four more slender pinnacles rise. About 120 graceful leaf sprays climb to the tip of the elegant spire.

A stone-roofed porch leads to the dim interior, with a medieval south arcade, a 19th century north aisle, an elaborately carved cover to the modern font, and an alabaster reredos showing the Ascension, its sculptured figures painted red, blue, white and gold. An engraved floorstone comes from 1485, and in a niche on one of the old pillars is a fine modern figure of St Oswald.

Near the church is Holy Trinity Hospital, founded in the 17th century for 16 poor bachelors or widowers, and made new in 1833. It is a charming block with a chapel, in a setting of lawn and shrubs and trimmed yew hedges.

South of the town is the modern church of St Alban, a fine, spacious place with the fresh bloom of youth. The walls inside are of cream Bath stone, the nave arcades have clustered pillars, and the chancel is entered by a wide, lofty arch. Lancet windows light the aisles; the fine east and west windows and those of the clerestory are in 15th century style. Very beautiful is the Kempe glass filling the east window, with Our Lord enthroned and figures of Gabriel, Mary, St Hugo, and St Cecilia in a company of nine saints. So high is the chancel that this great window is not hampered by the splendid oak reredos below it.

Near this church is King Edward's Grammar School, new-built in 1854. The school shared in Scott's immortal expedition to the South Pole, for it gave the sledge drawn by the pony Michael.

Here in 1683 was born Samuel Wright, the notable Noncon- formist preacher of whom someone wrote:

> Behold how papal Wright with lofty pride
> Directs his haughty eye to either side,
> Gives forth his doctrine with imperious nod,
> And fraught with pride addresses e'en his God.

The Village of Little Kate Greenaway

ROLLESTON. It will be interesting to thousands who may not have heard of it, for here came a child who was to grow up to delight the hearts of a whole generation with her pictures of children. She was Kate Greenaway.

It was in this village that she spent a happy childhood and found an ideal background to her growing mind—country children, orchards aglow with blossom, the sights and sounds of the seasons. Here she drank in the spirit of Nature and grew up with her mind full of poetry and music and beauty. She studied children wherever she found them, and was able to exhibit her first pictures of them when she was only 22. She imagined an idealised childhood and dressed it in the costumes of her own devising, now familiar to us all. Who does not know her incomparable gowns and the poke bonnets of her little girls? She never grew stale, never overtaxed her skill or allowed her inspiration to grow dim. She illustrated poems and books and Christmas cards, and her pictures have gone all over the world, so that when she died at Hampstead, early in her fifties, her work was almost as well known in Germany and France as in England.

She was brought here, as young as the youngest child in her pictures, to stay with her great-aunt Mrs Wise; but it was in a little red brick house where the road sets off to Fiskerton that she spent many of her happiest days with her aunt's old servant, Mary Chappell, and her husband Thomas, whom Kate loved to paint in his smock and tall hat. It was to this cottage-farm that she came for holidays long after she went to live in London, for Kate Greenaway never forgot this village in the green meadows where the River Greet turns the old mill-wheel on its way to the Trent.

Beyond the Chappell's house is the farm where lived Mrs Neale, with whom Kate and Mrs Chappell used to go to Newark market. The child loved every minute of the time, going round with the butter and wondering why people bought groceries when they could afford peppermints. Still farther along, where two oaks make an arch over the road, we catch a glimpse of the Odd House, a farm with a background of woods. It was the home of Kate's Aunt Aldridge, who would sometimes take her to market in a high dog-cart, giving her dinner with the farmers and their wives at one of the inns.

By the smithy is the base of an old cross, and not far away is part of another in a field where remains of fishponds and a moat mark the site of the old manor house pulled down over a century ago. It was the home of the Nevilles, who were lords of Rolleston from the 13th century till the time of Elizabeth. Two stones carved with their arms carry the hinges of the door of one of the barns.

The church has something of Saxon England. There is early herringbone masonry in its walls, and fragments of Saxon crosses came to light in 1895. Three blocks carved with knotwork are believed to be parts of a shaft, and a smaller fragment built into the wall is remarkable for having the name of the maker of the cross in neatly cut Saxon capitals, and small letters which mean, *Radulf made me.*

The outer walls of the splendid tower have been faced with new stone, but the original work of the Normans is seen in its lower walling inside; the rest of the tower is 15th century. The Norman south doorway has been rebuilt stone by stone; on it is what may be a consecration cross, and a stone with remains of a sundial which may be Saxon. In a niche in an aisle is the fluted bowl of a Norman shaft piscina.

The chancel arch and the nave arcades with clustered pillars are 13th century. Among the medieval windows is an unusual one like a quatrefoil in each aisle, about 600 years old. There are two medieval coffin lids, and fragments of others are in a wall. The tiny font is 17th century, the chancel screen has a 15th century base and a new top, and the tower screen is the good work of a local craftsman of our day.

A rare treasure is a portion of the original paper register which was continued after the day of parchment registers had come. It has nearly 40 leaves stitched together, covering the years 1584 to 1615, and is full of quaint notes made by Robert Leband, a vicar who was drowned by falling from a bridge. His notes tell of current events, local gossip, the weather, the price of corn, and odd things about his flock. He had a good habit of sometimes putting unfavourable comments in Latin. We read that Joane Peele was "so singular a housewife as Rolston could not match." The good vicar must have known less noble types, for we read again that we must not trust a woman, even when she is dead.

A memorial of 1706 is to John Twentiman, a vicar who made interesting entries in the registers in beautiful handwriting.

The Deserted Graves

RUDDINGTON. Its three thousand people make it one of the biggest villages in Notts, busy for the most part with hosiery and lace. For half a century it has had a fine big church in place of a medieval one which had seen much change.

Imposing outside with battlements, roofs of green tiles, and a spire crowning a tower in which much of the older one survives, it is dignified inside, with a finely timbered roof looking down on the lofty nave arcades. There is rich carving of wood in the modern chancel screen, and of stone in the pinnacled sedilia. With the stained glass filling many of the windows are the Twelve Apostles in the south aisle. The face of the Good Samaritan in one window is that of a village doctor who died at the end of last century.

Between the village and Edwalton is a deserted graveyard with a few headstones, reminding us of the lost village of Flawforth which was once important enough for its church to be the mother church of both Ruddington and Edwalton. When the church fell into disuse its windows were used in the rebuilding of Ruddington chapel, and when it was finally pulled down in 1773 much of the material was used in making Ruddington's churchyard wall. Flawforth will not soon be forgotten, for three wonderful alabaster figures once in its church are preserved at Nottingham Castle.

One of the Saddest Figures in History

RUFFORD ABBEY. Two miles from Ollerton, it is a charming neighbour of the ducal homes of Notts, a piece of Tudor England with many additions which have only added to its beauty. Its fate, like that of many great English homes, is in the balance as we write, but it stands as a noble structure and its story lives on.

The story goes back to the middle of the 12th century, when Gilbert de Gaunt founded an abbey here. The vaulted refectory is now the servants' hall, almost all that is left of the ancient place which, at the Dissolution, was granted to the Earl of Shrewsbury. It was his daughter-in-law (Bess of Hardwick) who built the Elizabethan house, and it was the marriage of a grand-daughter that brought Rufford to the Saviles, with whom it remained till 1938.

Among its treasures are beautiful tapestries and fine portraits. One is Van Dyck's portrait of Lord Strafford, who stayed at the abbey when the Marquis of Halifax (one of the fickle ministers of James the Second) was a boy; Strafford wrote him letters on the follies of Court life. It was Lord Halifax who added the Stuart wing to the house, where his brother Henry, a famous diplomat, was born in 1642.

It was in the chapel here in 1574 that the Earl of Lennox married Elizabeth Cavendish, Bess of Hardwick's daughter, the only child of the marriage being Arabella Stuart, whose portrait hangs in the drawing-room.

One of the saddest figures in history, Arabella Stuart was born in 1575, daughter of the Earl of Lennox, brother of Lord Darnley, and was next in succession to the throne after James the First.

She was early the centre of plots to set her on the throne in place of Elizabeth who, though sometimes speaking of her as her successor, imprisoned her. At the accession of her cousin James, Arabella's partisans urged that she, being British born, had a better right to the throne. A plot at the time aimed at the deposition of James and the crowning of Arabella, who was entirely innocent of complicity. The only offence the luckless princess committed was (in 1610) in secretly marrying William Seymour, a descendant of the Tudors. She was 35, he 13 years younger, and they desired only to be left alone; but James, roused to jealous fears, sent Seymour to the Tower and banished Arabella to Durham. She escaped disguised as a man, took ship for France, while Seymour escaped from the Tower and followed in another ship. A storm kept the ships apart, and Arabella was captured off Calais and brought back to England.

Arabella languished for four years a prisoner in the Tower, guiltless of all crime. First her health, and next her reason failed, and in 1615 she died, a melancholy ruin. Her husband remained in France until after her death, when he returned to England, fought as a Royalist, and at the Restoration was made Duke of Somerset. Arabella lies in Westminster Abbey, in the tomb of her aunt, Mary Queen of Scots.

The gardens of the abbey, set in a deer park of over 500 acres with a lake (filled by Rainworth Water), are very beautiful. The house is seen at the head of a lime avenue leading from handsome entrance gates on the highway. In the park itself once stood a shelter in which William Mompesson lived when he came to Eakring as rector. Over three years had passed since he had seen his folk at Eyam die one by one from plague, refusing to leave the village lest they should spread it to the outer world; but the inhabitants were still fearful that the brave parson would bring the plague to them, and Mompesson took refuge in the park.

Enshrined in Trees

SAUNDBY. Three miles from Gainsborough and half as far from the Trent, it is charming with its few cottages and farms, its big house, and the church, all mantled in trees. Some of the finest trees grow in the churchyard, reached by way of the buildings and haystacks of the Manor Farm; one magnificent cedar has a trunk 16 feet round and branches making a circle of 80 yards, and another has lost the great arms which reached too near the chancel. They are worthy companions of a gracious church much rebuilt in the last half century.

The tower, with eight pinnacles, is 15th century; the nave arcade of two bays is 13th, and separated from it by seven feet of wall is a 700-year-old arch leading to the chapel. The beautiful font with a band of diamond pattern on the bowl comes from the close of Norman days, and a medieval piscina, elaborate with pinnacles and a finial, has a head carved on the projecting drain. The altar table is Elizabethan, and a Bible of 1611 has a leather cover with tiny flowers engraved on its metal bosses and clasp.

One of the windows has St Martin giving half of his cloak to a beggar at the gate of Amiens; in another he is asleep and dreaming, seeing in a vision Our Lord wearing the other half of the cloak. In a medley of old fragments in the tower are the small figure of a woman and the tiny face of a man. The screens, the roofs, and the door with splendid hinges letting us in, are good craftsmanship of our own day.

A battered stone knights of the 14th century lies in the nave, wearing armour and a helmet; his feet are gone, but the lion on which they rested is still here. There is a floorstone with a brass inscription to William Saundeby, who made the church new before he died in 1418, and a canopied monument is to John Helwys, lord of the manor till the end of the next century.

The Three Old Bells

SCARRINGTON. Trim houses and wayside lawns help to make this quiet village in green meadows. There is a fine stone dovecot in a farmyard, and the small dim church has a few things old and interesting.

Its striking feature is the 14th century tower with a spire lighted by two tiers of dormer windows. Its lofty west doorway is adorned with ballflowers and a string of four-leaved flowers. Still ringing in the tower are three bells believed to have been ringing before the Reformation.

Between the nave and aisle is a 14th century arcade of three wide arches on pillars with stone seats. A century older is the priest's doorway. There are three old tie-beams, a Jacobean coffin stool, and a small font made in 1662.

The Man Who Took Away the Bauble

S CREVETON. An old-world village untroubled by the bustle of the highways is this place of a few homes, though the Fosse Way where the Roman legions marched from Leicester to Newark is less than a mile away. It gave the county its famous historian in Robert Thoroton, and has something to remind us of another family who made a stir in their day, the Whalleys.

Not far from the church (but belonging to Car Colston) is Brunsell Hall, part of the fine 17th century house where lived Dr Brunsell, rector of Screveton during the Commonwealth. The timbered house near the rectory has remains of 400 years ago, and the rectory itself is partly on the site of Kirketon Hall, the old home of the Whalleys.

One of the Whalleys was physician to Henry the Seventh. Another was Richard, who won the admiration of Henry the Eighth by his grace and skill in military exercises; his remarkable monument is in Screveton Church. He also became notorious for the part he played in the destruction of the monasteries; and for his services in this business he received Welbeck Abbey, though he had to part with it to raise money for the fines imposed on him for sharing in the intrigues of Protector Somerset.

One of his descendants was the Edward Whalley whose mother was an aunt of Oliver Cromwell, and who was himself the only Roundhead in the Whalley family. It was he who carried away the Bauble when Cousin Oliver dissolved the Long Parliament, and he had charge of the King after his capture by Cornet Joyce at Holdenby House. After the Restoration he was stripped of his estates and he fled to America and died in exile after 14 years of hunted life.

Almost hidden from the road and reached by a long row of limes is the pretty church in a lovely churchyard. Much of it is 13th century, the time of the nave arcades; the sturdy 15th century tower was altered in the time of Elizabeth. Three relics of an earlier church are a loose fragment of Saxon knotwork (once part of a tomb), part of a Norman coffin stone engraved with a cross, and an exceptionally beautiful Norman font with interlaced arcading. The south aisle has a beautiful piscina, there are two Jacobean coffin stools, and a splendid 15th century chest nearly seven feet long is encircled by a score of iron bands. An old miserere in the chancel, carved to represent Winter, shows a man in a loose wrap warming himself at a fire; a later one has St Wilfrid. The arms of Charles the Second, carved in oak, are under the tower.

One of the finest monuments in the county is the magnificent tomb of Richard Whalley, which has been moved from the chancel to the tower. He has a long beard, and lies in armour with his head and his feet resting on whales. In the panels of its elaborate screen are the kneeling figures of his three wives, and small figures of their 25 children kneel behind their respective mothers. A quaint inscription tells of their father's virtues.

The Village that Launched the Mayflower

SCROOBY. All the world has heard of Scrooby, for it launched the Mayflower, though its little river is far from the sea. It was the home of William Brewster and the meeting-place of the old Fathers of New England.

It lies by the Great North Road, bounded by the River Ryton, which leaves the mill wheels quiet now, a happy hunting-ground for the children who play in the old mill race. On its way from the mill to the Idle the stream flows by the manor farm, known as Brewster's House, standing at the side of a hummocky field in which once stood a fine manor house of the Archbishops of York. The greatness that came to Scrooby, from early in the 13th century till its decline after four centuries, was enough to make it famous if the Pilgrim Fathers had never been, for it was the scene of much magnificence.

Here were seen the retinues of many a knight and squire. Margaret Tudor called here on her way to Scotland to be made a queen. Here Henry the Eighth held a Privy Council, and Cardinal Wolsey spent some months here on his last sad journey north. Archbishop Sandys, friend of Lady Jane Grey, often stayed here till his death in Armada year. The story of the Brewsters belongs to about this time; and so does the beginning of the end of the so-called Archbishop's Palace.

In its decline part of the old house or its outbuildings was used as a post-house and inn, and William Brewster the elder filled the important office of Post. His son William, who was to sail in the Mayflower, carried on the business.

There is very little in the village that can be identified with him. It is thought he may have lived in what is now the manor farmhouse, which has been built at different times and has remains perhaps of his day in a lofty arch in an outside wall, some stone window frames, old roof beams in an outbuilding, and an old dovecot. A tablet on the house says it marks the site where Brewster lived from 1588 till 1608, and where he originated the Pilgrim Church of which he became Ruling Elder.

Some think he lived at the old inn in the village street, now a dingy block of cottage and reading-room with what was the old smithy between them; and the old cottage by the churchyard actually has an inscription saying that he lived there as Post to Queen Elizabeth and James the First. It is all very uncertain.

But we know that his house, wherever it was, was a meeting-place for the Brownists or Separatists. We know that he worshipped in Scrooby church, as did others who became Pilgrim Fathers; and we know that what is called Brewster's Pew was certainly, in one form or another, part of the church furnishing in his day. The handsome bands of vine and grape which make the back of the pew, and other pieces in two charming little chancel seats, were part of the chancel screen of about 1500. The pew has a massive 15th century traceried bench-end, and the two chancel seats have smaller old ends in similar style.

The font he knew has been sold to America, and the old stocks have gone there too. A floorstone to Penelope Sandys recalls the Archbishop whom Brewster would know in his younger days, and his son, Sir Edwin Sandys, who became Governor of Virginia and granted the Pilgrim Fathers the tract of land on which they settled.

The church itself, set in a churchyard of beautiful lawn, was made new in 1390 and much modernised last century. Adorned with fine battlements, it has some Tudor windows, a 14th century porch with a stone roof, and a 14th century nave arcade. A massive spire twice struck by lightning rests on a lovely old tower of rare design, its four angles chamfered near the top to make it eight-sided below its crown of battlements and four lofty pinnacles. Two fine pinnacles on the chancel have tiny heads at their base.

The Gipsy King

SELSTON. The finest views of this colliery village are from the neatly tended churchyard, with lovely trees, where we look out to the Derbyshire hills and Crich Tower high in the west. It is a fitting resting-place for one who loved the open country, and under the shade of a lofty lime near the 15th century tower lies Dan Boswell, King of the Gipsies. On the broken stone now flat on his grave a few words are still seen, and though the epitaph is gone it was odd enough to be remembered:

> *I've lodged in many a town,*
> *I've travelled many a year,*
> *But death at length has brought me down*
> *To my last lodging here.*

The church is old and beautiful. The entrance archway of the porch has capitals carved with grotesque faces, some with foliage coming from their mouths; it is about 1200. The splendid south doorway has a round arch on shafts with rows of ornament between them. The round arches and pillars of a Norman arcade divide the nave and north aisle; the south arcade, the plain chancel arch, and the arcades between the chancel and its chapels, come from the first years of the English style.

The clerestory and the east window are 15th century, and a pretty recessed window in the chancel comes from the end of the 13th. The effect of the lofty tower arch framing the old west window, glowing richly with modern figures of Our Lord, Nathaniel, and Philip, is charming. St George and the Dragon in a small window is in memory of nearly 50 men who died for peace.

In the bright Children's Corner is the bowl of the Norman font which came back to church in 1900 after being a trough at one of the inns. On an ancient floorstone is the crude figure of a priest holding a chalice. A great stone in the tower has a rare cross, and in an outside wall is a stone engraved with a dog gnawing a bone. A little old work is left in the roofs, and among the quaint stone heads supporting the beams in the nave are a man and a woman like Darby and Joan. The charming oak pulpit, with rich vine borders, is of our century.

On an alabaster monument lie the great figures of William Willoughby and his wife, he a young knight in 17th century armour, his face worn away; she in a gown with pointed bodice and full skirt, long sleeves puffed at the elbow, and ruffs at her wrists. An inscription has their names, and high up on the wall is a tablet with the original epitaph, on which are the words, "yet left ere he went a pair of female babes besides his infant heir, a hopeful imp, a right young Willoughby."

The Pride of the Stanhopes

SHELFORD. Delightful is Shelford when seen from the Malkin Hills which bring us from Radcliffe-on-Trent. With its houses and farms clustered round the old grey church, in a luxuriant patchwork of pasture and ploughland and winding river, Nottinghamshire has few prettier or more typical scenes to show us. So peacefully does it lie off the beaten track that it is hard to realise that one chapter of its long story fills one of the blackest pages in the tale of the Civil War, when the night sky was all aglow with the burning of the home of the Stanhopes.

They came to the village when Henry the Eighth granted to Sir Michael Stanhope the small 12th century priory, and here they lived for about a hundred years, pulling down the priory and building a manor house. It was an eventful century in the story of the Stanhopes, who were one day to have three earldoms.

Sir Michael was brought to the block for loyalty to Protector Somerset. His grandson Philip paid James the First £10,000 for a barony, and in 1628 Charles Stuart made him Earl of Chesterfield. After being captured by the Roundheads and buying his ransom early in the Civil War, he retired from the struggle and left his son to fight for the king. Philip Stanhope, his fifth son, fortified Shelford House which, with the garrison at Wiverton Hall, was for a long time a source of harassment to Nottingham Castle under Colonel Hutchinson, hindering the transport of food and troops both by road and river.

In 1645 the Parliamentarians determined to reduce Shelford and Wiverton before the final siege of Newark, and offered Colonel Stanhope favourable terms to surrender. After a scornful refusal, in which Philip Stanhope threatened to "lay Nottingham Castle as flat as a pancake," General Poyntz with Colonel Hutchinson and Colonel Rossiter set out to capture the stronghold, and the first thing they did was to burn out a party of Shelford snipers who were lodged in the church tower, having drawn up the ladder and the bellropes and taken a small cannon to the top with them. Colonel Stanhope refused the summons to surrender in these words:

> Sir, I keep this garrison for the king, and in defence of it I will live and die, and your number is not so great, nor you so much master of the field, but that I am confident soon to lessen your number and see you abroad; and, for relief, we need none. Therefore I desire you to be satisfied with this answer from
> Your servant Phil. Stanhope.

The order was given to storm the stronghold. After a gallant defence Colonel Stanhope was mortally wounded, about 140 of the Royalists were slain, and the rest were taken prisoners. The manor house was set on fire that night, and a small part of it which survived is in the house we see.

Many Stanhopes lie in the church, and their monuments, with a funeral helm and a gauntlet, are now in an aisle enclosed by a screen made from the timbers of the old roof. There is an inscription to Sir Michael who lost his head on Tower Hill, and a tomb with the alabaster figure of his wife. Three of their children round the tomb are in swaddling clothes.

The church is rich in fame. The famous 4th Earl of Chesterfield was brought to rest here after being buried first in London, and is mentioned on a tablet. Statesman and wit, he will ever be remembered for the letter his belated patronage called forth from Dr Johnson after the publication of his Dictionary beginning:

> Seven years, my lord, have now passed since I waited in your outward rooms and was repulsed from your door.

A wall monument by Chantrey, showing the graceful figure of a woman, is to Lady Georgiana West, who died in 1824 at 22. Another of the Stanhopes was Eliza Ellis, wife of Welbore Ellis who became the first Baron Mendip and wrote her praise in her epitaph here, ending with the lines:

> Such my Eliza was, and shall no verse
> Record these virtues or adorn her hearse?
> Forbid it Justice, Gratitude, and Shame,
> He who best knows attests it with his name.

A story is told of the village tailor here who early last century must have thought there was no harm in robbing the dead to clothe

the living. For a long time he was supplying customers with waist-coats of rich red velvet at a very moderate price, and there seemed to be no end to his supply of beautiful material. But the truth came out when someone saw the connection between the fact that he was sexton as well as tailor. Having access to the vaults, he had been stripping the coffins of the Stanhopes of their handsome funeral trappings to make waistcoats for his customers!

Much of the beautiful church is 14th century, but the tower which had such a dramatic share in the Civil War, and the clerestory above the lofty nave arcades, are 15th. The chancel has lovely modern glass of the Crucifixion with Peter and Paul in the new east window, and the Four Evangelists in four old lancets. In a beautiful window in the north aisle the Wise Men are bringing gifts to the Holy Child.

Older than anything else here is a fine fragment of a Saxon cross on a window-sill; nearly three feet high, it is carved on one side with the Madonna and Child, the Babe without a halo and holding what seems to be a scroll; on the other side is a winged angel, and knotwork adorns the edges. A chest is 16th century, the font 17th.

Two storied possessions the church has belonging to our own day. One is an oak angel holding a wreath above an inscription to a farmer of Whatton who, hearing the cry of a boy who had fallen into the River Smite when in flood, rushed to his help and was drowned through the river bank giving way. He was William Lamin. The other is a wooden cross with a metal Crucifix. For long it was an odd piece of wood lying in the churchyard, till a stranger one day asked the vicar if he might have it. He took it away with him, and the vicar was delighted to have it returned to him a few months later in the shape of this lovely cross, carved by a master of his craft. The vicar who showed it us with pride when completing his 50 years here in 1932 was still here when we called again in 1938.

The Letter-Bag of Lord Chesterfield

HOW quiet, how remote, is the resting-place of the notorious Lord Chesterfield! During the closing days of his long life (1694–1773) Philip Dormer Stanhope, 4th Earl of Chesterfield, asked how he fared, answered that he had been dead two years but did not choose to have it known. Dead to fame he will never be, to a fame based on shining qualities of intellect marred by heartless cynicism, with the worship of social graces and the accomplishments of the polished rake. Two things make him memorable to posterity, the letters he wrote and a letter he received, the hundreds of shameless letters to his son, and the letter addressed to him by Dr Johnson. Was ever such a letter-bag as his!

The Chesterfield Letters, brilliant, scandalous, immoral, are overcast by the shadow of tragedy. Their author hoped to make his son the perfect man of the world, master of guile, of social deceit, of every art conducive to worldly success which was not incompatible with a veneer of dignity and conventional breeding. The son was incapable of absorbing his lessons. He wilted under the blazing lustre of his father's overpowering counsel. He married secretly, died prematurely, and left an impecunious widow who, to Chesterfield's dismay, published the letters soon after her husband's death.

Dr Johnson's letter to Chesterfield was the result of the nobleman's neglect to help him while he was struggling with poverty during the preparation of his Dictionary. It is perhaps the most famous letter in our language.

Stories on the Walls

SHELTON. Mantled in trees and bounded by the River Smite, this quiet home of a few people is part of a wide countryside which is golden in summertime with waving corn. It sees the sails of Elston's windmill, and hears the bells of Bottesford.

The big house and the small church look across a stretch of fine parkland, the lawn of the house and the churchyard coming in friendly fashion to low grey walls by the wayside. The house has two sundials and on the lawn is a great beech.

The church lost its old tower a century ago. The chancel is made new, but it has two 13th century lancets, and over the modern east window is the old hood adorned with heads. A charming row of three old lancets in the aisle has tinted glass shedding a mellow light, and above them is the medieval corbel table.

The arcade of slightly pointed arches on round pillars comes from about 1200. A face smiles from the rich hood of a lovely piscina in the aisle, and the 14th century font is like a chalice. There are two Jacobean coffin stools, and old work remains in the restored chancel screen. Its embattled cornice is fixed on to the wall above the wooden chancel arch. A modern door with beautiful ironwork hangs in the south doorway, which has in it parts of two Norman doorways.

The great treasures of Shelton are two exceptionally fine Saxon stones carved with knotwork, perhaps from two coped tombs. Fragments of old carved stones are built into the vestry wall, and in the churchyard is a stone coffin.

Vivid and tragic stories are told by some of the memorials in this tranquil place. One tells of the tragedy of Samuel Maltby and his wife in the Indian Mutiny. He was severely wounded while escaping down the Ganges, and was afterwards massacred at Bithor; his wife was taken from there to Cawnpore, where she was thrown into a well by order of Nena Sahib.

We read also of William Vere Smith, who died of fever at Bulawayo, going through two Matabele campaigns; of Francis Vere Wright who lost two fingers near Viterbo in 1860, "in the making of Italy"; and of Walter Banks Wright, who died in Benares from the heat. Another soldier of the Wright family has been lying since 1920 in the churchyard, a white cross carved with a sword and a belt marking his grave. The arms of a soldier of three centuries ago are carved on a stone set in a pillar of the arcade; he was William Warburton, a Royalist buried here in 1669.

Shelton's peace memorial cross in the churchyard is to one young man of 21, who fell in the last year of the war.

A Lost Tree's Three Counties

SHIREOAKS. In the pleasantest part of this mining village the church stands by the wayside, shaded by limes. Built by the Duke of Newcastle in 1862, in 14th century style, it has a lofty tower with a short spire, aisles and an apse, and steep roofs painted in medieval colours.

Edward the Seventh, as Prince of Wales, laid the first stone, and he and Mr Gladstone gave some of the poor glass in memory of the duke who died two years after its building. Other memorials to him are the reredos, the sedilia, a table (all elaborately carved in marble and alabaster), and the mosaic lining the walls of the apse. The reredos has a group of 16 figures in the Crucifixion scene, also four angels, four saints, and symbols of the Evangelists.

Nothing is left of the ancient oak which gave the village its name, and threw its shade into Yorkshire, Derbyshire, and Notts. The boundary itself has changed, and the spot where it grew is now wholly in Notts. John Evelyn described the old tree as being 94 feet round, covering a patch of about 700 square yards.

He Crowned Our Most Pathetic King

SIBTHORPE. This bare little village has a few fine things to treasure, and the memory that one of its sons crowned one of our kings.

For 700 years a fine stone dovecot, nearly 100 feet round and with over 1000 nests, has stood near the church and seen Sibthorpe's great days come and go. The big house is no more, and the glory of the church has waxed and waned. It grew into a fine collegiate church after Thomas de Sibthorpe founded his chantry here about 1325, and was given by Henry the Eighth (with all its lands) to Richard Whalley and Thomas Magnus.

Magnus was a benefactor of Newark and friend of Wolsey. It is said that after his downfall the Cardinal asked if he could stay with him at Sibthorpe, and a letter from Magnus, still extant, explains that his house had but poor accommodation, so that whether or not Wolsey came is uncertain.

There are twenty Irish yews in sombre formation by the small church, so oldfashioned that it is still lit with candles. It has lost the north aisle and the chapel where masses were sung, but the arches of the old arcade are still seen in the wall. The sturdy tower of about 1300 has a modern parapet, and Georgian work is in the nave and the porch. The beautiful 14th century chancel has windows with leaf tracery, and its lofty 13th century arch rests on shafts with foliage capitals.

Over a founder's recess in the chancel is an elaborately carved Easter Sepulchre, showing four Roman soldiers crouching in their sleep and Our Lord risen, with two adoring angels. The font is 17th century, a plain little chest is over 500 years old, and there are solid oak benches a century younger. In the sanctuary is an old chair.

On a magnificent alabaster tomb lies the Elizabethan figure of Edward Burnell, wearing a ruff and a gown opened to show the tunic and breeches; his head rests on a book, he holds another in his

258

uplifted hands, and his feet are on a weird skull. It was erected by his widow Barbara; she also set up the fine monument in Screveton to Richard Whalley, whose third wife she was before marrying Burnell.

The man who crowned the king was Thomas Secker, born here in 1693, the son of a nonconformist farmer. He was educated at the nonconformist academy of Timothy Jollie at Attercliffe and sent to study divinity at the expense of Isaac Watts. In 1733 he was appointed King's Chaplain, two years later he became Bishop of Bristol, then Dean of St Paul's in 1750, and finally Archbishop of Canterbury. One of the greatest of our English Primates, he was wise, kindly, and hard-working, and a notable preacher, and he crowned George the Third, perhaps the most pathetic monarch who ever sat on our throne.

The Forester and His Lady

SKEGBY. The village has grown on the steep sides of a valley, and its church stands high at one end, looking down on the big house.

Much of the old church has been lost in the rebuilding made necessary by the mine running under it, but there is old work left in the base of the tower, a 13th century arcade in the nave, and a tiny 700-year-old piscina which has a woman's face carved on the drain. Built into the walls inside and out are 12th and 13th century coffin stones, carved with crosses, a chalice, a sword, and shears; one is only 27 inches long. A medieval stone on the wall has on it a kneeling priest.

The treasures here are two fine stone figures, once lying down but now standing against a wall. One is a lady with a wimple and a long gown, her hands in prayer and her head on a cushion held by angels; the other is a forester with his hunter's horn. They are thought to be Edmund Spigurnell of 1296 and his wife. Part of their home still survives in the 12th and 13th century remains in the ruined building by a farmhouse near the station.

An engraved brass to John Miller who was killed at Suvla Bay "at daybreak" in 1915, has two angels holding the inscription:

> *And to keep loyalties young,*
> *I'll write his name golden for ever.*

The Face in the Ruff

SOOKHOLME. A tiny village with a simple church all neat and trim, it has its share of Norman England in a wide chancel arch with roll mouldings and a font bowl shaped like a bucket. It has lost a third of its old length, but there is still much Norman masonry in the north and south walls, and a few windows are medieval. A fine piscina and a crude stone bench for the priests are 600 years old. There is an old chest, and the nave roof has two fine old beams and two ancient bosses, one carved with a quaint face with a pointed ruff all round it.

The Dragon on the Norman Arcade

SOUTH COLLINGHAM. A delightful neighbour for North Collingham, it has gabled houses, wayside lawns, overhanging trees, and winding roads revealing odd corners of unexpected charm. On the three-cornered green is an ancient elm 17 feet round its trunk, which is now a mere shell with rustic poles filling the gap between its yawning edges.

Perhaps its most charming spot is where the church stands in a garden of roses and shrubs, with beech and sycamore trees shading the velvet lawn; it is a beautiful churchyard lovingly tended. From one of its gates we see a pretty group of thatched cottages, and a holly arch frames a picture of the rectory garden, where a splendid oak has a wonderful spread of branches.

The church is neat and lovely in and out, with old and new happily blended. Some of its oldest work is still its chief possession. Exceptionally fine is the Norman arcade of the nave with rich mouldings and carved capitals, and an extraordinary corbel showing the head of a dragon-like creature with the bearded face of a man in its wide-open mouth, the face seen only when we stand below the corbel. The head of a man with his tongue out (as if at the beast) looks across the nave from the English arcade of the 13th century.

The tower is 13th and 15th century. It is a charming bit of the church inside, with its cream walls, its rows of benches, and a lovely arch with detached pillars. The massive font is 13th century and there are three old piscinas. In the 13th century doorway through which we enter hangs a splendid door, which is part of the excellent modern woodwork throughout the church. The benches have traceried ends and some linenfold, the pulpit has carving of vines, and the nave roof has floral bosses. A little old timber is in the roof of the north aisle.

Most of the windows are 15th century, and corbel heads with a striking family likeness adorn them outside. One of them glows with life and rich colour illustrating the 104th Psalm with scenes of night and day and the Providence of God. One angel holds a golden sun and one the crescent moon; there are birds in trees, reapers in the cornfield, grapes in the vineyard, purple hills and snowclad mountain tops, a stream running through green pastures, sheep grazing, cattle drinking, a heron in the water and a swan by her nest; while a great owl is flying above the forest trees in the night sky, and a lion and its mate are prowling through the land.

Another window shows John the Baptist, Mary Magdalene with Magdalen College in the background, and the vision of St John with the seven golden candlesticks and the seven stars. The peace window to 16 men shows a group with fighting saints, including David and Joan of Arc. The brass tablet to their memory is engraved with a rose, of which the petals and the centre are set with nine actual badges of their regiments.

The Coloured Walls

SOUTH LEVERTON. Gay gardens add to its charm, and its wayside church will not let us pass it by. It has grown old graciously, and stands in a lovely churchyard.

Its high unbuttressed tower is mainly Norman, with 15th century battlements, and is charming inside, where its pointed arch opens to the nave and the lovely glass of its 13th century lancet sheds a rainbow light on the great Norman font. The window shows Our Lord blessing the children, and is in memory of Maria Overend, whose gifts helped the restoration of the church at the close of last century.

One of the finest possessions of the church is the great Norman doorway, its detached shafts supporting an arch with handsome zigzag enriched with sunflower pattern. It frames a modern door with beautiful hinges, and as it opens to let us in the walls are seen like masses of mosaic, tinted buff, orange, green, and gold.

The 13th century nave arcades have pillars of grouped shafts crowned by foliage capitals, and among the corbels are two pairs of curious animals seeming to be fighting. Under the south aisle roof inside is a huge gargoyle-like head with staring eyes and open mouth.

The chancel is made new, but in its side walls are eight 13th century lancets.

A tapering stone with traces of carving is the oldest possession of the village, for it is believed to have been the lid of a Roman coffin. A floorstone with a cross is only two feet long, and the fragment of another ancient stone has crude carving of feet and a shroud. The chalice is Elizabethan, and three bells are 17th century.

A pleasant house called the Priory has an old gabled end whose walls, four feet thick, may be part of a monastic building. On the edge of the village is a derelict windmill.

The Beckoning Tower

SOUTH MUSKHAM. The few farms and houses of this quiet retreat are sandwiched between two busy roads, the great iron road where we see the Flying Scotsman racing by, and the Great North Road which comes for most of the two miles from Newark on the arches built by John Smeaton to raise it above the meadows flooded by the Trent. Much of Smeaton's work remains after nearly two centuries, though some of the walling is renewed, and a fine new bridge of graceful arches carries the road over the river in place of one built on piles.

The massive tower of the church beckons long before we reach it. It is the glory of the village. Its 13th century base has narrow lancets, 14th century windows light the stage above, and the splendid top storey is 500 years old. The belfry windows have embattled transoms, and hoods adorned with finials and heads; and one of them has a niche with a robed figure, perhaps St Wilfrid, holding a crozier and blessing all who pass by.

The oldest work in the pleasing little church is herringbone masonry seen inside and out of the north wall of the chancel, the carved bowl of a Norman font (with a 17th century cover), and the small north doorway of the 12th century. Less than six feet high, the arch of the doorway is almost round, a blending of the Norman and English styles.

The beautiful medieval door which lets us in is heavily ribbed and studded, and has two holes (now filled in) made by bullets of the Civil War. The nave arcades and the wide chancel arch are about 1400; the chancel has six 13th century lancets; the east window is 15th century. There are a few fragments of old glass, the piscina and aumbry are medieval, the south aisle has a few old roof beams, a table is Jacobean, and there is an ancient almsbox. Three bench-ends and four splendid poppyheads in the chancel seats were found under the floor during restoration; they are 15th century, the poppyheads carved with roses, a double-headed pelican, winged and crowned grotesques, and four crabs with nippers and claws.

An odd relic of the days before organs is the clarionet with which old William Redfern used to lead the village choir. There is an old stone coffin in the churchyard.

The Peace of the Byways

SOUTH SCARLE. The peace of the byways belongs to this border village with a big house, farms, a stone dovecot with a cheery red roof and lots of pigeons, and a charming old church. From the edge of the village we have a fine glimpse of Lincoln Cathedral.

The church shows its loveliest work as we open the door; it is in two Norman bays of the north arcade. Their arches are richly adorned with remarkable elaboration of zigzag ornament, their hoods are of tiny chevrons carved point to point, and the capitals have foliage and scallop.

These two bays are the original length of the Norman nave. A smaller arch at their east end comes from the 13th century, when the church was enlarged by transepts and the present chancel was built. This small arch, and the corresponding one in the 13th century south arcade, became part of the arcades when the transepts were opened to the aisles two centuries later; separating them from the other arches is eight feet of walling which is actually part of the Norman chancel. Between the Norman arches is the fine stone head of a man looking well content to have a place in so lovely a scheme; and two wide eyes have been looking across at the Norman work for 700 years. There are stone seats round some of the pillars. Fine 13th century arches to the tower and chancel, a 15th century clerestory, and a medieval roof with bosses and angel corbels with shields, complete the nave.

The rest of the sturdy tower is 600 years old, with battlements and pinnacles a century younger. The beautiful double piscina, the bowl and base of the font, and two lancets are 13th century. The 500-year-old screen is much restored, and a massive old ladder climbs to the belfry. A great chest, a pillar almsbox, and some bench-ends with tiny poppyheads, are other old relics. Under the tower are two ancient floorstones with crosses. Another in the chancel is engraved with the portrait of Sir William Mering of 1510, in armour and with his sword. His hair waves to his shoulders, and his hands are at prayer; his youthful face has wide-awake eyes, and his feet rest on an alert dog with a collar.

In a niche over the 15th century entrance to the porch is the tiny crowned figure of St Helena, the patron saint, and from the windows happy little stone faces smile down as we come and go.

The Wonderful Minster

SOUTHWELL. Is there in England, we wonder, a greater surprise for most of those who come, for here is the least-known cathedral in our Motherland, with a dignity and beauty unsurpassed. The rushing tide of life has passed it by and left it standing in a quietude of loveliness, like some dream of time gone by before our century came.

A small place still, a "city" with only 3000 people, it has a proud and ancient tale to tell. It was the first of our Stuart kings who came this way and was astonished to find so great a church in so small a place; it was his son Charles Stuart who rode out of these streets on his last journey as a free man. It was here in Southwell, at the Saracen's Head, that he stayed a few hours before giving himself up to the long captivity which brought him to the scaffold. The inn is still as he saw it; he would ride through these great gates; he would see these beams before he mounted his horse and surrendered to the Scots encamped at Kelham.

Southwell had seen history before he came, for its wells brought the Britons here. There is witness to the Romans and the Saxons in the noble Minster which has grown from a very early church and a rebuilding perhaps in the first half of the 11th century. Here came Archbishops of York to rest awhile from their labours, some of them indeed for their last long sleep. There are still fine fragments of their medieval house, which has been rebuilt in our time and is now the Palace of the Bishops of Southwell, for Southwell was made a

The Noble Fane from the South

The Impressive Nave and its Mighty Norman Arches

SOUTHWELL, LEAST KNOWN OF ENGLISH CATHEDRALS

The Canopy of Wolsey's Seat
in the Choir

Norman Doorway and Medieval
Ironwork

The Delicate Beauty of Southwell's 14th century Screen

THE CENTURIES-OLD BEAUTY OF THE IMPRESS

Norman South Doorway

Central Arch of the Screen

The Madonna and Angels on the Stone Screen at Southwell

LAGE CATHEDRAL OF NOTTINGHAMSHIRE

The Kneeling Figures on the Tomb of Archbishop Sandys

Heads on Sedilia   Chapter House Doorway   Heads on Sedilia

Norman Capitals in the Chancel

THE RARE AND DELICATE LOVELIN

The Natural Carving by the Chapter House Door

An Outer Wall

The Western Gate

Modern Bench End

A Beautiful Norman Capital in the Nave

SOUTHWELL'S STATELY MINSTER

Three Fine Heads Carved in Stone

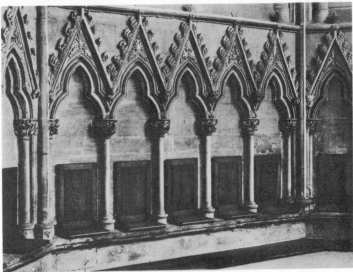

Chapter House Stalls

Three of the Lovely Chapter House Capitals

THE WONDERFUL MEDIEVAL CARVINGS IN

Three Quaint Faces from the Middle Ages

The Intricate Canopies of the Sedilia

The Fine Stall Canopies in the Chapter House

UTIFUL NORMAN MINSTER AT SOUTHWELL

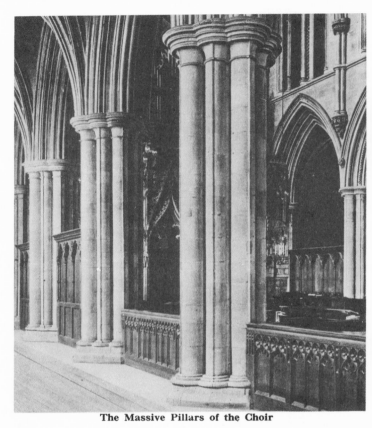

The Massive Pillars of the Choir

The Carvings on the Modern Choir Stalls

IN SOUTHWELL CATHEDRAL

bishopric in 1884. Now the diocese has been transferred from the province of Canterbury back to York, to which, until nearly a hundred years ago, it belonged for about a thousand years.

Here Wolsey came in the summer after he had fallen, like Lucifer, never to rise again. While he was at Harrow and Cambridge, Byron spent his holidays here with his mother at Burgage Manor House, and it was because of his friendship here with Miss Pigot (the Eliza of his early poems) that his Hours of Idleness were published through a Newark printer. Several fine houses in beautiful gardens and parkland add to the charm of this old town on the River Greet, the birthplace of the composer, Reginald Spofforth, who wrote Hail, Smiling Morn.

Of one garden hereabouts an interesting tale is told. In the neighbourhood of Southwell is Easthorpe, and in a garden there stands (or lies, for it is on its back) an apple tree of historic interest to botanists. It began its life at the beginning of last century in a plant-pot, into which the lady of the house set two or three pips from an apple she was eating. Two or three seedlings grew up and the strongest of these was planted in the garden in Trafalgar year. It grew, but did not bloom for years. Then the house came to be inhabited by a Mr Bramley. The tree now bore a good crop of apples, and one day Mr Henry Merryweather, of Southwell, met a gardener carrying a fine basket of them. "It is Mr Bramley's apple," he said, " and a very fine one too ; it grows in his garden at Easthorpe." Mr Merryweather went to see Mr Bramley, who said he had named the apple Bramley's seedling, and Mr Merryweather might take what grafts he liked. Mr Merryweather eventually sent to the Fruit Committee at Chiswick 16 apples weighing 16 pounds, and the fruit received a fine certificate so that Mr Merryweather went to Easthorpe and said "Now, Mr Bramley you have the honour of raising and I have the honour of sending out the finest apple on earth." So Bramley's seedling came into the world, and the old tree which grew from the plant pot is still to be seen, its long life over but its trunk supported on two props. It might have been possible, by some miracle of arithmetic, to count the apples that have grown on this one tree, but no man knows how many trees have grown from one apple a lady of Easthorpe ate about 140 years ago.

It was the Archbishop of York who began the Minster we see about 1110, after he had released the people of Notts from the annual pilgrimage to York on condition that they came to the church of St Mary of Southwell. Before the middle of the 13th century the small Norman choir had been replaced by the choir we see, a superb example of the Early English style at its best. The vestibule and the exquisite chapter house to which it leads were built between 1290 and 1300, and the richest stone screen in all England was set up 30 years later. The 15th century gave windows to the aisles, and the great west window, whose virtue it is that it throws light into the nave.

We come to the Minster through one of its old gateways, its Norman arch under a stepped gable with a medieval niche. By it are two beautiful yew pyramids, planted over a hundred years ago and still tended by the Southwell nurserymen who gave the world the famous apple known as the Bramley Seedling.

As we walk between the churchyard lawns, the fine west front is before us, standing as it stood in the 12th century except for the great window, and the square broached spires (the pepper-pots) with which the twin towers were crowned last century. The fifth storey of one of these high towers is enriched with Norman interlaced arcading, while that of its companion has a series of pointed arches. The west doorway is splendid with zigzag ornament, which also adorns many of the windows and the stringcourse running round the Norman part of the church. On both sides of the west doors is beautiful old ironwork in scrolls.

A stately square tower rises from the middle of a cross. The Norman two-storeyed north porch (a charming feature of the exterior) has a barrel roof looking down on arcaded walls and a recessed doorway with seven orders of ornament. It frames a 600-year-old traceried door.

We should enter by the west doorway, for here the grandeur of the Norman nave bursts upon us. Sturdy round columns with carved capitals with strength enough to last for ever support the moulded arches. Over them runs a stringcourse like the edge of a saw. Then comes the triforium, with wide arches on short shafts, and above these the smaller arches of the clerestory passage, which is lighted by the small round windows seen outside.

Very solid and impressive is this great nave, leading to the four colossal arches bearing up the central tower. They are carved with exceptionally bold cable moulding, and the capitals on which the eastern arch rests are among the earliest Norman work here, their dainty carving showing the Annunciation, the Nativity, the Entry into Jerusalem, Our Lord washing Peter's feet, and the Last Supper (portrayed with a gap at the table). For forty years these capitals were hidden by the organ; now only part of the organ is on the stone screen, and the carvings are revealed.

The north and south arches of the crossing open to transepts as old as the nave. The nave has a 19th century barrel roof, but the aisles have their original Norman vaulting. The undercutting of the capitals and the ornament in the mouldings, are striking features of the lovely vaulted 13th century choir, which has a triforium and a clerestory. We come to the choir through a pair of charming iron gates in the middle bay of the stone screen; a gift in memory of a mother, they were made in our time by the blacksmith of Brant Broughton.

The screen itself is a miracle in stone. It has looked as we see it for about 600 years, and is marvellous for its fine sculpture even in this place where the artist's chisel has produced what John Ruskin called the gem of English architecture.

Enthroned high up in this wonderful screen sits the Madonna, a beautiful figure with an angel beckoning her. On each side of the doorway are three stone stalls; one of them, carved at the back in about 200 diaper squares, was Cardinal Wolsey's seat when he lived at the bishop's palace after his fall. Along the top of the screen runs a row of carved heads, and over the stalls are exquisite canopies elaborate with foliage and finials, and heads hanging from the cusps. Everywhere on this screen we see the genius of the medieval artist at his best. Altogether there are 289 figures, an immense number when we consider the little space into which they are crowded.

To those who wonder at the quaint and curious things we sometimes find in our cathedrals, the Southwell screen is a wondrous picture book, for it is easy to gather from it something of the medieval craftsman's mind. It was not just a joke that he made plants grow out of a mouth, or chiselled ugly people; his strange grotesques were not just passing fancy. In those days before books this was the way of teaching; these things were the people's library, their picture gallery, their Bible. An ugly man was a bad man, the man with his tongue out was a gossip. Those who will interest themselves in these things will find these ancient sculptures full of good philosophy, with virtues and vices personified. We find here the head of a woman who seems to be in terror, and looking across we find the reason why, for there is a man like a brute. On one of the brackets is David playing the harp; on another is Saul falling on his sword in his tent; small as it all is, the pain in Saul's face is clearly seen. There is an exquisite suggestion of an angel listening, with the forefinger held up in a way familiar to us all.

We can see at a glance, looking across the choir to the sanctuary, that the beautiful seats for the priests must have sprung from the same mind and been done by the same hands as the screen. The five seats in the sedilia (the sixth has gone) are superbly canopied, but the canopies have been broken and were restored at the beginning of the 19th century. They seem no worse for it, but remain one of the most captivating achievements of craftsmanship in the country. The seats are divided by slender columns round which cluster the tiniest human figures tucked away among the foliage. There are about 75 of them, and about half are the originals. Groups of figures run along the top; a group showing the Flight into Egypt has a very fine head of Joseph which it is difficult to believe was carved in the middle of the 14th century. The tiny cusps have gems of sculpture hanging from them, and the roofs of the canopies are vaulted and bossed.

An admirable place is Southwell to those who believe the best days of the world have not yet been, that all the best work has not been done, for here, in this choir so full of beauty, the work of our own time is worthy of the old. Where this 14th century stone is wonderful, the 19th century woodwork is wonderful too. It is as if the man who set these seats in this great choir was moved by the spirit of beauty about him. It was Charles Henry Simpson who carved this marvellous range of oak stalls in the last years of the 19th century. They are of a delicate beauty everywhere, crowded with gems of carving which carry the mind to the chapter house a few yards away, where the carving has made Southwell famous through the world.

In these oak choir stalls is every kind of conception that comes to a carver who studies Nature in her infinite variety. There are many kinds of nuts and berries, mistletoe, honeysuckle, bullrushes, sunflowers, catkins, and lilies of the valley. There are thistles, clover, buttercups, and wild roses. There is a holly tree which would prick us if we touched it. There is bracken with leaves too delicate to touch. There is an arm-rest with primroses and butterflies, and ears of wheat with mice playing among them. There are birds in a fig tree, a serpent in an apple tree, a lizard in an oak tree, and two pigs eating acorns that have fallen. There are bats and fishes and toadstools, and peas in a pod, and we think the artist must have been very fond of music, for he has put among all this foliage something of the music of the countryside, a fiddle and a harp, a bird singing by its nest, and a lark at heaven's gate.

Much of the carving runs right through the oak, and everywhere it has the variety of the garden and the fields. The pulpit matches the stalls in teak; it is very fine, with a Madonna and Child in the centre panel under the canopy.

We are prepared in this shrine for a noble revelation of our English architecture, and we come with great expectations to this famous chapter house. We cannot be disappointed, for we have only to open our eyes to feel that we are in the very Ark of Beauty. We come into it through the vaulted vestibule, charming in itself, opening off the north choir aisle by a lovely doorway carved all round with leaves. It has a dignity of its own, as if it knew where it is leading us. We see in the wealth of carving on its arcaded walls a remarkable sculpture of a lay priest pulling the hair of a regular priest, a lady with a brooch, a quaint creature like a baboon, a blackbird pecking berries, and the face of a man who seems to be winking.

So we come to what is probably the most beautiful doorway in any cathedral in England, divided by a single clustered shaft, with exquisite carvings of leaves and flowers. It is a noble entrance to a place beyond compare, of which it has been said that it is among chapter houses as the rose among flowers. The doorway is recessed with a series of pillars, and the capitals of three on the right are carved from a single stone with oak and mulberry leaves and buttercups. The maple leaves round the doorway spring from one wyvern's tail and run into another. The chapter house inside is built like York's, an octagon without a central column. It has 36 seats, with triangular canopies over them, and the carving of these canopies is one of the stone wonders of the world. We do not know who did them, but among the figures is one of a monk who may, we like to think, have been the artist himself, for his natural hair curls under his cap. Why is he so real? Perhaps it may be that he is the lifelike artist who gave this place immortal fame in art. To him all things were real, and all work was life.

There are corbels where they never could be seen; but long before Longfellow said so this disciple knew that the gods see everywhere, and the corbels nobody sees are as fine as all the rest. The craftsman made a slip in his calculations, not finishing in line at the door, but he covered it up with a beautiful leaf. Over the doorway he put the head of a smiling man, and a dog to keep him company, looking down on all who come and go. Just inside the doorway he carved the head of a girl, with hair that might have belonged to the 20th century girl we saw standing beside it.

This unknown genius of Southwell copied his work from Nature; he took it from the fields hereabouts, and it is always true. His foliage may be tightly massed, but the stems are always there. His heads have plant symbols of the spirit of good and evil issuing from their mouths. He has a bird carrying its young from the poisonous ivy. He has two dogs with a hare run to earth, carved among ivy leaves, and we remember the gamekeeper's explanation that the hare seeks the ivy when it is about to die. He has a marvellous carving of acorn-cups from which the nuts have fallen, to be eaten by the pigs hidden below, a fancy the carver of the choir stalls was to copy nearly 600 years later. He has what has been called a May Queen, a woman with hawthorn leaves springing from her head like wings. He has monks with jester's caps, fabulous beasts, and on the top of a shaft from which the vaulting springs he has a goat eating ivy (he knew that it is harmless to them) and a herdsman blowing his horn.

The chapter house is built of stone quarried hereabouts, the stone which crumbled in our Houses of Parliament after only a hundred years. Here it is hard (with all this intricacy of carving) after six centuries, and from the canopied seats to the vaulted roof its condition is remarkable. It is flooded with light through its transparent windows, in which are set about a hundred pieces of 13th, 14th, and 15th century glass.

The east window of the choir is made up of two tiers of lancets, and has glass of remarkable interest in the lower tier, showing the Baptism of Christ, the Raising of Lazarus, the Triumphal Entry into Jerusalem, and the Mocking and Scourging. The windows are bold and aglow with colour, and some of the figures are supposed to be of historic characters, Martin Luther among them. The great interest of this Flemish glass is that it is from a church destroyed in Paris during the French Revolution. It found its way into a pawnshop and came to Southwell a few years after Waterloo. It is thought these windows may have been seen by Marie Antoinette on her way to execution.

There is a great window in the south choir aisle made into a mosaic with a thousand fragments of 13th century glass. The best of the modern windows is one of our own time by Christopher Whall, showing in glowing colours the Crucifixion and the Vision of St John. Some of the vivid glass in the aisles is interesting for its quaint scenes, one showing the Temptation of Our Lord, with Satan's eyes gleaming and a cloven hoof peeping from his robe. Another has Paulinus (who Christianised this part of the Trent valley), holding a model of this Minster, which some say he founded. The bright red and blue glass in two round clerestory windows of the south transept was made by two boys, who took it into Norwell Wood to burn in the colour.

Much of the impressiveness of this stately Minster comes from the fact that it is not encumbered with memorials. The monument which draws all eyes unto it is the lovely alabaster tomb of Archbishop Sandys. He lies with two angels at his head and two at his feet, and in a panel his wife kneels with a perfectly charming group of eight children behind her. The tomb is as old as the Spanish Armada. In the south choir aisle lies the oldest stone figure here, a 12th century priest. A very holy place has been given to Bishop Riddings, 43rd headmaster of Winchester and first Bishop of Southwell. He kneels at prayer, magnificent in bronze, stretching out his hands as we used to see him. Of the second bishop, his successor Dr Hoskyns, there is a bronze showing him in his robes, and his kindly face comes to life as the bronze turns on a spindle at the touch of a finger.

The most pathetic of the small group of monuments here is one of our own time which we believe to be unique. It is in a chapel off the north transept, and is a beautiful altar of sacrifice made from aeroplanes shattered in battles over France. The panels are made from broken propellers, the cross from cylinders, the vases from aluminium, and the plates from copper. The whole of this altar as we see it was at the very heart of the Great War, every fragment crashed by the guns. The pieces were put together by mechanics in the repair sheds of an aerodrome, and the altar was used there in the church hut until the aerodrome was closed. It stands here as a memorial to men of the Royal Air Force from a camp at Norton Woodseats, near Sheffield.

A little chapel off the choir has another altar with a story. It was found in a farmhouse in use as a chest, and appears to be a piece of 14th century panelling in which are painted figures in dark crimson, with black, green, and white circles over them. It is thought it was made into an altar by a village carpenter in the 17th century.

Many small things we find to stir our interest here. In a case by the chapter house door is a charter of Philip and Mary concerning land taken away from Southwell and given back to it; Philip is called King of England, France, Spain, and Jerusalem. Here also is a rare 14th century manuscript Bible, in beautiful coloured writing. In the Library is the precious manuscript known as the Liber Ambus, a folio written on vellum with nearly 500 pages. It grew through three centuries, begun in the 14th, continued in the 15th, and finished in the 16th.

The splendid brass eagle lectern is medieval, and has a story. It belonged to the monks of Newstead, and was found in one of the lakes there early last century. It was bought by a watchmaker at Nottingham, who, on taking it to pieces, found in the pedestal a bundle of legal deeds and documents concerning the privileges of the monks. The documents were still intact, and are today divided among the collections at the British Museum and at Newstead. The papers were hid in the lectern and put into the lake for safety on the breaking-up of the monastery by Henry the Eighth, the monks expecting to return. They never did return, and the lectern held its secret in the lake for nearly three centuries.

The story is told also of one of the two muzzled bears on the gables of the transepts that it was stolen by a workman and found in a garden, ultimately returning to its lawful place. It is good to think of these bears guarding the great crowd of carved figures like themselves in this old Minster. Inside and out there may be about 3000 sculptured heads.

A story of our day belongs to the high altar. It so happened that the 700th anniversary of the choir in 1934 was the Jubilee of the Mothers Union, and to celebrate the events every member of the union in this diocese gave a penny towards the cost of the altar.

Those who come to be surprised at Southwell and stay to love it will find themselves sitting perhaps on an old bench in the south transept. Men have sat on it for 500 years, and it seems to us the right place to sit and draw a last inspiration from the Stones of Southwell. These benches were once used for a court, and it was such seats that gave rise to the legal phrase "sitting on the bench." As we sit here we see, a yard or two away, the old stone seats by the transept walls built in the days before benches for those who could not stand in the church; it was such seats as these which gave rise to the saying that the weakest go to the wall. Interesting it is to sit and think of these things, and to hear Jerusalem my Happy Home played by the old chimes, given in 1693 by Thomas Wymondesold.

But it is not only of such things that we are thinking: we are remembering that as we sit on this old bench and look along the transepts we are in the presence of Roman and Saxon and Norman, for we lift a little trap-door below our feet and look at a tesselated pavement that has been here 1700 years; the Romans made it. We look along the north transept to a doorway at the corner and there is a tympanum with David (now headless) fighting a lion and Michael slaying a dragon; the Saxons made it. We look up into the great central tower, with stupendous arches impressive enough to endure for ever; the Normans made them. We look through the 14th century screen and see the marvellous carving of the oak stalls done as it were the other day; a 19th century craftsman made them. It may be doubted if we can sit in any other English cathedral with so much work spanning 17 centuries about us.

The clock goes slowly round in this cathedral village, a little place apart from the rushing world. The bishop's garden is shaded by 15th century walls, with an old fireplace and trefoiled arches open to the wind and rain. The Provost's lawn has a Roman pavement under it, and his herbaceous border looks up to the Minster's square tower with its hundred Norman columns. (The Provost's little dog lies

T

under a tree with his name on a stone, close by the only weeping pear tree we have seen). We came upon a good old man whose family has cleaned the brass of the Minster for three generations, and upon a charming old lady who used to ride about the village in a Sedan chair.

And in this quiet corner of the world the Jackdaw of Southwell is more famous than the Jackdaw of Rheims. We found him hopping about unafraid. He belonged to a choir boy who kept him in a cage but set him free when the cats began to worry him. Jack flew a little way, but not too far, and made his home in the village. He met the children coming from school, and every day he flew three-quarters of a mile to the home of an errand boy, where he would stop and call "Jack" till the boy came out.

Southwell is the sort of place where these things happen, a gracious ebbing place for the tide of life. We found the Provost (as they call the Dean in this place where nothing is quite the same) happy with his bees and his flowers, and he told us that for 17 years he had been here and 17 in the heart of London. On his desk in London he kept a photograph of an angel; he had no idea what it was, but kept it as a lovely thing. Then he came to Southwell and found it in the centre of the famous screen, the Beckoning Angel. It had been beckoning him all the time, his sister said, and we can only pray that when an angel beckons us it will be to some such heaven as Southwell is.

Nottinghamshire's Farthest South

STANFORD-ON-SOAR. It is the Farthest South of Notts, pleasant with trees and red gabled houses. By the grass-bordered road the village pump stands under a shingled roof with a graceful birch at each side; and a carved oak lychgate frames a pretty picture of the church, with stately elms and sombre yews about it. Under one yew, magnificent with a spread of branches covering a patch of ground 70 yards round, Charles Stuart and Sir Henry Skipworth are said to have conferred before the siege of Leicester.

Quiet as the village is, it has seen much change. With the coming of the railway the course of the River Soar was diverted, and there is now a high embankment between the river and the village. Near the church a small hump-back bridge which once spanned the stream stands among weedy shallows. It saw the passing of the ancient manor house by the church, and the building of a great house by Robert Raynes in the time of Charles Stuart, on what was then a barren hill over a mile away. The present hall is on the same site, but the bare hill has changed, for a tree-lined road brings us to a park with glorious elms and limes and lovely grounds, widely known as the home of Sir Julian Cahn, whose cricket team is the delight of thousands who come here to see it play. During last century the village was almost rebuilt by the Ratcliffs whose initials are on some of the houses and on the attractive pump.

There are blocks of Mount Sorrel granite in the base of the splendid 15th century tower of the church, whose oldest part is the 13th century arcade opening to the south aisle which was widened two centuries later. The north arcade is 14th century, and the fine clerestory was built about 1500. The chancel is made new, and the modern porch is on old foundations. Old relics are a piscina, a stone altar with five crosses, part of a coffin stone and a fragment of 13th century moulding in the vestry wall, and small original figures of angels at the ends of the tie-beams in the nave. The peace memorial lectern is part of the good woodwork of our time, and the modern font of richly tinted alabaster has lovely groups in white marble of Jesus with the children and Mary with Him as a Babe and the boy John the Baptist.

On the chancel floor is the fine 14th century brass portrait of a priest in robes, holding a chalice; it is one of only two ecclesiastical brasses in the county, and may represent Adam de Rothley. On an alabaster floorstone are the charmingly natural engraved figures of two Illyngworths of the 15th century, their faces rather worn.

In a recess in the wall of the north aisle, which he may have founded, lies the strange figure of a 14th century civilian with short hair and beard, high cheek bones, tightly closed lips, and a very long neck. He wears a closely-buttoned gown, has a sword, a dagger, and a pouch, and holds a heart in his folded hands. Part of his legs are missing. For a long time he has been known in the village as the Indian.

It was Thomas Lewes, a London alderman who bought the manor from the Raynes family, and the raised vault of this family and the Dashwoods (whom they married) spoils the south aisle. Among their memorials is an inscription to Samuel Vere Dashwood, rector for 49 years of last century; and a charming little monument of 1911 to Elizabeth Dashwood has the head of a woman with two children standing out in white marble on a blue ground.

Echoes of Troubled Days

STANTON-ON-THE-WOLDS. Its cottages and farms are clustered on the windswept Wolds, and the tiny church is almost lost in trees. From the golf links by the churchyard there is a fine view of the Trent valley.

After years of neglect, the church was made neat and pleasing by the beautiful lady who sleeps in Widmerpool Church. It has only a nave and chancel under one roof, with a bellcot, but the nave has traces of Norman work in its walls, and the round bowl of a Norman font is cemented to the floor. A medieval lancet lights the west wall, the shapely little east window is 600 years old, and one with dainty tracery under its square head is only a little younger. The old piscina and aumbry are here, and the tiny 14th century doorway in the porch has a modern door covered with the lovely scrolls of two hinges.

Two echoes of troubled days this village has. Colonel Hutchinson is said to have escaped from the house by the church when surprised by a party of Royalists one day in the Civil War; and we are reminded by a floorstone to Sir John Parsons of a family who, impoverished by the Civil War, came to live in the manor house, part of which still survives in the farmhouse by a clump of trees below the church. The family fell lower still, for in the 18th century one of its members was transported to America (after years of thieving and forgery), and was hanged at Tyburn for coming back.

The Saxon Cross

STAPLEFORD. We come to it with amaze that half a century could bring about such change, for fifty years ago it was a quiet village. We leave it filled with wonder that in this world of change some things endure so long.

Stapleford has given away its rural charm and accepted its place in industry. The great house, rebuilt in 1797 by a sailor of Nelson's day, is no more, and the little river near where it stood no longer turns aside to give power to the old mill. The stocks and pinfold are no more, but the gabled manor house, rebuilt near them in

1689, is still standing proud and trim. The church has something left of 700 years ago; in its shadow is a priceless thing which has stood while half a hundred kings have ruled in England; and close to the village is what is said to be the most curious natural object in the county, older than man can tell.

It is more than a century since Stapleford's great sailor died. He was John Borlase Warren, whose ruling passion as a boy was for the sea. He took part in the Colonial Wars, the troubles arising out of the French Revolution, and the fight against Napoleon. He was made a baronet and an admiral. One of his victories, for which he received the thanks of Parliament, was over the French fleet when it was carrying troops and supplies to the Irish rebels in 1798; he captured a ship of the line and three frigates.

A man of many parts was Sir John. He took his MA in 1776, and soon afterwards bought Lundy Island to accommodate his yacht and crew. In the intervals of naval service he lived at Stapleford Hall, representing the county town as MP. His last years were spent in the village, but he died when visiting Greenwich and was buried at Stretton Audley. He was greatly beloved for his courtesy and never-failing generosity. On re-entering the navy he bought out all the officers of the service who were imprisoned for debt in the Fleet and King's Bench prisons. The National School in the village is a monument to him for it was founded by his widow. In the church is a memorial to their only son who was killed at Aboukir.

Attractive outside, the church has a tower and spire from the three medieval centuries. The nave arcades are 14th century, the north a little older than the south. From about 1300 come the doorway letting us in (sheltered by an 18th century porch), some windows in the south aisle, and the east window of the chancel with its beautiful example of early tracery, formed by the simple intersection of the mullions. The font of this time has an unusual domed metal cover of about 1660. An oak carving of the Last Supper is foreign work, and was once the reredos. Two of the bells are believed to be 16th century.

For some generations the Teverys of Long Eaton were lords of Stapleford. Engraved on a floorstone are the portraits of Robert Tevery of 1571 in armour and his wife in Elizabethan dress. Gervase Tevery and his wife are lying on a massive monument; and kneeling on the floor are charming figures of three daughters and an only son, a tiny tot in a bonnet, all four battered through having been moved about since they were placed here 300 years ago.

A bright little chapel has been built in memory of about 200 men who did not come back from the war, its east window showing St Oswald, St George, and St Edward.

In our own time Stapleford's great treasure has been moved from its place in the street and set up in the churchyard. It is the famous cross, which has stood while England has seen the rise of all its royal dynasties. It was here when the Saxons worshipped in a little church of wattle and timber, and perhaps before there was a church at all. This tapering shaft of a Saxon cross, ten feet high and perhaps 1200 years old, is adorned with a mass of crude and worn interlacing work, and has on one side what is believed to be the symbol of St Luke, a horned figure with wings, treading on a serpent.

The cross is the oldest Christian memorial in the county, but older than anyone knows is the Hemlock Stone a mile away at Bramcote, standing proudly on a mound in a dip of the hills. A huge isolated mass of rock, with layers of harder stone protecting the softer sandstone below, it has resisted wind and weather through the ages.

From the high ground above the village we see the fires of Stanton's furnaces, which have so greatly developed in our time and now make pipes to carry water to teeming thousands in our towns.

In November 1936 a VC died here, a native of Grantham who joined the Navy in the second month of the war after working at Stanton ironworks. He was Walter Richard Parker, Lance-Corporal, who received the VC for bravery in Gallipoli, crossing a fire-swept zone at least 400 yards wide and attending the wounded in an isolated trench. The trench had finally to be evacuated, and Parker helped to remove the wounded, though he himself was seriously wounded during the operation.

One of Sir Walter Scott's Villages

STAUNTON. Hiding in a charming corner where the county meets Leicestershire and Lincolnshire is quiet Staunton, with a fine setting in the English scene and a fine place in our literature. A flagged path embowered in trees leads to the great house and the church, in delightful company, one rich in memories of the family who have been lords of the manor from the Conquest, the other with a goodly array of their memorials.

The long two-storeyed house, still the home of a Staunton and still partly 16th century, stands in a park with a lake at the foot of the sloping lawn where we hear the murmur of the River Devon and the little Winter Beck. It was after staying here that Scott made Staunton the Willingham of his Heart of Midlothian, describing it as "one of those beautiful scenes which are so often found in Merrie England."

A humble bell-rope and a beautiful golden key with a peacock under a crown keep alive the long association of the Stauntons with Belvoir Castle seven miles away. It began when the Norman lords of Belvoir granted the manor of Staunton to an ancestor, on the tenure of Castle Guard which made him responsible for the castle's defence. The high tower at Belvoir is known as Staunton Tower, and when a sovereign visits the castle the golden key of the tower is presented by the head of the family. Now and then the Stauntons give a bell-rope to Bottesford church in memory of the days when its bells gave warning of approaching danger to the castle.

They have shared proudly in the story of our land. William was summoned to the military muster at Nottingham in 1297, Hervey was Chancellor of the Exchequer and Chief Justice in the 14th century. At the time of the Civil War William Staunton was the head of his house, and when Charles raised his standard at Nottingham he attended the king and followed him to battle. Staunton Hall was looted by the Roundheads, and their bullet holes are still in the fine old door.

The beautiful church where many of them lie was made partly new last century, but the high tower, the lofty arcades, the aisle windows, and the charming north doorway are all from the close of the 14th century. The oldest relic is the fine Norman bowl of the font, enriched with interlaced arcading, its modern base set on a step which is part of a 15th century gravestone. There is an Elizabethan table, and an old almsbox made from the stump of a tree. The chief treasure of all is a beautiful oak chancel screen, with an inscription asking prayers for the soul of Simon Yates, who erected it in 1519.

The oldest of the monuments are two battered figures, one cross-legged and wearing fine chain mail, the other headless and almost legless: they may be the son and grandson of the founder of the house. An inscription to William de Staunton (of about 1250) is on

279

a tapering stone which must have been an earlier memorial, for the arcading on its thick edge is about 1100.

The remarkable monument of a 14th century Sir William shows him as in his coffin, the lid cut away to show the upper part of his figure, and again to show his feet on a dog. Lady Joan, in a wimple and a long gown, her feet on a lion, lies on a low tomb of 1366, adorned with shields and quatrefoils. There are floorstones to her mother and her daughter. An inscription of 1757 is to Jane Degge, youngest daughter of the Harvey Staunton whose death brought to an end his family's direct succession for over 600 years without a break. Through an heiress the estates came eventually to the wife of a clergyman, who assumed the old name.

It is believed that very few families have a more complete set of documents relating to a property possessed by them from Norman times. They are preserved from 1190 and run into thousands, and among them are four original charters relating to the emancipation of Hugh Travers, the serf who carried the Cross to the Holy Land in place of Sir William de Staunton, marching with Coeur de Lion to Jerusalem. Born in bondage to de Staunton, he was set free for his crusading, shared all the perils of the expedition, suffered plague and shipwreck, and came home a hero.

STOKEHAM. Few villages can be smaller, but it has a fine view over 14 miles of England's pleasant land to Lincoln's towers.

The tiny church is neat and smiling since restoration in 1928 saved it from its sorry plight, and its ancient tale is told by the Norman tub font and the rubble of much of the walling. The south side of the nave was built when the aisle was destroyed, and in it are the three arches of a tiny arcade.

There are two 13th century lancets, and the 15th century east window has the head of a man on its hood, smiling as if content that his church is so kindly restored. The pretty piscina is 14th century, there are old rafters left in the roof, an oak chest may be 700 years old, and in the churchyard is a stone coffin.

Knight and Lady Hand-in-Hand

STRELLEY. It lies off the beaten track, an unspoiled village with luxuriant lanes and a wealth of trees. From Norman days to Charles the Second there was an unbroken line of Strelleys in this place which gave them a name and a home, and it was their boast that twelve successive generations were knighted. They were renowned for their service to county and country, and were among the biggest landowners in Notts. One joined Earl John in his rebellion against Richard, others shared in the struggle with the barons. About 1356 Sir Sampson de Strelley made himself a lasting memorial by rebuilding the church which shelters their tombs. The last but one of them gave Bulwell a Free Grammar School which still stands, though no longer a school. In 1678 they sold the estates to Ralph Edge, who was three times mayor of Nottingham and has a memorial in the church, standing close to the hall, where his descendants were still living when we called. It is an 18th century house on the old site.

In the peaceful churchyard, where a fine old yew overhangs the road, is Sir Sampson's 14th century church, with remains of the earlier one in the wall of the south aisle, and a tower belonging to all three medieval centuries. The clerestory is about 1500, and of the old glass shields and medallions some are 14th century and some Flemish work of 300 and 400 years ago. The font is 14th century.

A great possession is the almost perfect 15th century chancel screen, with beautiful vaulting. The Jacobean pulpit with a lovely canopy has some older tracery, and two old misereres in the chancel are quaintly carved with a bishop holding up a cross and a crouching grotesque with limbs branching into foliage.

On a beautiful tomb in the middle of the chancel, enriched with 14 angels holding shields, lies Sir Sampson, a knight in armour holding the hand of his lovely lady who wears a richly jewelled head-dress; Sir Sampson's head rests on the crest of a strangled Saracen's head. Of the floorstones to others of the family round the tomb two have traces of figures, and one has a fine engraved portrait of a knight. Two are to brothers and their wives: Sir Robert Strelley who fought at Agincourt, and John of 1421. Another stone has fine brass portraits of Sir Robert Strelley of 1487 and his wife Isabel, sister of Cardinal Kemp.

On a traceried tomb with a handsome canopy adorned with figures in niches and angels lie the alabaster figures of John de Strelley of 1501 and his wife Sanchia Willoughby. John is a knight with his head on the family crest, and sitting on the back of the lion at his feet are two weepers.

In the south transept are two Flanders crosses and a Book of Remembrance of the men who did not come back to Strelley and Bilborough. In Strelley all came home but one. In the cemetery facing the churchyard is a stone peace memorial crucifix.

The Tower on the Roman Road

STURTON-LE-STEEPLE. Gladdened by gay gardens and grass-bordered roads, it carries some of its story in its name, for this town-on-the-street lies in the line of the Roman road from Lincoln to Doncaster, and is dominated by a splendid tower. With a lovely crown of battlements and 12 pinnacles, 9 windows, and a lofty arch, the tower is 600 years old in its lower half, and the upper storeys are 15th century. It is almost the only part of the church which escaped a fire at the beginning of this century; the rest has been reconstructed on the old lines with much of the old material.

The chancel is said to have been the original Norman church, and with the Norman masonry in its north wall is a Norman window now open to the vestry. The north and south doorways are Norman, and so is the bowl of the font, which came from the vanished church of West Burton; it is charmingly set on a flight of steps in the tower. An old piscina is restored, and the chancel screen is part of the beautiful modern woodwork here.

The oldest of the monuments is the stone figure of a woman in a wimple and a long gown, her hands at prayer. Though she has lain here 700 years her features are still clear. She was Lady Olive, and is believed to be one of the Thornhaughs who built the nave at the end of Norman days. They lived at Fenton half a mile away, but only the laundry and a few stone ornaments are left of their old home.

For a time Fenton belonged to a family who bore its name, and it is believed that Edward Fenton, the Elizabethan seaman, was born here. One of the bravest and most skilful of naval heroes, he accompanied Martin Frobisher in the voyage of discovery of the North-West passage, and was pilot in the Admiral's ship in the fight that led to the defeat of the Armada.

Standing erect under a pillared canopy against the tower wall is the figure of Dame Frances Earle, blackened by fire, with a wrap over her head and draped round her. She was the mother of one of the Thornhaughs, and died about 1699 when 80 years old. Their most interesting memorial is a floorstone with arms inlaid in coloured marbles, marking the resting-place of Sir Francis Thornhaugh, the great Parliamentarian and friend of Colonel Hutchinson, whose wife wrote an account of his brave death at the Battle of Preston.

Two Famous Naval Men

SUTTON BONINGTON. One village made out of two, with the churches of old Bonington and Sutton, it rests on a slope of the Soar Valley, looking across the river into Leicestershire. As we travel its pleasant mile-long road we find reminders of men who linked this place with great events in distant seas, and with one of the heroic achievements of our race.

At one end of the village is the gabled Hobgoblins, now two dwellings with something of an ancient house of the monks of Repton Priory; at the other end is a quaint old house with the upper storey of timber and fine herringbone overhanging the lower storey of Charnwood Forest stone. Halfway down the street is a tiny black and white cottage whose beams rise from ground to gable like a great letter A.

Facing this cottage, St Michael's Church stands back from the road in a terraced churchyard. The tower and its lofty spire, rising to 135 feet, come from the close of the 14th century; the south arcade is 13th century, the north arcade and much of the aisles are 14th, and the fine clerestory is 15th. There are stone seats round some of the pillars. The most interesting possession is the 600-year-old font carved with quatrefoils, its unusual feature being three projecting brackets, level with the rim. The oldest relic is part of a 12th century coffin stone in the outside wall near the modern porch.

The chancel was made new last century. There is good modern woodwork (including the screen and the stalls), and beautiful glass which sheds a rich glow. Among the windows in memory of the Pagets of Sutton Hall is one with St Michael and St George, to a soldier who died from wounds in the Transvaal. One with the Women at the Tomb is to Ralph Owen Yearsley, who in 1913 ended 47 years as vicar here.

Two memorials in this quiet church, a brass tablet and the pews, relate to a wider world; both are the gifts of one woman, married in turn to two famous figures who found a haven here from the perils of the sea. The tablet is to Admiral Sir William King-Hall, who, born a year after Waterloo, joined the navy at 13 and served in every sea, winning great distinction in the Chinese War of 1856. A deeply religious man, he conducted services aboard, advocated total abstinence before it was popular, and promoted charitable organisations.

His widow continued to live here after his death, and in 1894 married Sir Alexander Armstrong, a second hero the village came to know. A naval surgeon, he sailed in the Investigator in the middle of last century, searching for the lost Franklin expedition and, having passed along the North Coast of America from the West, reached Banks Land, from whose north-eastern corner the ice was crossed to Melville Island, and the long-sought North-West Passage at last achieved. Armstrong, who had helped to keep the crew alive for years in the Arctic, died here in 1899. His widow reseated the church in his honour.

The tiny towerless church of St Anne nestles high on the hillside, with an ancient bell swinging in the gable. What is left of the old church (after much restoration last century) is 14th century, the time of the nave arcade, the piscina in the chancel, and the font. In a recess in the chancel lies a knight in 15th century armour, a giant seven feet long with his feet on a lion; he was called Old Lion Grey. His identity is uncertain, though his collar of suns and roses assures us that he was a Yorkist.

Admiral King-Hall lives on in memory here, as at St Michael's, a window to him showing Christ walking on the sea with Peter, a miracle he must often have expounded to stay the troubled minds of his men beset by tempests in far latitudes.

The glory of this little church is its lovingly tended garden of roses, lawn, and trees, where we look over the village to the hills of Charnwood Forest.

The Village Queen of Sheba

SUTTON-CUM-LOUND. It has little but its church, but that is much. It stands with limes and sycamores above the village. Its 15th century tower, with eight pinnacles and a lofty arch, has two bells which have been ringing since before the Armada. The stone-roofed porch and the rest of the walls are all embattled, and are adorned with pinnacles and a gallery of sculptured heads. Some are cunningly fashioned at the foot of the pinnacles.

The old doorway through which we enter has the original folding door with its old plate and ring. Over the doorway is a round arch which seems to be Norman. A beautiful 14th century arcade divides the nave from the aisle, and a similar arcade is between the chancel and its chapel. The lofty Norman chancel arch has been rebuilt, three lovely sedilia and a piscina are medieval, and a fine founder's recess has a feathered arch with pinnacles and a finial.

Three poppyheads of 23 old bench-ends are carved with an eagle, a happy-looking angel, and the trim head of a lady the villagers call the Queen of Sheba. The handsome bands of vine carving in two old benches in the chancel belonged to the old chancel screen, and remains of a 15th century screen are in the modern screen of the chancel chapel. An old pillar almsbox has three locks, an oak chest is 17th century, and another chest is shaped from a solid block of oak, its small cavity covered by a heavily iron-banded lid which is secured by an iron bar on the front of the chest. At the ends of the hammer-beams of the modern roofs of the nave and chancel are stone heads, most of them crowned.

A brass inscription tells of John Farmer, who was vicar here for nearly half a century, both he and his wife dying in 1921.

At Barnby Moor, a mile from Sutton on the Great North Road, is a famous old posting house known to every traveller between London and York before the coming of the railway. Known as the Bell Inn, it became for many years a private house, and part of it even a chapel, but it is now brought charmingly up-to-date as a hotel.

Amazing Timothy Hall

SUTTON-IN-ASHFIELD. This home of 20,000 people busy in factories and mines carries in its name the memory of days when it was a small village abounding in ash trees on the border of Sherwood Forest, and of the great family to whom it belonged.

It was Edward the Confessor's village before the Conquest, and Saxon names survive in its roads; but its story is far older than Saxon, for a silver coin of Caius Claudius Pulcher 93 BC has been found in a garden in the town, and in the library is the skull of a chieftain whose skeleton was found in St Michael Street in 1892. He lay in the middle of seven men whose feet were all turned towards him, a form of burial in the later Stone Age.

Four centuries ago this village saw a tragic figure pass through its streets a few days before he was to die. He was the fallen Wolsey, who spent the night at Kirkby Hardwick a mile from here when journeying slowly to Leicester. He may have seen the manor house not far from the church, for its oldest part comes from the early 16th century.

Here came George Whitefield to preach, and here was born, in 1812, that amazing Spencer Timothy Hall, who could plough and reap, stack and thresh and winnow, make a stocking and a shoe, write a book and print and bind it, and cure all sorts of ills. Perhaps the most astonishing Jack of all Trades of his day, he sleeps at Blackpool, but he is still known as the Sherwood Forester, and will long be remembered here.

A long avenue of limes leads us from the road to the churchyard, which has an ancient yew said to be 700 years old, with a trunk slender for its years and shorn of half its spreading branches. In its shade are 18th century stones of the Brandreth family, relatives of the Jeremiah Brandreth who was executed as leader of the pitiful Pentrich Rebellion (in which Shelley interested himself) during the general unrest after Waterloo. A stone by the path leading to the porch is in memory of Ann Burton, who, if she did nothing worth recording in her life, achieved something remarkable at the end by dying on the 30th of February in 1836. It is one of several records we have found of days that never were.

The church is of light-coloured local stone, and has some interesting old remains in spite of severe restoration. Built by the Suttons in the 12th century, it was given by them to Thurgarton Priory, and John de Sutton in the 14th century left money to build the tower and spire. An ancient floorstone in the chancel, engraved with a great bow and arrow, is said to have had an inscription to one of the Suttons. Another interesting relic of the family was found when the sexton was digging a grave in 1870. It was a tiny 14th century metal seal with a ring for hanging it round the neck, carved on one side with a fleur-de-lys and on the other with a monk and an acolyte sitting with open books. Above the monk was a squirrel cracking nuts.

The nave arcades come from the close of Norman days, and the

286

chancel arch is half a century later. A lovely 13th century fragment is at the east of the north arcade, its three shafts crowned by a capital with three heads. The round bowl of a Norman font has been rescued from the vicarage garden. The top of a small shaft piscina, with scroll ornament, is a century older than Magna Carta.

Names of over 200 men "who gave their lives for their country and their souls to God" are remembered here. One has a memorial window, and an inscription tells of another who perished while attending the wounded near Armentières.

Just outside the town on the road to Mansfield is a fine reservoir made by the Duke of Portland in 1836 for irrigation of his meadows. It helps to grind flour in the stone mill close by, made new but still known as King's Mill, its name perhaps recalling days when kings came to their royal manor of Mansfield to hunt in the Forest.

The Rare Old Screen

SUTTON-ON-TRENT. It touches the Great North Road, and goes down in an unbroken sweep of meadows to the Trent. At one end of the village a lovely old church adds beauty to the road; at the other stands an old windmill with derelict sails. A turn of the road near the church leads by a wayside stream to pretty gardens, one delightful with a rockery, old-world pump, and well.

The church came into Domesday Book, and its 13th century tower with a 15th century top still stands on its Saxon foundations, though it lost a spire a century ago. Deep battlements, with gargoyles below them, enhance the beauty of a remarkably fine 15th century clerestory, and faces adorn the windows all round the church.

A handsome addition is the early 16th century Mering Chapel, which may have been brought here from Mering across the river. Pinnacles enrich its buttresses and rise from its parapet, which is carved with flowers, shields, faces, and gargoyles; one gargoyle shows two lizard-like creatures coiling round a head. A beautiful roof looks down on the rich work inside, where great windows with fragments of rich old glass fill it with light. The walls are enriched with arcading, shields, and brackets, and the lovely piscina is one of three in the church. Two arches between the chapel and the chancel rest on a beautifully carved pillar, and under one of them is a great tomb, perhaps of Sir William Mering. Dividing the chapel from the aisle is a rare oak screen of about 1510, with delicate carving of tracery, bands of quatrefoils, and trailing flowers. Its loft, seven feet wide and almost like a gallery, overhangs both sides. It is a pity so fine a screen has been spoiled for the sake of the organ.

The sides of the chancel arch are late 12th century, but the arch and the nave arcades are a hundred years later. The bowl of the font may be 17th century on a medieval stem: its pyramid cover and the altar are Jacobean. Among the poppyheads of 15 old stall-ends are birds, bearded faces, a grinning face, and two women smiling at each other.

Lovely for its 14th century stonework and for its modern glass is the east window of the north aisle, shining with figures of St George, St Gabriel, the Madonna, and St Ursula. Except for some old fragments, it is the only coloured glass in the church.

A Day in the Civil War

SYERSTON. Close to the Fosse Way, but untroubled by its stir, are its few farms and cottages with a tiny old church.

It is surprisingly pleasing inside, with walls aslant, traceried windows, and timbered roof. Except for its battlements the tiny tower is 13th century, and one of its two bells is older than the Reformation. The buttresses on each side of the church are as old as the tower, the entrance to the porch and the doorway into the church are 14th century. The chancel, made partly new, has its old piscina, a wooden arch on richly carved stone corbels, and a neat modern screen. The glass of the east window, glowing in rich colour with a scene of the Crucifixion, is to George Henry Fillingham, in whose memory the church was restored in 1896.

The treasure of the church is an exquisite little oak pulpit of 1636, its eight sides, backboard, and canopy all a mass of carved panels. The font, on a traceried shaft, is 600 years old.

Syerston had a day of adventure in the Civil War, when two or three hundred Royalist Cavalry, quartered here and at Elston a mile away, were surprised by Colonel Hutchinson, Governor of Nottingham Castle. The colonel took many of them prisoner, but their leader, Captain Thimbleby, refused to surrender and was killed. A rescuing party dashed from Newark, but the colonel reached Nottingham safely with his captives.

Scrooby   The Old Church

Scrooby   The Manor House

Ollerton **The Stately Beeches**

Wilford **A Charming Corner**

The Splendour of the Norman Doorway

TEVERSAL. Crowning a green hilltop, looking out to Hardwick Hall in splendid trees two miles away, it is a charming oasis where we forget the collieries and find treasure wrought by men who knew not coal.

Avenues of limes wandering through the village bring us to a delightful architectural group in stone—the old church, the rectory, and the manor house old and new, its harmony of gables and mullioned windows as background to fine lawn and flowers.

The glory of the little church is the remarkable south doorway built by the Normans, fascinating for a series of 19 medallions (continuous in the arch and sides) carved with a great variety of patterns and symbols including stars and crosses, three fishes, a bird, a snake, a holy lamb, and a priest. Round these are other carved stones, and on the end of the hood are a quaint little figure and a beakhead. It frames a 15th century doorway still swinging on its three old hinges. This fine doorway was perhaps at the west end till the tower with stepped battlements was built in the 15th century.

Two of the tower walls project into the western bays of the nave arcades. The south arcade is Norman, leading to an aisle which was widened in the 15th century. The 13th century north arcade, with two great corbel heads like masks, and capitals enriched with nailhead, opens to a narrow aisle with 14th century windows. A bracket in this aisle and the chancel arch are 13th century.

The Normans made the plain font. Fragments of ancient carved stones are in the outside walls and in the floor of the porch. In the south aisle wall is a tiny coffin stone with a cross, and above its east window is a stone with 1684, the initials I. M, and the cross of the arms of Molyneux which we see on the gate of the manor house. The nave roof has 15th century timbers and bosses, and quaint wooden figures at the ends of the beams. The altar table is Jacobean, and the chest is decrepit with its very long life.

Side by side in the south aisle are two finely engraved floorstones. One has the portrait of Roger Greenhalgh who may have built the manor house in the 16th century; his hair is falling to his shoulders, his fur-trimmed gown has a sash tied in a bow, his hands are in

U

prayer, and his head rests on a cushion under a canopy. His wife's stone has a great cross.

In this aisle is the splendid pew of the house of Molyneux, who followed the family of Greenhalgh as lords of the manor. Looking rather like a four-poster bed with its richly panelled canopy supported by four spiral columns and capitals carved with foliage, it comes from 1684, its dark oak harmonising well with the box-pews of the nave and chancel. On the chancel walls are the elaborate Molyneux monuments, three of the 17th and 18th century having an array of five busts. A marble plaque has the head of the last baronet, Sir Francis of 1812, who was for 47 years Gentleman Usher of the Black Rod.

There are two memorials to 20th century lords of the manor, the Carnarvons, one of white marble with painted arms and the beautiful head of a woman is to Gwendolin Herbert, daughter of the third Earl, who died in 1915.

The Pictorial Walls

THORNEY. In this quiet little place, delightful with orchards and glorious trees, the traveller will find a few ruins of an ancient church, and a modern successor of a remarkable kind. The old remains are two arches and pillars of a medieval arcade, a 15th century window and the top of another, and fragments of carved stones, set up in the churchyard which is screened from the hall by mighty elms and limes and beeches.

The church of today was built in Norman style in the middle of last century, and is an unusual sight with its mass of carving inside and out, its huge blocks of stone needing the mellowing touch of time. We may imagine that the builders sought to make it a pictorial encyclopedia of church ornamentation in Norman England.

The arresting west front of the church faces the road, and is full of detail. The doorway has pillars all differently carved, a round arch with every manner of moulding and figure in cable, ropework, dragons, heads of humans and animals; and a hood with zigzag lines and wheels ending in crowned heads. Above the doorway are three lancets with pillars at their sides, and over them is a wheel window. A stringcourse with rings and chip carving ends at each side in a great projecting dragon's head with a curled tongue. There are 17 of these dragons round the church.

Crowning this remarkable west wall is a bell turret with two bells swinging in a round-headed arch with more carving, and below the turret are six grotesque corbel heads, part of a gallery of over a hundred which encircle the building and adorn the elaborate little turret between the nave and chancel.

Lofty hammerbeam roofs with carved beams and stone corbels of winged angels and heads of human folk look down on the spacious interior of the nave and chancel, dimly lit by narrow windows. The rich carving continues in the chancel arch, on the sedilia and piscina, and on the priest's doorway. The stone lectern and the pulpit, entered by a flight of steps from the chancel, are a study in themselves, the pulpit showing Bible scenes, the heads of the Twelve Disciples in tiny medallions, and the symbols of the Four Evangelists.

The fine modern font is elaborate with arcading and a band of scroll work; and, as if not to be outdone by the new, the battered Norman tub font is here with its intricate arcading and lattice, fragments of knotwork mixed with foliage and quaint figures, and a plaited band round the rim of the bowl.

Over a mile away is Wigsley, one of three Thankful Villages in Notts, for the seven men who went from it to the war all came back. The names are on the Roll of Honour in the little Methodist chapel.

Old Church, White House, and Red-Roofed Barns

THOROTON. Every Nottinghamshire man knows it as the village which gave its name to the ancestors of Robert Thoroton, the county's historian. Everybody loves it for its rustic charm of green-bordered road, its round 14th century dovecot, wide views of serene countryside, and the old church in company with a white house and red-roofed barns.

The exquisite tower and its graceful spire (with three tiers of dormer windows) have been a landmark for nearly 600 years. A stair turret projects from the tower; buttresses climb to the lovely parapet of open quatrefoils on a corbel table of great heads, with gargoyles at the corners; and a niche on the west side, over 12 feet high, has sculptured figures at the sides of its elaborate canopy.

The chancel is made new and the porch is modern, but the nave has a Norman arcade and a 14th century one. The plain round font is Norman. Older still is a charming little Saxon window which allows the dawn to steal into the vestry like a finger of light. Deeply splayed inside and out, it is less than two feet long and four or five inches wide. Built into the outside wall above it is one of the stones of the vanished Norman chancel arch.

The Silver Cup

THORPE. The sight of its small church from the Fosse Way calls us to this secluded village near Newark. Standing beyond the rectory lawn at a bend of the road, it was rebuilt in 1873 except for the low 13th century buttressed tower with a pyramid top. The font is a curious combination of an old step, a 14th century shaft, and a small bowl which may have been a Norman stoup; its domed cover is 17th century. Three other relics are a pillar piscina, a piscina niche, and a Jacobean coffin stool.

A window showing the Women at the Tomb is in memory of one of Kitchener's Fighting Scouts in South Africa. Nearly six centuries ago Sir William de Thorpe was fighting at Crecy, and was one of the company who saw Calais surrendered to their king; here in the church lies the battered stone figure of his widow, wearing a wimple, her feet resting on a dog, her arms broken.

One of the treasures of the altar is a silver cup given by Henry Druell as a thankoffering for his safe return from London in 1665, when the plague was raging.

Old-World by the River

THRUMPTON. Even the swift-flowing Trent lingers here, making a backwater where the ferryboat waits; and red houses and farms climb gently past the arched and turreted entrance of the gabled hall to the little church above the wayside. It is an old-world corner.

The great house with mellowed brick walls stands by the river, sheltered by woods which clothe the hillside. It was refashioned in the 17th century by the Pigots, who gave it the carved oak staircase at the time of the Restoration. Before the Pigots, Thrumpton was for centuries the home of the Powtrells, who lost their estates through being concerned in the Gunpowder Plot; and Henry Garnett, one of the conspirators, is said to have known of the hidden stairway here, and of the secret room cut out in the cellars, even if he did not use them. Now the hall is the home of Lord Byron.

Among the magnificent trees in the grounds is a group of elms which were saplings when the Tudor dynasty was rising to its Golden Age. Two towering larches are perhaps unsurpassed in the county, and four cedars are living memorials of notable events, commemorating the Jubilee of George the Third, the crowning of George the Fourth, Queen Victoria's Jubilee, and the end of the Great War. There is a charming rose garden prettily laid out with tiny paths.

In the stillness of the lovely churchyard with its glorious elms and limes, a soldier in uniform lies in a recess of the church wall, a memorial to three men who did not come back, striking in its lifelike simplicity.

Pleasing and cared-for (though dim with coloured glass) the church was much restored when the chancel was made new in 1872, but it has its 13th and 14th century low tower, and the massive old font stands in the churchyard. Memorials of the Pigots, Emmertons, and Westcombs are in the tower. It was through the Emmertons, who followed the Pigots, that Thrumpton came to the Byrons.

George Alvey, who was born in the village and worked for the Byrons all his life, had just ended his 82 years when we called. For 70 years he was a bellringer, and was never known to be absent. For 45 years he served as clerk and sexton.

The Lovely Doorway

THURGARTON. It nestles at the foot of low hills two miles from the Trent, and through it runs a stream spanned by many little bridges, by one of which we saw the kingfisher flash past.

A lane with time-worn flags beside a mellowed wall (a deep cutting overhung with orchard bloom in spring) winds steeply up to the Hall and church in close and happy company. From the end of a path hedged in by box and yew, a dainty rockery corner opens out to a garden with a magnificent cedar among its wealth of flowers and trees.

Still known as the Priory, the big house is on the site of a monastery founded by Ralph d'Eyncourt, whose grandfather came with the Conqueror and received 67 lordships as his share of the spoils. For 300 years after the Dissolution Thurgarton belonged to the

Coopers, and was garrisoned by Sir Roger for Charles Stuart. It was John Gilbert Cooper, whom Dr Johnson called the Punchinello of Literature, who pulled down what remained of the old priory and built the present house, leaving the undercroft below. Dr Riddings, first Bishop of Southwell, whose fine bronze figure kneels in his Minster, lived in the house for ten years till his death. Its stretch of lawn is a perfect setting for the beautiful west end of the church.

The lovely 13th century fragments of the old priory church were restored last century when the chancel and north aisle were built. For over 700 years its one remaining tower has stood at the north-west corner, crowned with 15th century battlements. Stately and massive, lighted by lancet windows and adorned with lancet arcading, it has a fine arcaded stairway and a charming west doorway richly carved and deeply recessed. A rare gem is the deep west doorway of the nave, with eight shafts at each side and much ornament; it is one of the loveliest 13th century doorways in all England.

After the charm of the outside, the interior is gloomy and disappointing. Three bays of the old arcades remain on each side of the nave, some of the massive shafted pillars over 18 feet round. The south aisle is absorbed into the Hall. From the 14th century come one or two windows, the altar stone with five crosses, the sedilia, and two engraved floorstones. There are three old miserere stalls, and a chair is made up of Jacobean carving.

Darby and Joan

TITHBY. A pleasant neighbour of Bingham, this quiet company of cottages and farms gathers round a plain little church with a very big key, standing among elms and limes and chestnuts.

Its queer tower is fairly modern except for the buttresses, and it wears a pyramid cap. From the 14th century come the nave arcades, the priest's doorway, the lovely ironwork on an old chest, and the font (on which the date 1662 tells of its restoration after being cast out by the Puritans). There are two old roofs, an old piscina, and an old poppyhead seat. Among the odd things here are a row of hat pegs on the chancel wall, an eight-sided pillar boarded round, a brick pillar climbing through the gallery from the floor to support a tie-beam, and a strange assortment of chairs and pews.

There is a 15th century inscription to Thomas Chaworth, one of the family who were lords of Tithby for many generations and built the first Wiverton Hall close by. In the churchyard is a cross to Lina Chaworth-Musters, who died at the hall in 1912.

Under a tomb in the churchyard lie Tithby's Darby and Joan. They were John Marriot and his wife Mary, who both lived to be 94, John dying in 1866 and Mary following him the year after.

> *He first deceased her, she a little tried*
> *To live without him, liked it not, and died.*

Nottingham's Airport

TOLLERTON. Its oldtime peace is disturbed by the hum of many planes, for it has become Nottingham's Airport, with an aerodrome covering 140 acres.

The hall and the church, with a brave array of towers and turrets, pinnacles and battlements, stand sheltered by trees in company with the white rectory. Facing the church is a fine cross with St George and St Michael in its lantern head, keeping green the memory of three men who did not come back. Near a row of four fine chestnut trees is a quaint building with an archway which once led to the forge.

The great house was rebuilt in 1794 by the last of a Norman family who lived here for 700 years. It has become a Congregational College bearing the name of Dr J. B. Paton, a famous nonconformist whose hand was in a hundred movements for uplifting the people of his day. It was the rebuilder of the house, Pendock Barry, who made the church new some years later, and set up the small block of almshouses with an arched entrance and a courtyard. He built the embattled way from the house to the mausoleum he added to the church, where we see his monument of 1847 with other memorials of the family.

The oldest possession of the neat little church is a rare Norman shaft piscina, three feet high and handsomely carved with diamond pattern and scrolls. It was brought back to church from a neighbouring plantation some years ago, to keep company with a dainty modern font, shaped like a chalice and seen through an outer case of eight sides carved with open tracery. A roundel of old glass has a hooded head, and the nave arcades may be 13th century.

TRESWELL. It looks out to Lincoln cathedral 15 miles away when the day is clear. Its simple little church, with warm buff tints in the grey stone walls, is in a churchyard with fine trees (horse-chestnuts, limes, and firs) bounded on one side by the little Lee Beck, and on another by the rector's garden.

The lofty tower is 15th century. From the 14th come the doorway within the pretty rebuilt porch and the fine little chancel with beautiful tracery in its big windows. Built into a wall is about two-thirds of a fine Norman coffin stone, with stem and crosshead carved in relief. The north arcade is 15th century, its end arches, like the tower arch, resting on embattled corbels. The massive font is 500 years old and is carved with flowers in quatrefoils. The villagers take communion from a silver chalice of Elizabeth's day.

The Last of His Line

TROWELL. Collieries and ironworks are in its near view, but from the crown of the hill and the top of the church tower is a fine panorama of the Erewash Valley, and richly wooded hills with Charnwood Forest on the horizon. In the 15th century tower are the works of the old clock which used to tell the time in the biggest open marketplace in England, the great space in front of the Council House at Nottingham.

The clerestory is as old as the tower, and the nave arcades are 14th century. From the close of that century come the buttresses, the stone-roofed porch, the square-headed windows, and the beautiful font with quatrefoils and an embattled edge. The 13th century chancel has its old sedilia and piscina, a narrow arch reaching nearly to the roof, and a modern east window with angels looking down on Mary, Our Lord enthroned, and St Helena by a great cross. It is one of only two coloured windows, both showing fine figures in jewelled raiment; the Crucifixion is in memory of a rector's son who did not come back.

A wall monument to William Hacker (who has been sleeping here since 1668) recalls a family famous in the county; his cousin led Charles Stuart to the scaffold. In the farmhouse facing the church is part of the old home of the Hackers of Trowell, and it was here that the last of this line, Sir John, broke his neck by falling downstairs in 1735. He lies in the church.

What God Hath Built

TUXFORD. The Great North Road runs through this quiet old town where Scott's Jeanie Deans stayed the night on her weary journey to London.

Most of its interests are within a stone's throw of the cross-roads and the old market square round which it clusters. The ancient church is near the 18th century hall, and opposite the hall is the Grammar School with the inscription over the doorway, "What God hath built let no man destroy." Though a school no longer, it is little changed since it was founded by Charles Read of Darlton, who made a fortune as a shipper 300 years ago. One of the rules he left for Tuxford School was that the boys should sweep out the schoolhouse in turn on Saturday afternoons or else be fined sixpence. The inn in the square (built after a fire in 1702, which destroyed much of the town) reminds us of the days when Tuxford was an important posting station for the half-dozen towns round it.

Looking over the town from the Retford road are three windmills whose work is done. At the other end, by the side of the Newark road, stands a stone pillar marking the grave of a rebel buried there in 1746.

The church outside looks even older than its years, for the soft Tuxford sandstone is badly weathered. A few feet of herringbone masonry in the west wall of the south aisle takes its story back perhaps to Saxon days, but the church is chiefly medieval. The tower and spire are 14th century except for an older window and doorway, and the spire, which has four dormers halfway up, has the singular appearance of being broached though it rises within a parapet. It is an interesting example of the passing of the broach with the coming of the parapet.

The 15th century south porch and a doorway a century older bring us to a nave crowned by a fine clerestory, its windows only a little shorter than the similar ones in the aisles: it was built in 1475 by Sir John Stanhope, whose arms are on the battlement. The nave arcades are 14th century, except for the 13th century pillars on the north side and the half-pillars on the south. The chancel was made new in the closing years of the 15th century, but its arch, part of its north arcade, and its piscina, are 700 years old. There is fine 15th century tracery in the modern chancel screen; the nave roof has some timbering and bosses of that time; and on the ends of the roof beams are ten painted angels resting on stone heads. The 17th century font has a fine pyramid cover and a suspended canopy, both richly carved, the canopy having the inscription "Francis Turner made this 1673."

The east end of the south aisle was the chantry of St Lawrence, and in its east window we see him in old black and yellow glass, holding his grid. On the wall below is a quaint stone sculpture of about 1400, showing the saint lying on the grid under a rich canopy, and figures of three men rather battered, one with the bellows having lost his head. The old piscina is still here, and resting on a bracket carved with a bearded face is part of a draped figure. Built into the wall of the modern north porch is a gravestone showing the head and shoulders of a priest recessed in a quatrefoil, a chalice below his praying hands.

The north chancel chapel was widened in the 18th century to be a burial-place for the Whites, lords of Tuxford for many generations. The alabaster figures of Sir John White of 1625 and his wife lie on a tomb, their heads resting on tasselled cushions, both without hands or feet but wearing beautiful ruffs. Sir John, with a pointed beard, is in armour; his lady's mantle and gown have exquisite borders, and she has a fine chain round her shoulders. Charles Lawrence White, mortally wounded in 1814 at Bayonne, has a white wall monument with a carving of his grave and those of three brother officers.

One of two ancient figures in the chapel is a cross-legged knight with a broken sword, his feet on a battered beast; the other is a slender woman in alabaster, wearing a long gown adorned with roses, her feet on two small dogs; one is biting the other's ears and the other his companion's paw.

Beautiful glass of our own day fills two chancel windows. In the east is a Te Deum window glowing softly with cherubs in the tracery, a choir of minstrel angels, Our Lord in Glory, and four fine figures of saints. The other, in memory of Armistice Day, shows Thomas Becket robed in red and gold, the Madonna and Child in blue and white, and Peter in brown and gold. The modern pulpit is richly carved with a border of vines, and figures of St Agnes, St Anne, and Our Lord on the Cross.

A Diamond for the Crown

UPTON. It sees from its slope the delightful countryside where the little River Greet runs to the Trent, and it has a fine view of the valley from its churchyard, seeing Lincoln Cathedral on a clear day.

Elms and a great chestnut are among the beautiful trees about the church, whose glory is its splendid 15th century tower. Buttressed to the top, it is crowned with eight pinnacles clustered round a central one, known as the Nine Disciples. Up in the tower is a priest's room with a fireplace, and holes in the walls where doves nested in olden days. It is one of the very few tower dovecots still left in our churches.

Medieval windows fill the church with light. The nave arcade with clustered pillars, the rebuilt chancel arch, and the small arch between the aisle and the shallow transept, are all 13th century. The transept has a tiny peephole, and has been restored in memory of ten men who died for peace. The 14th century font has been brought back from the churchyard. By the pulpit are fragments of two earthen jars which were used in olden times as amplifiers of sound, the first loud speakers. The greatest possession here is a lovely chest over six feet long, adorned with iron bands and stars with tiny roses and trefoils; it may be 13th century.

Here was born one of a great host of 19th century men who made their way from small beginnings and built up our knowledge of the world. He was James Tennant, who began work at a shop dealing in minerals and shells, and grew up to be Professor of Mineralogy at King's College. He was one of a family of 12, his father an officer of the excise; his mother belonged to a yeoman family living in Upton for two centuries. Young Tennant was able to hear Michael Faraday's lectures at the Royal Institution, and Faraday became his friend. He was one of the first experts to confirm the genuineness of the first diamonds found in South Africa, and he was in charge of the cutting of the Koh-i-nor for Queen Victoria's crown.

The Queer Old Head

WALESBY. It lies in the byways, with Hanging Hill Plantation and the fine mass of Bevercotes Park on one hand, and on the other a pretty spot where the Whitewater flows by willow banks.

It is proud of its fine little church with a 15th century tower, and of the glorious trees in the churchyard; two splendid beeches bring us to the door (though one is now only half of its old self), two others are in a majestic row of limes, and there are ancient yews.

Its oldest possessions are a plain Norman doorway and the fine Norman bowl of the font; over the doorway is a modern porch with fragments of 13th century arcading in its walls, used now as a vestry. The north doorway, with part of an ancient coffin stone for a step, opens to an interior filled with light by charming medieval windows. The nave arcade comes from the close of the 13th century, its short arches on tall pillars.

The restored piscina in the 14th century chancel has a strange old head supporting the projecting drain, the face all awry, and resting on the hands of two arms coming from the wall. Over the piscina a small crowned head is wearing away, and on an old bracket in the aisle lies a stone corbel carved with a face. The 17th century pulpit has panels carved with thistles and leaves, and eight oak benches 400 years old have set the pattern for the new ones.

Twentieth Century Craftsmen

WALKERINGHAM. It is a mile from the Trent, where the ferry takes us into Lincolnshire. Its all-embattled church, rising from a trim belt of lawn and a bright border of flowers, has the old twin-gabled manor house for company, and close by is a fragment of the old market cross on three great steps.

The church has nothing older than its 13th century nave arcades, the pillars resting on fine square bases made eight-sided at the top. From the 15th century come the tower, the clerestory, and most of the windows, and two arches in the north wall of the chancel. These arches rest on a 13th century pillar, and on their hood are three quaint little heads. An old face peeps unexpectedly from the wall of the north aisle.

Much old timber remains in the roofs; there are three old benches, a Jacobean table, and an elm chest with its original ironwork (over 400 years old) and a new lid. The altar rails are very beautiful with trailing vine and grapes and ears of wheat hanging from the rail, and four splendid poppyheads carved with foliage and partridges among growing corn. We found the vicar and the sexton working here like two medieval craftsmen, adapting the 400-year-old screen to let more light into the chancel; using the upper part to enclose the vestry (where there is other old screenwork), and embodying the 17th century pulpit with the base.

On an elaborate monument kneel Francis Williamson and his wife, he in rich attire, and she in a full-skirted gown and flowing headdress of Stuart days. Three sons kneel below, and a rhyming epitaph bids us use this monument as a mirror in which to see ourselves:

> *Then thoughts and cares for long life save,*
> *And be undressing for the grave.*

Strange Tales

WALLINGWELLS. Its great days are gone, and with them the glory of the big house and the beauty of the fine park. A modern house turned into flats, it has stones in some of its walls which come from Norman days, for in it were built materials from Ralph de Cheurolcourt's nunnery of the reign of Stephen.

Buried near the house are several stone coffins and in one opened about a hundred years ago was found the body of Dame Margery Dourant, the second prioress. Her body was in perfect condition, and with her were a pair of shoes and a silver chalice.

A curious tale of natural history we heard in Wallingwells, which for long had a witness in the great house. One of its curios was a stuffed heron with an eel coiled round its neck, the bird having been found by the lake with the eel still alive. The heron had pierced the head of the eel with its long bill, and the eel had strangled the bird, each killing the other.

Another village story is of a squire and his son of last century, who were hawking at Scarborough. The boy was overtaken by the tide and washed out to sea, and would have been drowned had not the hawk fastened to his wrist struck out with its powerful wings and dragged him ashore.

The Church in Peril

WARSOP. With the River Meden dividing it into Market Warsop and Church Warsop, this small mining town on the border of the Dukeries was mostly open forest as late as the 18th century.

Looking down to its busy neighbour, Church Warsop is delightful with the old church high above the road, the grey stone rectory with a splendid beech, and a long stone farmhouse by the churchyard which is said to have been the old rectory and has a fine pigeon cote. The present rectory (embodying part of a Tudor house) was the home of the Fitzherberts, lords of the manor, till they went to Nettleworth Hall, of which we have a good view from the Mansfield road.

Built by William Wyld in the time of Elizabeth, the hall was rebuilt by another William in 1785, after it had been destroyed by fire. One of the family was Gervase Wyld, who settled here after making a fortune out of the Spaniards as a merchant in Andalusia, and later fitted out a ship at his own expense to fight them in the Armada, providing his men with arrows tipped with iron bands. He lived to be 93.

Old yews grow about the church, which came into Domesday Book and still has much old work to show. Except for its 14th century top storey, the tower is chiefly Norman, with an original buttress, a small Norman window with a Maltese cross cut on one side, and a fine Norman arch with cable moulding on the capitals. The priest's doorway, and a blocked doorway in the north aisle, are also Norman. From the 15th century come the lofty entrance to the porch and the north arcade of the nave. The doorway letting us in, the south arcade with stone seats round two clustered pillars, and the lovely sedilia and piscina, are from the end of the 13th century. The chancel arch of this time was raised three feet in the 15th century by placing short shafts on the old capitals; and the clerestory comes from the end of the same century.

The east window glows richly with the Crucifixion and the Ascension, in memory of Sir Richard Fitzherbert of 1906, rector and lord of the manor. Some 15th century beams are left in the roofs of the nave and chancel. The chancel roof is enriched with six gilded angels, and bosses with flowers, an angel with a shield, and a lion; two bosses in the nave have a woman's head and a grotesque with hands in its mouth.

An effective addition of over 400 years ago is the vestry on the south side of the chancel, but its outer entrance and its pinnacles are modern work. It has two quaint gargoyles, and three small windows with old glass made up from fragments found in the chest, among the oldest fragments being a 13th century head of a woman saint. A 14th century head with a beard and a curious brimmed hat reminds us of the merchant in the Canterbury Tales who wore a "Flandrith bever hat."

A 16th century floorstone is built into the tower. There are several brass inscriptions to the Wylds, but no memorial to the grand old man of 93, and even the entry in the register telling of his death has been almost nibbled away by mice. An elaborate wall monument tells of John Rolleston of 1681, who was secretary to the famous Duke of Newcastle (General for a time to the royal forces in the Civil War), and is said by his efforts to have saved Welbeck when the rest of the duke's estates were lost. We read how Oliver Dand, a rector, "continued peacefully through Royalist and Cromwellian times" and died in 1661; and of Samuel Martin who was rector 53 years and has been sleeping outside the chancel since 1859, when he died at 89. There is no stone to mark his grave.

Of our own day is the beautiful oak reredos with rich tracery and canopied figures of Peter and Paul.

Such was Warsop church when we saw it first in 1933; since then it has been in a cradle of wood and steel, unique measures having been taken to protect it from damage while coal is mined underneath it. The walls and pillars are underpinned by steel girders buried in cement; similar girders support the walls above ground, arches have wooden supports, and some of the window mouldings and glass were removed for safety. It is thought the church may sink over four feet before the subsidence is complete, but as we went to press it was expected that the cradle of wood and steel would soon be removed.

The Beautiful Gates

WATNALL. It is two hamlets, Watnall Chaworth and Watnall Cantilupe, making up a charming village which we remember for its neat cottages, stately trees, and the fine entrance to the drive of the great house, all in happy company on a lovely bit of road with holly-crowned walls.

Well worthy of admiration are the great iron gates of Watnall Hall, shaded by mighty trees. Probably wrought by Huntingdon Shaw, the Nottingham blacksmith of renown, they bear a gilded eagle's head, the crest of the ancient family of Rollestons, who have lived here since the time of Queen Elizabeth.

To that time belongs part of their house, standing on high ground in a park of 60 acres with fine old timber. It looks across to the hills of Annesley, where lived Mary Chaworth, Byron's first love; and from there she came to dance at Watnall's famous balls.

We remember the village, too, as the beginning of a fine little ride down the hollow and up the hill to where the bells in Greasley's lofty tower call the folk to church. It is a lovely mile, with beauty all the way.

WELLOW. It has its tall maypole on the green, and lies in a charming setting under Wellow Park, winding ways abounding in glorious trees.

At one of its lovely spots a wooded lane comes from Rufford to Wellow Dam, a placid pool in a wayside common; another delightful lane has splendid views of Sherwood Forest as it climbs to the edge of the park, bringing us to a field with the moated site of a fortified house that belonged to a lord of the manor in the 13th century.

The much-restored little church has a sturdy 14th century tower with a corbel table under 15th century battlements and pinnacles. The nave arcade is about 1300, and one of its corbels is like the head of a monkey. Several windows are medieval, and a lancet comes from the close of the 12th century. Under the tower is a font bowl at which Norman children were baptised, now used no more. The modern stone pulpit has a figure of St Swithin.

The Adventure of the Stone Man

WEST BRIDGFORD. Here, across the Trent Bridge from Nottingham, are the famous county cricket and one of the county football grounds.

With its rapid growth from an old village to a pleasant place of over 13,000 people, has come the growth of the church, and the small building of long ago is now the southern part of a spacious place. The 15th century tower (with earlier masonry in its base) still stands at the west end of the old nave, and into the old porch have been built two 14th century windows from a vanished wall. Here still is the 14th century arcade, and in the old chancel (now a chapel) are lovely canopied sedilia with quaint tracery. The old aisle has its double piscina and a 13th century lancet; the font is 600 years old.

The two 14th century east windows of the old chancel have lovely new glass showing St Giles with his hind and St Hugh with a swan at his feet, holding a model of Lincoln Cathedral. Four panels in each window tell the story of Jesus, showing Mary as a child, the Nativity, the shepherds in the field, Simeon and the Madonna; the Wise Men, the Return from Egypt, Jesus in the workshop and with the Doctors. A charming medieval window which was above these two now rests in the porch, and a modern copy is in its place. The

Wollaton   **The Magnificent Hall**

Thrumpton   **The Hall by the Trent**

Ruins of the Ancient Priory

Norman Nave

Norman Doorway

THE PRIORY CHURCH OF WORKSOP

east window of the new chancel glows richly with beautiful glass of the Crucifixion and six saints.

Fine roofs with bosses of leaves and flowers and heads look down on us everywhere. On the roof beams and on the chancel arch of the old part of the church is a strange company of stone heads of animals, human grotesques, and a quaint fellow like a Red Indian with feathers round his head. Rivalling these is the fine modern gallery under roofs and on arches, showing heads in medieval head-dress, queer creatures with human faces, and musical angels.

The charming woodwork is old and new. The chancel screen of about the year 1400, still in its original place with an extension at one end, has rich tracery tipped with flowers and leaves, and a cornice adorned with heads of humans, a lion, a muzzled dog, and a fox running away with a goose.

The fine little modern screen between the old chancel and the new has a rich cornice with cherubs and vine and grape. The modern reredos has exquisite carving of vines and olive branches growing round a great canopy, and two angels in niches with a crown of thorns and a sphere; and three recessed panels have a striking paint-ing of the Good Shepherd against a golden sky, a lamb on His shoulder, a sheep at one side entangled in thorns, and a holy lamb on a mountain top, triumphant.

In the abundance of detail in the small carved panels on the backs of the chancel stalls are a little Elizabethan ship in full sail and a man on the quayside leaning on the wind, a quaint fish in waves, a goat nibbling leaves; one charming scene shows a man returning to his cottage at the end of the day, his head bowed, his scythe on his shoulder, while the sunflowers are closing their petals with the setting sun, and the crescent moon appears. Carved in relief on the stall ends are birds, a crouching animal and a monkey, a squirrel, a wild boar, a bear with a rugged staff, an ass feeding, a workman sawing a plank, a man resting his head on his hand, and angels at prayer.

Within a 14th century recess belonging to the old chancel and now in the new, lies the sadly battered figure of a mail-clad knight with crossed legs. Known as the Stone Man of West Bridgford, he has found a peaceful resting-place after a strange adventure, for until 1893 he had been standing a long time on duty as a boundary stone in a field near the spot where Melton Road and Loughborough Road meet. We cannot be sure who he is, but he is over 600 years old, and may be Sir Robert Luteril, a lord of the manor.

WEST DRAYTON. It has a handful of farms and cottages and a tiny church off the Great North Road. A footbridge from the churchyard and a field path towards the hamlet of Rockley bring us to a delightful spot where the River Maun goes racing by the white walls of the old mill house, now a charming dwelling.

We enter the simple church by the doorway of the Normans, the shafts on each side supporting an arch carved with zigzag under a scalloped hood. Near it is an old stoup. A Norman coffin stone, carved with a cross and a sword, lies outside below the west window; the fragment of another of the same time is built into the wall inside. The only old windows are the east and the west, both 15th century, with pleasing modern glass.

The Beautiful Lady

WEST LEAKE. A small village on a little hill, it has a stream winding from the Wolds to the Soar, and a big house of which we have a lovely peep through an arch in the garden wall. From a green sward by the roadside, sheltered by a splendid chestnut tree, the peace memorial lychgate opens on a churchyard in which a fine yew, great limes, chestnuts, and sycamores watch over a church where a lady has been sleeping since the beginning of the 14th century. She lies in a canopied recess in the chancel, wearing a wimple, one dainty hand holding the folds of her gown. She is a beautiful figure which has been said to be almost without equal among others of its time. We may believe that she was a founder or rebuilder of this place.

In a recess of the transept he may have founded lies a man of perhaps a generation after her, with curly hair, a heart in his hands, and his feet on a dog; he wears a gown patterned with crosses in circles, and may have belonged to the family whose name was that of the village. Another medieval civilian, wearing a belted gown, lies in a richly canopied recess in the aisle.

There is nothing older here than the small Norman doorway, now built-up, and some 12th and 13th century coffin stones. The chancel and the long nave arcade are 14th century, though the aisle itself is made new. Two stout oak benches are at least 400 years old.

In West Leake Woods, where he loved to roam, is a rough-hewn cross in memory of Frederick Strutt, the first Lord Belper's son. He was a naturalist and archaeologist who knew all about the countryside, and left behind a collection of local books, prints, and maps.

The Wonderful Ladder

WESTON. Church spires are rare in this part of the county, but this quiet place by the Great North Road has one of its own and looks to another three miles away, at Tuxford. The pleasing church stands facing a row of six fine chestnut trees, and has an ancient yew in its churchyard, where we found a stone with the simple epitaph, "Alas, poor Suroye." Here too is part of the shaft of the old cross, with a sundial high enough for only the tallest of us to be able to read.

Two stages of the tower are 13th century, the top storey and the spire coming from the 14th. A scowling face is among the corbels on the 14th century nave arcades; another (round which the pulpit is fitted) shows a face baring its teeth, as if at the parson. At the base of a corbel supporting the 600-year-old chancel arch is a queer little figure which seems to have the body of a snake with the bearded face of a man.

Except for old fragments, the only coloured glass in the medieval windows is of dainty formal pattern in the east. The chancel has its old sedilia, and the south aisle a piscina. A worn stoup is near the door, and a fine chest is 500 years old. We measured a stout old ladder to the belfry at 67 inches round.

There is fine old carving of tracery and elaborate arcading in the modern chancel seats and the screening of the vestry. Thirteen bench-ends of the 15th century have tracery and roses in quatrefoils; there is a Jacobean altar table, the nave roof is 1768, and fine floral bosses adorn that of the chancel. The tub font was here when Gilbert de Archis gave the church to the monks of Blyth in the 12th century.

WEST STOCKWITH. It is like a quayside where the Chesterfield Canal comes into the Trent, which is a tidal river here and is joined by the Idle. Its old windmill has lost its cap and found a gabled roof, now housing people instead of grinding corn. Its houses

THE KING'S ENGLAND

line a dingy street on a bank of the river, looking across to Lincoln-shire on the other side; but the village keeps its red brick church neat and clean within. Built over 200 years ago in memory of William Huntingdon, it has a marble monument with his lifesize figure in a half-reclining attitude, showing him holding a drawing of a sailing ship. The inscription describes him as a ship's carpenter, and tells of the charities he left to this village where he worked. The reredos and altar rails are in memory of 17 men who did not come back.

The Butterfly on the Belt

WHATTON-IN-THE-VALE. The last resting-place of a man whose famous son died bravely at the stake is this pretty village, where houses with tall chimney stacks are scattered about a network of roads. It stands on the River Smite, crossed by a wooden bridge not far from a church which is famed for its monuments.

Alterations last century included the rebuilding of the chancel and of the central tower with its sturdy spire. A transept was destroyed, and the Norman arch once on the south side of the tower is now on the north, hidden by the organ but seen outside. From about 1300 come the north porch, the inner doorway, and the nave arcades. The double piscina is medieval, and the font is 17th century.

The east window of the south aisle is a fine frame for glass by William Morris and Burne-Jones, with figures of Our Lord, Peter, and John, on heavy backgrounds of orange tree, flowering rosebush, and pomegranates. Below them are scenes of Jesus making the blind to see, the lame to walk, and raising the dead. The east window of the other aisle, showing Our Lord ascending in a company of angels with Mary and the Disciples below, is in memory of Thomas Dickin-son Hall, who last century rebuilt some of the farms and cottages and built Whatton Manor, a charming house in Elizabethan style standing amid beautiful plantations on the edge of the village.

Part of the church was once used as a school, and the splendid monument of Sir Hugh de Newmarch of about 1400, defaced with innumerable names and initials, bears ample evidence of that time. He lies on a tomb with 20 shields, an alabaster knight in chain mail and SS collar, one leg missing and one half of the other foot left to rest on a lion. His worn belt must once have been fine, for one of the medallions has carving as fresh as the day it was done, and has on it a kind of butterfly with wings spread out like fans, and a quaint and vivid face. It is a little gem worth finding.

In a restored recess of the north aisle lies the stone figure of Robert de Whatton, who was vicar here from 1304; his hands are at prayer, and he wears the simple dress of a canon of Welbeck Abbey. Sir Richard de Whatton of 1322, with his legs crossed and wearing chain mail, lies on a splendid stone tomb with shields.

Very fine is an alabaster floorstone with the engraved portrait of a man with flowing hair, wearing a long gown with a purse. It is the most stirring of all Whatton's possessions, for it is the portrait of Thomas Cranmer of 1501, who doubtless brought his famous son to worship in this church before he grew up to be Archbishop of Canterbury and to die for his faith. Born at Aslockton close by, the Archbishop is said to have loved to listen to Whatton's tuneful bells.

Other old relics are a richly carved founder's recess with ball-flowers, battered now and without a tenant; and the head of the old village cross which was found last century in a cottage wall at Aslockton. It is elaborately carved with figures of Peter and Paul, St James with two others, and Our Lord with Mary and John.

The Sleeping Lady

WIDMERPOOL. In the heart of the Wolds, amid some of the loveliest woodland scenery in the county, is this charming village, where a delightful walk leads to the church in the lovely grounds of the hall, a stone house with tower and terraces, and a dell which is a fairyland of flowers and trees.

We shall not soon forget the little church, for it shelters an exquisite thing. In a dimly lighted chamber lies a beautiful woman asleep, her head on a cushion, a spray of lilies in her hand, a smile on her lips, and on her tomb the words:

> *Thinking that our remembrance, though*
> *unspoken, may reach her where she lives.*

It was an Italian sculptor who fashioned her in white marble here, working with great skill on every detail of her gown, her dainty lace, her cushion with a tasselled cord, her patterned pillow, and her coverlet of lovely folds. She was Harriet Annie Robertson, the lady of the Hall, who with her husband bore the cost of the charming restoration of the church. They were beloved by all who knew them.

There are many cedars among the fine trees here, one near the church growing higher than the 14th century tower, which is almost all that is left of the old building. St Peter stands in a niche on the porch, and a door with lovely hinges lets us inside, where the glory is in the chancel. Bosses of leaves adorn its vaulted roof, the windows have clustered shafts with capitals of flowers and foliage, the stone reredos has rich carving of a holy lamb and the signs of the Evangelists, and angels are singing in the tracery of the stalls.

A lovely relic is the 14th century font, which has been given an oak rim carved with flowers. The register tells of a child baptised in it on the day Charles Stuart was beheaded, and an echo of his day clings to the churchyard, where in two unknown graves sleep two soldiers slain at Willoughby Field in the closing years of the Civil War, when the king's men were routed.

A Poet's Inspiration

WILFORD. Its memories are of a curious scholar, an adventurer, and a poet who loved it when its charms were often sung and its landscape often painted.

The poet was Henry Kirke White, who found here and at Clifton the inspiration of much of his best work. Born in Nottingham, he came with his books to stay in the village while preparing for the university, and lodged in a cottage with a garden reaching down to the river. There he would dream as he looked out on a scene which was Wilford's great joy, a never-to-be-forgotten landscape of swift-flowing river, meadowland carpeted with crocuses in spring, and Nottingham with its castle silhouetted against the sky. He lies at Cambridge, where he died, but it was in Wilford churchyard that he longed to be, for he wrote:

> Here would I wish to sleep. This is the spot
> Which I have long marked out to lay my bones in.
> Tired out and wearied with the riotous world,
> Beneath this yew would I be sepulchred.

Kirke White, who has a modest place in literature, was born in 1785, the son of a butcher who took him early from school and set him to deliver meat before apprenticing him to the stocking loom. Inheriting his talent from his mother, who had been a schoolmistress, the boy showed fine resolution in study and, being transferred to the office of a firm of lawyers, made such progress in Latin that he was reading Horace within a year, and had begun the study of Greek and modern languages. From an early age he wrote verse, and he wrote "Clifton Grove" to raise his university fees. Friends helped him to Cambridge, where his natural abilities placed him first in every examination and promised a dazzling career; but his health broke down and he died at 21.

The reviewers had not been kind to his poems, but Southey championed him royally, wrote his life, and published his works. The sympathy of Byron was stirred, and he wrote:

> *Unhappy White! while life was in its spring*
> *And thy young muse just shook her joyous wing,*
> *The spoiler came; and all thy promise fair*
> *Has sought the grave, to sleep forever there.*
> *'Twas thine own genius gave the final blow*
> *And helped to plant the wound that laid thee low.*

Posterity has not endorsed this high opinion, but all the stricken poet's work was written before manhood rounded his broken youth. Yet his name still goes sounding round the world, for the hymn "Oft in danger, oft in woe," is one of half a score of hymns by which congregations still remember him.

Wilford has changed since those days, and a coalmine and a power station stand across the river where the poet saw flowers, but the toll bridge which replaced the ferry has helped it to keep some of its quiet charm. It has still the green with a delightful group of homes founded by Lord Trent for veterans of the Crimea and the Mutiny: the old church has the 18th century rectory for company, and an old tithe barn and the old inn are close by.

To the old school, founded by a rector 200 years ago and rebuilt last century, came Gilbert Wakefield as a boy of nine in 1765. We do not wonder that he grew up to be a great scholar when we read what he says of his schooldays here:

We came into school at five in summer, and, with less than two hours for breakfast and dinner, continued there till six at night.

He lived on into the first year of the 19th century, a learned man of great impetuosity and extreme opinions, which in the end brought him to prison for libel. He had declared that the working classes would lose nothing by a French invasion and had roused a storm of protest by his controversial attitude on various subjects. A kindly man, he was fanatical and extreme, full of sympathy but lacking restraint. Born at St Nicholas's rectory, Nottingham, he lies at Richmond.

Wilford church is mainly medieval. The low tower and the fine chancel are 15th century; from the close of the 14th come the porch, the nave arcades and the chancel arch, and most of the south aisle, which has a piscina of 1300 and four floorstones of the 12th and 13th centuries. The old stairway still climbs to the loft and the roof. There is beautiful modern craftsmanship in the handsome chancel screen, the screen of the tower and the vestry, and the benches with traceried ends. A fine Kempe window has twelve minstrel angels, and a vivid window with the Wise Men is in memory of Kirke White. His medallion portrait is on a wall.

When we came to the village George Smith had just died in his hundredth year, after spending half his life as parish clerk.

Under a railed-in tomb in the churchyard sleeps Captain John Deane, who began life as a butcher's boy and ended it as a British Consul. He spent the last quarter of his life at Wilford, and built here two houses still known by his name. Once on a barren island Deane and his crew were reduced by privation to such terrible straits that the living ate the dead. Rescue came when all but the last hope was gone, and Deane with the surviving few returned to England, penniless.

Misfortune had not broken his spirit, however, for in 1714, when he was 35, he was appointed to the command of a ship in the Russian Navy. He remained for seven years in the service of the Tsar and then, remembering that he was still an Englishman, resumed national duty and for 17 years was a capable and respected member of the consular service, with posts at various ports in the Netherlands. It was as a veteran of nearly threescore years that he eventually returned to his native county to become a citizen of note. Having escaped so many perils at sea, he experienced his greatest danger at home, for in a field adjoining his grounds he was robbed and almost murdered by a thief, who expiated the crime on the gallows.

This was John Deane's last adventure; he lived to be 81, to die in peace, and to be buried here in the old churchyard.

The Famous Willoughbys

WILLOUGHBY-ON-THE-WOLDS. It gave its name to a great family seven hundred years ago, and has a fine old church where some of them lie. A part of their old home remains in the farmhouse and cottage near the church. The first of them was Ralph Bugge, a rich Nottingham merchant who bought land here in the 13th century; his son changed his name to Willoughby. In the next century they were in possession of Wollaton, and had begun a long association with that village which ended only in 1924, when the splendid house they built in Elizabeth's reign became one of Nottingham's great possessions.

Their splendid monuments are in the 14th century chapel of the church, which has nothing older than the 12th century nave arcades. A hundred years later are the tower and spire, the chancel (with modern windows), and its arch. The clerestory is about 1500. The font, the fine piscina, and part of a stone altar, are medieval, and a 20th century screen is a thankoffering for peace.

The stone figures of Sir Richard de Willoughby (a cross-legged knight of 1325) and his wife represent the parents of another Sir Richard—a famous Lord Chief Justice, who lies on his alabaster tomb in his robes of office, with a sword and a roll in his hand. It was his marriage that brought Wollaton to the family. The alabaster figure of his son Richard lies between the chapel and the aisle, on a tomb enriched with heraldic shields. On a splendid tomb with sculptured figures in 18 niches lies Sir Hugh Willoughby of 1448, wearing richly decorated armour and a wreathed helmet. With him is one of his wives in a long gown, a cape tied with a tasselled cord, and a mitred headdress. There are also two ancient stone figures of women in wimples.

A small brass in the floor of the north aisle marks the resting-place of Michael Stanhope of Shelford, who was slain "in Willoughby Field in 1648, being a soldier for King Charles the First." This was the last struggle of the Civil War in Notts, when the Royalists under Sir Philip Monckton were routed by Colonel Rossiter. Tradition says the skirmish took place in a field near the church, and that the villagers climbed the church tower to watch the fray; it is more probable that the site was nearer the Fosse Way, which passes by the village after entering the county at Six Hills, where Notts points a finger into Leicestershire. On this famous road, near Willoughby, is the site of one of the five Roman stations in Notts, Vernometum.

The Great Beech

WINKBURN. One of the county's hidden villages, lying in the valley of the tiny River Wink, it has a few houses and farms, an inn, an ancient church by the great house, and wonderful trees.

We see fine groups of almost every kind of tree as we come from Hockerton through the spacious park; and masses of lofty veterans lead from the old gabled schoolhouse to the small church looking very weary of its years. The pride of them all is a magnificent copper beech at one end of the hall; it is one of the largest in the land, 13 feet round its trunk, its great branches touching the ground in a circle of about 90 yards.

Standing at the head of terraced lawn with flights of shallow steps, the hall is chiefly 18th century, with a top storey of the 19th, and some panelling inside belonging to an earlier manor house. Over the doorways in the central hall is a series of panels carved with scenes from Aesop's Fables.

The oldest part of the church is the tower, which is for the most part Norman; the belfry windows are adorned with zigzag and cable moulding, and the Norman archway to the nave is carved all round with heavy zigzag. In an ancient frame of carving with a small figure of a saint, on an outside wall of the tower, is a later stone telling of restoration in the 17th century. One of its three bells of 1633 was lent to Southwell Minster when the bells there were being recast.

A lofty Norman doorway, carved all round with beak-heads, opens to the interior, which is quaint with 17th century furnishing, box-pews, spiral altar rails, a small altar table, a commonplace screen, and a charming three-decker pulpit with a canopy. There is a Jacobean chest, and a decrepit one much older. The font is 17th century. There is bright glass in memory of the Burnells who, after the Dissolution, followed the Knights Hospitallers as lords of the manor.

Engraved on his tomb are the arms and portrait of William Burnell of 1570, his features worn away; he was auditor to Henry the Eighth, and brother of Edward Burnell whose fine monument is in Sibthorpe church. William Burnell of 1609 kneels in his wall monument, a lifesize figure in armour, holding a long metal sword; the inscription tells of the marriages he made for his four daughters.

After nine generations at Winkburn, the male line came to an end when Darcy Burnell died in 1774. His initials are on the great lead cistern by the porch, and his elaborate monument has lifesize figures of a bowed woman and an angel holding a plaque with his portrait. His descendants have sold the estate in our time.

The Fleet Dives Underground

WINTHORPE. It seems like another world as the prosaic road from Newark brings us into its leafy glade and to its delightful houses and gardens, spacious roads, and gracious trees. By the inn at the side of the green the little River Fleet dives underground (as London's Fleet does) to come out smiling by the old village cross, and join a tiny willow-bordered brook as it rushes on.

It lies between the Fosse Way and the Trent, to which the fine grounds of the hall go down. During the dry summers late in the 18th century, foundations of a great bridge, believed to be Roman, were exposed in the river near by. The village came into story in the Civil War as one of a chain held by Parliament during the last siege of Newark.

Built half a century ago on an older site, the lofty church of brick and stone is attractive with many arches, and a tower and spire 105 feet high. An elaborately carved stone reredos has figures in niches.

The Great House and the Wonderful Book

WOLLATON. It has come into Nottingham with all its splendour, but a new road leaves the heart of the village secluded down a shady lane. The old pump stands in its shelter in the square, and here, too, is the inn with foundation stones said to be part of the home of the Willoughbys, as is the stone cottage facing the church where some of them lie, the spire rising from the treetops.

For 600 years the story of the Willoughbys has been the story of the village, beginning when one of them married an heiress of the Morteins and ending but a few years ago. Some of them have helped to make the history of their county, and their country, and some of even a wider field; one of them built here as fine a house as any of his time. Sir Richard was Lord Chief Justice in the 14th century. Sir Hugh was the famous navigator who set out to discover the

North-West Passage, and perished with his company off the coast of Lapland. Sir Francis of 1672 was a famous naturalist whose son became Baron Middleton. It was another Sir Francis who built Wollaton Hall in the time of Elizabeth, a splendid house with features of the Gothic, Tudor, and classic styles. Dutch gables and pinnacles crown its four corner towers, a fine Prospect Room looks out from the central block, and the Great Hall inside has a handsomely carved stone screen and a fine hammerbeam roof. We can well believe, looking at the towers and turrets, domes and parapets, that it has a window for every day of the year, for it seems to be covered with them. It took eight years to build, and cost Sir Francis £80,000, in addition to the cost of the Ancaster stone, which was defrayed by Wollaton coal. It is believed that John Thorpe was its architect, and that Robert Smythson (who sleeps in the church) carried out the work with the help of craftsmen from Italy.

The park, with nearly 800 acres, has long been the glory of Wollaton. It has noble trees in plantations and groves, lovely gardens, and deer browsing by the lake in a woodland hollow. On the building of the seven-mile wall enclosing the park an apprentice is said to have served the whole of his seven years.

We may all see this fine place today, for in 1924 Lord Middleton sold the estate to Nottingham, and the house is now the home of the city's Natural History Museum. The builder has been at work in the park and the seven-mile wall has been disturbed. The gardens are still fine, and there is a lovely cedar grove near a splendid flight of steps, with a peep of the golf links beyond. Unforgettable is the sight of the marvellous camelias in a house which cost £10,000 to build. Yet Wollaton holds nothing finer than the magnificent lime-grove, three-quarters of a mile long, which leads from the great stone gateway to the hall; and nothing more entrancing than the panorama from the leaded roof of the Prospect Room, with a view of Belvoir Castle 20 miles away.

In the trim churchyard joining the garden of the white-walled rectory stands the church, much restored last century, when it was given a south aisle and a chapel to serve as the family pew. The three eastern bays of the north arcade are 14th century, the time of most of the old work. Two sides of the tower stand on open arches, through which we can walk outside the church.

Among the Willoughby memorials are the fine brass portraits of Richard of 1471 and his wife, he in plate armour and she in long cloak and gown. They lie on a tomb in a canopied recess, and below them lies a stone corpse. On a tomb between the chancel and the chapel lies Sir Henry Willoughby of 1528, with small figures of four wives beside him, and a stone corpse below. Three sons and three daughters are on the tomb, and it is thought that the third son may be Hugh, who was one day to be found frozen to death in his chair, with his will and his ship's log beside him.

On the death of Sir Francis, who built the hall, Wollaton passed to his daughter Bridget, who married her cousin, Percy Willoughby. Their memorial is a stone on the chancel wall, with a Latin inscription in beautiful raised lettering.

A priceless treasure, a rare gem for this village church, is the book of service and song which was used here for nearly a hundred years before the Reformation. Its great pages, about 22 inches by 15, are worn at the edges, but their rich illumination is almost as fresh as when they left the artist's hands 500 years ago. When Edward the Sixth's Prayer Book came into use this book was taken to the Hall and remained in the keeping of the family till Lord Middleton gave it back to the church in 1925. Here it lies in a glass case, the pages being turned over now and then. We saw it at Christmas, when the open page showed a charming picture of the Nativity, with the ox and the ass, a woman holding up the Child to Mary lying in bed, and Joseph sitting by. We saw it again at Easter, opened to show Our Lord stepping out of the Tomb. The book is almost complete. It was written and illuminated before 1460, for it belonged then to a rector of Wollaton whose executors bought it for ten marks and gave it for use in this church for ever.

The window pictures are a pleasing part of the church, two in the chancel being the work of Christopher Whall. One shows St Francis surrounded by a company of 30 English and foreign birds, with the chaffinch, robin, thrush, blue tits, sparrows, love-birds and doves among them, and St Nicholas with two children, one with a doll. It is in memory of a rector who loved birds and children, and who served here for 46 years. The chapel was restored in his memory, and has been given an oil painting for a reredos, showing in soft colours the scene in the Upper Room at Emmaus. The other Whall window is to James Cosmo Russell, who won the DSO and fell at Ypres in 1917; the window has figures of St George in gold and St Michael in silver, each standing on a dragon.

Heroes Frozen on Their Ships

SIR HUGH WILLOUGHBY, born early in the 16th century, won distinction and was knighted as a soldier. His military career ending with the fall of his patron Somerset, he turned from the land to the sea.

Sebastian Cabot having discovered North America when seeking the North-West Passage, Willoughby was made admiral of three little ships to seek an Eastern way to Asia along the north of Europe. With Richard Chancellor as pilot-general he sailed in May 1553, but the vessels were driven apart by a storm. Chancellor found his way into the White Sea, made a sledge journey to Moscow, and laid plans for the foundation of our foreign commerce. Willoughby, recovering his second ship, sailed with it to Nova Zembla, the first Englishman to penetrate so far into the Arctic. Turning south, he reached the wild and inhospitable coast where Lapland joins Russia, with neither food nor clothing for an Arctic winter, the severity of which was not then understood.

Nothing was heard of them for about two years, but we know from Willoughby's diary that they spent some months at the end of 1553 in sending out three men south-south-west to see if they could find people, three others westward, and three south-east, all of whom came back after their long journeyings without finding any people or any sign of habitation. The last entry in Willoughby's journal is in October, and it tells us that "thus remaining in this haven the space of a week, and seeing the year far spent, and also very evil weather (frost, snow, hail as though it had been the deep of winter) we thought best to winter there."

Still nothing was heard of them, and the year 1554 passed with no news. Then in the spring of 1555 some Russian fishermen found Willoughby's two ships (Bona Esperanza and Bona Confidentia) on the icy coast, as silent as the grave, and on them were their crews, six merchants, two surgeons, Sir Hugh Willoughby, and in all about seventy men, frozen to death. With Willoughby were his diary and his will, the signature of the will making it clear that he was alive in January 1554.

There have been few more tragic spectacles than that upon which these Russian fishermen looked; we think of Scott and his comrades found in their tents half a world away down south as we picture these ships with their frozen crews in the great White North:

> *He with his hapless crew,*
> *Each full exerted at their several tasks,*
> *Froze into statues; to the cordage glued*
> *The sailor, and the pilot to the helm.*

Here Ends a Romantic Tale

WOODBOROUGH. The last resting-place of the most astonishing figure in an astonishing family, and the birthplace of a village evangelist who left the world better than he found it when they laid him in his native churchyard, Woodborough lies in the valley, looking up to hills rich in ancient encampments. Its lovely corner is where the steep hill comes down from the Plains; here roads meet by bright gardens, a fine drive leads to the great house, and a stream goes on its way to the Dover Beck.

Once it was a busy centre of the old stocking knitters, and the rattle of the hand-frames is still heard in some of the cottages. To one of the knitters was born in 1769 a son whose knowledge of the Bible earned him the name of the Walking Concordance. He was George Brown, brought up to be a knitter, but with a thirst for learning which took him to the village school and ended in fifty years of ministry, preaching the gospel from house to house. When he fell ill at Worcester they brought him home to Woodborough, where he died in 1833.

It was the home of some of the Strelleys from the time of Edward the Third to Elizabeth's day, and it is to Richard Strelley that Woodborough owes its crowning glory, the splendid 14th century chancel of the church. While his father was rebuilding Strelley church, Richard erected this stately chancel with fine windows, gabled buttresses with grotesque heads on each side, and beautiful sedilia and piscina. Modern days have enriched his 14th century work with a fine gallery of glass, and with fine woodwork.

The great east window (which Richard adorned with heads of his king and queen) has in it the Crucifixion, Paulinus, and St Swithin. In others we see the Madonna between saints, Apostles and Nativity scenes with fine horses and camels and rich gifts, David with his harp,

Dorothea with apples, Columba with a church, Chad with Lichfield Cathedral, Hugo with a model of Lincoln, and Cecilia with an organ. The peace memorial window has Gabriel, Michael, and Raphael, and tiny white and gold medallions with the Baptism, the Crucifixion, and the Road to Calvary.

The hand of a clever craftsman is seen in the poppyhead stalls, their shallow canopies carved with quatrefoils in tracery, and in the reading desks with symbols of the Evangelists; the craftsman was Mansfield Parkyns, who, after a life of great adventure, came to live at Woodborough Hall. He spent two years on the work with the help of two joiners, doing all the designing and most of the carving himself. It was a labour of love in memory of his wife, and it proved to be a memorial to himself, for we read that these choir stalls, the last work of his life, were designed, carved, and given on Christmas Eve 1893 by Mansfield Parkyns. He died on January 12, 1894, aged 70. He carved the screen across the tower arch, and designed the pulpit. He sleeps outside the church he helped to enrich.

Except for a few fragments, the rest of the church has nothing of the glory of the chancel. The nave and aisles are later in the 14th century, and the tower is perhaps 16th. Three massive old tie-beams support a mass of timbering in the fine steep roof of the nave, there are fragments of glass 600 years old, and there is a Jacobean altar table given as a thankoffering for the end of the Civil War. Older than all the rest are two 12th century coffin stones, a beautiful Norman doorway with shafts and three orders of moulding, and the Norman font (like part of a round pillar) adorned with bands of zigzag. Two old gable crosses are restored.

It is remarkable to find in this church the work of so romantic a figure as Mansfield Parkyns. Born at Ruddington in 1823 of a distinguished line, he inherited the brain, the brawn, and the unconventionality of his family, so it was in keeping with his qualities that, incurring censure for some mild escapade at Cambridge, he should leave without a degree, and set off for the East as a youth in his teens.

Three years later Sir Francis Galton and a party of friends, after a camel journey across the desert and a voyage down the Nile, reached a collection of mud huts which was Khartoum. They heard of a mysterious European in the town, and going to his hut, entered to find a white man, nearly naked, as agile as a panther, with his head shorn, and with a lepoard skin thrown over his shoulder.

One of the visitors immediately recognised the seeming Dervish as a fellow student at Cambridge, Mansfield Parkyns! The wild man had spent three years wandering in Abyssinia with a freedom and fearlessness which no other man had shown since James Bruce.

With all his wildness and wander-lust, Parkyns preserved a saving sanity. "Of the many travellers whom I have known," said Sir Francis Galton, "I should place Mansfield Parkyns as perhaps the most gifted with natural advantages for that career. He won hearts by his sympathy, and could touch any amount of pitch without being himself defiled."

He returned to England after an absence of four years, went out to the Embassy at Constantinople, then returned home once more. He wrote an excellent book on Abyssinia, confirming many of the amazing stories of Bruce; married a daughter of a Lord Chancellor, made an admirable chief official of the Bankruptcy Court; and, still enjoying a reputation as one of the most formidable of amateur boxers, devoted his leisure to woodcarving, to geography, and to the propagation of knowledge of native African and Western Asian languages which, with wonderful facility, he had mastered during his strange journeyings.

Gateway to the Dukeries

WORKSOP. Its attractions are a noble church with grand Norman remains, the charming gatehouse of a lost priory, and its place on the fringe of the Forest as the northern gateway of the Dukeries. For the rest, it is a straggling old market town on the River Ryton, with the Chesterfield Canal passing through. Among its few old buildings is the Ship Inn by the marketplace, picturesque with gables and an overhanging room.

Within four miles of the town stand Welbeck and Clumber in their glorious parks; nearer still is Osberton Hall, a modern house in lovely grounds, with fine pictures and an almost unrivalled collection of British birds; and a mile away is its own great house, Worksop Manor, in a fine park.

The story of the Manor begins with the renowned John Talbot, first Earl of Shrewsbury, who built a house here in the 15th century.

His house was greatly enlarged by a later Talbot and his famous wife, Bess of Hardwick, and it was here with them that Mary Queen of Scots passed one of the most miserable spells of her imprisonment. James the First was entertained here on his way to London for his crowning, and Horace Walpole came in 1756, five years before it was burned to the ground. The Duke of Norfolk, to whom the estate had passed, set 500 men to work on what he meant to be the finest house in England, but the death of his only son disturbed his plans when he had built 500 rooms, and in 1840 the Duke of Newcastle pulled most of it down, leaving enough of it to become the fine house we now see.

Workaday Worksop has crept up to the town's most precious possession, the lovely 14th century gatehouse of the Priory of Radford. Adorned with gables and buttresses and saints in canopied niches, it was guest-house as well as gatehouse, and has a big upper room with a fine window. The gateway itself has three fine arches, and its original black and white roof with moulded beams. It was probably built by Thomas, Lord Furnival; and towards the end of the century the monks added the charming porch to serve as a shrine for pilgrims, giving it a doorway on each side, a lovely window, a stairway to the upper room, and a very beautiful vaulted roof of delicate tracery, still in splendid condition.

As we stand under the gateway, one of the outer arches frames a charming view of a tall tapering cross on a flight of seven steps. It is restored with a new head, and was brought here from opposite the church gates, where in olden days Radford Fair was held round it; during the Commonwealth banns of marriage were published from the steps. The other end arch frames a delightful picture of the church, with its twin western towers about 90 feet high.

The story of the priory church of St Mary and St Cuthbert goes back to early in the 12th century, when Sir William de Lovetot invited the Black Canons to found a monastery, granting them the small Norman church already here. The monks set to work to build a larger church, which consisted at first of a chancel, transepts, and one bay of the nave, round a central tower. By about 1160 the rest of the nave was completed and given for the use of the parish, but at the Dissolution Thomas Cromwell and his master Henry the

Eighth destroyed the monastic part of what had become a noble church, leaving the nave, its aisles, and the two west towers.

So it has stood for centuries, a magnificent fragment of a great building which is being given back in our own day some of its lost glory. The grand Norman nave is 140 feet long and 60 wide, opening to aisles with stone vaulted roofs. Above the ten bays on each side is a handsome triforium and a clerestory of round-headed windows. The arches of the arcades and of the triforium are rich in ornament as clean-cut as if carved yesterday. The eastern bay of each arcade is different from the rest, for these two, with a fragment of the south transept, are the remains of the earliest work of the monks.

The big south porch (its beauty enhanced by the noble avenue of limes leading to it), has a stone-vaulted roof and a trefoiled niche in its east wall, and shelters a lovely doorway with a round arch on six shafts. It frames a beautiful door which is one of the precious things of the church, for, though patched here and there, it is the original door made of yew wood from Sherwood Forest late in the 12th or early in the 13th century. Its mass of exquisite ironwork, richly wrought in sweeping scrolls, is claimed to be the earliest example of its kind in England.

The deep west doorway, with shafts and zigzag ornament, has a lovely modern door with ironwork to match the old. A smaller doorway with a similar modern door opens to the north vestry, which had a beautiful vaulted roof, and was originally the parlour where the monks received their guests. Joining this north-west end of the church are slight remains of the priory cloisters. The north-west tower is about a hundred years older than its companion, and was raised when the other was built, both being finished in the 15th century. After the destructive work of Thomas Cromwell the ruins became a quarry of hewn and carved stone, from which houses, a farmhouse, and a water-mill were built. The mill and some of the buildings have been demolished, and a few years ago we found the stones of the old priory being used again in restoring the central crossing and the north transept. The south transept was rebuilt as a thanksgiving for the end of the Great War, and the beautiful lady chapel, with charming lancet windows, has been restored in memory of the men who did not come home. It is a memorial for a second time, for, in addition to the many names on the oak panelling of the fallen, there is an inscription cut in stone telling that the chapel was founded in the 13th century in memory of a Lord Furnival and of the Crusades in which he fell. His body was brought home by his brother and buried here. The architect of the restoration of the church and the gatehouse was Sir Harold Brakspear, his plans being carried on after his death by his son.

Lady Joan Furnival of 1395 lies in the nave, a battered alabaster figure wearing a lovely netted headdress, and a mantle over her long gown. Her husband, Sir Thomas Neville of 1406 (brother of the famous Ralph Neville, Earl of Westmorland), is one of the two battered knights lying on each side of the altar, both with legs missing below the knees. The other knight is a 14th century Furnival.

The south aisle has a 700-year-old piscina, the modern font has lovely foliage and medallions of the Four Evangelists, and the modern iron screenwork in the eastern bays of the arcades is delicately wrought with flowers. The chapel has an Elizabethan altar table, an oil painting of the Madonna and Child is by Domenichino, and the painting of the Holy Family is by Perugino. In a glass case is a skull, perhaps of one of the Sherwood Forest archers, *still penetrated with the tip of an arrow which carried death in its flight*. It was found near the porch last century, a grim and intimate touch with the life of the Forest in those far-off days. Big wooden figures of the Madonna and St Cuthbert are of interest for being the work of one of the congregation, who also carved the three figures of the Rood.

The custom of an old tenure is still observed at Worksop when a sovereign is crowned. The lord of the manor has to find a right-hand glove, and supports the king's right hand holding the sceptre.

Seventeen Silver Inkstands

WYSALL. Time brings little change to this quiet village on the edge of the Wolds. At one end of a short road shaded by stately trees is a beautiful church with something of perhaps a thousand years ago; at the other end is an inn with a pump trough said to have been hollowed out of the top of a Norman pillar. Below the village a brook flows from the heart of the Wolds, on its way to the Soar.

Wise restoration has left the church with all the dignity of lovely old age. We read its oldest story in the north wall of the nave—in rubble walling which may be Saxon, in a Norman doorway, and in a charming little Norman window.

The lovely font with a round bowl on five shafts saw the dawn of the 13th century, and from its close comes most of the tower, with an earlier arch resting on foliage corbels, and a 15th century window; its small spire is 600 years old. The belfry is reached by a wonderful old ladder with a handrail and candle spike. The nave arcade, and the aisle with a fine east window, are 14th century. From the end of the 14th comes the chancel, and the clerestory is 100 years younger.

The 15th century screen (with gates and a massive middle rail) has small holes in two panels which were used as peepholes to the altar. The oak pulpit of about 1400, perhaps the oldest in the county, has come into its own again after having been displaced by one of stone. Three sturdy oak benches are over 400 years old; there is an old chest, and two old miserere seats are carved with quaint faces. Very impressive is the old timbering of the chancel roof.

The dainty brass candelabra in the chancel was given "for the use of Psalm singers of Wysall church in 1773." A painted wood panel is a memorial to George Widmerpole of 1689, and on an alabaster tomb lie the splendid figures of Hugh Armstrong and his wife Mary Sacheverell, both wearing ruffs. The knight is in armour with a double chain round his neck, a book in his hand, his feet on a lion, and a pair of gauntlets at his side. His lady's Elizabethan dress is held by a long chain, her arms are gone, and a tiny dog is at her feet. Round the tomb are their seven children.

Proud he would be, this knight in his armour, if he could know that from his old village 17 men went out to the war and came home again; it is one of three Thankful Villages in the county. Wysall has no Roll of Honour, but every man was presented with a silver inkstand on which was engraved his name and the words, "With gratitude from Wysall for answering Duty's call in the Great War."

NOTTINGHAMSHIRE TOWNS AND VILLAGES

In this key to our map of Nottinghamshire are all the towns and villages treated in this book. If a place is not on the map by name, its square is given here, so that the way to it is easily found, each square being five miles. One or two hamlets are in the book with their neighbouring villages; for these see Index.

Annesley	B7	Cotgrave	C9	Harworth	C2
Arnold	C8	Cotham	E8	Haughton	D5
Askham	E4	Cottam	F4	Hawksworth	E8
Aslockton	E9	Creswell Crags	B5	Hawton	E7
Attenborough	B10	Cromwell	E6	Hayton	D3
Averham	E7	Cropwell Bishop	D9	Headon	E4
		Cuckney	B5	Hickling	D10
Babworth	D4			Hockerton	D7
Balderton	F7	Darlton	E5	Holme	E6
Barnby-in-the-		Dunham	F4	Holme Pierrepont	C9
Willows	F7			Hoveringham	D8
Barton-in-Fabis	B10	Eakring	D6	Hucknall	B8
Beauvale Priory	B8	East Bridgford	D8		
Beckingham	E2	East Drayton	E4	Kelham	E7
Beeston	B9	East Leake	B11	Keyworth	C10
Besthorpe	F6	East Markham	E5	Kilvington	E8
Bilborough	B9	East Stoke	E8	Kingston-on-Soar	B10
Bilsthorpe	D6	Eaton	D4	Kinoulton	D10
Bingham	D9	Edingley	D7	Kirklington	D7
Bleasby	D8	Edwalton	C9	Kirton	D5
Blidworth	C7	Edwinstowe	C5	Kneesall	D6
Blyth	C3	Egmanton	E5	Kneeton	D8
Bole	E3	Elkesley	D4		
Bothamsall	D5	Elston	E8	Lambley	C8
Bradmore	C10	Elton	E9	Laneham	E4
Bramcote	B9	Epperstone	D8	Langar	D9
Brough	F6	Everton	D2	Langford	F7
Broughton Sulney	D11			Laxton	D5
Budby	C5	Farndon	E7	Lenton	B9
Bulcote	C8	Farnsfield	C7	Linby	B7
Bunny	C10	Finningley	D1	Littleborough	F3
Burton Joyce	C8	Fiskerton	E7	Lowdham	D8
		Flawborough	E8		
Calverton	C8	Fledborough	E5	Mansfield	B6
Carburton	C5	Flintham	E8	Mansfield Wood-	
Car Colston	D8			house	B6
Carlton-in-Lindrick	C3	Gamston	D4	Maplebeck	D6
Carlton-on-Trent	E6	Gedling	C8	Markham Clinton	D5
Caunton	E6	Gonalston	D8	Marnham	E5
Clarborough	D3	Gotham	B10	Mattersey	D3
Clayworth	D3	Granby	E9	Misterton	E2
Clifton	B9	Greasley	B8	Morton	D7
Clifton, North	F5	Gringley-on-the-			
Clifton, South	F5	Hill	E2	Newark	E7
Clipstone	C6	Grove	E4	Newstead	B7
Coddington	F7	Gunthorpe	D8	Normanton-on-Trent	E5
Colston Bassett	D10			Normanton-on-	
Colwick	C9	Halam	D7	Soar	B11
Cossall	A9	Halloughton	D7	North Collingham	F6
Costock	C11	Harby	F5	North Leverton	E3

INDEX

This index includes all notable subjects and people likely to be sought for. A special index of pictures is at the beginning of the volume.

INDEX

INDEX

INDEX

INDEX

334

INDEX

INDEX

INDEX